BRIAN LITTLE

A Little is Enough

BRIAN LITTLE

A Little is Enough

With

SIMON GOODYEAR

Foreword by

GARETH SOUTHGATE

(England Football Manager)

Published in 2018 by Goodyear Publications
www.goodyearpublications.com

Some photographs are from a personal collection;
most photographs that require permission have been
granted copyright; a small number of photographs
are pending authorisation at the time of print.

ISBN (Hardback): 978-1-78281-320-0
ISBN (Paperback): 978-1-78281-318-7
ISBN (eBook): 978-1-78281-319-4

A full CIP record for this book is available from the British Library.

Cover Illustration by Dave Mills

Edited by John Hill

Proofread by Mike Leach

Designed and Typeset by Riverside Publishing Solutions, Salisbury

Printed and bound in the UK by Jellyfish Solutions, Swanmore

DEDICATION

To my family and friends who have supported me throughout my career.

I would like to pay tribute to former Aston Villa chairman and owner, Sir Doug Ellis, who sadly passed away aged 94 during the production of this book.

Also, I'd like to pass on my sympathy to my former club, Leicester City for the tragic loss of their chairman and owner, Vichai Srivaddhanaprabha, who died during the production of this book.

CONTENTS

ALSO BY THE AUTHOR

The Gerry Hitchens Story – From Mine to Milan

La Storia di Gerry Hitchens (Italian version)

The Bobby Thomson Story – The Real Bobby Dazzler

The Harry Moseley Story – Making it Happen

Memories Made in Aston

Peter Withe – All for the Love of the Game

Cherno Samba – Still in the Game

FOREWORD
by Gareth Southgate
(England Football Manager)

When I signed for Aston Villa from Crystal Palace in the summer of 1995 Brian Little was brave enough to pay a club record transfer fee of £2.5m. Actually, that record only lasted two days, because he subsequently signed Savo Milošević from Partizan Belgrade, but as a player, when a manager shows that faith in you, it does wonders for your confidence.

While I had signed as a midfield player, Brian also knew I had played in defence and through that initial pre-season in 1995 he tried me as part of a back three away at Portsmouth. That was a success and within two months I had been called into the England squad as a centre back. I will be forever grateful.

I think that clarity of how he wanted his team to play was a real strength. After a few months at the club, he'd been brave enough to offload some big personalities and good players in Dean Saunders and Dalian Atkinson, but clearly believed in the likes of Dwight Yorke who was really given his head that season. From the opening day 3-1 victory over Man Utd (the 'you'll win nothing with kids' game) the team played with confidence and as a very tight group. The team shape was clear, 3-5-2, we were hard to score against and played some exciting attacking football. He wanted us to pass the ball, his messages were clear and his coaching team were all on the same page. That season we finished 4th, won the League Cup and reached the FA Cup semi-final.

Brian had clearly looked at the type of professionals he wanted at his club – his values shone through in the way he treated us, spoke to us and asked us to play. Yet he was also prepared to go with more complex characters like Paul McGrath and Mark Bosnich, because he knew what they brought to the team. He wanted a disciplined team, but knew that we were men and so gave us our space as well.

I would say the other area Brian did well, was managing up. On the day I signed, Brian had done all the hard work, but he allowed Doug Ellis his moment to sweep in and complete the signing. I'm sure at times Doug was hard work for his managers, that might be a huge understatement, but Brian recognised that he had the club's best interests at heart and always seemed to manage that difficult relationship as well as was possible.

Finally, I think it's a prerequisite for a manager to care about the long-term future of the club he's managing. Brian had loved his time as a player at Villa and you sensed his pride at leading the club as manager. That pride and care has been clear when I've seen him at Villa subsequently, in advisory or ambassadorial capacities.

It will hurt him as much as it still surprises, that winning the League Cup in 96 with Villa, remains this historic club's last major trophy.

PROLOGUE

A look back at the extraordinary career of Brian Little
by Simon Goodyear

Brian Little was born in Newcastle-upon-Tyne in the early **1950s and brought up playing football for several local sides before leaving school at the age of 15. He was even scouted by the one and only Sir Stanley Matthews, who at the time was manager of Port Vale, but Brian was to join Aston Villa as an apprentice.**

Two years later, he turned professional and made his first-team debut as a substitute against Blackburn Rovers in October 1971 in front of 25,500 at Villa Park, and that season went on to help Villa win the FA Youth Cup by beating Liverpool. In the same year, he helped England Youth win the Little World Cup in Spain, by beating West Germany in the Final – on penalties.

Early in his Villa career, Brian was part of the 1975 and 1977 League Cup winning sides and in May 1975, his staring roles for Villa earned him his first (and only) cap for the full England team in a substitute appearance against Wales at Wembley. His appearance, although brief, was rewarded when he laid on England's second goal for David Johnson.

By the 1979-1980 season, Brian was a regular in the Villa side and a proposed £615,000 move to cross-city rivals, Birmingham City fell through because of a persistent back problem. One year later, after making 302 appearances for his one and only club, scoring 82 goals and having a clean disciplinary record to boot, just before Villa's victorious 1980–1981 season, Brian's career ended prematurely because of a knee injury.

Although football had been Brian's life since the age of 15, he briefly quit the game following his retirement and worked in a printing company, later to return to Aston Villa, among other things, working in the promotions department. Brian returned to football when he was appointed youth team coach in September 1982, the season that followed Villa's greatest ever triumph – winning the 1982 European Cup. Brian stayed at Villa for two seasons before leaving to take over at Wolves as caretaker manager before Graham Turner took over nine games later.

Middlesbrough was next up for Brian, two months after being released from Wolves, when he was recruited as the youth and reserve team coach by his former Villa teammate, Bruce Rioch. Like Wolves, Middlesbrough was financially troubled, but Brian became an important part of the club's coaching staff. As their form improved, and with two successive promotions, 'Boro found themselves in the First Division for the 1988–1989 season; however, the season ended in relegation for Middlesbrough, and in February 1989, he left Ayresome Park and became manager of Darlington.

Darlington were bottom of the Fourth Division when he took over; however, Brian was unable to prevent them from getting relegated to the Conference National League, but they were soon promoted back into the Football League at the first time of asking. The next season brought more success as Darlington won the Fourth Division championship.

Brian's success was by now being monitored by some of the bigger clubs, and in June 1991 Leicester City appointed him as a replacement for Gordon Lee. The Foxes had just avoided relegation to the Third Division and Brian was seen as the right man to turn the club's fortunes around.

At the end of 1991–1992 season, Leicester came fourth in the Second Division (second tier) and for the first time in his managerial career Brian had led a team to the promotion playoffs. They overcame Cambridge United in the semi-finals and faced Blackburn Rovers in the final, but the Foxes lost to a late penalty. At the end of the 1992–1993 season, Leicester qualified for the playoffs again in the renamed Division One (second tier). They beat Portsmouth in the semi-finals, but in the final were 3-0 down shortly after half-time to Glenn Hoddle's Swindon Town. Leicester fought back to bring the scoreline to 3-3; however, Swindon scored a controversial late fourth goal from the penalty spot to progress to the Premier League.

With a place in the new Premier League as the prize, Leicester finally won their third consecutive playoff final with a 2-1 win against local rivals, Derby County in 1993–1994 season.

In November 1994, Brian quit his role at Leicester and returned to Aston Villa to replace Ron Atkinson as their manager. When he arrived at Villa Park, they were at the foot of the Premier League. There were a lot of senior players at the club, such as Nigel Spink, Earl Barrett, Shaun Teale, Ray Houghton, Garry Parker, Dalian Atkinson and Dean Saunders, so Brian faced the task of building a new team.

A 1-1 draw with Norwich City on the last day of the 1994–1995 season meant that Villa remained in the Premier League for another season. In came a whole set of new players into the Villa line-up for the following season, the likes of Alan Wright, Gareth Southgate, Gary Charles, Ian Taylor, Mark Draper and Savo Milošević were drafted in. The new look Villa team gelled well, and the 1995–1996 season was the most successful season at Villa Park in recent history. The club finished fourth in the Premier League, reached the FA Cup semi-finals and won the League Cup with a 3-0 win over Leeds United at Wembley. Trinidad and Tobago striker Dwight Yorke had now firmly established himself as a world-class goal scorer and the Villans were on fire. Villa qualified for the 1996–1997 UEFA Cup and, although they were knocked out at the first stage by Swedish side Helsingborgs, they also qualified for the 1997–1998 competition after finishing fifth in the Premier League. In February 1998. Although he had managed to lead the team into the quarter-final of the UEFA Cup, with the club in the bottom half of the league, Brian suddenly resigned after just over three years as Aston Villa manager and was replaced by first-team coach, John Gregory.

After a short break from football, Brian was appointed manager of Stoke City in May 1998. His appointment was met with approval from the club's supporters. Stoke had moved into a new all-seated Britannia Stadium, but poor performances had led to the side being relegated to the Second Division (third tier). His only objective was to gain an instant return to the First Division (second tier) in 1998–1999. Stoke began the season in fine form winning 14 of their first 20 matches and they sat well on top of the division. However their form fell away after Christmas and ended up finishing in eighth place. In July 1999 Brian resigned as manager of Stoke.

During the summer of 1999, Brian was back in employment as manager of West Bromwich Albion. The club were languishing in the First Division (second tier), and he was unable to revive their fortunes. In January 2000, things got worse for Albion as the promising Italian midfielder Enzo Maresca was transferred, under the nose of the manager, to Juventus for £4 million as Albion battled against relegation, and then Brian was sacked in the March of 2000 after just eight months in charge.

Just one month after leaving the Hawthorns, Brian was appointed manager of Third Division (fourth tier) strugglers, Hull City. The Tigers were hit by huge debts, and by the end of the 2000–2001 season, had been saved from closure by new owner, Adam Pearson, and the club's future looked brighter. Brian took the Tigers to the Third Division playoffs, but lost to Leyton Orient in the semi-finals.

By February 2002 Hull City had suffered some indifferent form, but Brian was unexpectedly sacked after a home defeat to Macclesfield.

After another break of around 18 months, he made a return to football management with Tranmere Rovers, who were in the Second Division (third tier). His first season with the Merseyside club was a success. When he took over they were battling against relegation, but by the end of the season they had climbed up to eighth place and had reached the quarter-final of the FA Cup. In his first full season as manager, Brian guided Tranmere to a third-place finish in the newly formed League One (third tier), but they lost in the playoffs.

Tranmere began the 2005–2006 season as League One promotion favourites, but by the turn of 2006 they were facing a relegation battle. The club only avoided relegation with one game to go and, because of the club's poor final position, Brian left the club by mutual consent on 5 May 2006.

After yet another break from football, Brian took the reins at Wrexham in November 2007, but could not save the club from relegation. Wrexham were relegated to the Conference on 22 April 2008 after losing 2-0 at Hereford United; however, he signed a two-year contract, promising to revive the club's fortunes. The following season started well, with a 5-0 home victory against promotion favourites, Stevenage Borough; however, a run of poor results followed, with Wrexham being only four points above the relegation zone. Following a 3-0 home defeat against Rushden & Diamonds, Brian left Wrexham by mutual consent.

Conference North side, Gainsborough Trinity appointed Brian as their new manager during the early part of September.

He then began the task of building a squad of professionals at Trinity, picking up many players from the Football League and other ex-League players from the Conference, but despite boasting a large squad of experienced players Trinity narrowly avoided relegation to the Northern Premier League during the 2010–2011 season. On 22 August 2011 following two defeats, Brian was sacked as manager of Trinity, after almost two years in the post.

Brian was then appointed as Jersey FA's director of football in November 2014, to oversee the work of first-team manager Jimmy Reilly, who went on in the following May to lead the islanders to their first Muratti Vase Final victory in four years. Months later, Jersey announced their intention to join UEFA, and when Reilly stepped aside in early 2016, Brian was appointed to replace him and won the 100th Muratti in May 2016, but stepped down as manager the following month and left his position as director of football, which allowed him to concentrate on his commitments in an advisory role to the board at Aston Villa – a position which he still keeps (at the time of writing).

Simon Goodyear
www.goodyearpublications.com

Chapter 1

THE APPRENTICE
Aston Villa apprentice: 1969–1971

"Look, Listen and Learn"

Many people have asked me over time, "Why did you become a footballer?" Well, I had always been the sporty type at school; I played county and area basketball; I could have run cross country for the North East, but, quite frankly, it all got in the way of my football (and school). My dad once said to me, "I'd just be careful if I were you, you know if you finish in the top 10 the county will want you to run here, there and everywhere and they might be able to get you out of a football match, so be careful". He never told me not to be my best, but he was warning me not to get involved in every sport. When I did my cross-country trial, I remember being tired and thinking, "Crikey, if I have to do this every week I'm going to be absolutely shattered." So, I eased off and finished about 20th and it meant I wasn't selected for the squad, thankfully, and so it gave me a chance to concentrate on my basketball and football. I loved football more than anything else, but I was never the tallest or the strongest and I never made the county team. Strangely enough, I also enjoyed basketball, mainly because I thought taking the ball off the rebound from the backboard could be good for my timing and jumping.

When I was at school, I used to say to people I wanted to become a car mechanic, not that I knew anything about cars, but I liked them. We had a Morris Minor Traveller when we were kids, but it hardly worked and my brother, Alan and I used to sit in it, sometimes all morning, just having a laugh and a joke, pretending we were driving the car.

My dad was an electrician down the pits in a little village called Peterlee. It was a pretty mucky job with long shifts.

We had often be in and around the pits, usually attending the pubs and clubs for events. One day, when I was about 15 years old, he asked me to come to the mineshaft to work with him, and he said to me, "That's where I work," and for me, that was enough. He said, "You don't have to follow in your dad's footsteps, that's for sure". I guess that was the first time I'd really thought about what I wanted NOT to do when I left school. At some stage I had to leave home and if I wanted to be a footballer, I knew I'd have to work hard at it. The fact that I never really thought I was good enough to be a professional actually became part of my motivation to become one.

So, in answer to the question, why did I become a footballer, I just think it was something inside and in my blood.

Being brought up in a mining area became a major influence in me wanting to become a footballer Between the ages of 13 and 15, I'd been to a few clubs for trials, and if there was something that made me want to become a footballer more than anything else, it was the fact that my dad worked at the pit for such long hours that we hardly saw him. In fact, I recall one of my school report books where I wrote: "I want to be a football player and I want a nice house. I want to be a coach and work for TV when I retire." Looking back, I'd actually mapped out my whole life at the age of 15.

I remember playing for the East Durham boys' team, and amongst others there was a lad called Harry Wilson, who ended up going to Brighton and another called Colin Morris who went to Sheffield United and of course my brother came on later. From a tiny little area, there were several footballers that made it.

So, it was my dad who had an influence on me; he never pushed me, but supported me with my football and my parents came to every single game I played in, and they were exactly the same with my brother.

I'd had a few disappointments as a youngster. I played in the Durham county trials, but I didn't perform very well and after the game I was told I wasn't in the squad. I was so disappointed and began to say to myself, "If I can't even get into the Durham county side at 15, how am I going to be a football player? How on earth am I going to be good enough?" I'd had trials at several clubs, including West Bromwich Albion, Leeds United, Port Vale, Manchester City, but that was the first real doubt for me in my life, even though there were other top clubs chasing me to go for a trial with them; I began to think I wouldn't be good enough to get in any of those sides anyway, and that played on my mind a little bit.

However, I had a bit of luck in that my relative, Malcolm Musgrove actually played for West Ham in his younger days, but he was the first-team coach at Villa at the time and that's from where my first trip to Villa stemmed. Having been rejected by Durham, I began to think that a club like Aston Villa would be perfect for me. A message was sent to Malcolm saying I was doing OK at football, and the county scout, Brian Wilson, was sent along to watch me and on the back of that performance, I was invited to go to Villa Park.

At the time, Villa were in the Second Division, and during my visit to Villa Park, we went to see a game and straight away the club was sold to me; the atmosphere; the fans singing in the Holte End; the whole thing just grabbed me. Before I went to Villa Park to meet the officials there, I had been to Sunderland, West Bromwich Albion and Burnley, but I liked what I saw at Villa.

It was April 1969 when I signed a three-year apprenticeship contract at Aston Villa F.C. It was crazy looking back on that time, because if I remember rightly my wage was a mere £7 a week in year one; £8 a week in year two and £10 a week in the final year. On top of that, the club looked after my lodgings, with bed, breakfast and evening meals all paid for; food was also provided when I trained.

I also got to play the game I loved, so it wasn't a bad life really.

I travelled down to Birmingham with my dad to sign the contract; it was quite a daunting experience, truth be told, because at that time, I had no idea where or with whom I was going to stay. After signing the forms, I went back home to the North East for a month before I started in earnest. It was an exciting, but at the same time it was a worrying time. Had I done the right thing? There were opportunities to join a club closer to home and Birmingham was over 200 miles away, but deep down, I really thought Aston Villa were the club for me. There was just something about them that I liked.

Fast-forward to the day I left home in June 1969. I was a skinny 15-year-old who had barely left school. I remember that day well. Mam and dad were already up when I woke that morning; I guess they had mixed feelings and I'm not sure whether they were excited, sad or apprehensive. Dad had a Morris Minor 1000 Traveller, a collector's car these days, but then just the mode of transport for our 45-minute journey to Durham station to pick up my train heading south, to Birmingham New Street. My dad gave me £1, 10 shillings pocket money, which to me was a lot of money and he told me to buy something for my journey. He then gave me a big hug, shook my hand and saw me onto the train. There was no real fuss made, to be honest, and no tears in his eyes.

Having been informed by the club that I "wouldn't need to bring much," I only had one piece of luggage with me, not that I had a lot of possessions, anyway. I was also told that my training gear would be provided, and as time went by I'd have enough money to buy my own things. The trains were steam back then. The journey took three hours, and three hours on my own on a train was my worst nightmare. I was a poor traveller at the best of times. I hated public transport, mainly because smoking was permitted in public places and I hated the smell of cigarette smoke. The train was no exception. It seemed that everyone smoked in those days and I couldn't get away from it. The journey wasn't easy and I didn't enjoy it one bit. Nowadays I love travelling by trains, it was just the smell of the smoke in those days that I hated. You had to sit down somewhere and if the person next to you smoked, you just had to put up with it. Unsurprisingly I was glad when smoking was banned in public places some years ago.

When I arrived at Birmingham New Street station, I had no idea what to do or where to go. Bear in mind I was a 15-year-old and it was the first time I'd travelled on my own. I didn't do too bad to get that far. I exited the station, looked around and recognised a familiar face; it was Peter Doherty, the Aston Villa chief scout and he'd come to collect me from the train. Peter was a lovely guy whom I'd met before, and he welcomed me to Birmingham. We got into his car and he drove me to Villa Park. By that time, I still didn't know where and with whom I was going to be staying. Usually, clubs put you up in digs with another apprentice so I began wondering whom I'd end up with. I knew I was going to meet somebody new and possibly I'd spend the next three years of my life living with that person.

Coming from a small town in County Durham, moving to Birmingham was a big deal and even the journey from the station to Villa Park seemed to take an age. Even though it was in the late 1960s there was still a lot of traffic on the road and it was so much busier than it was back at home. When we arrived at Villa Park, Peter left me in the reception area and went off to find out where I was going to be staying for the next three years. It wasn't just me who had started that day, but several other lads arrived while I was waiting. I think I was one of the last people to arrive, as I'm pretty sure the other lads had been given their itinerary already. For me, it was a journey into the unknown – but ultimately, a journey I wanted to follow.

It was mid-to-late afternoon and Peter came back to meet me in reception and said we were going to meet the other lad who was going to stay in the digs with me. That lad was Roy Stark (Starky) and I when I first saw him I couldn't get over the size of him. Roy was twice my size and compared to me looked like a fully-grown man. I asked Roy what position he played and it didn't surprise me when he said he was a centre-half because I could see he was built like one. We both hit it off and little did I know at the time, but it was the start of my first friendship as a footballer. Roy turned out to be a great friend of mine in later life.

Once Roy gathered his belongings, Peter drove us to our digs in Boldmere, Sutton Coldfield, a leafy suburb north of Birmingham, about five or six miles from Villa Park. Again, it seemed like a long journey to me. Roy and I didn't really say a lot. I was quite quiet and shy and wasn't one for asking loads of questions in those days. I was probably really nervous and, given his size along with the fact that he was very confident in himself for a 15-year-old, Roy seemed a bit intimidating. He was definitely the more dynamic character of the two of us. He wasn't worried about leaving his parents and going to meet two strangers who would look after us for the next three years. Roy told me he was looking forward to the experience, whereas I probably wasn't ready for any of it, if truth were to be told.

When we arrived at the digs, Peter knocked on the door and we were introduced to our new 'mam and dad', so to speak. From the first moment that Mr and Mrs Mallard both came to the door to let us in, I knew I'd be just fine with them. For about an hour, Roy and I sat down with Peter and talked to the Mallards about ourselves; what we liked to do; what we liked to eat and drink; just a general chitchat to settle us in more than anything. I was still nervous, but at the same time, I enjoyed it and felt more comfortable as the time went on. Peter stayed with us for a little while before heading off home and I distinctly remember him saying to us, just before he left, "Now lads, Mr and Mrs Mallard know exactly what you've got to do to get to Villa Park in the morning." That was quite intriguing, but also very welcoming to me.

I soon settled into my new home, and I felt straight away that I was with a couple of people who were genuinely looking forward to having two young footballers stay with them. It was really quite an unreal situation and looking back on it, it seems a complete contrast to how the youngsters enter the game now.

After Peter left us, Roy and I sat down together and had a bit of tea – beans on toast I think, my favourite at the time. The house was semi-detached with three bedrooms and I took an instant liking to my new home, and to the Mallards. They were brilliant. Mrs Mallard had a lovely personality and Mr Mallard was a very funny man with a great sense of humour, and his job as a postman suited him. I don't think I've ever met anyone who could fall asleep so quickly once he sat down after eating his tea.

As time went by, we both settled into a routine, but I remained nervous for a while. The Mallards were lucky enough to have a TV, black and white of course, and we'd always go to bed around 9pm. Roy, being more relaxed and comfortable with the situation would go to sleep before me. I was in a strange bed, in a strange house, with strange people. I was used to having my two brothers with me when I was at mam and dad's home so this was a massive change.

On our first morning, we got up bright and early, had some tea and toast for breakfast and headed out to catch the bus. Mr Mallard explained what our routine for the next day would be, but nonetheless it seemed daunting, as it was something else to get my head around. We had a 20-25 minute walk to the bus stop to catch the number 7, Outer Circle bus to Witton Island, which was the closest stop to Villa Park.

We both knew we were walking into the unknown, but hopefully to begin our new life as professional footballers.

Roy and I had been told to arrive at Villa Park before 9am on that first morning and we got there with plenty of time to spare. When we arrived at the ground we met up with the other lads, and then we were introduced to Ron Wainwright, the kitman. We were told his job was to basically look after the apprentices and to teach us how to do the chores, but more about that later.

Ron showed us into the away dressing room, where we were to get changed for training. A few of the first-year pros were also sent into the dressing room too, and then it was a case of sitting and waiting for everyone to walk in. With every lad that walked in we'd shake hands and introduce ourselves. Looking back, that first day is all a bit of a blur, to be honest. I only knew Starky, so it was going to take a while to get to know so many new faces.

After about an hour of talking between ourselves and trying to get to know as many people as possible, we got changed into our training gear. We were surprised to be told we would be all training together; our coach, Graham Leggat, came into the dressing room, introduced himself and told us we would be training with the senior pros. It was our manager, Tommy Docherty, who had bought into the philosophy of getting the apprentices training with the seniors. It meant that no matter what the senior players did, the youngsters did exactly the same.

We had a minibus to take us to training; we didn't have a fixed venue like most teams do now so we made use of about four different facilities in the local area. On that first day we went to a place called Barr Beacon, which was near Walsall. When we got there I couldn't believe it, because it was just a load of hills and no sign of a football pitch anywhere. Here we were, a bunch of 15-year-olds and expected to run up and down hills against the senior pros, the likes of Andy Lochhead, Bruce Rioch, Charlie Aitken and Ian 'Chico' Hamilton, all well-known players to the Villa faithful. To this day, I can genuinely say I've never run so far in my life as I did that day. That first morning was the most horrendous training session I've ever had in my life. I have never felt as sick as I did after that torture, and I don't use that word lightly. It was torture. In fact, it was quite strange watching grown men being sick all around you. Luckily I wasn't sick myself, but it was brutal for me just the same.

I promised myself I would not do that to anybody and I never made anybody run that far when I became a coach later in life.

I have a lasting impression of that first training session that has stayed with me since that day. I believe their plan was to see who would last the pace, and who would be 'last man standing'. It was absolute punishment at the highest level. I look back now, to when I was 15 years old. I could have run for the County Durham cross-country team and fortunately I was fit and could have run along with anybody. That morning, we must have run around Barr Beacon Country Park for what seemed like several hours, and anybody who didn't put the effort in was tortured by the coaches. It was a case of, "Keep moving and don't stop..." There was no method or point to it. Even at that young, tender age I had an opinion and it went something like, "What the hell are we doing here? What on earth is going on? This isn't right." For me, there should be some logic and structure to training sessions, but there was none that day.

I will never forget it, and I'll never forget how ill I felt afterwards. At that stage it was the toughest day I had ever encountered, but I can tell you there were some even tougher days to come. I think it was tough because we had no idea what we were going to do that first day. It hit us unexpectedly. We were apprentices on our first day and we were expecting to be in and around other young players, taking it easy, passing the ball to each other, but we ended up being thrown in among the most senior players at the club, running up and down hills. It was the craziest situation I think I've ever been involved in – and it was only day one.

When we returned to Villa Park, the club gave each of us some money to buy a well-earned lunch. There were two cafés near to the ground and Ernie's Café on Nelson Road was where all the senior pros went, so we were banned from going there. Funnily enough, I never went into Ernie's Café, even when I made the first team, as I wanted to be with my mates. Ernie's was the place they had their chat between training sessions; the place they moaned and groaned or whatever they wanted to do. We all had about 90 minutes in between sessions and the apprentices and young players had to go a bit further down the road, to a place called Pearl's Café. It was clean and tidy and had a pinball machine in the corner, and it soon became a second home to us. In time, Pearl got to know each and every one of our names, and got to know exactly what we liked to eat. It eventually became a familiar place, so much so that when I walked in, Pearl would say, "Here comes Brian: a well-done bacon sandwich?"

The café got us away from all the hard work and grind of training for a while, but it also became an interesting place to go to; it was a time to relax, sit down and chat, tell some jokes and have some laughs together. It was also a place where we got to know each other really well. From the bonding point of view, it was a great place because, over time, we'd spend hours and hours there 'chewing the fat'. However, I don't think any of us ate a great deal of food there, as we were all too tired to eat, especially after that first day.

The second part of the first day's training saw us going back towards Barr Beacon, to Cooksey Lane, which was a training complex with loads of pitches. The afternoon session wasn't as hard, thankfully, and consisted of a lot of shorter distance work; sprinting and running around the pitch a few times. It was much more of a dynamic type of training, but again, it was hard, and I dread to think how many laps we did. We just ran and ran, and ran and ran even more. It was a crazy day, and one I can honestly say, I didn't enjoy and I'm sure I speak for the other lads as well.

To get that day over and done with, and to get through it unscathed was an accomplishment in itself. When we returned to Villa Park to get changed, we all sat in a bath for a long time, to take in what we had just done and to try to recover from the aches and pains.

If we thought the day was over once we'd bathed and got changed, we were very much mistaken. The other side of being an apprentice then kicked – in the chores. Ron Wainwright was the kitman and the man who showed us the jobs we had to do. There were lots of them as well: cleaning the professionals' boots; cleaning the old wooden floors in the dressing rooms; cleaning the toilets; cleaning the shower rooms; we were even expected to sweep the terracing. You name it, we'd have to clean it. Each week, there was a rota and everybody would get their chance to learn a different job so we could each learn all the tasks and not get bored doing the same thing every day. I admit I wasn't ready for it. I mean, I'd never cleaned anything in my life and I mean anything. My dad used to clean my shoes and mam did the housework, but now I was expected to learn how to clean up after professional footballers.

We were all given jobs each day. They ranged from tidying up the boots to cleaning the boots to hanging the training kits up in driers. The kit wasn't washed every day in those days so we had to put it into large driers. The kit was sweaty and stunk like hell and it was just left out on the huge drying racks to freshen up, ready for the next morning. It was that bad that I can still smell the kit to this day. Thankfully, at least once a week the kit would be laundered, but on the days it wasn't, the smell of 25 or 35 stinky kits was horrendous. I don't know why they bothered with the drying racks, because the following morning, the kit stunk just as badly as it had when we'd hung it up. The very thought of those sweaty shirts hanging up will stay with me forever, that's for sure. However, as time went on, some of the lads, especially some of the seniors actually took their gear home every day to get it washed. Some of the pros like Bruce Rioch, Geoff Vowden, Fred Turnbull and Ray Graydon would do that without any hesitation, but they were in the minority.

Like at a lot of big clubs in those days, there was a 'boot room' at Villa Park. Cleaning the boots of senior pros was a hard job in itself, because it wasn't only cleaning the boots and trainers, it was sweeping up all the mud and dirt and keeping the room tidy, after training. Our boot room was an iconic place, just like the famous Anfield boot room. It was the place the boots were brushed, washed and hung and it was located underground, and you'd have to take them back upstairs to put them back on the appropriate players' pegs when they were clean. Each player would have their own boots, trainers and kit, all numbered from 1 to 40 and they would all have three or four pairs of boots each, so you'd end up cleaning around 100 pairs of boots of all shapes and sizes, every single day. On top of having responsibility for the boots, we were all given a number of professionals boots to clean that we had to prioritise. I remember my 'priority' pros were Bruce Rioch and Pat McMahon, who I thought were really decent fellas. As time went by, Bruce had a real influence on me, my initial impressions of him were very positive, but more about Bruce later. Pat was also a lovely fella and a good footballer and someone whom I later admired greatly.

Another tough job was scrubbing the wooden floors after training. We had large, heavy machinery to do that, but it was a hard job because the machinery was so heavy to push around the small changing rooms. We used brushes to get underneath the benches and into the corners so we could get all the dirt and rubbish out to avoid Ron catching us out. Not only did we have to clean the dressing room floors, we also had to clean the toilets, the bath and shower rooms. The bath was huge; it could hold up to 20 people at a time, they left a right mess afterwards and it had to be cleaned every single day. Health and safety wouldn't allow that these days, but in 1969 we knew nothing else.

And that wasn't the half of it. The tunnel had to be cleaned properly, the passage way had to be cleaned and mopped out every single day. Our own dressing room had to be done, and the coaches' kit and boots had to be cleaned. The amount of work we had to do, after the two sessions of proper training was phenomenal. I can't for one minute imagine the youth players these days doing any of that work.

Having said all that, we all learned so much about cleaning, about cleanliness and tidiness; we weren't allowed to walk past a piece of paper without picking it up and putting it in the bin. If we did and Ron saw us, we'd get a right rollicking. It was so strict that we were even told to pick up any rubbish off the floor, wherever it was and put it in the bin straight away. If we saw boots in the wrong place, we'd have to put them in the right place. Anything that was out of place, we were told to put it right. In fact, Ron used to hide pieces of paper in your job areas, underneath any nook or cranny, in the hope you'd miss it and we'd be given another rollicking. I remember Ron used to smoke and he'd cruelly hide his cigarette ends behind different places and say, "Let's have a look here – that's not done, do it all again." That meant we had to do our job again and do it properly, because if we didn't we'd soon get found out. It caused some great arguments amongst the apprentices at times. Looking back, it was the first bit of proper work I'd had to do in my short life, but with hindsight, it was a brilliant way to teach young people about discipline.

There were lots of jobs we didn't particularly like doing; however, there was one task that soon became a favourite of ours. If the groundsman ever said there was loads of rubbish that needed burning and he wanted a volunteer, all the apprentices would put up their hands. If you were lucky enough to get picked, you'd be expected to take all the rubbish to a patch of ground behind the Witton End stand at Villa Park, an open terrace that in those days, had a huge grass bank sloping from the top of the terracing to the bottom. Once we'd gathered all the rubbish, we'd have to burn it and keep an eye on the fire. Although I use the term loosely, it was a job everybody enjoyed because it got us outside, away from all the hard slog of cleaning and scrubbing in the changing rooms.

Even though at first we weren't very good at our jobs, once we were taught properly how to do them we became experts at cleaning. Having said that, I thought we were training to become footballers, not cleaners.

So, that was our introduction to being an apprentice – and that was only day one. Bring on day two!

If I had looked back on the timeline of that day, Roy and I would have left our digs at 7:30am and I think we got home at something like 7:30pm. I can remember Mrs Mallard asking us what we wanted to eat, and on that first day we both had a bowl of soup and then went straight to bed. We weren't that hungry and we were both knackered.

As I lay in bed that night, recapping the day, I said to myself, "Crikey, this is hard work. What have I got myself into? Am I really going to get through this?" I found it hard to get to sleep that first night; I was so tired; physically my body ached from head-to-toe.

It was a massive learning curve for all of us apprentices and there was a realisation that being an apprentice wasn't going to be an easy job at all, and not a job you could take lightly. If I found the first day tough, I thought to myself "What is it going to be like tomorrow, and the days after that?" I obviously wanted to be a footballer from an early age, but it certainly wasn't as glamorous as I'd first thought it would be.

In fairness to the boys who were playing in the first-team, whilst they had the grandeur of playing every Saturday in front of thousands of fans, I was genuinely totally gobsmacked how hard they had to work, day in and day out to get to where they were.

That first day certainly had a profound effect on me, and was a day that will stay with me for the rest of my life.

As time went by, the daily grind of the 12-hour day and the endless scrubbing and cleaning didn't become any easier. It was a typical apprenticeship in the 1970s. If there were to be any glory, there would only be glory in the years to come.

That first pre-season I was selected to go with the reserve team on a tour of Scotland and again, that was difficult for lots of various reasons. I saw, for the first time, the other side of football, a side where footballers, some who were in the reserve team and weren't happy about being there because they thought they were good enough to be in the first-team, were told to go on the trip regardless. However, as a 15-year-old apprentice, I was more than happy at being selected.

On that tour, we faced the likes of Ross County, and in our team we had a bunch of senior pros that weren't happy and as a youngster, in and amongst it, I heard and saw things that were, shall we say, very grown-up. For example, after the game with Ross County, the lads were allowed to have an alcoholic drink or two, and I'd have to sit around with them, drinking Coca-Cola, watch them down pints of beer and behaving like, well, you can imagine. For a kid from a fairly quiet background, what I witnessed was eye-opening, to say the least. To hear them talking and to see them drink the amounts of beer that they did, was a bit of a shock to the system. There was a drinking culture within football back then, that's for sure, and it wasn't seen to be bad for you providing it was done at the right times, especially when it was meant to help team-bonding. I found it really strange at that age, to be around adult football players who to say the least were acting wildly. At that tender age it wasn't something I'd witnessed before or had expected to witness. Maybe I was just a bit naïve.

****

The first-team dressing room was a terrifying place to be in for any apprentice to be in, even for Roy, but more so for me. There were 15 or 16 of us in that dressing room who were pretty new to the club and I'll mention just a few of the lads who made an impression on me in those early days. Firstly, Dennis Common was one of the first I met. He was another Geordie, from Blyth, and straight away I could see there could be a friendship there, probably based on the fact we were from the same neck of the woods. Dennis was the craftiest bugger in the group and would sometimes make up a job, go off and speak to the groundsman and skip his real tasks in the dressing room – and for that, I loved him to bits.

Then there was Alistair Cook, from Carlisle, who was a lovely lad and the same age as me. He was only tiny, had a lovely left foot and was probably one of the most enthusiastic lads I've ever come across; always bubbly, even doing his chores after training and always willing to help, which wasn't a common trait amongst footballers. Believe it or not, a lot of the apprentices would try and shirk their work and that became the most common source of argument amongst the group, especially when someone didn't do their job right and that would result in a load of infighting. Alistair was a top lad though, a brilliant apprentice and great to be around. Then there was Bobby Glaze, who I still keep in touch with to this day. Bobby was from the Black Country, a year older than me and in his second year, but he knew everything so he showed us the ropes. Bobby was very vocal and made sure the lads did their jobs properly. As a footballer, he was a tidy midfielder who wanted the ball all of the time and was a great character on the pitch. But just like with the Scottish lads, getting used to Bobby's accent was pretty difficult.

Greg Fellows was another Black Country lad and he'd been in and around the England schoolboys' scene for sometime. He was a big, strong six-foot centre forward and a real character in the dressing room. He knew everyone, claimed he knew everything, was really a funny lad, and as he came from a fairly well-to-do family he didn't like doing the chores at all. He was a good lad though, crafty with it, but if he could find somewhere to go to escape the cleaning, he would be there and he would bear the brunt of the flack that was thrown around for the jobs that hadn't been done. Another Black Country lad was Neil Ross. He was a funny lad who liked a laugh and a joke and would do anything for you. Neil was a good trainer, popular and was nearly always one of the first players to be picked in training.

Then there was Roy Stark, with whom I shared digs of course. Roy was from Nottingham and was the leader of the group and at 15 years old, he was more man than boy. Straight away, he was given the role of keeping the lads in their places, making sure everything was done and done properly. As a footballer, he was hard as nails and in subsequent years, he and my brother Alan formed a good partnership and were two of the toughest lads I've ever come across in football. He'd even look after me in our digs. We'd often go out at night for a walk around the streets of Boldmere and just talk or we'd meet up with Brian 'Jimmy' Melling, who had digs a mile or so from us, and a great friendship developed between the three of us. I'm not saying I needed looking after as a youngster, but my quiet background probably dictated that I needed someone to keep an eye out for me. Starky was more like a big brother to me in that first year or so, and I thank him for that.

Being in such a tight-knit group soon teaches you a lot about people. Among the group, we had eight Scots, including three Scottish schoolboy internationals who had been chosen to come all the way down to Birmingham to play football after being chased by quite a few of the bigger English clubs. I think those lads chose Villa because the new youth policy that the first-team manager, Tommy Docherty, brought in seemed to appeal to them. I think they had been 'looked after' by the club and had been promised a year's contract as a pro following their apprenticeship, which was unheard of in those days. Apparently, on Sunday mornings, Tommy Docherty and the chairman, Doug Ellis, would fly to places like Newcastle and watch two youth games, then fly to Glasgow where they'd watch another two games simply to get the signatures of the boys that were recommended by the local scouts. I remember being sold the youth policy by the club, which was that Villa were a big club and they wanted to start producing their own talent for the future. To prove that point, fast-forward a few years and several of the lads in my group did play for the first-team, including me, which was great and proved that the forward-thinking policy worked.

All of the Scottish lads had their own characteristics, and they were all great lads to boot. Gordon Knowles was a goalkeeper, and a really hard worker who always wanted to be a footballer; so much so, it was untrue. He so wanted to be the best, but unfortunately, it never really happened for him. He was a lovely lad and had a very polite, well-spoken Scottish accent. However, we had some lads who had strong Glaswegian accents and they tended to growl rather than speak to us, and we sometimes found it intimidating. Alex McMillan was one. He was a left back, a very excitable character and although he loved playing football he loved talking more. So. He was always in the middle of all the jokes that were flying around the dressing room. Billy Kellock was a big lad, six-foot two inches tall and an unbelievable passer of the ball from midfield. Billy was a fine footballer with a good touch and he was one of the crop of youngsters who went onto play a lot of league games, although his lack of pace probably stopped him progressing any higher than the second tier of English football. Micky Kearney was a great character, the man about town who became a good friend of mine. He always dressed well. In fact all the Scottish lads were well-presented and quite fashion-conscious. Some of them had their shirts handmade with their initials embroidered onto the collar and their clothes were on a different level. Micky was a decent player as well and went onto play for Reading and Chester later in his career.

Jamie Hughes was a year older than me, but he had sideburns even at that age. I had hardly started shaving, but he had full-on facial hair. He was a tenacious character who really got stuck in, but he never really made it in the game. Then there was Joe Burns, the classical Scottish footballer who came from Glasgow. When I went to introduce myself, I stood in front of him and said, "Hi, I'm Brian, Brian Little. I'm from Newcastle and I play in midfield." Joe looked at me and replied, "Just call me Joe, Joe the Blade." That stunned me and I just said, "Sorry, did you say Joe the Blade?" "Yeah, Joe the Blade" he growled. He was about the same size as me, but he was intimidating and I got the impression that you wouldn't dare mess him around. In fairness, he turned out to be a really great lad, but he frightened me to death on our first meeting. There was a lad called Micky Brady from Aberdeen, and he had quite a localised dialect that was hard to fathom at first and it took the English lads a long time to get used to his accent. Having said that, it was fascinating listening to all the accents in the dressing room. There were some great leaders amongst the Scottish lads, including the likes of: Jimmy Brown and Micky Kearney, who were all a year older and helped us settle in and taught us how to clean up after training.

We had a great mix of characters in our group, and players of varied qualities and abilities. We often had England v Scotland 8-a-side matches in training and it usually ended up being a competitive battle as you can imagine. We'd have a different captain each day and sometimes we'd even mix the teams up. If you were first pick you'd be 'king of the jungle', but if you were last pick, you'd be gutted. It created a great atmosphere after the main training had finished and it added an extra edge to those sessions. There was so much banter that went on but the aim of the exercise was to learn how to be competitive and how to react to and handle different situations. Football is all about how you handle certain situations and those first few months certainly taught us about how to react to different scenarios.

In the main, we all got on really well, but I have to say there were a few scuffles here and there. When you put a bunch of 15 or 16-year-old lads together from all over the country, who all want to do something in their lives or want to get somewhere in the football world, there will always be times when there is a little bother, and our group was no different.

****

When we had to go into the first-team dressing room (the home dressing room) for some reason or other, we'd head for Ron

Wainwright's office first of all. His office was in the corner of the dressing room and it was very much his domain. If you wanted something for the pro you were looking after, you'd have to knock on his door and ask him for the bit of kit the pro wanted. Despite having the unofficial title of 'kitman' he was quite commanding and in charge of lots of other things. However, certain pros would get their way with him, the likes of Bruce Rioch, for instance. Bruce joined the club during that summer in 1969 on, at the time, a record transfer deal of £100,000 and was a top-class professional. If he asked for something, it was handed to him, no questions asked. Bruce commanded respect, even at that early stage of his career. However, the cheekier ones who had been around for a while, often asked for stuff they weren't supposed to have, but Ron would tell them in no uncertain terms to "Get lost," or words to that affect.

It really was a strange environment to be around and to get used to, especially for a whippersnapper like me. If you were given the job of taking the tea into the pros' dressing room, you'd have to go to the canteen and ask the tea lady for as many tea bags, plastic cups and as much milk and sugar as she would give you _ which usually wasn't a lot. Once you'd made the tea, you'd have to take the huge teapot and the cups and put them on a table in the centre of the dressing room. There was a central column with a large table around it and that was the focal point of the first-team dressing room. You'd try and make a quick exit once the teapot and cups had been delivered, but the very minute you'd put the teapot down, there were shouts from here, there and everywhere, "Oi son, cup of tea, four sugars over here..." or "...cup of tea, two sugars, over here, sunshine." It was unbelievably intimidating and on top of all that, you'd hear all the banter that would go on between the pros. Looking back, it was hilarious, but to a 15-year-old it was all a bit scary. In fairness to the pros, they had a laugh at our expense, but it was just in good fun.

The things that went on in that dressing room, well, it was no place for the faint-hearted that's for sure. I once saw a pro cutting the toes out of someone else's socks while they were in the bath, and another time I witnessed someone filling a pair of shoes up with water. I even saw someone putting Vaseline in his mate's socks. All sorts of the most stupid things that you probably wouldn't believe would go on in that dressing room. When you'd walk in you not only saw those things go on every day, but you'd hear the cries of laughter from someone hiding behind a newspaper, when the unfortunate person found his socks with no toes, or his shoes filled with water. Hilarious, yes, but it was unforgiving as well. There were always certain people who would be picked on. Some would take it in good spirits and as a joke, but there were others who would get angry and annoyed that someone had put Vaseline in their shoes or something ridiculous like that. Sometimes, I witnessed the odd fracas, where it would end up with two senior pros squaring up with each other, but fortunately, mostly it was taken in good humour.

The dressing room was an unbelievably competitive place and every time I went in there I'd always say to myself, even at that early age, "Brian, look, listen and learn". I quickly established that some of the things I would learn wouldn't be healthy; some of the things would stand me in good stead; some of the things I might have to stand up to as time went by and those were the things I thought I had to be up and ready for. I was very much preparing myself for the future and, looking back now, I quite enjoyed that atmosphere in a strange way. It was a wonderful place, despite the fact that, if you were a weak person in those days, you just wouldn't survive. It was most definitely, the battle of the mentally strong and the physically fit.

There were some classic days during that first year as an apprentice. It was around the Christmas time of 1969 that we signed George Curtis from Coventry City. Now, he was a footballer who you could be genuinely frightened of – just by looking at him. He was a man and a half, and even though he was quietly spoken off the field, he was unbelievably tough and strong on the field of play, and because of George's presence, he was often the target of pranks. Some of the more daring lads used to do things to George. Even though they were terrified of doing it, at the same time, it seemed to be a challenge for them. That they wanted to do it seemed very odd to me. George came in one day and saw his socks had been cut to bits. He just turned around to the nearest person to him, on that day it was Lew Chatterley, who was about six-foot four inches tall himself, and grabbed him by his ears and banged his head against the wooden dressing room wall. George then turned round, held up his socks and shouted out to the dressing room, "Who's done this?" Everybody in the dressing room sniggered, but one person piped up, "I don't know George, it was probably only a laugh anyway". The other lads laughed and somebody else then shouted out, "Ahr, leave him alone George." Unfortunately, George wouldn't give up. He wanted to know who'd cut his socks up. In the end, George got Lew's shirt behind the back of his neck, pulled the scruff of his collar, hung him on his peg and left him there. Poor Lew was almost crying. As you can imagine, the rest of the dressing room were cringing and the lads who'd actually done it were hiding behind a newspaper, sniggering and pretending to be reading it, knowing they had got away with their prank. Barrie Hole was one of my favourite players at the time and was such a laid-back character. He would usually sit in the corner, with his legs crossed, smoking a cigarette, but on that occasion, he piped up and said to George, "George, just leave him alone. Put him down. This is ridiculous George." Barry never joined in those sort of stupid tricks. He just came in, did his work and went home. He loved his football, but he would just sit there, taking everything in after a game or training and do his own thing. Although he didn't say much, when he did he was the voice of reason in the group. To be honest, though nobody took much notice of him, as he was just a completely different character from most of the other lads. He was the one who'd usually shout out something like, "Sit down, shut up and behave yourselves." Then he'd go about his business as if he'd never said anything. He wasn't overly bothered if they didn't behave themselves, but he would say something just to let people know he was actually there. Most of the lads were hyperactive, jumping up and down, but Barry was the opposite. He was the classic old-school foot-baller; he'd have a cigarette before the game, and another one at half time and probably two before he'd even thought about going into the bath after the game.

The dressing room was pure theatre; it was a place where only the tough survived, and the weak got beaten up, and for myself and the other lads of my age to see that, it surely was an incredible place to be, even though we were probably scared stiff half of the time.

Those were the days!

****

One of the jobs, I've already touched on, that we had to do as an apprentice was sweeping up the terraces after a midweek matchday. We tended to do it together as a group, the day following a match. Along with a few of the older ground staff, our job was to sweep the terraces and burn the rubbish at the back of the Witton End stand. In fairness, we had a great laugh doing it and it was always one of the jobs everyone enjoyed – only because it got us out of the routine of cleaning up the changing rooms. Looking back, the amount of times we found coins or ten bob notes made the job worthwhile. Clearing the huge Holte End terraces was the worst job though. The sweeping up took a long, long time and come lunchtime, we would pool all the coins and notes and we'd go and buy ourselves some fish and chips to share from the shop at the back of the Witton End stand. We'd take half an hour out of the grind and eat our lunch on the steps of the Holte End, looking out onto the Villa Park pitch. We used those days to bond as a group, a group of lads, some of who would be destined to become footballers, but were spending their day sweeping the terraces at Villa Park.

Looking back, it was a good education I guess, but sweeping the terraces was a bind, it really was, and there were times when we'd have a right moan about it. On one occasion Jimmy Brown was allowed to skip the jobs the rest of us had to do. This was because he was about to make his first team debut at the ripe old age of 15 years and 349 days; the youngest ever player to play in the Villa first-team at the time, a record that stood for many years. There were many times after that when Jimmy got called up to the first-team, and we'd be left sweeping the terracing while he would be told to rest up before the game at the weekend. Instead of keeping out of the way, though, Jimmy would sometimes take to the Villa Park pitch to show off; he'd do some tricks with the ball or he'd kick the ball from one end of the pitch to the other and bang the ball in the back of the net. I wouldn't say it was a problem, but he got a lot of stick from the lads and he wound some of us up by doing it. While I thought he shouldn't have to continue doing his jobs with the rest of us, I didn't think it was right him displaying his skills in front of us as it was kind of showing off.

With Jimmy in mind, fast forward for a moment to when I was 17 years old, and I had signed professional, but instead of jacking in the cleaning jobs, I decided to continue doing them, until I was pretty much transferred into the pro dressing room on a full-time basis. I didn't want them grumbling behind my back, not that they would have done so because my brother, Alan, was there by then and he would have sorted them out if they had started moaning about me behind my back, that's for sure.

****

I did get involved with the first-team during that first year as an apprentice, even though I didn't play. I travelled to several away games with the lads; the club always took a young player along with the kitman to away games and this was seen as a bit of a privilege, and it was seen as a way of slowly introducing young players to the first-team environment. I had quite a few journeys with the first team and it was quite flattering, but I was left at home if I was required to play for the intermediate team.

I also played for the reserves several times during that first season. One of my very first games was at Old Trafford and I was only 15 at the time. Before we travelled up to Manchester, I remember the reserve team coach giving me some words of encouragement, "I know you're only 15, but you can run and whoever you're playing against, if it's a senior pro you'll be able to run him off the park. You'll be great." As it turned out, the Manchester United player who was playing directly opposite me was a fella by the name of Paddy Crerand, probably one of the finest players around in his time. Paddy was getting on a bit, probably 30 years old and late into his career, but my coach told me not to worry about the person who I was facing as he wouldn't want to run past me. How wrong was he? I think I collapsed after about 65 minutes; I couldn't get anywhere near Paddy Crerand. He was so good it was untrue, and whenever he got the ball, no matter how quickly I tried to close him down, he would get a yard or three on me, to such a point that at the end of the 65 minutes, I had nothing left – I was absolutely shattered. I've had the pleasure of meeting Paddy on many occasions over the years and every time I see him I remind him of that story and he just looks at me, giggles and says to me, "I know. You played against me and you struggled." Stories like that just don't happen any more, because until youngsters reach adulthood, they don't tend to play against men, but back then I was 15 and had played against one of the best players around at the time, even though he was double my age. It was great experience for me.

That first season was blumming hard and I can't really say anything positive about it. However, there was one game that stuck in my mind and it came during the early part of October 1969. The first-team had only won one game up until then, but we absolutely battered Huddersfield Town 4-1 at home and I remember the manager, Tommy Docherty, and his assistant, Arthur Cox, jumping up and down in the dug-out. Pre-season, the club had spent big money on players like Bruce Rioch and expectations were high for a push towards promotion to the First Division. Being part of that squad, even though I didn't play, was the best experience I'd had as a footballer so far and I wanted more. We really did play well that day and everybody thought it signalled the turnaround in fortunes. However, that joy at winning was short-lived.

The season started to get worse when Graham Leggat, the youth team coach, who had only been on the staff a short time, left the club by securing himself a job in Canada, and was replaced by Frank Upton and his appointment signalled the start of a cycle of changes at the club. Then, on 19th January 1970, with Villa bottom of the Second Division, Doug Ellis sacked Tommy Docherty and he took Arthur Cox with him. Former Villa player Vic Crowe then took charge of the senior team, along with ex-Villa inside forward Ron Wylie.

At senior level, Vic was far calmer than Tommy Docherty and Ron Wylie was more meticulous than Arthur Cox, who was very strong with the senior players. Even though Ron had retired, he was one of those coaches who would play in amongst the players. Whilst he couldn't run around all day, you'd certainly want Ron Wylie on your side in those 5-a-side games because he was such a good footballer.

Frank Upton was employed as our youth team coach. When Frank first came to the club, he frightened me to death and certainly made an impression on me. He was a big, strong man who wanted to be organised and disciplined and at first, I was quite wary of him. However, Frank Upton was brilliant for me, and he had a massive impact on my development. I owe a lot to Frank because he spotted that I was good enough to play higher up the pitch. When I came to the club I was playing out wide or in midfield, so I had to learn a different way to play the game; he taught me to look at the ball; to look at the person who was about to play the ball and to look at who was playing against you. He taught me how to adapt my game, from one week to the next, because not all players would give you the same problems. Some weeks you had to run beyond people, other weeks you had to play short and back into them. He was a brilliant man manager and a brilliant coach. He recognised some of my weaknesses and frailties and kept talking to me about them. Under Frank, the game of football began to become clearer and more natural to me and it all began to fall into place. I soon found out that the more I practised things on a daily basis, the easier it became and I started picking things up pretty quickly. I already had the ability, but my skills began to rise. I became aware of everything around me. Sometimes, I surprised myself with the things I did, like doing overhead kicks and silly things like that. Somehow, I developed in a way that was quite surprising, but I loved it.

Although I looked scraggy and unkept, I was totally dedicated to the game; my hair tended to be a bit long and scruffy; I also liked to play with my socks rolled down around my ankles, but I loved training and wanted to improve all the time. I also began to look at other people; some players were nervy before, during and after a game, whereas I was never like that, and I don't know why. That I was fear free was all part of my development and that helped my game. I look back at some of my mates who never made it in the game, and it was because of their fear of trying different things, just in case it didn't work. My mentality had a huge impact on my career.

Those three significant changes in personnel had a massive affect on me as time went by. However, that season didn't get any better. Even off the pitch, the jobs we had to do in the dressing room seemed to become harder and the negativity around the club seemed to rub off on the lads. Suddenly, there were a few niggles and irritations flying around the dressing room. When Vic came in you could sense there was more calmness about him and he was far more low-key. However, there was a real fracture around the first team dressing room; even as an apprentice and on the fringes of the first team, you could feel the tension and hear the arguments amongst the players. Personally, I didn't get embroiled in it, but there was an atmosphere there, that's for sure. I think I'm right in saying Barrie Hole actually went on strike at one point because of the way he was being spoken to. Barrie was normally relaxed about things, but he wasn't going to be messed around. Players were falling out with each other and you could sense something wasn't quite right.

Even though Vic had five months to save the club, we only managed to win eight games all season and lost exactly half of our games, he ultimately couldn't save us and we got relegated to the Third Division for the first time in the club's history in that 1969–1970 season, and for the size and magnitude of Aston Villa, it was a disaster. Even for an apprentice like me, it was really hard to take. It was a painful experience seeing the demise of Aston Villa, who were deemed to be a great club. In fact, I'd go as far to say it was the worst period of my football career. For a young lad to witness that, it was strange, but at the same time, without a doubt, it was educational,.

Changes were afoot, and those changes would become instrumental for both the future development of the football club and for the development of my football education. For instance, we signed Andy Lochhead and Davie Gibson from Leicester City, and they would prove to be key figures for the club and for me, later in my career. I also look at the influence Ian 'Chico' Hamilton had on me, because unlike some of the other senior players who tended to look down on me and would preach to me, 'Chico' took me on as being like one of his mates. He was a great lad, great fun and I loved being around people like that; we were always having a laugh and a joke and he took everything with a pinch of salt, which I thought was the right way to do it.

****

It wasn't all work and no play for us apprentices. If we were given some time off or if we managed to get away from training at 3pm, we'd catch the bus into Birmingham city centre. As there were quite a few Scottish lads in the group, they liked their fashionable clothes, but every now and again, I'd treat myself to a new pair of flared trousers that, although it's hard to believe nowadays, were the fashion in the early 1970s. I don't know why, but I had to have the largest flares going, anything between 28 inch to 30 inch flares, and to go with the trousers, I used to wear platform shoes. Thinking about it, walking around in those platform shoes was probably the reason why I've got bad knees today. It was like walking on stilts. The number of times people stopped me and said I looked bigger than they had thought was because I was wearing two-inch platform shoes. We spent what little time we could uptown, shopping and going into Lewis's for a coffee or an ice cream sundae for a treat. Those were good times.

We were just ordinary lads doing pretty ordinary stuff in our free time, like going shopping, going to the café or the pictures and generally hanging out. Alcohol usually wasn't involved. We just enjoyed each other's company and had a laugh and a joke. It was fairly strange, travelling on the bus or train in those days because the public would be fascinated by the sight of a group of football players travelling on public transport and many were probably fans themselves. Having said that, we had a wide circle of friends who were also football fans and some of whom we had got to know by travelling on the bus or train. Through them we got invited to several parties. I remember one particular party very well. It was just before the end of that first season. Roy and I, together with Micky Kearney and Alex McMillan, were invited to a party in Lichfield and we were told it was an overnighter. It sounded good because we didn't have to rush and get the train back home. We made it to Lichfield and got stuck into the party, having a really good laugh, talking to plenty of people and generally having a good time. However, all of a sudden, at about midnight, we heard a loud scream. It turned out to be the girl whose house it was and she'd discovered something quite valuable had been broken and she became hysterical about it, so she told everyone to leave the house immediately. At the time, we were all trying to help her and we were banking on staying over in the house. It was late and there was no public transport back to Sutton Coldfield and we couldn't afford a taxi. What were we going to do? She was adamant that we all had to leave and I distinctly remember the four of us walking all the way from Lichfield back to Sutton Coldfield, which was a distance of about 10 or 12 miles. We set off at midnight, and I can't remember what time we got back to my digs, but it must have taken us a fair few hours. For the first couple of miles we were having a laugh and a joke and singing songs, but the last 8 or 10 miles were horrendous. We finally got back and as it was so late, all four of us piled into my digs and we ended up top and tails sleeping in the single beds.

I remember another night out with the lads. We hadn't gone far, maybe ten-pin bowling at the local bowling alley in Sutton

Coldfield. When I first arrived at the Mallards' house, I recall Mrs Mallard saying if I arrived home after midnight, the door would be locked and I wouldn't be able to get in. With that deadline fixed in my head, on one occasion I got back really late, probably 12:30am or maybe closer to 1:00am. As I tried to put my key in the door, I noticed it wouldn't turn at all. Out of respect for Mr & Mrs Mallard, who were getting on a bit, I thought I couldn't knock on the door and not forgetting she did warn me about being late, I went round the back to see if she had left the back door open. So, I climbed over the fence at the front of the house into the side garden, walked around to the back door and found that was locked as well. I was thinking, "Oh my God, what do I do here? I can't knock on the door and wake them up. No way." I knew I would upset her if I did that, but I just about made out a shed in the corner of the garden and instinctively thought I could sleep in there. When I tried to open the shed door, guess what? That was locked too, so the only alternative was the greenhouse. I knew there was a folding chair in there because Mr Mallard used to sit there, probably watching his tomatoes grow. Fortunately, the greenhouse was unlocked and as it was pitch black, I couldn't see anything. After fumbling around a bit, I eventually found the chair, unfolded it and spent a very uncomfortable night in the greenhouse. It was a night I won't forget, that's for sure.

For months afterwards, I got absolutely taunted by Mr and Mrs Mallard for spending the night in the greenhouse, mainly because they said I should have woken them up after all. Incidentally, they told me they had a great crop of tomatoes that year.

At the end of that first season, there was some bad news for us apprentices. We were told we couldn't go home during the summer. This news came as a shock to us all and the reason why we couldn't go and see our parents was because we had to help the groundsman lay a new pitch at Villa Park. I was barely 16 years old and had never done anything like that in my life, and to this day I've never done anything like it since and I don't intend to do anything like it in the future.

While there were a couple of tractors on hand, most of the work was done manually, with the use of wheelbarrows, shovels and rakes. For five weeks during May and June, we worked with Bert Bond, the head groundsman, removing the old turf, moving sand around, moving soil around, digging and fetching. It was the most horrendous job I've ever done. However, I think the club wanted us to use it to help us bond as a group, and to some extent I could see their point. We used to sit down at lunchtime with Bert and he'd tell us some brilliant stories of his days in the RAF. We'd sit there and have a real laugh and joke and now and again we'd all think he was telling us some 'porkies', as some tales seemed a bit far-fetched to say the least.

Even though it was hard work there aren't many people who can say they have helped dig up Villa Park and re-seed the pitch ready for the next season.

****

At the start of the second year, my brother Alan joined the club as an apprentice and also came to live with me at the Mallards', as Roy Stark had moved out and so had the Mallards' son, leaving a free bedroom. Jimmy Melling moved in, to make it three apprentices staying at the Mallard's. I always loved being with my brother and all three of us had a great laugh together.

****

In those days, you didn't have a 'mentor' as such, but senior pros always helped the youngsters and talked to you all the time about football. People like Bruce Rioch, Andy Lochhead and Davie Gibson were my 'mentors' and I loved being around those guys. Davie, especially, was a football genius and he taught me so much about the game during my early years. He was so energetic, enthusiastic and the most talkative player I've ever come across. I also loved playing in a partnership and Andy Lochhead was the type of player I loved to play with, where his job was to get involved with the rougher stuff on the pitch and my job was to pick up the bits and pieces, be around him and create opportunities for him. Andy would always tell me that his game was rough because the big centre-forwards would always try and kick the big centre-halves at their first opportunity, and vice versa. There was always contact between the two sets of players. Andy always preached to me that I should read where the ball was going, look at the positioning of where he and the centre-half were and read where the ball was going to drop. However, sometimes it would drop in between them because the ball was the last thing they would look at. They'd sometimes look at the player first and then they went for the ball. In today's football, either the centre-forward or the centre-half would be sent off (or both), but that's how it was in those days, rough and tough.

Back in the 1970s, football was an unbelievably physical game. It didn't matter how ferocious your first tackle was, you'd nearly always get away with it. I should know because I was the victim of quite a few first tackles during my time. If you had a big centre-forward in your side, it was his job to check who he was up against, just like it was my job to pick up all the pieces. Football was all about winning your own battles, winning the physicality side and hopefully, you'd have a player or two in the team who might have something a little bit special. Being that type of player, I was a marked man, or at least I was, once teams knew all about me. When I first came onto the scene, everybody knew who Andy Lochhead was, but nobody knew about me, or what I did. Even though I played alongside Andy, it was unbelievably good for me for a short while because I had freedom on the pitch to express myself, without players targeting me.

I found myself in the reserve team at the start of the 1970–1971 season and I can still see that first Central League game and the names on the teamsheet in my head: myself, George Curtis, Neil Rioch, Malcolm Beard, Bruce Rioch, Lionel Martin, Geoff Crudgington, Micky Wright, Lew Chatterley, Davey Rudge and Paul Child was sub. For me, as a 17-year-old, playing in and amongst those pros, it was an incredible day and a great experience, but for the senior pros, it wasn't a good day, because they wanted to be in the first-team. However, it took me about four or five games to score a goal, and ironically, the first goal I scored was away at Newcastle, which was brilliant for me, as it was in my hometown. I then went on a little run of games where I was scoring goals for fun and by October time, I was probably the leading scorer in the reserve team.

I recall the youth team went to Dusseldorf for an event, I think it was the International Youth Tournament around 1970, but as I recall, I don't think I took part in any of the games. If I'm correct, we beat AC Bologna from Italy 4-2 on penalties in the final; it was another good experience for me all the same.

In December 1970, I got an unexpected, but lovely Christmas present and it proved to be a fantastic day. There we were, in the League Cup semi-final in front of 58,600 at Villa Park and playing a Manchester United team that included: Rimmer, Saddler, Dunn, Crerand, Ure, Morgan, Fitzpatrick, Best, Charlton, Kidd and Law. Crikey, no wonder I remember that game, even if it was because of the strength of the United team. Watching that game from the stands, I saw flashes of brilliance from some of their players, the likes I've never seen before. The goal came from a long ball which found Brian Kidd and he brought it down out of the air, zipped round and Fred Turnbull flew into him, but Kidd got past him and John Dunn, then side-footed it into the net. While I was there waiting for the likes of Charlton and Best to do all the things you'd expect, it was a brilliant goal from Brian Kidd that I saw and remembered the most.

The comeback from Villa then started shortly after their goal, when Brian Godfrey picked the ball up on the halfway line, lobbed a high ball into the box to find Andy Lochhead, who rose above everybody and headed a bullet header into the net. As a young lad, who hadn't even made his first-team debut yet, I just thought, "Wow, this is fantastic and such an incredible atmosphere." Later on in the game, Willie Anderson latched onto a flick on by Andy Lochhead, and he lobbed it into the box to find Pat McMahon jumping above everybody to fire the ball into the net with a header.

Why was it such a great day for me? Well, as an apprentice at the time, I cleaned Pat McMahon's boots. I was his bootboy, and he was that happy after the game he gave me £10, which was a lot of money, considering I was only on £8 a week. It was more than a week's wages. It was an iconic game for any Villa fan of that era and it was a Christmas that I will never forget.

Chapter 2

DESTINED TO BE A STAR
Aston Villa first-team player: 1971–1974

"Was I nervous? Not a chance!
Did enjoy it? Absolutely!
Did I want more of it? Yes, of course I did!"

The 1971–1972 season was special for so many reasons – no more so that is was the season I broke into the Aston Villa first-team.

As a young lad of 18, I had been training full-time with the first-team squad for a good while. Pre-season was hard, but different, in a good way, with Vic Crowe at the helm and assisted by Ron Wylie. It was all about possession and possession was key. We tended to play loads of small-sided games: two v two, three v three, for example. You'd play these games in a circle, with everybody on the outside, and you played one-twos off each other. You were absolutely shattered afterwards though, but it was all good fun, good practice and sometimes, Ron would make you do it until we literally couldn't walk anymore; some players were that tired they'd kick their opponents just to stop the game for a few minutes in order to catch their breath. While that was going on, the players on the sidelines looking on would be screaming and shouting at the player who'd kicked out. It really was rough, but great at the same time. However, for me, I found it amazing that when you had the football at your feet how much energy you suddenly found and it gave you the desire to get past your opponents and score a goal; it gave you a completely different mindset and Ron was brilliant at it.

When we played those small-sided games, one of the senior players would select the teams and more often than not, Davie Gibson would be a captain and he'd always pick John Gidman (Giddy) and myself. At the time, Giddy was a terrific athlete; he was brilliant and he'd run all day long. Looking back, he's probably one of the best full-backs I've ever seen in a claret and blue shirt. So, they'd be Davie and two up-and-coming players and during those games, Davie would always give encouragement to us youngsters, and very often, we'd win the games.

Ron was only 38 years old at the time and he was in incredibly good shape. He had been a really good footballer in his time, and because he had become a coach, he knew how to talk to players and how players think. When he was coaching, it was more with the ball, along with some running and he'd always work our socks off. It was different because we weren't just running for the sake of it, as we had done on my first day as an apprentice. We felt there was value in the training, because we had a ball at our feet most of the time, and that was absolute Heaven for me, and something I took on board when I became a coach myself.

However, if there was something I could be critical about it was Friday morning training at Villa Park. We'd start off by running around the perimeter of the ground several times in a 20-minute warm-up. In theory, you were able to stop and stretch if you wanted, but you had to do a certain number of laps within that period of time. We set off in different groups and each had a different mentality to get the edge of the other groups. I tried to stay near Giddy and Davie Gibson, mainly because they would do the session properly, unlike some of the other lads who were less enthusiastic and would skip certain things. After the running, we'd have a game in the main car park – I say game, but it was more like 'killer-ball', where something in the region of 30 players would join in and play on the tarmacked ground for half an hour. In the most competitive environment you could imagine, it was crazy because players would pick up bruises, grazes, scratches or worse. It was like playground football, with no rules. The amount of times people got pushed against the wall was incredible. To me, it defied logic. It didn't make sense then and still doesn't now, but that's the way it was. It was the only time I felt disappointed about training, but it was deemed by others as the place to be. When the 'killer ball' had finished, we'd go back into the ground and to do some quick sprints on the pitch and that finished off the morning session, and then it was time to go down the road to the café.

At around 1:30pm, we all went back to the ground and that was the time the teamsheets for all three teams would go up on the board, in readiness for the games on the Saturday. You'd see the faces of the players in the reserve or intermediate team drop because they'd be gutted, more often than not, that hadn't been picked for the first-team. Bear in mind there was only one substitute in those days so there was less chance of anyone getting into the first-team squad. The senior pros were paid to play, not great money, but it was reasonable for the time, and focused players on getting into the first-team in order to get their appearance money. A lot of the senior lads had a family to look after and a mortgage or rent to pay, but if you weren't in the first team there was no appearance money, so they were gutted. However, there was a very small fee for winning a reserve team game, but basically you wouldn't be happy if you were a senior pro and found yourself in the reserve team on a Saturday afternoon. That was the hard fact of the matter.

In those early days, we'd always have practice matches during the week, maybe on a Tuesday morning, a Tuesday afternoon or a Wednesday, and very often it would end up in carnage. However, it was a chance for the reserve team players to stake a claim to get into the first team for the Saturday game. It would be a full-scale match – first team v reserve team, and they were brutal. It was madness even to think about playing in such a game, given the players involved: George Curtis, Harry Gregory, Bruce Rioch, Andy Lochhead, Fred Turnbull, Trevor Hockey and youngsters like my brother, Alan, who was every bit as tough as those guys I've just mentioned. I've seen practice matches stopped because some players crossed that imaginary line. I saw Bruce Rioch and Trevor Hockey being sent off time and time again for fighting each other on the pitch. There was so much competitiveness at times that it verged on nastiness among that group of players, and sometimes that wasn't healthy, but it did show that every player was ultra-competitive. Everybody was desperate to be in the first team; everybody wanted to play in front of thousands of people; everybody wanted their appearance money. It was a brutal period to be a senior footballer at Aston Villa.

During the pre-season, we went to Germany, and it was the time I realised timekeeping was a big thing for me, and specifically making sure I was early for everything – in fact it became something of an obsession in later life. We had to go down to Heathrow on the team bus and when we got there, we all sat down at a table in the main part of the airport and I recall watching three or four of the lads playing cards. I sat there thinking that I was a young lad just about to embark on my first tour, and who not having been anywhere significant in the past, didn't really know where I was going but somehow I realised how lucky I was. I didn't get involved with the game as I thought I'd just stick by them and watch them play cards. I didn't realise we were meant to go over to the departure lounge until we spotted the coach coming towards us with a grim look on his face, and he told us we'd missed the plane. I was distraught; it was absolutely ridiculous that we could miss our plane, because we were in the wrong place and several of the lads were engrossed in a game of cards. It was a lesson learnt for me. It was an absolute nightmare.

The next plane to our destination took us via Amsterdam, so by the time we got there, it was the next day. From that day on, it left me scarred and it was the only time in my life I've been late. Now, every appointment I have, I make sure I'm early, because I dislike being late and I hate rushing for anything. When I go to watch games now, I leave hours before I am supposed to and I always like to be the first there. Even when I was doing my coaching badges at Lilleshall, it became a bit competitive because some of the other lads on the course wanted to beat me and be first to the session. It may come as no surprise that when I became a coach I was strict on timekeeping. I now have something of a reputation of being early, which I don't see as a bad thing and it means not many people want to travel with me, because I always arrive so early. It's got so bad that if somebody agrees to pick me up and they're late, I end up going in my own car.

****

Aston Villa were a First Division club playing in the Third Division of English football. The 1971–1972 season, our second season in the Third Division, kicked off with less than 27,000 watching the first-team at Villa Park against Plymouth Argyle and a 3-1 win, with Willie Anderson, Pat McMahon and Geoff Vowden getting the goals. We were expected to do well that season, and it took a bit of time for us to lose a game, a 2-0 defeat to Bolton, and if I'm correct, Roger Hunt scored for them. The first major disappointment came in mid-September, when we lost at home to Mansfield Town. It was a big shock, but we bounced back to win the next three. The crowds were beginning to creep up, and by October there were over 30,000 at Villa Park to see another home defeat, this time to Rotherham. We would have gone top with a victory, but it wasn't to be. It was an up and down period and our fans were probably wondering what was going on. It wasn't that we weren't playing well. We were, but the team just had, had a few blips along the way.

I was amongst the goals in the reserve team by October. I think I was probably the top scorer and it was because of my goals that I got called up to play in the first team, with the team going well in the Third Division. My call-up came a month or so before my 18th birthday, just before the game against Blackburn Rovers on 30th October 1971. In that game I came on as a substitute in a 4-1 victory at Villa Park. Ironically, I came on to replace Davie Gibson and I felt a million dollars when the 25,500 fans gave me a tremendous round of applause as I took to the field. Was I nervous? Not a chance! Did enjoy it? Absolutely! Did I want more of it? Yes, of course I did!

I can honestly say I wasn't nervous that day – I was never nervous playing football, because I just loved being out on the pitch and showing people what I could do. The Villa fans inspired me that day, as they did every time I played. During the game my confidence grew and I did things that I just couldn't explain, like flicking the ball over my head or spinning the ball back to myself. I loved doing the tricks and showing off, and so did the crowd that day. I honestly don't know where I got the confidence to do those things. Funnily enough, later on in my career, those tricks used to irritate Ron Saunders, because he wanted me to control the ball, simply by stopping it, not spinning it with the end of my toe and touching it past the player. He just wanted me to do the simple stuff. However, I ignored Ron most of the time and I just tried to play my natural game, regardless of what Ron wanted me to do. I took that with me every time I played football, even in training, just trying little bits here and there. I worked for ages with bouncing balls and being able to flick it over my head and keeping it in my stride. I just didn't like to do things the normal way, but more about that later.

That victory against Blackburn raised expectations amongst the fans and within two weeks, we had over 37,000 to watch us beat Notts County 1-0 at home, with a goal from Ray Graydon. He was an out-and-out right-sided wide player but he always chipped in with the goals, whereas Willie Anderson on the other side wasn't a goalscorer, he was more of a provider. Suddenly, a momentum was building up, and that was the key; there was something good about the team, and it was brilliant to be part of it, even if I was sitting on the sidelines most of the time. The balance of the team was spot on, with the likes of Charlie Aitken, who was a phenomenal athlete and a shrewd cookie; George Curtis, who was the biggest, toughest and roughest footballer in the team; Fred Turnbull was a talented, but underestimated centre-half; Jimmy Brown had an unbelievable attitude for someone so young; Andy Lochhead, well what else can I say about him, and we had Geoff Vowden, who was silky smooth, clever and used to feed off Andy Lochhead.

By January 1972, we were pretty much top of the league, the club was buzzing and responding to the momentum. From then on, we only lost three games of football until the end of that season. Although I didn't play in it, one game that really sticks out in the memories of people who witnessed those days watching Villa in the Third Division was the home game against Bournemouth in February 1972. This was that memorable game when 48,110 attended Villa Park, and the Holte End was absolutely packed to the rafters. I can still see that game in my head. I can still feel the atmosphere – the place was rocking, it really was. Bournemouth were right up the top of the league at the time, along with ourselves and they had one of the best centre-forwards in the league in Ted MacDougal, who was scoring goals for fun. Ted scored the opening goal for the visitors with a typical diving header, and then Geoff Vowden scored our equaliser, with Andy Lochhead grabbing the winner. It was a very iconic game in Villa's history, and just about summed everything up about that season and that team for me; that game really cemented the belief that we could get promotion and back into the second tier.

Following the success of the youth team during that season (more about the Youth Cup later in the book), I was called up to the first team for my full debut in the last home game of the season against Torquay United in front of 37,000 fans. By that time, we'd signed Ian Ross (Rossco) in the February of 1972 from Liverpool, to play alongside Fred Turnbull at centre-back.

Rossco was a shrewd cookie; he was very calm and used the ball well. We were chasing promotion, but I never would have imagined that so many people would have turned out for that game, but they did. Vic Crowe, the first-team manager, only told me just before the game that I was playing, and I so was excited as I joined the Youth team lads on a parade of the pitch before the game, holding the FA Youth Cup, which we'd won. It was brilliant for me to join my teammates and celebrate in front of so many people. I just loved every minute of it. To top it off, we beat Torquay convincingly 5-1, and I set up a goal or two, and scored the fifth. Although I didn't really think I'd arrived on the scene as such, I felt I was part of something special, nonetheless. It is hard to explain to people how I really felt, but it could come back to that momentum thing again. Sometimes, if you play in front of a great crowd like that at Villa Park, and they are right behind you, it's just a phenomenal thing to be involved with and the momentum starts to kicks in.

From going top in January, we stayed there right the way through until the end of the season. We were promoted to the Second Division as League Champions, with Brighton finishing second and Bournemouth in third. Our record was phenomenal, winning 32 out of 46 games. We had an incredible season; we had an incredible bunch of players, and it was a season I will never forget. I always reminded myself where I had come from and what I needed to do for me to stay there. I was really looking forward to what I thought was going to be a massively important period of my life.

****

Before making my first-team debut against Torquay, the youth team were also going through a fantastic spell. We started in the FA Youth Cup in November 1971 and we beat Boldmere St Michael 8-0 in the first round and I scored a hat trick, Tony Betts scored two, Giddy scored two and Bobby McDonald scored the other. Looking at our team, we had: Jake Findlay in goal, Bobby McDonald, John Gidman, Nigel Dyer, my brother Alan, Roy Stark, Micky Brady, Jimmy Melling, Tony Betts, Dougie George and myself. It's incredible looking at that team because quite a few of those lads came through and went on to play for the Villa first team in later years.

CHAPTER 2: DESTINED TO BE A STAR

Our second game was a 7-0 victory against another Third Division club in Port Vale with Greg Fellows scoring a hat-trick, Jimmy Melling and Giddy getting one apiece, and Tony Betts scored a couple. We used to call Tony 'The Camel' because he did all of my hard work and I'd get all the glory. That's a little bit unfair I guess, but he was a great lad to play alongside. We then beat West Bromwich Albion 3-2 and following that, we hit something that was quite unique in youth football.

We were then drawn against Birmingham City and they had a phenomenal team, with the likes of Trevor Francis, Joe Gallagher, Stevie Bryant and Kenny Burns who were already first-team players. Before the game, there was a lot being said about both teams and there was even a centrepiece spread in the local sports newspaper comparing me with Trevor, with huge pictures of us either side of the local broadsheet newspaper. It was quite strange having such a focus on two 17-year-olds before a youth team game, but I guess we were the hottest prospects in the Midlands at the time. We played the first leg at St Andrews and drew 1-1 in front of a staggering 21,000 fans. We won the replay at Villa Park 2-1 in front of an attendance of nearly 19,000, with my brother Alan scoring the winning goal, which for me (and him) was very special. So, that meant the two games had over 40,000 people watching a bunch of youth team players, which was pretty much unheard of, but it was brilliant to play in both of those games in front of such big crowds and the atmosphere at both grounds was incredible.

We had great spirit in that youth team and that was one of the main reasons why we were winning games, and for a Third Division club, we were probably punching above our weight. However, there's a lot to be said of something called, 'momentum' in football as I've mentioned before – what it does for players, how it makes them feel, and how it makes the fans feel, too. To sample momentum at whatever age is a great thing. I was at a football club that was on the move again and the direction was upwards; the first team was right up there, battling for promotion in its first season in the Third Division; the youth team were winning; the crowd were incredible; the media attention was intense and the belief inside the players at all levels was fantastic. I was part of a group of young players that were beginning to make the headlines and some were pushing for places in the first team and beyond.

One of the older players in youth our side was Jimmy Brown, who, as I've already mentioned, made his debut for Aston Villa's first-team as a mere 15-year-old. Jimmy was now 18, but if I'm perfectly honest, he was levelling out and wasn't the same player he was two years previously. However, people like myself, Jake Findlay, John Gidman and Bobby McDonald were all getting better and progressing. We had a great feeling about the way we were playing as individuals, and as a team, and the first team had a positive feel about it too. When you sample that sort of momentum at a club like Aston Villa, you will never forget about it and that period was something special. During that 1971–1972 season, I experienced what effects momentum has on a team.

We suddenly found ourselves in the quarter-final of the FA Youth Cup and were drawn against Chelsea at Stamford Bridge. They were a team who were fancied to do well, along with Arsenal. Both had some really good youngsters, including some England youth players in their squads. However, we had nothing to fear from Chelsea and came away with a 1-1 draw, and I scored our goal, which was great for me. It was a tough game on a massively open pitch and we had worked our socks off because we had to. We came off the pitch absolutely shattered, but it was a fantastic result nonetheless. The replay ended up goalless and went to extra time, but we came away winners by 3-0, with two goals from Dougie George and another from Tony Betts.

Talking of Arsenal, our names were drawn together in the semi-final, the second of the most fancied sides in the competition that year and we were about to face them. The first leg was away at Highbury, which was a great place to play football, it really was. It was my first trip to Highbury, an incredible stadium and I loved every minute of playing there. Looking back, I always say that apart from Villa Park, Highbury was my favourite ground to play at. There was just something about it; from the first moment you stepped into the building there was an aura about the place. Maybe it was the marble floor that made it look palatial; it was grand and old-fashioned, but it just looked brilliant.

The game was a tight affair, as you'd expect and we drew 0-0. We had a good side out for the second leg, no real changes apart from a young lad called Dave Smith. There were nine players in that team who were 18 years old, but most teams in the competition had been made up of lads around 15 or 16 years old, so we had a real advantage in terms of age and experience at that level. We'd been together as a group for the best part of three years and we had two of the toughest lads you could ever come across in Roy Stark and my brother, Alan, who were both rock solid centre-backs. Alan eventually got a reputation as a destroyer; he'd destroy anybody who came anywhere near him. At times, he could be brutal. He'd get stuck in there with the best of them. I've already mentioned watching Bruce Rioch and Trevor Hockey in my early days, and the way they competed against each other in training, and sometimes it spilled over between them, but on the odd occasion Alan as a 16 or 17-year-old would hold his own against either of them. If they went in hard, Alan would go in every bit as hard. Anyway, in the return game at Villa Park, our experience showed and we beat Arsenal at home by a single Bobby McDonald goal.

The youth policy that was set up by the club at the start of my apprenticeship in 1969 was starting to show signs of fruition. Apart from myself, there were four fellow apprentices from my intake in that team: Jimmy Brown, Jimmy Melling, Roy Stark and Dougie George. In goal, we had big Jake Findlay, who had ousted Gordon Knowles, the Scottish schoolboy international to take the goalkeeping gloves. Technically, Gordon was excellent, but Jake was immense. Jake was a funny lad, had a great sense of humour and made us really solid as a team; we had real confidence in his ability.

It was an incredible feat for us, to think where we had come from and to reach the final of the FA Youth Cup for the first time in the club's history within the space of less than three years.

So, we were to face the mighty Liverpool in the final, and again, it was a two-legged affair. We won the first leg at home by 1-0, a penalty scored by Giddy and it was a great feeling to take a lead to Anfield. Although Liverpool had a good side, in that game at Villa Park the one player in their side that stuck out to me was Phil Thompson. I think he was the only player who actually cut it at the top level for them if I'm not mistaken, but if you look back at our team, a lot of us went on to play league football in our careers. I must mention here that there was only one non-British player on either side in the final. We had seven English and four Scottish lads in our team, whilst Liverpool had 10 Englishmen and one Irishman. It was a different era where homegrown talent was given a chance to shine.

I genuinely feel the Liverpool lads thought the one goal deficit wasn't a bad result and they were going to win the game at Anfield. Just like in the game against Chelsea, it was a tough game, and unfortunately for us, Bobby McDonald got sent off. Again, like in the Chelsea game, it went to extra time, but we ended up winning the game 4-2 to win the FA Youth Cup. Winning the cup was something we had only dreamt of as a Third Division club and we were all proud as punch. To think we had beaten a decent Liverpool side in front of a combined attendance of over 32,000 was a brilliant thing to achieve. Moreover, as a Third Division club we'd played 11 games and scored a bucketfull of goals to win the trophy, which was even more of an achievement.

However, there was a sour note to the evening. Even though Bobby McDonald worked his socks off throughout the game, he wasn't allowed to pick up his winners' medal because he'd been sent off and that spoilt the evening for all of us. I found that ruling pathetic and really quite unfair if I'm honest and to this day I'm convinced he never received a medal. There is a particular picture I can think that shows us all celebrating our win, all chuffed to bits wearing our medals and Dougie with the trophy on his head, but it also shows Bobby McDonald with his sweatshirt on – and no medal round his neck. I bet he must still be gutted about being punished for being sent off. From a personal point of view, for many different reasons, that final will always be one of my favourite games that I've played in.

Many footballers believe in superstitions. They put their left sock on first or they sleep upside down before a game, but I can honestly say that I've never been superstitious in my life. I don't believe in all of that nonsense, and in fact it makes me cringe. I just believe in doing things naturally or because it feels like the best thing to do at the time. Having said that, when I arrived at Anfield before the second leg of that final, I found that I had a penny in each pocket of my shorts. I'd no idea why or where they came from, but as I walked onto the pitch before the game I remember walking up to the penalty area and I threw the penny in the back of the net, walked off and thought nothing of it. Knowing I had another penny in the other pocket, I ran the full length of the pitch and threw it into that goalmouth. Why did I do it? I have no idea! The strange thing was, I ended up scoring a goal in each half. Now, if I was superstitious I'd have ended up chucking pennies into every goalmouth I came across during my subsequent career, but I never bothered again. Maybe I'd have scored a lot more goals in my career if I had?

We didn't just have success in the FA Youth Cup. I must also mention we got to the semi-final of the Southern Junior Floodlit Cup, which saw us play in three games. First up was a 2-1 win against Arsenal at home and I scored, along with Micky Brady. It was a very small competition so we went straight into the quarter-final, where I scored the two goals to beat West Ham at home, but in the semi-final, we lost to a very strong Chelsea side.

****

The FA Youth Cup Final was a stage that showcased all 22 players to the big, wide world and to the international scouts that were watching, so when I was selected to play for England Under-18s in a friendly game against Scotland at Villa Park, I was full of confidence. Maybe I'm doing myself a bit of an injustice here, but I felt at the time that I was only selected because I was a Villa player, there to boost the home crowd more than anything else. There were four Villa youth team players playing in that game: myself and Giddy for England and Jake Findlay and Bobby McDonald for Scotland, so it was all geared towards getting a decent crowd at Villa Park. It ended up 0-0 and it was a pretty average game, but I was proud to have put on the England shirt for the first time. If you put that into perspective, only three years previously, I was playing for Acre Rigg Secondary Modern School (I don't think it exists now) and I couldn't even get into my county team. That's how far I'd come in such a short space of time, and I was very proud of that fact.

The lads who'd won the FA Youth Cup all went on holiday to Majorca that year; however, Giddy and I missed the trip because we were called up into the England squad for the 1972 Under-18 European Championships in Spain. Now, if we had thought the 1971–1972 season couldn't get any better for us we were wrong because England won that competition. I didn't play very much during the competition, as I was kept out of the team by the brilliant Trevor Francis. Trevor was a phenomenal player, even at that age and he was probably the quickest footballer around at the time. He'd been playing senior football for Birmingham City since the age of 16 and we had a great, friendly, rivalry between us as people and as players. As I've said before, there was a lot made of us, being similar types of players and playing on opposing sides, but he'd predominantly kept me out of the England side and probably did for years to come. However, there were also a couple other lads fighting for the same spot in the England side to play alongside Trevor. The first was a lad called Alan Green from Coventry City and he was given the nod in front of me a few times, too. Alan subsequently, went off to the US early in his career to become one of those pioneer players of US soccer. The other lad was Steve Cammack, who was playing for Sheffield United. Steve was a hard-working and honest player, but if there was any chance of me getting into the England team it was at the expense of Steve. However, it didn't work out like that and more often or not Steve partnered Trevor up front for that England youth team.

Apart from Trevor, the England Under-18 side was made up of some really good players at the time such as the late Kevin Beattie. If there was ever a 'man' at the age of 18, Kevin was that person. He was immense in the centre of our defence. Then there was Kevin Lock, who was likened to Bobby Moore in some ways. He looked like him I suppose and he was probably moulded in the same way, being from West Ham. Some players get labelled for this and that a bit too early in their careers and I think Kevin Lock fell into that bracket. He was a very talented player, and he and Kevin Beattie made a tremendous defensive line-up. I've already mentioned Phil Thompson, another top player from that side, who played in midfield in those days, even though he played at the back throughout his Liverpool first-team career. During the two weeks away in Spain, we had a bit of fun with Phil, having just won the FA Youth Cup with Villa against his Liverpool side so we had the pleasure of rubbing it in a bit. Just like the group of players we had in the Villa youth setup, we had a great bunch of lads in the England youth setup too.

In the group stages, we were with Belgium, Yugoslavia and the Republic of Ireland. It was a pretty tight schedule; we played a game every two days in the group stages and if you got through to the final it was all over within two weeks. It was the first time I'd been away with the national team and it was good to get to know everyone and in particular, their tastes in music while we travelled on the team bus to and from games.

Everyone had diverse tastes and we all had a chance to give the driver our own cassette tapes to play. The team spirit was great and we enjoyed each other's company.

I didn't play in the first game against Belgium, a 0-0 draw and it was a bit drab anyway. Our second game was better, as we beat the Republic of Ireland 4-0 and that game gave us a massive boost in confidence. In the final game against Yugoslavia, who'd beaten Belgium previously, we won 1-0. Competitions in those days weren't long and drawn-out like they are now and suddenly we found ourselves in the semi-final. Poland, who had beaten France, Norway and drawn with the Netherlands in the group stages, were our opponents. Again, we went into the game full of confidence, knowing we'd meet West Germany or Spain in the final, if we could beat Poland. As it turned out, we beat the Poles 1-0 at the Campo de Mestalla in Valencia to reach the final and it was an incredible occasion. It was a tremendous stadium, the oldest in Spain and I remember walking around it before the game, looking at the high-sided stands in amazement – it was quite a sight. In the other semi-final, West Germany and Spain drew 2-2 and inevitably, the Germans won on penalties.

The final was at Barcelona's Camp Nou and it had reminders of 1966 I guess, as we beat the Germans 2-0, and even though I didn't play in that game, it was great just being part of the squad and warming up on the pitch. It was my third taste of success in the space of a few weeks: with gaining promotion with Villa and winning the FA Youth Cup, now I was a European Under-18 champion. It ended an unbelievable season and one I will never forget.

****

It must have been around that time that I passed my driving test. I'd always been into cars and motorbikes and still am, but I was hopeless at saving money, so my brother, Alan helped me buy my first car at the age of 18. It was a 1500cc Hillman Minx, registration number POP 831G, dark blue in colour, and even though it was useless, it was mine (well ours). I think it cost us £250 and Alan leant me £125, so in effect, it was half his car, even though he didn't drive. However, we made a pact that if he wanted to go anywhere, I should take him and I was fine with that. I was just desperate to get a car. It had a column change gearbox, bench seats at the front and at the back; it was a real old-fashioned car. It was that bad, I had to pump the brakes to make it stop.

Although the car was an absolute nightmare, it was great to have the freedom to go out and about. One day, somebody went into the back of us when we were both in the car. Well, that was the worst thing anybody could have done, because within five seconds Alan shot out of his seat and headed towards the other car and dragged the poor driver out of his seat. He pinned this fella against our car and shouted, "Look what you've done to my car..." If I hadn't have been there, I think Alan would have battered the other driver, but instead he kept his cool. I'd learned the hard way that you never mess him around or break anything that belonged to him, and that fella found that out too. It was a classic and I had to sit and watch, saying to him, "Al, leave him alone. It's not that bad. We can get it fixed." Alan kept on, "He's going to pay for it..."

I think it's fair to say we had a few more scrapes in that and other cars over the course of time. In later years, I became a bit obsessed with cars and motorbikes and I hate to try and add up how much over time I've spent on them. I've had loads and loads of cars, I can tell you.

****

During the early 1970s, the first-team used to do some training in a gym at Birmingham University every Tuesday, and I learned a lot from those sessions. I learned a lot of things that I shouldn't do before and after training, as well as things that I should do before and after training. During training there were very often fights, basically because everyone was so tired, some people couldn't keep up and trip people up and that sometimes turned into a physical fight between two grown men. I witnessed lots of scraps like that, but the physical work that caused those fights was hard, as hard as I've ever encountered as a footballer.

We used to sit at each end of the gym and Ron Wylie used to give the lads at one end of the gym a number between one and 10, and he did the same to the other lads at the other end of the gym. If you were say number five and Trevor Hockey was number five, too, you'd think to yourself, "Oh no, not him, please not him!" Everybody knew Trevor wasn't the tidiest player in the world, because if you were going to go past him, you'd end up on the deck. It wasn't so bad for the younger lads, but for the senior lads like Bruce Rioch, if ever he got matched with Trevor Hockey, then that would be serious carnage. Only they could answer if they didn't like each other, but they were both super-competitive, even in full-on training matches; sometimes it was taken beyond friendship and competitiveness and turned into pure nastiness. For people like 'Chico' Hamilton, if he was tired, all he'd do was stick his leg out to trip up his opposing player and he'd be on the deck. The amount of little niggles that started in that gym was untrue.

One of the classic match-ups was Charlie Aitken and Bruce Rioch. Charlie was the fittest man in that squad. He was always into training early and he always trained properly. He was such a bubbly man, a wonderful man, and he was a player who never really needed to use contact in his game – he just used his brain, together with his pace and power to get past people. Charlie was a clever player and it was no wonder he played the amount of games he did for Villa. He still holds the club appearance record. I don't recall Charlie ever getting into an incident with anybody. He got on with everybody in the squad and always went about his business in a professional manner. However, there was one particular day when he drew Bruce on a one-on-one and for the first few steps, Bruce was right into him, but Charlie started using his fitness, pushed the ball past Bruce and flew past him. Bruce couldn't catch him and reached a point where he was getting angry. Bruce then just left the ball in the middle and started chasing Charlie around the gym. It ended up very comical. Charlie stood in the corner and when Bruce came up to him, he'd do a little shimmy and run past Bruce. In the end, Bruce just lay on the floor absolutely shattered. Charlie was just too fit for him. We didn't often have those comedy play sessions during training. If ever there was a scuffle, it usually ended up in a proper fight. There was no way Charlie was going to scuffle with Bruce, but if that had happened, there would be only one winner, and it wouldn't have been Charlie.

Tuesday training soon became quite notorious and we'd very often be given the Wednesday off, simply because we'd all be shattered. Because I was young and new to the first-team, I used to go with the flow, so on a Tuesday lunchtime after training the lads went into Birmingham city centre to a place called The Longboat, off Broad Street, a little pub on the canal. There were several occasions when I woke up in the cinema in New Street wondering how I was going to get back to my digs. I genuinely couldn't remember how on earth I had got there. I soon realised that some of the senior lads didn't come to the pub after training and I began to wonder why, so then I came to the conclusion they weren't there because it wasn't the thing to do because it often ended up in carnage. The realisation of who was and who wasn't there soon kicked in with me and I soon stopped going. However, all I wanted to do was to get in amongst the lads and do a bit of team bonding, but it eventually got out of hand. I am certain the management team knew what we were doing, and I'm pretty sure they encouraged us to have the Tuesday afternoon off and have a good time, which very often included alcohol on the agenda. That was one occasion where I followed the saying, "Look, listen and learn" to the full. While I wanted to be popular amongst the lads, the idea of going out getting bladdered just didn't appeal to me and I soon had a reputation as someone who didn't go out with the lads. Whilst I did go out with Giddy on occasions, going out with a large group didn't appeal to me at all, but the experience stood me in good stead in the future.

****

During the January of the 1972–1973 season we played Bayern Munich at Villa Park and looking back on it, that game turned out to be the standout friendly game of my career, simply because of the quality of the opposition. Their team was incredible and included such names as Sepp Maier, Johnny Hansen, Paul Brietner, Georg Schwarzenbeck, Franz Beckenbauer, Gerd Müller, Uli Hoeneß and Wilhelm Hoffmann, and the Aston Villa News & Record matchday programme referred to them as the 'Europameisters'. It was a great experience to play against Beckenbauer especially, because he was such a majestic and famous player. From a personal point of view, I remember eating egg and chips a few hours before the game, only because I had nothing else in the house at the time. It didn't seem to do me any harm to be honest as we drew 1-1 with the German champions in front of a disappointing 23,000 crowd.

Looking back at that game, and at that period in time, we never used to swap shirts with the opposition, not like players do now. I don't know why, but I wished I'd have swapped my shirt with one of those German guys. I always think to myself, "Why didn't I get hold of Franz Beckenbauer's shirt?" It really grates on me, but players just didn't collect things like that back then although some fans probably did. Maybe it was because the shirts didn't have names on the backs, like they do now. Having said that, if I had collected shirts, I would have a magnificent collection by now.

****

At the end of the 1972–1973 season, we embarked on a special bit of history as a club. After finishing a respectable third in our first season back in the Second Division, we headed to unknown territory for our end of season tour. I don't know if it was true, but we were supposedly the first English football team to travel to the East African state of Tanzania. This was an era very much before African football had made its name, and looking back, I think we were pioneers by going out there, certainly to the area we went to. We headed for a place called Dar es Salaam and none of us knew anything about the country or the area, but it was an incredible experience and very much a test of character.

Before we left Birmingham to embark on our journey, there was a great atmosphere amongst the lads and the staff, and everybody was looking forward to the adventure. In fact, we were making plans well in advance for when we got to Africa, with Jimmy Cumbes, our self-proclaimed 'head of entertainment' for the tour, making all the plans. It was destined to be a fun trip. However, the tour didn't start well. As we headed down to Heathrow to catch our flight, the team bus broke down and we were stuck on the motorway for hours. Fortunately, we weren't flying out until the next morning, as we were due to stay in an airport hotel, ready for an early flight out of London. That was just the start of things to come.

The next morning, we boarded the flight and as the aeroplane taxied out onto the runway, all of a sudden we stopped for 15 minutes. The captain addressed the passengers stating we had a problem with the plane, so we'd have to pull over. Three hours later, we were still sitting there on the plane. There were no announcements and nobody knew what was going on. The captain then made a long-awaited announcement, saying

"Everything is OK and we are going to try to get a slot." He didn't sound too reassuring though, but at least we had started to taxi along the runway. By this time, some of the lads who hated flying were getting restless and panicking and were really knocking the booze back. We eventually took off and the panic was over, or so we thought. As we were flying over African airspace, we had to make an untimely stopover to refuel, and we landed in terrible weather. After three hours sitting on the plane at Heathrow, plus an eight-hour flight to the middle of nowhere, we were told we could get off to stretch our legs while they refuelled the plane. We left the plane and had to hang around the small terminal building with not much to do for two or three hours. By the time we got back on board, the rain had worsened, and when we took off, thunder and lightening started. I've always enjoyed flying, but we took off in a storm and if there was one time I was frightened it was that day. The pilot tried to reassure us that we weren't in any danger, but looking outside we were all very concerned for our safety. It really was horrendous.

We eventually arrived in Dar es Salaam, got off the plane and onto a rickety old bus. The roads were awful, sandy and full of potholes and we went through loads of shantytowns on the way to the hotel. I'm not sure if it's still the same today as I've not been back since, but how Africa was at that time was an eye-opening experience. However, all of a sudden we arrived at this incredible hotel called the Kunduchi Beach Hotel and it was right on the beach. So, from the time we left the plane to reaching the hotel, we had gone from one extreme to another in no time at all. Only 300 yards from the gates of the hotel, there were shantytowns and sandy roads. How people lived in the area was a complete mismatch.

If you can picture the scene, the hotel complex was like any other in the world; a beautiful white 5-star hotel complex set on one of the most incredible beaches you're likely to see anywhere. As a 19-year-old, I was completely overawed by it and 44 years later, I've still not seen anything quite like that place.

As we settled in, Jimmy Cumbes took charge of the proceedings and he organised the first night's entertainment. I can't remember the game exactly, but I think it was called 'Captain Bluff' and there was a little process where you had to sit around a table with a drink and follow some instructions when it was your turn. The instructions were all about touching different parts of

Making my debut as a substitute against
Blackburn at Villa Park in October 1971

Scoring my first league goal for Villa against Torquay United in 1972

My first and only England cap

My dad with his two little footballers-to-be. Alan is to the right of dad

At home with my one and only England shirt

The great (Sir) Stanley Matthews with myself (left) and
my brother, Alan (right) at Port Vale in 1967

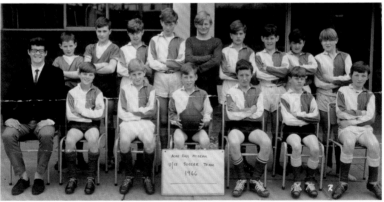

At Acre Rigg School in 1966 – I'm on the
front row, second in from the left

The Story of my Life

I am now lying in my bed resting as I am eighty seven years ~~od~~ old. Looking back ~~as to~~ the first job I had which was an apprentice footballer. I trained and was this for a few years. And at last I had my first game for my club and turned professional as I stayed on ~~for~~ for football for many years. Having many exiting moments. I retired from football into a television reporter on sports I did this for fourteen years and then retired at the age of forty five years old. I then went on tours and other things.

Dreams come true don't they?
Written when I was at school, probably circa 1965

10. In consideration of the observance by the said player of the terms, provisions and conditions of this Agreement, the said **F.J. ARCHER** on behalf of the Club hereby agrees that the said Club shall pay to the said Player the sum of £**7. 0. 0** per week from **25th April 1969** to **25th November 1969** and £ **8. 0. 0.** per week from **26th November 1969** to **25th November 1970** and £ **10. 0. 0.** per week from **26th November 1970** to **25th November 1971** and £ per week from to and £ per week from to

11. This Agreement (subject to the Rules of The Football Association) shall cease and determine on **25th November 1971** unless the same shall have been previously determined in accordance with the provisions hereinbefore set forth.

Fill in any
other pro-
visions
required

As Witness the hands of the said parties the day and year first aforesaid

Signed by the said **F.J. ARCHER**

and

BRIAN LITTLE

In the presence of the Parent or Guardian of the Player

(Signature) *R. Little*

(Occupation) *Electrician*

(Address) *67, Grisedale Road*
Peance, Co. Durham

Brian Little

(Player)

J Archer

(Secretary)

My first contract as a footballer – an apprenticeship contract with Villa in 1969

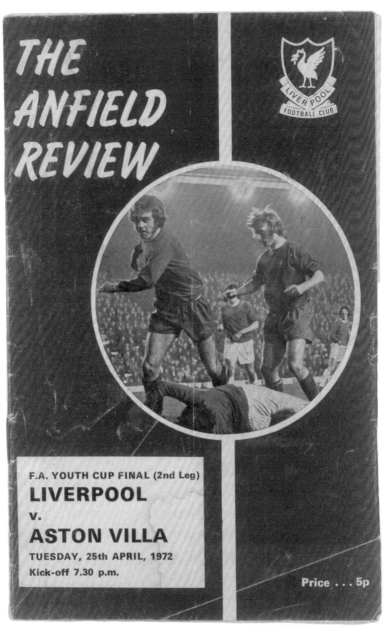

THE ANFIELD REVIEW

F.A. YOUTH CUP FINAL (2nd Leg)
LIVERPOOL
v.
ASTON VILLA
TUESDAY, 25th APRIL, 1972
Kick-off 7.30 p.m.

Price . . . 5p

The 1971 FA Youth Cup Final programme – I scored twice
and it helped me get into the England Youth set-up

This is where my football career started –
Deanhouse Junior School, Peterlee

In amongst the thick of things during the 1975
League Cup Final against Norwich

Celebrating a goal against a strong Liverpool side in December 1976. It was probably the best game ever played at Villa Park. Villa won 5-1.

your body with your fingers and thumbs. So, the first player had to say, "I dedicate the first drink of the night to Cardinal Bluff" and the game begun with the first person having to: tap the table top once with one finger (both hands), tap the table underneath once with one finger (both hands), snap their fingers once (both hands), pick up their beer with one finger and thumb, hit the table with bottle, tap bottle in the air and then drink as much as they could. Everybody in the circle then had to repeat the process until we'd gone round the table; however, with Jimmy in charge, if anybody messed up, they had to finish the drink and start again with a new one. That continued for as many rounds as it took, until the last person remained, and he was the winner.

It was Jimmy's initiation for everybody at the club – I think it came from his cricketing days. It wasn't my type of thing and I usually stood on the side watching the lads get it all wrong and some got horrendously drunk it has to be said. It was great fun and a great idea to get a bunch of young lads to bond with each other and it started the trip off in great shape. In fact, it was that good that even Mr and Mrs Ellis played it.

We were meant to be in Africa to play several games of football, but as it was the end of the season we didn't intend to take them too seriously. Even though we were probably one of the first English clubs go there and play football we weren't expecting anyone to turn up to watch us; however, when we got the stadium for our first game, there were at least 50,000 people packed in to see us play. It was absolute bedlam. The stadium was primitive even to 1970s English football standards; there was fencing around the outside of the ground but you could see people climbing over the fence to get in and not paying. It reached the point where the riot police were called in, and at one stage they were trying to control the crowd with tear gas. Of course, the tear gas drifted onto the pitch and affected all of the players. It was crazy and we had never expected anything like it. The game eventually finished 0-0.

Just before the kick-off in another game, witnessed by the crowd of 35,000 people, the opposition decided to have a sit-in for some reason, right in the middle of the pitch and refused to play. Some of their coaches came onto the pitch at one stage and tried to pull the players up off the ground to get them to play, but they wouldn't budge. Eventually, the captain of the team stood up, went to the sidelines where the manager, directors and organisers of the game were, clapped his hands and the other players stood up and we started the game. It was all very bizarre. We only found out afterwards that they sat there in protest at being underpaid to play in the game, so we assumed they had been promised more money, as they had agreed to play.

Apart from going to and from the stadium, we weren't allowed to go outside the confines of the hotel at night as it was deemed too dangerous, but we did go into Dar es Salaam town during the daytime as a group with a tour guide and some of the lads bought wooden souvenirs.

It was an incredible experience for people like Jimmy Brown and myself, who were the two youngest in the group. Some of the lads went off to the Angolan Safari Park in Kenya for a three-day trip, but I, along with some of the others, chose to sit around the hotel complex and sunbathe for those few days. When I look back, it was one of my few regrets and I always remind myself of the mistake of not choosing to go on safari. However, those who stayed had our own trip organised by the hotel to a deserted island, about three miles off shore. The hotel didn't skimp on luxuries either, as they shipped out their own chefs to cook food for us and we were well looked after for the day on the deserted island in the middle of the ocean. We spent the day sunbathing, swimming, snorkelling and barbequing and it was an absolutely brilliant day. We were all told to take a tee shirt, but some of the lads didn't and I remember Neil Rioch getting sunburnt while he was snorkelling.

We had some great times during the trip, but the biggest laugh could be heard after we had thrown the chairman, Mr Ellis, into the swimming pool. It was towards the end of the tour and Mr Ellis had been fishing during the day and as the story goes, he told everyone that he had caught a huge fish. We weren't sure that he did, but we took his word for it. While we were all sitting around the pool area waiting for the evening entertainment and the barbeque to start, having a drink and a laugh, Mr Ellis appeared on the scene, waiving a huge fish above his head and telling everybody how he'd caught it. Apparently, he'd gone out to sea especially to catch a fish for the barbeque – but only he knows if that was true. Anyway, we'd all contemplated throwing Mr Ellis into the pool some time during the trip, but we couldn't make up our minds who was going to do it and when, until Andy Lochhead stepped forward right at that opportune moment. Nobody was ever going to say anything to Andy so he walked towards Mr Ellis and picked him up, and threw him straight into the swimming pool, fully clothed and the fish still in his hands. As soon as Mr Ellis hit the water everyone took their tee shirts off and chucked them at him. Mr Ellis, being one of the lads, emerged from the water and stood up in the pool with a big grin all over his face as he took it all in good spirit. It was very funny to see and was the swansong of the trip.

We ended up playing four games, drawing three of them and winning the other on very basic pitches. The African lads we played against were athletic and keen, although they lacked the skills that our lads had, but you can see how much they have developed over the years. Even back then, there was an immense amount of talent out there, without the coaching and organisation they needed. Our lads didn't take the games overly seriously, but the trip was pioneering and enjoyable.

That trip was an incredible experience and very much my first experience of the big, wide world, and it remains my favourite end of season tour. It was a little bit frightening at times and the football was very difficult, but most of all, the antics that went on were really educational for a 20-year-old, to say the least. There were some concerns though, mainly about how people lived in the area and that was something we weren't prepared for. Having said that, we did mingle with some of the locals, who walked along the beach to sell their crafts to the tourists, and that was an experience in itself.

****

I wouldn't say the 1973–1974 season was good for me; it was a season where I had the chance to establish myself in the first-team, and that's just what I did. Even though I played 38 games, I only scored eight times, but as a 19 or 20-year-old, it wasn't bad really. I had a dozen or so games out with injury, but I consistently played throughout that season under Vic Crowe. I had a few strike partners during that season, namely Bobby Campbell, Alun Evans, Sammy Morgan and then of course I played with Keith Leonard, a partnership very much in its infancy, but one that established itself in the following years.

That season was a tough one, and pretty uneventful for the team, as we only finished 14th in the Second Division. I remember leading up to the end of the season Vic talking to me about trying to sort out a better contract. I wasn't earning much money, but I'd established myself as a regular in the first-team. In fact, if I'm not mistaken, I think I was out of contract at the end of that season. We didn't have agents in those days, so it was up to the player to sort his financial package out directly with the manager, and as for me I didn't really know what to do or who to talk to if I'm honest. Managers were very powerful in those days, but Vic was a nice guy and he genuinely wanted to look after me financially, and made waves about doing just that.

Chapter 3

THE SAUNDERS ERA
Aston Villa player: 1974–1980

"I can't tell him what to do, he'll only do whatever he wants"
Ron Saunders, former Aston Villa manager

We had finished 14th in the Second Division in the 1973–1974 season and unfortunately for me, that saw the departure of Vic Crowe, a manager whom I got on especially well with. As I've previously mentioned, Vic had promised me a new contract, but as he was sacked and replaced by Ron Saunders in the summer of 1974, that never materialised. I was gutted, not just because I didn't get my new contract, but I enjoyed working with Vic and he was a good man. I was left in limbo, unsure what was going to happen, once Ron Saunders came in.

Ron Saunders had been dismissed by Manchester City, three weeks before the end of the previous season, with the club just outside the relegation places, even though he had guided both Norwich City and Manchester City to League Cup Finals in successive seasons, losing both by the odd goal.

When the club announced Ron was to be our new manager, I decided to waste no time and decided I wanted to see him, mainly because I was worried about my position in the team. Having just broken into the first team I wanted to understand where I stood, so I had to make an appointment with his secretary in order to have a chat with him. However, before my appointment with Ron, I went to see Vic to thank him for everything he'd done for me. He'd been good for me and I enjoyed his company very much so I thought going to see him was the least I could have done. When I met him, I told him I'd made an appointment to see Ron and he actually gave me some advice about how to handle my contract negotiations with him;

he told me to sit down and listen to what he had to say, but also to get my point across to him; he told me to speak honestly and openly, which wasn't a problem for me. It was all good advice and I took on board what he said.

Ron had the reputation of being a tough cookie; he was a manager who didn't mess around and from that first moment of meeting him, I knew who was in charge of this football club. Although not quite as firmly as four or five other players like Jimmy Cumbes, Charlie Aitken, Chris Nicholl, Ian Ross, I considered myself as an established player at the club. I'd played a lot of games during the previous season, and without a doubt, I was the youngest. I'd rehearsed for a long time before I went into the office: how much money I wanted; what sort of deal would be right for me; and such like; all the advice that Vic had given me.

I would have been 20 at the time. I have never been loud and airy, although I could have been pretty stubborn at times, but I knew where I needed to be in monetary terms compared to other players, whether that was right or wrong, but that may be a football thing. As a footballer back then, without the help from your fellow players, we didn't have a clue what weekly wage to ask for, unlike players of today, who have agents to do their deals for them; we basically had to go into the manager's office and ask for what we thought we were worth in the hope the manager thought the same. That was the theory anyway.

I've mentioned before that I'd only been late once in my life (at Amsterdam airport) and I promised myself I'd never do that again, so when that day came, I arrived nice and early at the Villa Park offices for my first meeting with Ron. When I was called up to his office, I knocked on his door and walked in, not nervous but just a bit apprehensive. Ron then gestured for me to sit in front him at his desk and before I could open my mouth, Ron looked at me and his first words to me were, "Well what's your name then?" I was a bit taken aback. He knew I was having a meeting with him so he must have known my name. To this day, I think that's the one thing that wound me up the most about Ron in all the time I've known him. I thought to myself, "Oh great, here we go. This isn't going to go well." It wasn't the welcome I'd expected, but in hindsight, it was the sign of things to come. In short, I got blown out of the water completely by him. I can't remember the figures, but Ron offered me roughly half of what I was expecting, or hoping for. The contract consisted of an average basic wage; he did offer me reasonable appearance money, but the overall offer was peanuts compared to what I knew other players were earning, and the meeting turned into a shambles for me, to be perfectly honest.

I think what bothered me about that first meeting with Ron was that he never once tried to find out anything about me. He didn't make me feel very comfortable. He didn't want to have a conversation with me. Maybe I was probably asking too much of him; I expected him to have looked at my stats, known who I was and tell me what he expected of me for the coming season, but there was none of that at all. I wouldn't say Ron was aloof, but he obviously hadn't done his homework on me. Maybe I had hoped there would be some rapport between us, but in all honesty, there was nothing there. I really thought it was a poor way to treat me, and it was something that remained with me.

Those were the days when some footballers would ally with the local newspaper and when things like that happened, you'd go to the local journalist and ask him to put a story in, stating the facts of the contract or whatever it was. However, I didn't go down that route as it seemed pointless to me. The written offer eventually came through the post to me. I didn't sign it straight away, but I did sign it a few days after reading it. In those days, if you didn't sign a contract you just didn't know where you'd end up. It wasn't as professional and organised as it is nowadays, with the agents controlling the players and dealing with the clubs. Can you imagine a player in my position nowadays? The agent would be banging on the door of the manager or the Director of Football demanding to know what's happening with his player. However, in the 1970s, more often than not, if the all too powerful manager didn't agree with what the player demanded, you couldn't do much about it other than stick at it or find another club. On that particular day, Ron certainly made it known he was in charge and didn't agree with my wage demands. From that day on, I had the feeling he and I were going to have a problem and I left the meeting fairly disappointed.

Even though we got of to a shaky start, trying to negotiate a good deal for myself, I have to say my first impressions of Ron Saunders as a coach were good. However, as time went by, there were some training methods I didn't agree with, but more about them later. During that first pre-season, we did a lot of hard running, up and down hills, but thankfully it wasn't as boring and repetitive as it had been under Tommy Docherty. Ron had been a boxer in his youth, and was a fitness fanatic, so he knew what he was doing. For our pre-season training, Ron would pick three or four separate hills; some long hills; some steep hills; some short hills, and it was all about power, timing and how quickly you could recover. For example, he'd pick a hill with a certain gradient and get us to run 10 yards, but that was about power; it was about getting 10 yards as quick as you could. Then he'd find a low gradient that was not so steep and he'd make you run 40 or 50 yards, where you needed power again, but you could build it up to get stronger. The general rule was, the steeper it was, the fewer repetitions you did; the longer and the less the gradient rose, you'd do more repetitions. There was always a variation of four or five different options: you'd sprint up the 10 or 15 yard one and you'd build power up the 30 or 40 yard one. All the different gradients had a slightly different amount; if you were doing the short and sharp one, you'd do 10, 15 or 20 repetitions; if you were doing the longer one, you'd only do 4 or 5 repetitions.

Then there would be a rotation so we ended up running up and down every hill doing the different drills. It was unbelievably hard work, but doable, and to a point I could understand what he was trying to do, building up our stamina and strength. It also pushed us to the limit and it built up team spirit because we were pushing each other, too. In fact, I quite liked the idea of those drills; many of the drills I've mentioned here I took on board and used them when I became a coach or a manager myself.

However, the one training session that I hated was the hurdles. I remember a lovely fella called Ted Small, who was the club's 'handyman'. He would sometimes get called up to the training ground to make things – yes, make things. Ron loved hurdles, so Ted had to make 20 wooden hurdles, which were used for some of our training sessions. The hurdles were lined up all in a row with just a wide enough gap to jump over, but we ended up hopping over them and we had to raise our knees to our chests as we jumped over the 20 hurdles. Another drill was to jump over two, then back over one, over two then back over one until you reached the end. Once you reached the end you'd effectively jumped over 40 or 50 hurdles. It wasn't surprising some people couldn't get over the hurdles and fell over through fatigue. I still believe to this day, a few of us in that team had knee problems later in our careers because of the times we crashed into the hurdles; we had a spate of cartilage operations in the team over the course of the next two years, and I really believe that they were caused by us doing those exercises with the hurdles. Those drills really tested our bodies to the limit and I, for one, stood up for myself and told Ron what I thought of them and that it wasn't the best exercise to give footballers, but of course, he took no notice of me. Not surprisingly, I decided never to use that drill when I became a coach.

We also did lap progressions, where you'd run a quarter of the pitch, jog a little bit, then run half the pitch, then jog three quarters of the pitch and that was followed by a full lap. In between each lap, you'd have a quarter of a lap to catch your breath, get your energy back and then you'd have to jog (not walk) for a few minutes. He used to call it the 'increase-decrease' drill and it was an unbelievably physical exercise. Again, it was doable and that was actually one of the methods that stuck with me later in my managerial career.

In some ways, Ron was a breath of fresh air, but there were a lot of things he did that I didn't agree with, didn't like or couldn't accept as being the right thing to do. One time, he brought in a gentleman by the name of Tony Ford as a training instructor, and his background wasn't football. He was a professional weightlifter and, although a lot of the lads enjoyed doing weights, I hated it. One of Tony's favourite drills was to get you to pick someone up and run with them in the air. The number of times I refused to do that was untrue – I just didn't believe in it. If you ask any sports scientist, fitness coach or physio these days that would be the last thing you'd do as an exercise. You just wouldn't see anybody pick up anything, let alone another person and run. Another time, Tony got us to run up and down an embankment, situated over the far side of the Bodymoor Heath training ground. He then asked us to pick up the person next to us and carry them up and down the embankment. Frank Carrodus was next to me at the time, he looked at me and knew I wasn't going to do it and I didn't. I thought to myself, "Tony, are you going to make me a better footballer by carrying someone up and down a hill?" Then I said to him out loud, "He's too heavy. I can't pick him up and run up and down the hill and I won't do it." Not surprisingly, I got sent back to the changing room that day, and a few times subsequently, just because I refused to follow his instructions. I wasn't being awkward about it, but

Tony hadn't given me any indication of how that exercise would have benefited me. There was no indication how it would make me fitter and, more to the point, become a better footballer, so I declined participation quite a few times in fact. Still to this day, I think I was right and made the correct decision to refuse doing those drills. As it turned out, I did have a bad back and although running up and down hills was OK, carrying someone was not and that was another reason why I hated that drill.

For various different reasons, I tended to get fined for either refusing to do certain things or for being a bit too argumentative, and often it resulted in me losing my loyalty bonus. Our contracts were minimal in terms of fixed wages, but there was decent appearance money on offer for playing in the first team, and at the end of each season you'd receive a loyalty bonus, so every time I refused to do something it was written down in the book as 'dissent' and it actually stopped me getting my bonus for probably three years in a row. I told you I was stubborn, didn't I?

Ron was a very hard man and loved physical exercise, and hated people abusing their body. He hated the smell of alcohol on players' breath and pretty much punished everyone in the team, whoever you were, even if only one person smelt of alcohol. His favourite trick was to stand close to you, give you a hug, not in an affectionate way, and shake your hand, but only to see if he could smell alcohol on your breath. God help us if he did, because we'd all end up with even more, hard physical work to do. Back in those days everybody liked a night out, as it was a way of bonding with your teammates. However, Ron didn't like it, unless, that is, when we won football matches and he'd offer everybody drinks on the team bus on the way home. He'd also hand out cigars of all things as rewards to his players, something I really hated and never once took one.

I have to say, there was so much about Ron that I liked, but the truth is, I just didn't get on with him. He never tried to get on with me and he never tried to find anything out about me as a person or as a footballer. However, Ron was brilliant at working with his team; once he'd got the exercises out of the way, and we went onto the training field, Ron was superb. He worked his defenders and midfielders tirelessly, more than the attackers I'd say. Ron would often play his back four, his midfield players and leave out the strikers until the last fifteen minutes. As a striker, I'd have to stand and watch while his team of eight outfield players would play against ten outfield reserve players, and that I didn't like because I wanted to be involved all the time. He used to drill his team to work on the opposition so they didn't score. Occasionally the reserves did score against the first team, but more often or not the first team would hang in there and not get beaten. He worked hard at that drill, time and time again, giving the opposition the ball in different areas of the pitch and his team defended so they didn't give anything away. It was repetitive and for people like me, it wasn't great because sometimes I'd only be involved for the last ten or fifteen minutes when he'd bring me on for the remainder of the match. He was fanatical about organisation and discipline and the understanding of how to defend, even if you were under pressure with fewer men in your team and that I agreed with.

Our training ground was at Bodymoor Heath, near Tamworth and every morning we'd come in and the kitman would hand out the clean training gear. The first team were often asked to wear a claret shirt so the kitman would have had his instruction of what the fifteen or sixteen first-teamers were and who was going to train with the reserves. Usually, most of the first-teamers were nailed on, but there were one or two who were on the periphery of the first team and they didn't get a shirt and would have a moan about it. When we went out training, Ron had another trick up his sleeve. He'd walk out with a reserve team shirt in his hand and you'd look at the three or four people who were on the edge of the first team and you just knew he'd come up and throw the shirt at one of them and send them to the far end of the training ground where the reserves trained. Once you saw him walk across the training ground, heading towards us, you just knew someone was about to be chucked out. Some people took it on the chin, but a few just melted as he destroyed them on the spot in front of everyone. There was no reason for it and I really believe he planned it on purpose. If you were in that first-team group you tried everything to stay there because you didn't want it to happen to you. For me, it wasn't right and I couldn't grasp the concept. He did it on purpose, that's for sure and he seemed to gain so much pleasure from shattering someone's confidence. You'd think that was silly, but he had that air about him that frightened some people and totally knocked the stuffing out of some of the players. It was his way and he had this thing of wanting to show people he was in charge and he was the one making the decisions. In short, Ron was pretty cruel at times, a control freak if you like, but you just had to get on with it, otherwise you'd get hurt. I never warmed to it at all and as you can imagine, we had a few run-ins.

****

The 1974–1975 season in the Second Division with Ron in charge started with three straight 1-1 draws, followed by a 6-0 home win to Hull City, which made a few people sit up and take notice of us. I think I scored one goal in the opening half a dozen games, but I then picked up an injury that kept me out for a good 10 games. During that time, my brother Alan played in the first team, making his debut in a 2-1 away win against Oldham in early October 1974 and that made me very proud indeed.

The pitches back then were awful and didn't help with the type of football we wanted to play, but all that pre-season fitness work we did with Ron Saunders started to bear fruit. Ron hardly ever gave us any time off; possibly if we had a midweek game we may have been allowed to have a day off, but if we didn't have a midweek game we'd be training all throughout the week. Having said that, Ron's idea of a day off was being in at 9am to do 45 minutes of hard work and being out of the gates by 10am. He was worried if we had a full day off we'd have gone out the previous night, so he made sure we'd be doing some sort of exercise. His thinking was that if we had played on a Tuesday, there would be no way we could go out the previous night because we'd have to be up early and in at 9am to the training ground. Of course, a lot of the lads still enjoyed a good night out so that took some getting used to, but like everything you adjusted to his methods. You had to or otherwise you were out of the door. There were exceptions of course; one or two of the lads did go out on the night before a day off on the Wednesday morning and let me tell you, the next day they wished they hadn't. Those 45 minutes were unbelievably hard and of course, he got the hurdles out, and those lads who went out, boy they felt it.

Ultimately, all the training had a positive affect on us, because we were probably one of the fittest teams in the league, if not the country. The results bore witness to that, and during the season, we just got stronger and stronger. I started to build up a good striking partnership with Keith Leonard, who in my eyes was one of the best players in the league at the time. He was as brave and as strong as an ox, with wonderful upper body strength and had a little streak in him in that ensured he could look after himself, which was important in those days. As I've said before, strikers had to look after themselves because the centre-halves were hard warriors and didn't take any prisoners. Just as centre-halves didn't want to lose a game, the centre-forwards wanted to win the game, and more often than not, that was the biggest battle on the pitch. It has to be said, Keith did as much damage to centre-halves as they did to him and he really did look after himself. You could tell from first challenge in a game that he'd be in a battle with the centre-half, and Keith won most of his tussles on the pitch. I'd always know when Keith had won, because he would give me a little smile and say something like, "Go on. You just go and do what you want now."

Looking back at my early career, playing alongside Andy Lochhead, who also put himself about a bit, I'd say Keith was a younger version of him. Keith wasn't just a fierce competitor, he had a good touch as well, and even though he wasn't quick I'd pick up a lot of balls from him because he led the line brilliantly, and we struck up a great understanding for a short period of time. Unfortunately, Keith's career was cut short to injury less than two years later.

There was one game, away to Orient that springs to mind when I'm talking about Keith and clashes with centre-halves. The first clash between Keith and their centre-half, Tom Walley, was seriously unbelievable. It looked like a nasty challenge between them and they both ended up on the ground for a minute or two, with Keith getting up first, but Tom stayed down and looked as though he'd broken his nose. The physio (the trainer with a sponge) came on and cleaned the blood from his face and he somehow managed to get to his feet. I looked at Tom and he looked terrible, but he somehow managed to stumble to his knees and when he got his balance, wiped his face with his shirt, pulled his sleeves up, pulled his shorts and socks up and Keith just looked at me and went, "Woooo!! I might lose this battle today." Keith did lose that battle in the end and we lost the game 1-0. How Tom Walley got up and continued playing I will never know, because Keith really scuttled into him with some force. Maybe it's too much to believe we ended up losing that game because the centre-half won his battle against Keith that day. I don't know, but it was how the game was lost from our point of view.

In the second half of the season, I began to find my scoring boots and scored quite a lot of goals during that period. We managed to win 10 out of the last 11 games in the league, with the only defeat being at Orient. Several other games stick out in my memory of that season. We played Oldham at home, but the funny thing about that game happened just before half time, when we were awarded a penalty at the Holte End and I picked up the ball to take it. I'd scored two already and was determined to get my hat trick and everyone was looking at me in disbelief, until somebody said, "You can't take penalties, Brian." I can still see Ron Saunders jumping out of his dugout, screaming from the touchline, "Don't let him take that f***ing penalty. Do not let him take it. Get on the ball." However, I defied Ron and stood my ground, "I am! I'm taking it!" By now, the whole team were all looking at me as if I had gone mad, because I was refusing to take orders from the gaffer, "Don't do it. Don't do it. If you miss he'll hurt you so hard." I was still standing my ground and told my teammates, "I won't miss." Ron was still screaming and swearing at me, calling me all sorts of names I can't repeat, "Put that f***ing ball down." So, what happened? Of course, I missed the penalty. To be fair, I felt the goalkeeper was going to dive so I tried to play it right down the middle, on the floor and without pace. It was almost as if the 'keeper had dived, got straight back up, picked the ball up and walked down the tunnel for half-time. What I wanted to do was to be really clever and to chip the 'keeper, but I ended up running towards the ball and side-footing it at the 'keeper, who didn't move. The ball went towards the 'keeper so slow he could have run around the pitch and still had time to save it.

"Oh dear, I will be in trouble," I thought. No sooner had the referee blown for half-time, than Ron was waiting to pounce and he followed me off the pitch, hammering me all the way into the dressing room and once the dressing room door had closed, he absolutely slaughtered me in front of my teammates, even though we were winning 3-0 and flying, and I'd scored two of them. A dialogue continued between Ron and myself that I have to say was totally unrepeatable. He made it quite clear he didn't want me to take that penalty, but I did, and I can still see all the lads cringing, shaking their heads as they witnessed a tirade of abuse from the gaffer. I bet they were saying to themselves, "He's done it again. He's wound the manager up."

And I did – big time!

In the second-half, I got my hat trick and we won the game 5-0. Incidentally, I was never asked to take a penalty in senior football again, and to be honest, I'd learned my lesson that day. When I look back though, it was funny thinking that everybody was telling me not to do it. They all knew, and I guess so did I, what the consequences would be at half time, but I'd made my mind up and just went ahead anyway. That was typical of me.

The away game against Sheffield Wednesday in late April was another one of those games that stick out in my memory of that season. We were 3-0 up at half-time and we were playing unbelievably well and ended up scoring one more in the second-half, and I scored two that day. We eventually clinched promotion on the penultimate game of the season, at home to Sunderland, who were chasing promotion as well. Unusually for me, I'd been out with a friend of mine the night before, not drinking mind you, but as I was driving home to my digs in Sutton Coldfield, I saw a group of lads so I stopped to offer them a lift. As I wound the window down of my new Vauxhall Viva, I noticed they were a group of Sunderland fans, but I still offered them a lift and dropped them off in the city centre. I don't think they knew who I was, and I didn't let on, but they knew I had a similar accent. In those days before social media and TV sports channels, you didn't have a clue about other teams' players and what they looked like, apart from the very famous ones. Anyway, the next day, we played Sunderland and Ian Ross and I scored the goals to win us promotion to the First Division. It was watched by a massive crowd of over 57,000, including 8,000 away fans and it was one of those iconic days, because it ended with a mass pitch invasion, with Villa fans celebrating the clubs' promotion back to the First Division.

Ron had developed a really good team during that season. When you look at some of the great teams, even some of the great modern-day teams, you tend to look at the midfielders being by far the most energetic players in the team. Ron's teams' were no different, and one of his early signings was a lad called Frank Carrodus, who he signed from Manchester City. Looking back at watching, playing and coaching football for 50 years, Frank was as good an athlete as anybody I've ever come across.

He ran up hills quicker than he ran down them; on the football pitch he ran back at the same speed that he'd run forwards. He had unbelievable energy and I would have loved to be able to run like him. While he wasn't the most gifted player in the world or the best player in the team, and I think he'd accept that, he did have enough talent to play football at a very high level. He had an incredible effect on the team and he was the driving force of the group. In today's game, they monitor how far players run during every single game, but I would love to have known how far Frank ran during each game he played in. He never moaned about anything and if there was ever an unsung hero in our team during that period, Frank was that person. He was simply phenomenal and a different class.

Apart from recruiting Frank, Ron also brought in Leighton Phillips from Cardiff City for £100,000, and those two players proved to be very shrewd signings for Ron. We had many other good players in that team, including Ray Graydon, who was what I'd call a model professional. In an era when team bonding was all about going out and having a good time with the lads, Ray was over and above all that. He always looked after himself, worked hard and was really serious about his football and would talk about the game to anybody who'd listen and he's still like that to this day. It didn't surprise me that he went into coaching after he retired from playing. He was probably the most under estimated player in that team. He made so many goals and also scored so many from wide positions. He also had a terrific way of coming in at the far post and ending up slotting the ball home.

We did well in the League Cup that season, which started in the September with a home tie against a very strong Everton side, consisting of players like Mick Lyons, Howard Kendall, Joe Royal and Bob Latchford. You tend to remember the players in the game rather than the game itself. We drew at Villa Park 1-1 with our goal coming from Chris Nicholl and their goal scored by Bob Latchford, two giants of the game. I don't remember too much about the game, more the battles between those two players. The tie went to a replay at Goodison Park; I didn't play in that game through injury, but we won that 3-0. I seem to recall Ron playing Bobby Campbell and Sammy Morgan up front that night, which was a completely different combination from what he would normally put out. We then got drawn against Crewe, and I missed that game too; Sammy Morgan played up front with Keith Leonard that night. Imagine playing against those two? Crikey, if there were two centre forwards who could put themselves about, it was those two. They both scored in front of a capacity crowd in a 2-2 draw and it was a hell of a hard game. I was back fit for the replay at Villa Park, and my brother Alan was on the bench. We beat Crewe 1-0 through a 'Chico' Hamilton goal. We were progressing well and playing teams who were beatable.

The next draw gave us Hartlepool, and again we had a tough night in front of another capacity crowd. I played with Bobby Campbell, so that was another new partnership up front; there were injuries here, there and everywhere. We only managed another 1-1 draw in that match, and so it was back to Villa Park in front of 17,000 on the 25th November 1974, my 21st birthday and a game I will never forget, because I scored two goals to help the team win 6-1. Not only that, Alan came on as a substitute so we played in the same side for the first time, and that capped off an incredible day for me, personally. Alan was tough as nails and played in midfield in those days; he was a proper lad to have in your team and I was delighted for him to have finally made his debut. If I remember, Ray Graydon got a hat trick that night. That performance signalled a run in the side until pretty much the end of the season, and as a group, we started to believe we could do something special. It was a run of games where we didn't lose many at all and the team started to click. From memory, I think we only lost five games from that Hartlepool game until the end of the season.

If there was ever a cup run that you would think you'd have been given a chance to go all the way in, it was the season 1974–1975. Some may say we had an easy run-in, but I'm not so sure. From that day on, we were starting to think a little bit about Wembley. We thought we must have half a chance, and lo and behold we got a draw Colchester United. Again, it was another hard game, even though they were another small club, but for them, playing us was their cup final. Another away tie and again, Alan played in the first-team with me and actually scored the winning goal for us. So we progressed through to the semi-finals. How proud our parents must have been on that night. We were then drawn against Chester, another giant-killing team, in the two-legged semi-final. The first leg was away from home. It was an unbelievably competitive game and we drew 2-2 in front of 19,000 with goals from Bobby McDonald and Ray Graydon. Somebody I must mention here is a lad who played in that game but not many people will know of: Frank Pimblett. Frank was a really good footballer, but Ron was a bit hard on young lads like Frank, and he seemed to make it difficult for him to get a chance. He really should have kicked on at Villa, but never did. I'm not really sure how many more games he actually played for Villa after that – probably not many. In the return leg at Villa Park, the 47,732 that turned out got the biggest fright of their lives, because Chester took us all the way to extra-time. With the score at 4-4 on aggregate, guess who popped up to score the winning goal? It was a marvellous moment for both me and my teammates as we finally won the tie 3-2 on the night and booked out place at Wembley. We had gathered momentum during the season and were playing some good football; we'd also developed a great team spirit amongst the group so reaching the final seemed like just reward.

Our prize was to play Norwich in the final at Wembley on the 1st March 1975. For two second tier clubs to be in a final was unusual even in those days. Norwich themselves had worked their socks off to reach the final, maybe even more than us, because they had to beat their local rivals, Ipswich and then Manchester United in the semi-final. We were two, well matched sides on the day, with some good players on both sides on the park. Our team was:

Cumbes, Robson, Aitken, Ross, Nicholl, McDonald, Graydon, Little (B), Leonard, Hamilton, Carrodus.

During that final, I remember their centre-back, Dave Stringer followed me all over Wembley, but our game plan was perfect. It was that game that finally opened the door for me at international level, because lots of people were there to witness it. Nobody will ever forget Mel Machin handling the ball from a Chris Nicholl header that was going into the net and Ray Graydon's famous penalty, which was saved by Kevin Keelan, but Ray slotted home the rebound.

That year proved to be a successful year for both Villa and Norwich, as we were both promoted to the top flight, with Villa finishing second behind Manchester United. Both Villa and Norwich made a bit of a statement that year, so it was a terrific advert for our league. To play in the final at Wembley was amazing for me personally, and it was fitting for us as a team that all our hard work proved worthwhile. To win the League Cup was an incredible feeling. It was incredible considering I'd only left home six years previously and it probably cemented my chances of playing for England that summer. Was I nervous? Not in the slightest. I loved every minute of it; loved the big stadium; loved the big pitch; loved the atmosphere. It was a brilliant day and an experience I will never forget.

Incidentally, I ended the league season playing 44 games and scoring 22 goals in all competitions; I was right up there, in amongst all the more senior players like Jimmy Cumbes, Charlie Aitken, John Robson (Robbo), Frank Carrodus, Ian Ross, Chris Nicholl and Ray Graydon, who'd all played over 45 games. I was also up there in terms of goals, along with Ray Graydon, who scored a phenomenal 31 goals as a winger.

So, at the end of a very successful season for both Villa and myself personally, I was called up into the England squad aged 21, along with John Gidman, for the Home International game against Northern Ireland. I wasn't selected to play, nor was I named on the substitutes bench; however, I was selected to be a substitute for the next game, at Wembley against a strong Welsh side on 21st May 1975. The England manager, Don Revie, told the media before the game that I was fit and ready to play and was singing my praises, saying I had the ability to beat defences. Other England players like Kevin Beattie were also calling for me to play. Some newspapers were saying I was the most exciting prospect for the 1978 World Cup; however, England didn't qualify so that subsequently ended that debate.

Before the game, Kevin Keegan had walked out of the team hotel; nobody knew where he'd gone, so he would miss the game against Wales. It wasn't ideal preparation, but we got on with it. With 19 minutes of the game to go, Wales were leading 2-1 and Revie told me to go on to replace Mick Channon. The crowd responded to my appearance and although it was my debut I wasn't nervous at all. I was ready and willing to play my part, be it a short one. Within five minutes of coming on as a substitute I made an impact. I took the ball out wide, crossed it into the box and David Johnson headed home at the far post for his second goal to make the score 2-2. We'd salvaged a draw.

That brief appearance in an England shirt was a very proud moment for me; however, it was also my last appearance. I think everybody was expecting me to start the next game against Scotland, but Don Revie had other ideas. I wasn't even included in the squad. Revie was quoted as saying, "I couldn't play him against Scotland because we needed experienced players", and said, "The atmosphere will be different". The England fans were not happy, and some called it a disgrace that I had been over-looked. In all honesty, I doubt he fancied me as a player, even though there was some heavy competition in that England side at the time.

However, I can say I have played for England at Wembley, and not many people can say that.

****

The end of season tour following that successful 1974–1975 season was to the Caribbean, and to a small French island called Martinique. It was the most incredible place and we were there for 10 days of pure sunshine. Our hotel was fantastic and so was the beach it looked out on to. The idea was to chill out, but we did have a couple of charity games to play in.

We had some great characters at the club during that era and John Burridge ('Budgie') was one of those. He signed for us from Blackpool during 1975 and he ultimately replaced Jimmy Cumbes in goal. He also replaced Jimmy as our unofficial 'head of entertainment'. Anyone who remembers Budgie will know he was an absolute fruitcake, and I mean that as a term of endearment. He was a great lad, though and he was the most energetic and athletic goalkeeper I've ever known. I've never had so many laughs in my life than during the spell Budgie was at the club. He was deadly serious about everything and loved his work. He absolutely loved being in goal and probably worked harder than anybody else I've known in my life.

Budgie was in his element on the tour and he'd be in the pool area, showing off and everybody was trying to keep out of his way, up the other end of the pool. We were a group of 20 young footballers and all daft as brushes and Budgie was there to entertain everybody, and wherever he went, he was loved. Very often, he'd do something just for a laugh, whether it was doing one-arm press-ups, walking along the diving board on his hands, doing a double somersault into the water or going through a whole warm-up routine. Budgie would always do something to keep himself fit, while entertaining the lads. So, there he was doing his exercises, while the rest of the lads were lying in the sun having a beer, but we all left him to it.

Martinique was a beautiful place, but we were all bored out of our brains; it was out of season and there was nothing going on, that was, until Budgie decided to perform on one particular day. There were a couple at the opposite end of the pool made a point of staring at us in dismay, and you could see they weren't happy, just because we were having a laugh and a joke, so Budgie decided to aggravate them even more. Being a brilliant gymnast, he climbed onto the diving board, bounced up and down a couple of times, dived into the pool and went right under the water. He then swam to the bottom end (underwater) and without stopping. As he came out of the water he jumped straight up onto the edge of the pool, right by where the couple were sitting, shook himself off like a dog and splashed water over the couple on purpose. He then jumped onto his hands, walked around the pool, went up to the diving board and performed the routine again. He did it three times and every time he did a circuit, we'd give him a round of applause. At the time I felt sorry for the couple that had to bear the brunt of his tricks, but they clearly didn't like us and Budgie had put them in their place.

We had a lad in the party called Keith 'Corky' Masefield, who was probably drunk for the whole time we were in Martinique. He was a strange lad because he spent the whole 10 days in his underpants. Every time we saw him, 'Corky' would be walking round in a daze, wearing a pair of Y-fronts, bless him. He just didn't care, and why would he? He was never sober.

We all attracted a lot of attention while we were there and the locals loved to be entertained by us, singing, telling stories and having a laugh and a joke; everybody got to know us in the short space of time we were on the island. One night, we all went to our usual harbour bar, dressed up in tight tee shirts, three-inch heeled shoes and flared trousers and having a great time, singing and dancing; the locals loved it. I think most of us were wearing what's called 'bling' nowadays, and I'm sure we thought we were all pop-stars. It was a crazy time, but nothing untoward ever happened when we went out. It was always good-humoured fun.

One night, Budgie had been out and about for the day and he walked into the bar and straightaway, he sensed there is an opportunity to entertain the crowd. There was a big crowd there so he decided to do one of his routines and started to do some press-ups, then he jumped onto some tables and then he somersaulted back off the tables. He was on incredible form, but then he decided to take it one step further by jumping up the metal struts that held the gazebo together and started to do pull-ups, showing everybody how strong he was, lifting his head up above the bar several dozen times. For whatever reason, he decided to swing round, rolling around like a trapeze artist. I told you he was as daft as a brush. So, after doing it once, he did it again. However, on the second occasion, he pulled the gazebo down and the whole thing collapsed on top of everybody. While everybody else started screaming or laughing, we were thinking, "Oh no, what the hell have you done this time, Budgie?" while we were trying to scramble out from underneath the gazebo. As we emerged out of the collapsed gazebo, we noticed the owner of the bar, a mate of ours, standing in front of us with a cricket bat in his hand, shouting in his Caribbean accent, "What have you done you stupid lot?" All of a sudden, somebody shouted, "Run! Run!" and everybody, I mean everybody, started to run down towards the jetty area. Giddy and I were wearing three-inch platform heals but we were overtaking everyone; we shouldn't have been able to run with them on, but somehow we were legging it down the road and we didn't realise we were wearing them. Then, diverted from the crowd, Frank Carrodus came flying past us towards the jetty and dived headfirst into the sea. However, the sea wasn't even a foot deep so his whole body collapsed and his head almost stuck in the sand as he dived. Giddy and I killed ourselves laughing when we saw Frank, face down in the water. When Frank finally got out, his face was dripping with blood and his forehead and nose were scraped to bits. We got him patched up and somehow back to the hotel. It was like a scene from a comedy sketch.

The next morning, the whole team decided we should go round to the bar and apologise. We had a bit of a whip round and gathered some money together and went to see the owner, whom we had upset. As it turned out, he was OK with us and said he wanted us there every night as we were so much fun.

We didn't go back to that bar every night, after all, probably due to embarrassment. However, one particular night, a few of us went to the local casino and we all chipped in. maybe a few hundred pounds, for a betting pot. None of us were experts or big gamblers, but we stuck Giddy in the chair to play Blackjack and on the first hand, we were expecting him to put a tenner in, but no, he stuck the whole lot on the first hand. I think that resulted in some interest from the locals and other tourists, who were observing us around the table. Some American tourist asked us who we were and thought we must have been really famous, as we gambled a large amount of money. As luck had it, Giddy came up trumps as he won the hand and doubled our money. Because of that success, we decided to play there on at least three or four nights after that. By the end of the holiday, it didn't come as any surprise that we'd lost everything that we had put in.

Put it this way, it was four or five nights of pure life education that money could not buy.

****

One memorable game from the 1975–1976 season was the local derby at Villa Park against Birmingham City in September 1975. Over 53,000 fans packed the stadium to watch an incredibly competitive and rough game, as rough as it can be. They had Kenny Burns, Trevor Francis, Peter Withe and Joe Gallagher playing for them. From memory, they scored first after Kenny Burns pumped a long ball into the box, which was flicked on and Budgie pulled off a decent save, but it rebounded off him into the path of Trevor Francis, who as usual tapped the ball in. At that stage, the home crowd didn't go quiet, but they actually increased the volume in the stadium. On that occasion, Ron played John Robson in midfield. He wasn't known as a midfielder, but he could play there. He could run all day and that's quality you need as a midfielder. There was instance where Robbo went through with the ball and hit a blistering shot with his left foot from 30 yards towards the Holte End but it missed the net.

It was some time into the second-half before we equalised. We had started to ping balls into the box to be flicked on, and one of them found 'Chico', who turned and rifled the ball into the net and the whole stadium erupted. There was a nasty incident in the second-half where Kenny Burns nearly sliced Robbo in half. Robbo came flying through and Kenny just stood there and stamped at him. How he didn't hurt him more, I don't know. Then Leighton Phillips, or 'Blodwin' as we called him, was absolutely livid as he came over, flying into Kenny and people were trying to hold him back, as he'd lost it completely.

We had Andy Gray, who'd just signed for us, sitting in the dugout next to Ron Saunders that day; little did we know what effect he'd have on us in the future. However, our winning goal on the day came from a long goal kick from Budgie and it found Frank Carrodus, who leapt like a salmon to flick it on and I found myself chasing the ball with Kenny Burns; Kenny looked odds on favourite to get it as he put in a sliding tackle, but as he slid, his left leg went under his body and he lost his balance, so I nipped in with a half challenge and the ball ricocheted into the box. I took a step to one side and side-footed it into the bottom corner. We won the game 2-1 and if you ask any local Villa fan of that era, they will always remember that game. It was a brilliant day, but I will remember it because of the Villa fans. They were immense.

I also remember the Birmingham City kit that day; it was royal blue with a big white stripe down the middle, and is often called 'the penguin kit'. It just didn't work for me, but it is an iconic kit, nonetheless. If you compare that to our classic claret and blue kit with the 'V' neck and collar and the round badge that's still my favourite kit and we looked immaculate in it.

Another one of my favourite games, maybe even my absolute favourite game was the 5-1 defeat of League champions Liverpool at Villa Park in December 1976 when I scored one of the goals, and we were 5-1 up at half-time in front of more than 42,000. It is no exaggeration to say it was probably the best 45 minutes of football ever seen at Villa Park. It was the game that sent shockwaves around England, and indeed Europe, but for me, it was just such an incredible game to be involved in. Liverpool were by far the best team in Europe, if not the world at the time, with the likes of Keegan, Neal, Thompson, Hughes, McDermott and Heighway in the side, but we destroyed them by half-time.

For my goal, I received the ball from Giddy, who was in an inside-right position, around 30 yards away from the goal. I did a little shimmy, turned onto the inside, then onto my left foot (my weaker foot) and curled the ball past Ray Clemence into the top of the net. John Deehan and Andy Gray scored two each. It was such a great game in a time before wall-to-wall football coverage and mobile phones, so it was a pity the TV cameras weren't there because no video coverage of the game exists.

CHAPTER 3: THE SAUNDERS ERA

****

Budgie was always up to something. I remember we went away for a team bonding exercise to Selsdon Park around the Christmas period of 1975. It was meant to be a relaxing few days to get away from it all, but for Budgie it was far from that. There was a golf course on site and Giddy and I decided on the first morning we'd be first on the course. It was a bit foggy early doors and while we stood there on the first tee, waiting for the mist to lift, having a laugh and a joke we could hear something rustling a few yards down the fairway. It sounded like there was someone down there making a noise in the bushes. As the mist lifted a little, we could just make out a figure in the bushes – it was Budgie running up the hill. He was only wearing a big, heavy jacket and all of his pockets were full of sand and he also had a rucksack on his back that was full of sand, too. Not only that, he had several bags in his hands – full of sand. Still to this day, I can't believe what he was doing. While we were supposed to be away having a bit of fun, Budgie's view of fun was to try to keep fit, running his backside off carrying bags full of sand. As he ran past us, he nonchalantly said, "Morning lads," and carried on running, as if it was the normal thing to be doing. Giddy and I both stood there in amazement, laughing and thinking he was an absolute crackpot, which he was, but it was so funny thinking about it now.

Talking of Budgie, he'd come into training some mornings and say something like, "Nobody's going to score past me today, lads," and we'd ask why, "...because I was practising at home, last night and I caught every orange. You should have seen me. I was diving off the sofa, catching everything." Apparently, his wife used to throw tennis balls or oranges towards him while they were sitting watching TV and he'd dive off the sofa to catch them before they hit the ground. He really thought that exercise would make his reactions sharper. Seriously, that's what he'd tell us. In training, most of the lads would usually try and blast the ball past the 'keeper, but sometimes, I'd do something different, maybe chip the ball over him in order to catch him out. When I did that Budgie wasn't happy and he'd scowl at me and say something like, "You'd never do that on a matchday." My response was, "To be honest, Budgie if I was playing against you, I would." When that happened he'd get angry and kick the ball as far down the training ground as possible so I'd have to go and fetch it.

There's a great story that really sums up Budgie and it happened when we played Rangers in a so-called friendly match in October 1976, which was infamous for being abandoned after 53 minutes when the away fans invaded the pitch. There were some incidents during the first half as we led 1-0 through a Dennis Mortimer goal, but it was at half-time when trouble flared with hundreds of Rangers fans causing trouble in the Holte End. Supporters at the back of the Holte End surged towards the front forcing frightened supporters to spill onto the pitch. The second half had kicked off by the time the field was cleared and all fans returned to the terraces. In the Holte End, bricks, stones and bottles were thrown by yobs who had completely ignored the game that was still being played. When Frank Carrodus put us 2-0 up on 52 minutes, the violence erupted again, with the Villa fans joining in the fighting and for a second time the fans invaded the pitch.

In order to escape the pitch invasion Ron Saunders and Rangers counterpart Jock Wallace ordered the players off the pitch and they all ran like crazy down the tunnel to escape the mayhem. I saw Rangers fans being caught and arrested by the police, hands tied behind their backs, shouting and swearing at us and as we were running off the pitch they started kicking out at us. There were all sorts of things going on. It was absolutely horrendous, and I'd never witnessed scenes like it at a football match before.

The Villa Park tunnel in those days was at the corner of the Trinity Road and Witton End stands and it was very narrow. There were steps down, then steps up, leading to the dressing rooms, and there were very often scuffles breaking out between opposition players, owing to the tightness of the area. Anyway, as we reached the top of the steps, I heard Budgie say, "I've left me gloves in the back of the goal." I asked him what's he was going to do and he said, "I can't leave me gloves in the goal, can I?" Despite what was going on out on the pitch and in the stands, Budgie ran down the tunnel and back onto the pitch to get his gloves out of the Holte End goal net. Somehow he got through all the madness; somehow he got his gloves; somehow he got back in one piece. Well, that just sums him up, really. He had no fear and only Budgie would bother to go back out into the mayhem to retrieve his gloves. As I've already told you he was as daft as a brush, in the nicest possible way.

Fruitcake!

Some of the other lads in that side are worth a mention here, because they were all great guys and even better players. Giddy and I became really good friends from the day he joined us from the Liverpool youth set-up in 1971. We looked after each other on and off the pitch, roomed together and had some really good fun nights out. Then we had the likes of 'Chico' Hamilton who was another fun guy and so laid back it was untrue. He loved a night out with the lads too and he also smoked, which wasn't unusual in those days. Ian Ross was our captain and like most players of that era, he liked a night out and he also smoked. It's crazy to look back now, how many players smoked and had a beer, but it really was the norm. Then we had John Robson, who became a very good friend of mine and was a lovely lad, God bless him. He played either left or right back and sometimes played in midfield. I can't get by without talking about Chris Nicholl. We had a brilliant relationship, because we were just so different. He was deadly serious and wanted to know everything, whereas I was happy-go-lucky and I played 'off the cuff', but that's why we clicked, I guess. Chris was a terrific centre-half and the big man always tested himself with everything he did, and he wanted to test himself against the best players he could. Ron Saunders very often got us to wear running spikes, because he claimed they would make us run faster and were lighter on our feet. As I was quick, Chris always had to run against me, but unfortunately for the big man, he couldn't get anywhere near me. Every single sprinting session, he wanted to test himself against me. In fact, I was also quicker at turning than him and I was quicker with my reactions. However, Chris wanted to challenge me day in, day out, challenge himself and he wanted to beat me so much it became an obsession for him; I could count on one hand how many times he beat me. That goes to show what he was like; he was competitive; he wanted to get closer to me; he wanted to catch me, but more often than not, he couldn't. For example, we did a drill where we'd lie on our belly with our hands and legs in the air and when the whistle went, we'd have to jump up and start running. By the time I was half way to the finishing line, big Chris had only just started to get up onto his feet.

The 1976–1977 season was another tremendous season for Villa and I played in some of the favourite games of my entire playing career. We won the League Cup in 1975, and that was a tremendous occasion, but our 1976–1977 League Cup run was equally special. We kicked off with a home tie against Manchester City, a team we'd only lost to at Maine Road, a week earlier. I remember that game like it was yesterday, because as a forward, I just couldn't get into the game, and we lost 2-0. Dennis Tueart was a forward who played for City, and for some reason I had it in my head that he was miles better than me; he was bright; he was alive; he was here, there and everywhere. So, ironically, we played them a week later at Villa Park, and Dennis's performance at Maine Road was all the motivation I needed. So I told myself I was going to be alert, alive and play out of my socks – I was so ready for that game, and on the night we won 3-0, and I think I scored two goals. My first was a flashy goal with an overhead kick from a corner into the top corner, and my second was from a flick on from Chris Nicholl, I slipped it through my legs, back-healed it, then slotted the ball into the bottom corner. We were outstanding as a team on the night in front of 34,000 and we were up-and-running in the League Cup. I remember as a kid, watching Dennis play for Sunderland. I was really impressed by him, and his performance against us taught me a lot about football. Reflecting on that game, I owed that performance and that brace to Dennis Tueart, because he inspired me so much in the previous game, and made me want to show the world I was as good, if not better than him.

In the next round, we played Norwich at home and had a comfortable 2-1 win, with big Andy Gray scoring them both. That was followed by another home tie against Wrexham, and another big victory by 5-1, and I scored another brace. Things began to hot up, and the crowd of 41,000 began to sense another cup run. In the quarter-finals we drew Millwall, at home again, and 37,000 saw a 2-0 victory. Chris Nicholl and I scored those goals. I loved it when either of us scored, because we were great friends and still are. I loved his attitude when he played. I used to wind him up when I made out I wasn't serious about my football. He was outwardly, deadly serious about the game, whereas, he claimed, I was inwardly deadly serious about my football. He would let the world know how competitive he was on a football field, whereas I was the opposite and made out I didn't care, but inwardly I was unbelievably determined to show everybody how good I was. I demonstrated that during that Manchester City game, earlier in the season. I didn't outwardly shout it out how much Dennis Tueart had inspired me to do well in the League Cup game, but I inwardly wanted to show everybody I could play.

We were really flying by then!

Ron Saunders had built a terrific team and it had begun to take shape, playing a 4-3-3 formation: Budgie in goal, Giddy at right-back, Chris Nicholl and Leighton Phillips as centre-backs, John Robson (God rest his soul) playing left-back; a midfield three of Gordon 'Sid' Cowans, Dennis Mortimer and Frank Carrodus, with Andy Gray, Ray Graydon and myself up top. When you look at that team, Dennis Mortimer was so dominant running with the ball; Sid was probably one of the best passers of the ball we've ever seen, and Frank, was the fittest man on the park. It was a good team. The balance was right and the signs were good for us.

The League Cup semi-final first leg, against Queens Park Rangers at Loftus Road, ended in a disappointing 0-0 draw. Then we had the second leg at Villa Park, in front of an amazing 48,429, and it was a great game of football which ended 2-2. Ron had brought in John 'Dixie' Deehan to play alongside Andy Gray and myself, and that move gave me a load of freedom. It was another dimension for me, playing with Dixie. Basically, Andy and Dixie held the central area so my role was to play in a diamond formation from time to time or play in wide areas on other occasions. Although Ron was a total disciplinarian, it was the period in his reign he gave me a free licence to express myself. He still had a moan at me from time to time and would say things to people like, "I can't tell him what to do. He'll only do whatever he wants," but deep down, he was encouraging me to play with complete freedom. In possession, football's a great game to play, but we had to work hard at it out of possession. My role was to stop the full-backs, so I could swap wings, or if the full-backs were adventurous I could sit in a diamond position and play.

With the second leg ending all square, we had to have a replay, as there were no penalties in those days. We had to play a reply at a neutral venue, at one of my favourite grounds, Highbury. It was a game I will never forget and it turned out to be a very special evening for me personally, mainly because I scored a hat-trick to take us to the final. I can still visualise each of the goals.

Two of them were simple goals, slotting into the bottom corner; for my third, Dennis Mortimer made an incredible run through the middle and beat a few players, got to the by-line and saw me coming into the box and I shot from 15 yards to make it 3-0.

The final at Wembley against Everton was another special occasion, but it was a poor game and probably the worst game I've ever played in, it was that bad. It was a great Everton team, too: Duncan McKenzie, Bob Latchford, Ken McNaught (who Ron later signed on the back of his performance in the final), Mick Lyons and Bryan Hamilton. I think the most exciting thing about the game was that one of the band members lost his spur and everybody was looking for it before the game. It would have been very dangerous if we'd of left it on the pitch, and so it was fortunate that somebody found it.

The replay was at Hillsborough in front of 55,000, and it was another average game, with two sides that were evenly matched. It didn't seem that either team could beat each other, so the least said about that the better. Then, we went to Old Trafford for the second replay, and were watched by another 55,000 people. Something had to happen, and fortunately it did, but only after extra time. The game is probably best remembered for a 40-yard goal from Chris Nicholl, and in a 2010 poll it was voted in the Top 25 of all-time League Cup moments. It was very special and it was a another special game for me too, because in the dying minutes of extra time, Dennis Mortimer made a great run and slotted the ball out wide to Gordon Smith, who put a cross over and the ball passed the Everton defender, Terry Darracott and it landed into my path for me to slot home my second and our winner. Were we the better side? Maybe not, but it didn't matter. We were probably the fittest team in the First Division and we needed to be. At last we'd won the League Cup again, after 330 minutes of football.

When you're playing in a football team that you know you enjoy playing in, that you love and you know you can win football matches, you can play against anybody. You can score goals against anybody. Well, the 1977 Villa team was probably that team. It was a great season and we beat lots of teams convincingly and we won the League Cup for the second time in three years. That season, the three of us, Andy, 'Dixie' and I, scored a hatful of goals. I think we scored 73 goals between us in all competitions, which wasn't a bad return, and I scored 26 of those, including 10 in the League Cup. It was a great experience and good to be part of that team.

After winning the League Cup in the previous season, we recorded some good results in the UEFA Cup in the 1977–1978 season. We opened our European adventure with a resounding 4-0 home win against Turkish side, Fenerbahçe, with Dixie Deehan scoring two and Andy Gray and myself also getting on the scoresheet, and in the return leg, Dixie and I scored the goals to give us a 6-0 aggregate win. We then disposed of Polish side, Gornik Zabrze 2-0 at home, with big Ken McNaught scoring both goals, and we earned a draw in the away tie, so it was 3-1 on aggregate. The away leg was memorable because when we arrived in the town, there were hundreds of people walking the streets all holding candles. We never got to the bottom of what was going on, but it was quite daunting. Our guide for the day was quite solemn when he spoke about it because some of the lads on the bus were having a bit of a laugh at it. He was quite serious and wanted everybody to respect what was going on that evening. It was quite a strange place to be in and we were glad to return home and through to the next round. Then came my favourite Spanish team, Athletic Bilbao at home where we won 2-0, which was a great result as they were a good young side at the time. We drew 1-1 in the second leg and progressed to the next round. There was something I liked about Athletic Bilbao; I loved the way they brought through their youngsters; I loved the atmosphere in the ground; I loved the stadium.

All of a sudden, we were in the UEFA Cup quarter-final and dreaming of glory. We'd been drawn against the mighty Barcelona, a side that had mega talent, with the likes of Johan Cruyff, Johan Neeskens and Miqueli. To put their side into perspective, they had lost 3-0 away to Ipswich in the first leg of the previous round, but in the return leg, just a couple of weeks later, Ipswich were put in their place in front of 100,000 baying Catalan fans, losing 3-0, and then 3-1 on penalties.

Interestingly, one of Ron Saunders' favourite tricks was to read the opposition teamsheet out to us before the game. Once he'd read all the names out, he always scrunched it up and threw it in the bin and would say something like, "What absolute rubbish." He'd usually pick out one or two players and talk about them, more often than not, dissing them. So before the Barcelona game, he started to read their team out and when he got to

Cruyff he said, "Joey Gruff – he can't play", screwed the piece of paper up and threw it in the bin, as if to say he didn't know who the great man was; everybody else in the dressing room knew exactly who he was. Looking back, it sounds funny, but at the time, Ron just didn't care about the opposition and was more interested on what we could do, which I guess was a good philosophy in a way, not bothering about the opposition and just concentrating on your own side.

The game itself was as rough a game as I've ever played in, but nearly 50,000 Villa fans witnessed a thoroughly absorbing game and we held the Catalans at bay. I remember hitting a shot that went straight into the goalkeeper's hands, but at the time I felt good about it, maybe because it was Barcelona and I'd done something positive. I will never forget the lad who marked me, Migueli, he nailed me, time and time again. It's fair to say that, although they were a fantastic footballing side, the Barcelona players bullied us, and I mean we got battered all through the game, and it was no surprise that they took an interval lead. Their goal came from none other than Cruyff, who was different gravy and it was a thing of beauty, from a player who was supposed to be "rubbish" according to our manager. He was in the centre circle when he took possession of the ball, ran unchallenged and then from a good 20-yards out, pulled the trigger and the ball swerved beyond Jimmy Rimmer. With only a dozen minutes remaining Barcelona scored their second and the great man got taken off owing to an injury, but he went off to a standing ovation from the Villa fans. They had all come to watch the Dutch legend play, and they showed their appreciation. However, within three minutes big Ken McNaught reduced the deficit when he got his head to a Gordon Smith cross. With time running out Dennis Mortimer chipped the ball forward, Allan Evans went in hard on their keeper and in the melee the ball fell to John Deehan, who was on hand to fire it in with his right foot. It was incredible. It was 2-2.

Playing against Johan Cruyff was amazing. I've never seen anyone move so quick over three to five yards. All he did was drop his shoulders and he flew past players. He was immense and electric. He had a trick or two in him, and one of them was the step-over, and that was his main strength and the thing he was most famous for. It was a fascinating game to play in, because even though they had a great reputation, John Deehan and myself knew we were in a game. We were kicked to pieces by their defenders.

Before the second leg, we had a tour of the stadium and saw the training facility; The Camp Nou was a fantastic place, even empty. In the game, I'm sure I scored first to put us 1-0 up in the 57th minute, and Giddy got sent off late on. However, they won the game with two goals scored within the next 20 minutes of our goal and they won the tie in front of 90,000 fans. If memory serves me right, Barcelona were beaten in the semi-final by PSV Eindhoven, who went on to win the UEFA Cup that year; Dutch football was really flying at that time.

I loved that cup run. It would have been brilliant to have made it through to the semi-final, but it wasn't to be; it was a massive step in the right direction for the club, nonetheless.

****

During the summer of 1978, we went on a pre-season tour of the former Yugoslavia (before it was broken up) and there's a funny story that just about sums up Ron Saunders to a T – and it's a story that both Giddy and I aren't very proud of and in all honesty one that we both regret.

Ron was a shrewd cookie. He knew exactly what he was up to, and on this one occasion in Yugoslavia, he taught Giddy and me a massive lesson. The weather in July was beautiful, but unbelievably hot, with temperatures in the high 80s. We travelled all over the place to play games, sometimes eight or nine hours on a coach in the stifling heat. Surprisingly, we had a full itinerary given to us, which was quite unheard of. Ron was very organised on that occasion and he'd put everything in writing so we could see exactly what we were doing day-by-day.

Within the itinerary, there was a line saying, "Day off. Night out," so we thought he was rewarding us for all the hard work we'd done and were going to be doing over the next few days. Of course, as soon as we saw that, we were on it and started planning the night out. We had it in our heads that we were going to look cool and smart and planned on wearing our tight tee-shirts, flares and high-heeled shoes. However, we also had it in the back of our minds that Ron was setting us up, even before we'd gone out for the night, because that was what he was like.

With the tour underway and a couple of games played, we had a long coach journey to Split. We arrived at the hotel around 6:00pm, with dinner at 7:00pm and according to our itinerary, we had a night out. We were all looking forward to a little bit of freedom and planned on eating our dinner as quickly as we could, then going out as soon as possible. After dinner, Ron told us he needed to talk to us before we left, which we thought was very strange, but typical of the man. He informed us, "The night out is cancelled." Well, that lit the torch paper and everybody started moaning, "You can't do that..." But Ron wouldn't listen and told us he'd changed his mind about the night out; he'd changed the plans and wanted us all to stay in that night and get to bed. Everybody suggested they were going to sneak out and defy the gaffer, but when it came to the crunch nobody had the balls to do it. I think most of the lads weren't surprised deep down, because he was capable of pulling a stunt like that, and on that occasion he did.

Giddy and I roomed together as always and we had our moan and also decided it too risky to sneak out. We thought Ron would have all the doors guarded so none of us could escape. We went to bed early and sat up thinking about things, but then Giddy said he had an idea: room service. "We'll just order some drinks on room service." I told Giddy he could do it because I wasn't interested in making the call for room service. Giddy then made the call: "Two gin and tonics, please." Within five minutes there was a knock on the door and the drinks arrived. Giddy paid and tipped the waiter and asked if he could order the same again in an hour or so. By midnight, two gin and tonics led to several gin and tonics all on room service and then we ordered another couple. However, when the same waiter handed us the drinks, he said, "The gentleman in room 201 knows you are having a drink." Even though we half thought it could have been Ron by that time we didn't really care as we were steaming. We then decided to have one more so Giddy rang down again to order; however, two minutes later, there was a knock on the door and we thought it was a bit quick for it to be the room service. The next thing I hear when Giddy opened the door was a massive slap. Ron absolutely whacked Giddy around the face. Ron, being an ex-boxer must have hurt Giddy and he shouted to us, "Get back to sleep." We got our comeuppance there, but I showed my bravery by lying on the bed, pretending to be asleep and snoring profusely. I'll never know if I conned him and if he really believed I was asleep.

We'd had a late night and had to get up for breakfast between 8:00am and 9:00am. We struggled to get out of bed because we'd had a few too many and we weren't in the best of shape. Then at 8:30am, there was a knock on the door; it was one of the lads, "The gaffer sent us to get you out of bed and he wants you down for breakfast now". We thought the worst so we went down for breakfast, feeling and looking really rough, and when I looked at Ron, he had that unmistakeable smirk on his face. He knew exactly what he was doing. He then said, "Just so you all know, the reason why you stayed in last night was because the game's been rearranged and it's now tonight." Honestly! Right from the start and the first gin and tonic we had, he must have known Giddy and I were up to no good, and I guess by midnight, he had thought, "Enough is enough. They'll be OK to get by and will be able to play football, but I'm going to teach those two a lesson" _ and he did to be fair. It was a massive lesson for both of us, and taught us not to try to be clever, big and attempt to get one over on the gaffer. No one ever got one over Ron Saunders.

In the game, we lost to Hadjuk Split 4-1 and I scored our goal when I leapt like a salmon to meet a cross from Giddy. I can still see the smirk on his face and can hear him say to himself, "Serves you two right." It was obvious we weren't as fit as we should have been for that game. We didn't play too badly, but we were still recovering from the night before. It certainly wasn't the right preparation for a pre-season football match.

It was typical of Ron Saunders, being clever and crafty. Ron had his ways and means of sorting things out and teaching people lessons; we didn't like it at the time, in fact it probably took me a few years to get over that episode and I continued to call him names two or three years on, but when I look back he wasn't just testing Giddy and me, he was testing everybody and it was only us two daft ones who actually did something stupid in the end.

Talking of pre-season tours, we had another tour in the late 1970s, this time to Spain and it was more of a bonding trip than anything else. I think we stayed in Mijas in southeast Spain and spent a few nights out in Puerto Banús. On one particular night as luck would have it (or bad luck, whichever way you want to look at it), Birmingham City were in town at the same time, which potentially was a recipe for disaster. However, we decided to join forces and book a joint table; there must have been around 20 of us, having a laugh and a joke, goading each other, and the star of the show was the Brummie comedian, Jasper Carrott, who was with the Birmingham City players on their tour. Jasper more or less held court round the table, telling jokes and organising the party atmosphere. Everybody was joining in. We had our own crown prince in Jimmy Rimmer, and his party piece was to take his false teeth out and drop them in somebody's drink while they're not looking or had left the room. We were quite wise to it, because we'd know to look in our drink first. We actually thought it was very funny, but Jimmy thought it was hilarious and he kept doing it time and time again, to a point it became silly and obvious. One on occasion though, you could see Jimmy was gunning for Jasper. It was in his head that he wanted to drop his teeth into Jasper's drink. So, while Jasper disappeared for a minute or two, Jimmy dropped his false teeth into Jasper's drink. We could tell Jimmy was up to something because every time he did something like that he would nod his head, roll his shoulders up and down and bounce up and down on his chair nervously, and he couldn't hold his giggling in. We'd all had a few too many by that stage, and we were all waiting in hope that Jasper wouldn't notice Jimmy's teeth were in his drink when he came back to the table. Jasper had been in complete control of his actions all night, giving us some great entertainment, but when he looked at his drink he saw a pair of false teeth in the glass. He then put his fingers in the drink, pulled the nashers out of the glass, put them down his trousers and rolled them around his private parts and then threw the teeth back at Jimmy. That scene was very funny, but to cap it off, Jimmy caught his teeth, put them into his own drink and then placed the nashers back in his mouth. His party piece got a huge round of applause from everybody on the table, including Jasper.

It was a classic night and a classic bit of fun; Jasper was streets ahead of Jimmy, but fair play to him for continuing the fun after being caught out by Jasper.

****

During 1979, there was a boardroom dispute that led to Mr Ellis being replaced as chairman by Ron Bendall. Ron was a big man, a very sombre character; I don't remember too much about him as I never really had a lot to do with him, but I remember one day, parking my car in the club car park before a game and saw Mr Bendall trying to park his Rolls Royce. I'd just got out of my car and I saw him reversing his Roller into the parking space. As he reversed, he stopped his car about 20 yards away from the wall and out stepped his son, Donald from the car. There were no reversing cameras in cars in those days and so Donald then guided his dad back towards the wall. He was waving him back and saying, "Keep coming, dad, keep coming..." All of a sudden I heard an almighty thump. His car absolutely whacked into the wall. Without batting an eyelid, Donald shouted, "That's far enough, dad. That'll do." I stood there watching it happen and thought to myself he'd just splattered his Rolls Royce against the wall, and Donald told his dad he'd parked OK, as if nothing had ever happened. It was just a silly little story that I will always remember and it just about summed up the mentality of the Bendall family, that they weren't overly bothered that the family Rolls Royce had crashed into a wall. In all fairness, they didn't seem overly worried about anything, least of all, Aston Villa.

****

My relationship with Ron Saunders has been well documented over the years, and also in this book. I'd had cartilage trouble and I'd also had a stomach injury that turned out to be a trapped nerve; I wasn't able to play my normal game and it affected me. I'd reached a crossroads in my career it seemed. I hadn't fallen out with Ron; I respected him and I owed a lot to him. I wouldn't have been in the secure financial position that I found myself in had it not been for what I'd achieved under his management. However, I found myself wanting to move on from Villa because my game hadn't progressed in recent times. I'd been at the club for 10 years and I felt as though I needed a new challenge.

During the summer break, I'd gone to Spain for a well-earned holiday and came back at the end of June, ready for pre-season training with headlines in the papers that Birmingham City were interested in signing me for a figure in excess of £600,000. Over a period of several years, I'd had conversations with Ron Saunders about me moving on and other teams being supposedly interested in me. Some of these teams didn't interest me and some weren't the sort of teams that would want to buy me anyway, and that's about as far as it went. I remember clearly Trevor Francis being sold by Birmingham and joining Brian Clough's Nottingham Forest for a then record transfer fee of £1m in the summer of 1979 so Birmingham were in the market for a new striker and the headlines sparked my interest a little.

With news of a serious offer from Birmingham City being received by Ron Saunders during the summer he called me into his office to discuss it. It wasn't uncommon for players to move to rival clubs in the same city or same area; lots of players did it in those days so for me it wasn't an issue. Nowadays, that sort of move would lead to outrage with local fans. When I met with Ron, I agreed to meet their manager, Jim Smith and talk to Birmingham about a possible move.

With Jim Smith on holiday in Portugal, I was asked if I was prepared to fly out there to meet him and of course, I agreed, even though that sort of thing was unheard of back then. I was also asked by their chairman, Keith Coombs to travel there with Dennis Shaw, a local journalist and Commercial Manager of Birmingham City. I knew Dennis pretty well so that wasn't a problem.

When we arrived in Portugal, we jumped into a taxi to go to the Vale de Lobo hotel. It was a beautiful hotel, situated right on the beach; it was a gorgeous day and everything was perfect. As I've said before, there were no agents in those days so I was there, effectively representing myself. It was a surreal and unique situation; I was in a foreign country about to talk to a football manager who was on holiday about a big money move. When we got to the reception, I asked for Mr Smith and was directed to the beach bar of all places. I spotted Jim with his wife in the far corner of the bar and headed over there with Dennis to introduce myself. We spoke for about ten minutes before Dennis left us to talk about a possible deal. I sat there for a minute or two expecting Jim to tell me what the club was offering me, but Jim just opened up with, "Well Brian, what are you looking for?" It took me aback a little bit I guess, and I had to think on my feet fairly quickly about a reply. I initially thought I'd ask for a little bit more than what I was on at Villa, but out of the blue I gave Jim a figure that was double my basic salary. I don't know where that came from and I initially thought the figure wouldn't open the door for me, but Jim just sat there with a piece of paper and a pen and wrote the figure down. Jim then looked at me as if he was prompting me to say something else, so I told him I wanted so much in appearance money; the figure I gave him was again, double what our appearance money was at Villa, and Jim duly wrote that figure down. The appearance money was around the same as our weekly wage, mainly because it was the incentive to make the first-team. After giving Jim the second figure, Jim looked up again as if to say, "Well what else…?" so I said, "I'd like a Ford Capri 3 litre GT". Again, Jim wrote that down too. In the space of two minutes, I'd effectively doubled my weekly wage and appearance money and asked for a new car, without Jim batting an eyelid. After that, I thought for a few seconds and told Jim I could do with some private medical insurance for myself, and my family, and Jim also made a note of that. To this day, I have no idea where any of that had come from or why I asked for that much. I didn't stop at that either, because I then asked for a 5% signing-on fee, which equated to £30,000. That 5% signing-on fee was a fairly standard figure for footballers in those days so that wouldn't have come as too much of a surprise for Jim, even though the other figures and requirements may have. That signing-on fee was a lot of money then and it would have certainly bought a very nice house in a nice area.

After I'd told Jim of my requirements to sign for Birmingham, he said, "I think that's enough now, Brian". Everything had gone swimmingly well by then and we continued chatting for the next 15 or 20 minutes, until I left Jim to get back to his holiday and I went back to the hotel.

During that trip to Portugal, Dennis and I shared a twin room and he'd pre-warned me that he snored at night and asked me to nudge him if he did it. I didn't really take much notice as I thought I'd be fast asleep anyway. However Dennis snored and snored for most of that night and the noise kept me awake. I'd never heard anything like it and I was too embarrassed to wake him up and tell him to shut up. I just couldn't get to sleep and I kept turning and tried to drown out the noise by putting a pillow over my head. It got to the point that I didn't have it in me to wake him up so I collected my bedding and put it in the bath and slept there all night.

In the morning, Dennis woke up and saw me sleeping in the bath and said, "What are you doing in the bath, Brian?" so, I told Dennis he was snoring too loud. It was a funny end to crazy couple of days. We flew back to Birmingham that morning and

I was asked to report to the ground the following afternoon to sign the contract, followed by a medical in Edgbaston.

When I arrived at St Andrews the following day, I met Norman Bodell, Jim Smith's assistant manager and he took me to the office to sign my contract. I remember walking across the pitch and noticed Norman trying to sneak a look at my contract and he kept shaking his head; he probably thought I was asking too much. Well, if truth be told, it was a heck of a contract for a football player in 1979. After signing my contract, Norman took me for my medical and it was there I discovered that I'd got an inherent back problem. I knew I'd had pelvic and hernia problems in the past, but I was unaware of having any back problems. I was diagnosed with having a complaint called a congenital abnormality of the vertebrae, sometimes called a slight displacement of the vertebrae. On the back of my pelvic and hernia problems, they linked the back problem with those issues and failed me on the medical.

When Jim found out about my medical, he was apparently really angry and upset. I'd unknowingly played all through my career without my back causing me any issues and now I'd failed an important medical. I was shocked and taken aback; I'd never even had a backache in my entire life, let alone a back injury. The specialist said that I'd probably had it since I was a schoolboy. Once Birmingham City found out about the specialist's report, they had no choice but to call the deal off. I was gutted, but there was nothing I could do about it; I had to accept it as it was.

I was still a Villa player. I hadn't fallen out with anybody at the club, least of all Ron Saunders. He even said I still had a future at the club. In some respects, the failed medical made me more determined to do well and prove to everybody I was fit and could still play a bit and that's exactly what I did.

I remember speaking to Ron and he was fine with me; in fact he was quite jovial and we had a laugh about it. He even took the mickey out of me for not being as fit as I should have been. However, in his head he wanted to replace me, Andy Gray and Giddy for the new season. He'd already signed Kenny Swain to replace Giddy and had Peter Withe on his radar to replace Andy and Gary Shaw was coming through the ranks. Ron welcomed me back into the fold and probably thought it would shut me up a bit and I'd get on with trying to get into the team. My relationship with Ron had always been a little awkward, a bit frosty if you like, but he knew I could play a bit and I think he always respected me for that and I'd always respected him for being a great manager.

Incidentally, in subsequent years, I found out Ron wanted to partner Peter with myself up front, so that convinced me he had had plans for me in the first team after all.

Anyway, when I told the lads about my interview with Jim Smith and my failed medical, and I mentioned my huge contract they offered me, they all were a bit shocked. The figures I'd requested were twice what any player at Villa was on at the time, so some of the lads decided they'd try their luck and ask the gaffer for a pay rise. In all fairness, some good came out of my failed medical and my hyped-up contract request, because every first-team player eventually received a revised contract, including myself. At the time there was a capped wage and all the lads were on pretty much the same, so we all received a healthy jump in wages and appearance money. Looking back, we should have been on that revised wage in the first place; it was what most top-flight players were on at that time.

I'd gone from hero to zero, back to hero again in the space of a few weeks. It was an incredible experience nonetheless. I think I've mentioned it already, during my entire time at Villa I'd never negotiated a contract myself; I was told what I was getting. Reflecting on that unique experience with Birmingham City, I might have made a decent agent in the future.

One date that sticks out in my memory during the 1979–1980 season is the 8th March 1980 when we played West Ham at Upton Park in the quarter-final of the FA Cup in front of a massive crowd. The place was bursting at the seams. We went there as favourites, even though they had a good-looking side, with Billy Bonds, Frank Lampard senior, Trevor Brooking, Ray Stewart Alan Devonshire and Stuart Pearson, and we were without four crucial players through injury or suspension: Allan Evans, Kenny Swain, Dave Geddes and Gary Shaw. Terry Bullivant and Ivor Linton played in their places with Terry Donovan playing up top with me. We were fancied to win, but it was a disappointing game. Trevor Brooking was outstanding in midfield for the Hammers and they were a bit better than us I have to say. The significance of it was that a penalty was awarded to West Ham right at the end of the game when a hand went up in the air. It was one of our defenders, either Ormsby or Ken McNaught, and a penalty was given. We ended up losing the game in pretty much the last minute; in fact it was the 92nd minute, and through a debatable penalty at that, and that was scored by Ray Stewart. We were seconds away from earning a reply on the Wednesday night at Villa Park. That would have meant some if not all of the players who missed the game would have played in the replay. However, the consequences of losing the cup game meant we had to play our scheduled fixture against Wolves two days later, on the Monday night. There are two ironies here. Firstly, former Villa favourite, Andy Gray was suspended for Wolves so he couldn't play against us on the Monday night. However, if we had drawn the FA Cup game against West Ham two days earlier, Andy would have been suspended for Wolves for their League Cup Final on the 15th March, which would have been an absolute nightmare for him. Of course, for those of you who can recall that final Andy scored the winning goal for Wolves in the 67th minute and they won the cup. How ironic was that? Secondly, for me, I got injured in that game against Wolves which was a game that was seconds away from not even happening; it was the game that turned out to be the very last full game I played for the Aston Villa first-team or for anyone for that matter. .

I suffered an injury during the Everton game in October 1975, and it was probably the worst injury I've encountered in terms of pain because my knee locked, and that resulted in a cartilage operation, but the injury that probably finished my career was against Wolves on 10th March 1980, where I twisted my knee in a tackle on the halfway line about 15 minutes from the end of the game. I somehow managed to hobble my way through to the final whistle, but it was just the most horrendous feeling. We lost the game 3-1, and that result topped off a bad day for me. Personally it was the worst day of my football career.

Although I tried to come back from that injury towards the end of that season, I ended up having another operation; I knew I would never be the same player, even if I did recover from it. I had about a month where I had my knee in ice every day, strengthening it with exercises and I even played against Leeds on the 18th April but I came off injured; I couldn't walk; I could never have got it strong enough to have fully recovered. I'm sure with the advances in surgery techniques and technology today, I would have recovered, but back then they just couldn't operate further to save my career. I always look back at that Ray Stewart penalty and think it was all down to fate that I played in that game on the Monday night, rather than the replay on the Wednesday. In hindsight, if we had played West Ham in that cup replay, I may have carried on playing football for a while longer, but hindsight is a wonderful thing and you can't change history. It was the game that pretty much finished my career, so when someone asks me "What was your worst game?" then that was it.

My very last competitive game turned out to be on 22nd April 1980 against Manchester United at Old Trafford and we lost 2-1; I am convinced that was the very last competitive game I played in; I know for a fact that I never played in the following season, the season Villa won the league. At the end of that season, I had another operation, on the other cartilage, but that wasn't that damaged. It was my ligaments that were completely shot to bits. Back in the early 1980s, there was no real treatment for those types of injuries. I remember a surgeon saying he was going to experiment with a ligament transplant of some sorts to make my knee ligaments join together and a bit tighter. It all sounded ludicrous at the time, so it never happened. I never recovered from that initial injury at Everton if I'm honest, or from the subsequent operations following the West Ham game. I never played football again because there wasn't a replay and that was down to fate. It could be said that an injury time goal changed my whole career. It was a disappointing way to end my career. However, I had managed to play 37 games during the 1979–1980 season, scoring six goals.

One of the other lads in the squad, Mike Pejic was having problems with a pelvic injury, and all the information and data about his injury and my own injury had been sent down to a consultant in Harley Street, so we both went down to London on the train together one day. That was the day we were both given the news, during separate consultations that we should both retire, in the opinion of the consultant that is. The consultant did a 20-minute examination of my knee, looked at he history of the injury and made a decision based on what he knew were the facts. He did a similar examination on Mike, and we both came away from Harley Street knowing that a letter was going to be sent to the club, saying that under his recommendation, Brian Little and Mike Pejic should retire from playing professional football. We were both gutted – and that was an understatement. After we heard the news, we both found a pub and had a half pint of beer and sat there for a while, not really speaking to each other, both really dejected and wondering what to do next with our lives.

The letters duly arrived at Villa Park and the process of our retirement began. We both bit the bullet and accepted the news that we were finished. The club had insurance for me, and they paid up a portion of my contract. I didn't have a huge contract anyway, and I didn't receive loads of money. I didn't have a personal injuries insurance contract, and so I was looked after as well as could be expected. There were lots of stories in the media about my payoff from Villa, and figures of £100,000 were mentioned, but it was nothing like that. I'd always looked after my finances, and I'll just say I was fairly happy with what I received.

During the time when I was trying to recover from the injury, I did a lot of work in the gym, but I probably knew, deep down, that I was fighting a losing battle. I also played in some reserve team games, but I didn't finish them. My knee just ballooned and I couldn't continue. I didn't put myself about as much as I normally did, but I still scored goals. However, after each reserve team game on a Saturday, I'd go home and spend the night with an ice pack on my knee and a polythene bag on the carpet so the ice didn't wet it when it melted.

My very last game in the Villa reserves was just before Christmas 1979, against Preston North End and I scored both goals; it didn't mean a lot to me; it wasn't a good time for me, to be honest.

With news of my retirement, the Villa fans were terrific with me; I received loads of letters of encouragement and the telephone never stopped ringing. I just couldn't moan about it. I could have been bitter about having to give up the game I loved at the age of 28, but I wasn't. What did I have to moan about, after all? I lived in a detached house overlooking a golf course. I'd played 300 odd games for Villa, winning two League Cup medals and being capped by England in a 10-year career. I only had to look at my old mate, John Robson, God rest his soul, who had to retire from football aged 29, as he'd sadly been struck down with MS just before I retired. I don't know how he handled it. He got himself a job after he retired and just got on with it. Just like John, I wasn't the type of person to just sit and mope around the house, and I had the attitude that if one door closed, another door would open.

Some people ask me if I regretted not being able to continue playing football and whether I should have tried the experimental operation, but I don't, because I've worked hard at opening a lot of other doors in my subsequent career that I might not have otherwise experienced. I see Mike Pejic from time-to-time and we both still say that day in Harley Street was all a bit of a blur.

Chapter 4

TO CIVVY STREET AND BEYOND
March 1980–June 1984

"What are you going to do with your life?"

Over the years, a lot of people have asked me, "How did you become a football manager?" Well, there's an easy, but lengthy answer to that. Even today, now I'm well into my 60s, a lot of people still don't realise that my playing career finished very early, and that had a major bearing on it. As a 27-year-old first-team footballer for Aston Villa and an England international, I should have been at the prime of my career; however, I had an injury that destroyed my career.

So, after I was advised by a Harley Street surgeon not to play football again, I was constantly asked by people, "What are you going to do with your life?" and "Where are you going to go?" I had no idea, because all I knew was football.

I was very fortunate to be at a huge club like Aston Villa, because there were many people there who wanted to help me. There was a fella by the name of Stan Buggins, who had his own printing company and was also Vice-President of Aston Villa. His company used to print the Aston Villa News & Record, the match-day pro-gramme. It was Stan who gave me my first opportunity outside of football, but this opportunity was also one of the major reasons why I was desperate to get back into football, too.

I started working for Stan on a part-time basis at first, a couple of days a week, whilst my insurance and contract with the club were being sorted out. Just going into the 'outside world' made me think, "Crikey, this is not for me." I mean, I had to get up at the crack of dawn to be at work by 9:00am, finishing at 5:30pm, with a lunch break for half an hour; there was just some routine and regularity about it that I couldn't adjust to. Yet, it was a decent enough job to be fair. Stan wanted me to learn about his printing company, which, I have to say, I didn't do very well. He gave me an opportunity to go out into the work place and try and get more business for him. Given I had a fairly well known face around the Birmingham area, I suggested to Stan I could easily get more business. However, I really didn't and it didn't work out as he'd hoped. I really couldn't sell what I was supposed to sell, because I couldn't grasp what the printing business was all about, and I quit after a few months.

It was a crazy few months working for Stan. Sometimes I'd have to go into the printing works, watching how things werre done and listening to people explain how things were put together; however, the information went in one ear, and came out of the other just as fast. Things that are probably fairly simple and straightforward for most people to learn, I just couldn't grasp. Why didn't I grasp it? Number one, I wasn't interested and number two, I was bored. Stan was a great fella and a massive Villa fan, but after those few months I just thanked him and said, "It's just not for me."

When I left the printing company, I went back to Villa Park and spoke to a couple of people who worked for the commercial side and asked if there was anything I could do to help. They suggested I could work in the club shop, sell some lottery tickets, go round the pubs and clubs or go and knock on the agents' doors and collect their tickets and bring them back in. After a few days, I managed to get myself a job, doing all the things I've just mentioned. I even travelled on the supporters' coaches to away games. One of the trips I went on was to Berlin, when Villa were in the European Cup. It was a crazy spell for me.

I spent a few months working in the club shop on matchdays with Pam and Dave Bridgewater, who are both still at Villa to this day, and Abdul Rashid, who went on to become the Commercial Manager. One of my jobs was to pop into pubs and clubs selling Aston Villa lottery tickets and I used to spend most of the time talking to the landlord about football. It was one of the ways clubs made a little bit of money in those days. I even had a company car. It was a Mini Metro painted in claret and blue, and it had the words, 'Aston Villa Development Association' written all over it. I just felt more at home, although I didn't totally enjoy what I was doing, but it was better than working at the print works, that's for sure. I didn't mind it because I was still involved in the football club and so I was happier, at least.

Shortly after the 1980–1981 season had ended, following Villa's winning league championship campaign, I was invited along to the civic reception at Birmingham Council House. That told me that I was still involved at the club; football and Aston Villa were very much part of my life. The club also awarded me a testimonial match on 18 May 1982: Aston Villa XI v England XI. It took some planning and the fact we managed to get the England squad there was brilliant. I played in that game, alongside Peter Withe, the player Ron Saunders bought from Newcastle to play alongside me in the Villa first-team before the start of the 1980–1981 season. It was a wonderful experience for me, and for him I hope. In the game, my Aston Villa XI won 3-2 and I scored two goals, but Peter says I scored a hat trick, in front of just over 9,000 fans. My second goal was a screamer _ an overhead scissor-kick. However, I hobbled off to a standing ovation after 28 minutes, just before my knee gave in completely and started to swell up.

While it was great playing up front with Peter Withe in my testimonial game, it would have been lovely to have played in that team, along with Gary Shaw and had a piece of the action, but it was never to be, unfortunately. Was I bitter or jealous about missing out on Villa's triumphs in 1981 and 1982? Absolutely not; however, it was strange not seeing my face on the team photo, but I had my own life to organise. I kept thinking there were millions of people worse off than me.

It must have been around the time that Ron Saunders unexpectedly left his post at Villa and Tony Barton took over as Villa manager, and the rest is history I suppose. In the subsequent days, my old strike partner, Keith Leonard, who was the Villa Youth Team coach, followed Ron Saunders to Birmingham City. That obviously left a gap at Villa Park for someone to look after the youth team. I'd actually done some coaching on the Aston Villa Community Scheme, where we coached some local youngster at the training ground. A lot of those lads couldn't really play football; it was just a way of getting out into the community. It never really occurred to me that anybody would ask me to step into a proper coaching role, but lo and behold, I bumped into Tony Barton one day and he surprised me with, "Hello Brian, how do you fancy looking after the youth team for a few games, just until things sort themselves out?" Well, I jumped at the chance and told Tony, "I'd love to. That's why I'm here. I don't want to leave the club. I'm more than happy to do that, and if I am any good at it, will I be given a longer chance?" I'd known Tony for some years, and we had a healthy respect for each other; I didn't mind the uncertainty as I was still involved in the football club. He really was a lovely fella. So, he offered me a little role as youth team coach on a temporary basis, and promised to consider me if I took to the role.

Although I hadn't been officially given the role full-time, at the age of 28, I had fallen into a caretaker post, more by chance than anything planned. It was like I was going through my second apprenticeship; it really was. I ended up only doing the role for a matter of two or three weeks before I was officially announced as being the Youth Team Coach, replacing Keith Leonard. I remember being quoted in the club programme, how proud I was to be back at the club and be part of something. I hadn't worked towards being a coach. In those days qualifications and UEFA licences weren't the be-all and end-all, but the fact that you'd played football was the most important thing. The role didn't pay well though. I did it for next to nothing in all honesty, but it wasn't a case of doing it for the money. I just needed that job. I made it clear to Tony, he could give me as little or as much money as he liked, and I said, "I just want to do this."

It's amazing recapping that part of my life, thinking about the first few team talks I gave. I always had plenty to say in the dressing room as a player and very often piped up with something controversial, but standing there in front of a bunch of lads, not much younger than myself, and making a statement or telling them what to do, was completely different. Hearing my own voice was weird really. Apart from taking part in some media interviews, it was pretty much the first time I'd done that sort of thing, standing in front of people who were there to listen to me. I wouldn't say I was necessarily ready for it. I was very much thrown in at the deep end, but I was trying my best and giving it a go.

****

That chance job lasted three and half years. I had a great time with the youth team lads, watching my team play in the Intermediate League on a Saturday. It was an open-age league, so I often had some of the older lads who were 18 or 19 coming to play in the team, players like Dean Glover, Ray Walker and

Paul Kerr who were essentially reserve team players looking to step up to the first team. I also had lads like Bernard Gallagher, Tony Dorigo, Tony Daley, Mark Burke, Darren Bradley and David Norton, lots of lads who were really good for me, and they eventually went on to make a good career in football. They were all destined to play in the first-team, and in the cases of Dorigo and Daley, they went on to play for England. I'm not saying I made them great footballers, or even England internationals, but I know I guided and encouraged them in their early days. In the case of Bernard Gallagher, God rest his soul, nobody would have thought he'd make a footballer, let alone a Villa first-team player with over 100 appearances under his belt. In contrast, Mark Burke, aged 15 years, was probably the most talented player I have ever worked with. If he was playing football today, he'd be an absolute genius. In the 1980s in football there was a lot of long ball, a lot of physicality, a lot of squeezing up to the halfway line. He couldn't quite come to terms with the physicality of the game; not that he couldn't handle it, more he had a different view of it. It didn't surprise me that he went off to play in Europe and Japan later in his career. He was definitely a player who came out in the wrong era. I think he would have been a fantastic player in today's game.

My man-management skills started to shine through even then, and I got on very well with most, if not all of the lads. Yes, I had to discipline some of them, and there were a few who were crafty sods, but by and large, they were great lads. At the age of 28 it was a great time for me, I'd never planned to become a coach so early, in fact I'd never really planned to become a coach, if I'm honest. When I stopped playing football, I realised how much I loved the game, and because of the way my career ended, there was no way I was ready for something new, let alone a coaching role and even less working in a printing works. There's a saying about being at the right place at the right time, and that was certainly true for me. Working in and around the club, seeing people on a daily basis and then being chosen by Tony Barton, I was certainly willing to give it a go.

It was a wonderful experience and I was very lucky to have been given the opportunity by Tony.

Having being an apprentice myself, I knew how hard it was for those lads, and I also knew the types of jobs they had to do, even though by then they didn't have to do as many jobs as we did in the 1970s. It wasn't just the coaching side I had to look after.

I hated those jobs as I've previously said, so I assumed those lads hated them as much as I did. I loved the fact that I was in control of a group of people

Jim Paul was the kitman at Villa for many years and wore seven or eight hats, but he also assisted the youth team on a daily basis. There were jobs to be done at Villa Park and the training ground at Bodymoor Heath that he was responsible for. For instance he had to look after the hostel and make sure all the jobs were done there; he needed to get all the kit ready for the lads on a daily basis, and there were jobs like tidying up the training ground after training. He worked his socks off, he really did. On top of all of that, he looked after the travel for the first team.

Very often the young players would help out some of the first-team players, especially the goalkeepers like Jimmy Rimmer, who asked us to do some shooting practice or to pump balls into the box so he could collect them. The lads enjoyed that side of it and Jimmy couldn't get enough of it. He'd work all day if he could so he appreciated our help.

One of the things that stuck with me from those days was having good people around me who were on hand to help me out. I remember Mr Eric Houghton, who was a player at Villa, managed Villa and was a director at Villa. He was wonderful to be around and he used to travel with us on the team bus. He was a true Villa legend, but was getting on in years and some of the things he used to say to me were simply fantastic. Some of the old-fashioned sayings he came out with were quite important to me and he taught me an awful lot about football.

Even though I still wasn't qualified to coach, I was capable of coaching a team nonetheless. What helped me in those early days was being able to show them what to do, as I was still fairly mobile so there were things I could do on the training ground. I could demonstrate how a ball should be played into the box; I could demonstrate how to go past people, and I think that was the biggest strength I had in those days. There was many a time when some of the youth team players, and even some of the first-team players, would come up to me and say, "You should still be playing today, Brian." I don't think they realised that when I got home at night I was in bits and I'd have to take it easy for three or four days on the training ground afterwards. However, I felt demonstrating things to them was important and I got involved as much as I could in those days. It was my way of coaching, being involved with the lads. I felt I grasped it fairly well and I spent three brilliant years as a youth team coach at Villa. I loved every minute of it.

As the years went by, I had to change and develop my coaching routine and cut out the demonstrations, as I had to learn how to coach from standing still and point out things, and move things around on a training ground. The one thing that I enjoyed most was the one-on-one situations, trying to understand the lads; what their rights and wrongs were; what the good and bad things about them were; what made them tick. I had to encourage them to do things that sometimes they didn't want to do, but never got them to do things that I didn't think was right, or do things that I wouldn't want to do myself. I guess you'd probably call that development, and that was something I found I was good at. It was my job to find out everything about every youngster I had on my books; the things about their make-up; the way they played; what they liked and disliked, but I had also to develop them to the best possible extent, and develop them as young men to prepare them in case they didn't become footballers. There were also other things I had to consider, like some of the lads probably wouldn't play for Aston Villa, but might move to a different club, or play at a different level even. I had to have in the back of my mind if they didn't make it at Aston Villa I wanted to give them the very best chance to make a living out of football elsewhere, or develop them as good people who stepped out into the big wide world outside football. So, the development part of the job encompassed lots of different things and I felt it was important to me to bring those lads on as people as much as anything else. Because I felt like that, I never dismissed anybody. I never gave up on anybody, even if I genuinely knew they wouldn't make it, and you could tell if somebody wasn't going to make it pretty quickly.

I had taken a lot of what Frank Upton had told me on board. Frank was a mentor to me, even though the word 'mentor' wasn't used back then, but that's what he effectively was. I went as far as making myself presentable when I came into work, having a shave everyday and putting a collar and tie on, unless I was travelling for a game. I made sure I had a proper appearance for the role I had, and I felt that was very important. For me to have that sort of discipline in my life was good, because as a player I was very free and easy, not a great one for discipline, but

I looked at Frank and observed how he appeared and how he presented himself as a coach back in the day, making sure we as apprentices were disciplined. While I didn't coach in the same way as him, I took on board some of his ways and I also had lots of my own little technical methods.

The thing about youth team coaching in those days was that you did a bit of everything. We had no physios in those days, so during matches I was the physio and carried the medical bag around with me. I also had to drive the mini-bus to the games and a multitude of other jobs, too. Scouting was something I got interested in when I was working for Tony Barton, as he'd ask me to go and see certain players play in local games. When I started watching first-team games, I realised there was a massive difference, not just in quality, but in ethics; the games the youth players played in were put on to help their development; the first-team players were playing to win games. Those first-team games were so important for the manager. I used to observe the manager in the dugout and see what he was doing and how he was reacting to certain things during the game, and I watched the players, of course. I soon began to think, "God, one day I'll have to do that. I'll have to do what they're doing in the dugout."

There was one incident that I remember to this day that had a dramatic affect on me, and the way I went about my coaching roles in the future. In March 1984, Tony Barton signed Steve 'Fozzy' Foster from Brighton, and he was a larger-than-life character. He was famous for wearing a headband. One day, I was listening to a rather heated conversation with Roy MacLaren, Tony Barton's assistant, and Fozzy, and it centred on why the club signed him, based on the fact that the club were trying to change him as a player. As a coach, I always had the philosophy that players should be signed on their strengths, and not change their weaknesses. Fozzy's argument was, "Why can't I play offside? Why can't I hold a line and play offside?" Roy was saying, "Because we don't play like that at Aston Villa. If we fall deep; we fall deep and we defend." Fozzy couldn't believe we signed him on that basis, because he had never played that way in his life, "Why sign me if you wanted me to play that way. Let me tell you, I will manage the back line; I will tell them to hold a back line; I will keep them straight, nobody goes behind me. I don't want to have to run after people all day – that's not my game." I felt he had strength in his argument; I really did.

During training one day, Roy took Fozzy out to an area of the training ground that was mapped out as 20-yards by 20-yards, with cones all around. Roy's theory was to try and get Fozy to stay close to people, playing in a two v two situation. All Roy wanted to do was to pass the ball into the two forwards, with Fozzy and another defender following people around, getting the ball off them. Once they got the ball off the forwards, the game stopped. It was pretty simple stuff; you did a lot of things like that in training. It wasn't uncommon. All Fozzy had to do was to follow and track the other person who he was marking. Well, for something so simple, it became absolute chaos because, Fozzy wanted to know which line they had to get to, and Roy would say, "I want you to get to the line behind you", but Fozzy kept saying, "Well, every time he steps behind me, I'm just going to put my arm in the air." It became ludicrous, because every time a man ran a yard behind Fozzy, he'd stand still and put his arm up. Roy told Fozzy he wanted him to mark the forward, not stand still, but Fozzy wouldn't have any of it. He kept saying, "No, if anybody stands behind me, they're offside." Fozzy refused to chase after the forward and in the end, didn't want to play the system. To a point, I saw his argument and when I look back on that now, I remember learning a lot from that particular situation as a young coach.

Why we signed Fozzy is another argument, given his strength wasn't chasing after people, and he had a point on that one. We tried to change the player's style of play and I guess there's a lesson in there. From a personal point of view, when I became a coach, that episode became an important lesson for me – sign players to do a specific role, rather than a player who is expected to do something he's never done before. I was learning on the job all the time.

It wasn't any surprise that Fozzy's time at Villa was short. He was sold to Luton eight months later.

Things changed dramatically when Tony Barton left Villa only a couple of months later, in May 1984 and Graham Turner came in, and it was then I became very unhappy. Things had changed and things didn't work out. I didn't have a bad relationship with Graham, but it wasn't a brilliant one either; I didn't feel any interaction between us and it was never going to work. There was also a fella called Don Dorman who came in from Birmingham City, and again, I didn't have the great working relationship I needed with him either, which doesn't mean to say he was a bad person or anything, but we just didn't get on that well. Sometimes, life says you don't click with certain people and Don was one of those people. I find it very awkward to work with somebody who I don't get on with. I think I'd found some of my young players had been taken away from me or something like that, and as their coach, I hadn't been consulted about it and I didn't agree with the decision, so one day, to everyone's surprise, I went into see Graham and told him that I disagreed with one or two things that Don was doing as my Youth Development Officer, and Graham said, "Well, if you're asking for me to support yourself or Don, I'm going to support Don." I told Graham that I understood his stance, but I also said, "Well, if that's the way it is, then I don't agree with what's going on, and I certainly don't agree with you backing him." I said those things, not in a nasty way, but in an honest way. I was told in no uncertain terms to shut up and get on with it.

Villa's first team were struggling at the time, two years on from their historic First Division Championship, European Cup and Super Cup glory, and the team was being been split up too soon for my liking. I've always stuck to my guns in life and I remember telling what had happened with Graham to Bill Shorthouse, who played in that great Wolves side in the 1950s. He was the reserve team coach and one of my first mentors at Villa and he was absolutely gutted for me. Bill was really old school and a wise old owl. He told things to me, about what I should and shouldn't do as a coach in those situations. He said things like, "Brian, just keep quiet. You don't need to say anything about that, even if you don't agree." Being the person I am, I replied, "Bill, I can't. If the manager asks me the question, I have to say what I think. I can't sit on the fence. I can't accept that somebody else is making decisions about things that I should be making." Bill told me to keep my peace and keep myself to myself. He said to me, "I'm not trying to be funny, but the manager's struggling, and if he's struggling he won't last long _ that's the nature of the game. You may find that the next manager is going to be your best friend." but I didn't have that type of patience in those days. I was very headstrong, and still am to a certain extent.

It came as no surprise that I left Aston Villa shortly after my meeting with Graham. Was it a silly thing to do? Well, no, it's just the way I am. I won't tolerate things like that and if I'm put in those situations, I will stick to my guns. Do I regret it? No! Did I think I was right? Yes! Graham and I were never a match made in Heaven, that's for certain. I didn't disrespect Graham for sticking up for Don at the time, but at the same time I didn't regret what I said to him either. I know for a fact that a lot of the lads were gutted when I told them I was leaving. It was a crazy and sad ending to a brilliant three years at the club, but I couldn't let that situation continue.

The ludicrous thing was, there I was, just walking out of a football job when I hadn't got anything else to go to. I had nowhere to go again, which was really stupid looking back on it, but that was me all over, I guess. I was jobless again after over three years learning my trade as a coach, but not for long.

Chapter 5

THROWN IN AT THE DEEP END
June 1984–February 1989

"You can stick your compensation where you want!"

Wolverhampton Wanderers were going through their darkest era ever; they were owned by a group called **The Bhatti Brothers back in the mid-1980s, and almost went into administration. Sammy Chapman was their manager and he'd read in the local paper that a chap called Brian Little was out of work, so he phoned me up to ask if I could come and help him out. Sammy had been the chief scout and for whatever reason, became the caretaker manager of the football club, something he'd never done before, so he contacted me and asked me to help him out with some coaching. Sammy couldn't guarantee me any salary, which wasn't surprising, but I reluctantly agreed.**

It turned out to be the most unreal experience I've ever had in football.

Molineux, the Wolverhampton Wanderers stadium, had been closed off on three sides as it was falling to pieces, leaving one stand that was set back from the pitch. Things were that bad, that every Friday, when the staff wages were supposed to have gone in, there was a massive rush to the bank in the hope that the money had gone through. The training ground was an absolute tip, and that's being kind to a tip. It had been left to rot completely. It was very difficult to train professional footballers day in, day out in conditions like that. Having said that, training the first-team squad with Sammy was an experience in itself.

Wolves were struggling in the Third Division after being relegated in the previous season (1984–1985); they weren't winning games, but it opened my eyes to a lot of things, and again, even though it wasn't a good experience, it was something I wanted to do and at the same time, I was trying to help the team win football matches; however, my help wasn't enough and we were relegated to the Fourth Division.

Sammy and I took pre-season and then started life in the fourth tier of English football as badly as we'd finished in the Third Division in the previous season, losing three out of the first four games. During the start of the season things got worse behind the scenes. On 2 July 1986 the Bhatti brothers' era came to an end when the official receiver was called in at Wolverhampton Wanderers Football Club. However, the club was saved from extinction when Wolverhampton Council purchased Molineux for £1.12 million, along with the surrounding land, while Gallagher Estates Limited, in conjunction with the Asda Superstore chain, agreed to pay off the club's outstanding debts, subject to building and planning permission for an Asda superstore on land adjacent to the stadium being granted by the Council. Shortly afterwards, Sammy Chapman was sacked by the administrators and I was then asked if I would run the team, something I wasn't happy about, but I rang Sammy and he told me I was the sort of person who should be running the team, rather than him.

So, I was appointed caretaker manager of Wolverhampton Wanderers on 31 August 1986 as successor to Sammy Chapman. It came at the end of the blackest spell in the club's history, when three successive relegations had dragged them from the First to the Fourth Division. At the time, Wolves were fourth from bottom and times were hard. Mixed results followed during the Autumn, as we were some way off the automatic promotion and the playoff places but at least we were clear of the bottom place in the league.

To say I had been thrown in at the deep end is an understatement!

The job of manager was something I had to handle, and handle pretty quickly. I say 'manager' but I wasn't managing as such, I was basically looking after the team. I wasn't in control of anything going on around me. However, I did make one signing, that of 34-year-old Alistair Robertson from bitter rivals West Bromwich Albion. Ali had been at The Hawthorns for 17 years and had made 500 appearances for the Baggies, so he would give the team some much needed experience in the middle of the park.

However, I didn't get to see Ali play that much as my 'experience' as being a 'manager' didn't last long – 36 days to be precise. I remember winning a game at Scunthorpe on the Saturday and going into the club on the following Monday when I was told I was going to meet the new people who were coming into the club. The news came as a nice surprise, or so I thought at the time. Just before I went into the meeting with the new owners, one or two people congratulated me, thinking I was going to be appointed the new manager. However, when I went in to meet the new owners, they thanked me for looking after the team, then told me I wasn't wanted at the club. They were openly ready to give me some money as a gesture for looking after the team as a send off, "I'm sorry Brian we can't see you staying here, but we're quite prepared to give you a little bit of compensation to help you out for the next few months," but typical of me, I told them in no uncertain terms, "You can stick your compensation where you want!" then walked out, and never went back.

The club had a succession of different managers during the crises of the previous three years, including myself, but a new era of managerial stability began on 7 October 1986 when Wolves ironically appointed Graham Turner, who'd been sacked by Aston Villa, as their new permanent manager, merely three days after the new owners had sacked me. In hindsight, it was a good job they sacked me, as I probably wouldn't have worked with Graham, anyway.

Maybe I should have listened to Bill Shorthouse and stuck around at Villa.

I was gutted at being given the sack, especially after loads of people were expecting me to be kept on. However, I enjoyed the experience of picking the team and trying to win games, not that I really knew what I was doing, but I was pleased with what I did during those 36 days.

Shortly after leaving Wolves, my old Villa teammate Bruce Rioch, who still lived in Sutton Coldfield, near where I lived at the time, contacted me, totally out of the blue, about a vacancy he wanted to fill at Middlesbrough, the club he was managing and asked me if I fancied being the youth and reserve team coach, after the position had been vacated by Eddie Gray. Like Wolves, Middlesbrough were a financially troubled club and had narrowly escaped bankruptcy with a cash injection from a consortium brought together by the current owner Steve Gibson in 1986.

It seemed like a great idea, because it meant I could spend some time with my mam and dad, who still lived in the North East. I was even considering moving there if things went well. After a few months, I sold my house in the Midlands pretty much straight away and bought a country cottage in Thirsk, which was a little way out of Middlesbrough, but it was a nice area to live in.

After my experiences at Villa, Wolves and Middlesbrough, it was because of Bruce Rioch that I seriously wanted to become a football manager. He taught me all the things I needed to know about being a manager of a football club.

Working for Bruce was a completely different experience from anything I'd known before. Bruce, Colin Todd, who was Bruce's assistant, and I used to go and watch football matches at least twice a week, did all the coaching including schoolboy level and, along with Barry Geldart, we did all the scouting as well. It was absolutely non-stop. Little did I know that, over the course of time, I was building up a dossier of young football-ers in my head – some of which I actually signed in the future. Bruce's enthusiasm, work ethic, organisation and discipline, all the things I probably didn't have at the time, or at least wasn't aware of, Bruce actually brought out of me over the subse-quent three years. When I say I had three incredible years with Bruce, I'm not exaggerating either. That was my education into how I became a football manager, and for me, Bruce was the master at it.

Working with Colin was also enjoyable. He had been a great footballer himself. He was a shrewd man and a player I'd played against many times, but he was also a good foil for Bruce. He had a different mentality towards things from Bruce, which wasn't a bad thing. For example, Bruce was meticulous and would try and over try things with people, whereas Colin would say straight away, "That's as much as he can do." He wasn't blunt as such, but his opinions were almost spot on, time and time again. He would often stop Bruce from spending too much time doing things that he shouldn't have been doing, and would focus him on the things that would probably reap more benefits. They had a fan-tastic relationship; they had a fantastic partnership; I learned so much off the pair of them, it was untrue.

Middlesbrough were in the old Third Division when I joined during the 1986–1987 season. They had some decent players in that team, the likes of Tony Mowbray, Gary Pallister, Colin Cooper, and Bernie Slavin, who were a great bunch of local lads, led by Bruce. Subsequently, some of the young Villa lads I'd coached were signed to help us out, including Dean Glover, Mark Burke and Paul Kerr. Although I didn't have much to do with the first team, I took an interest in the team's fortunes and helped out where I could.

I had a marvellous bunch of young players who were enthusiastic and wanted to progress. They were that keen, the club sometimes contacted me saying some of the lads were still training in the gym that was situated at the Ayresome Park ground at 7 or 8:00pm. They just wouldn't go home. They had an incredible love for football, playing and practicing in the gym, and that was nice to see. It was a brilliant football club with great people who loved the club.

As I looked after both the youth team and the reserve team, I had two games a week to manage; the youth team would play on a Saturday and we'd also have midweek reserve team games. We relied quite heavily on Steve Gibson, who at the time was a young director, and his company did lots of sponsorship for Middlesbrough and other local teams. Steve knew a lot of the lads who played for a local team called Billingham Synthonia, and quite often when we had a reserve game on we'd use five or six players from Billingham as well as our own apprentices. They loved it, part-time footballers playing against teams like Manchester United reserves.

It was a bonus for me that one or two of the lads actually got to play in the Middlesbrough first team in the time I was there, in particular a local lad called Owen McGee who played 21 games for the first team at right-back, and the fans loved him for his attitude and his cheekiness. I look back on that squad of youngsters and I know that they were all massive Middlesbrough fans, people like Nicky Mohan (who played for me at Leicester and Stoke City), Gary Robinson, Andrew Fletcher, Peter McGee, and Michael Trotter (who played for me at Darlington and Leicester).

The club was in so much trouble that we didn't have a lot of apprentices in those days. One of the best things I ever did was to take the lads on a bit of a team-bonding exercise. When I was an apprentice at Villa, we did everything from sweeping the terracing to digging the pitch up, and there were lots of things an apprenticeship taught you back in the early 1970s. It was similar at Middlesbrough, but not to that extent, even though the lads had to tidy up and keep the training facility clean and tidy.

So, following an away youth team game where we got absolutely hammered, something like 4-0, we were all gutted, to the point that I asked them all to come in the following morning, which would have been a Sunday, and be prepared for a day of hard work. It's imperative to get a defeat like that out of your system. I wasn't planning on running them all over the place, moreover, it was a time to sit down and talk to them and perhaps trying to do some sort of bonding session. I wasn't sure of the exact details of what I was going to do, just that I needed to do something positive to pull them together. I'm not sure what they were thinking; maybe they thought I'd run them into the ground physically, as I told them not to come in all dressed up.

The next morning, I was there waiting for the lads as planned. There were 12 to 14 of us and off we went in the minibus. At the time I still lived in the little village just outside of Thirsk, North Yorkshire, and I wanted to sell my little white detached cottage; it was in a bit of a mess and was in need of a bit of TLC. So, I took the lads to my home and gave them all jobs to do on it. "What we're going to do today fellas is to paint this house on the outside from top to bottom." There were other jobs as well, like tidying the garden and repairing the fence. I had a barbeque planned at lunchtime and told them there was an ice cream man who came round in the afternoon, so we would stop and have ice creams.

I'm not sure whether I'd get away with it these days, but I swear all 14 of us painted my cottage, garage and fencing from top to bottom, dug the garden over and at the end of the day, although there were a couple of spillages and it didn't all go swimmingly well, I'd got a brilliantly white, gorgeous cottage that looked brand new. We all had a great laugh and every one of the lads loved the day. In all honesty, some people these days may say it wasn't right, but let me tell you, in terms of team-bonding, in terms of a group of people who loved every minute of the experience, it was a magnificent day. It reminded me very much of being stuck at Villa Park for six weeks while we dug up the pitch and re-seeded it. However, I'm really pleased I did it. There was no malice meant and there was no harm done. In fact, I bumped into Andrew Fletcher at the Belfry recently. He played for me at Middlesbrough in the mid-to-late 1980s, and he reminded me of that story and said that was one of the best days of his footballing life. For someone to tell me that over 30 years on, is incredible and that just shows how mistaken were all those who wanted to criticise that sort of thing and that we had a great bunch of lads who wanted to have a great time, doing something useful. For me, it was something very worthwhile doing.

****

So, how did I make the transition from being a football coach to becoming a football manager? Well, it was a bit of a long trek if I'm honest and the experiences I'd had helped the transition: walking out of Villa when I probably shouldn't have done, being sacked at Wolves when I'd not done anything wrong, but the last three years of that seven-year period, working with Bruce Rioch were massive for me in terms of wanting to be a manager and how I became a manager. Bruce gave me all the motivation I needed, and I can't stress that enough.

When I worked at 'Boro, I developed things that I knew were within me somewhere, but being the type of person I was, they just hadn't come out in my personality until then. Some people still say I fell into being a football manager, but that's not strictly true, because I worked extremely hard at it, and did it the hard way. Prior to the development of football as we know it today, a football manager did everything: they picked the team, coached the team, spoke to the media, went scouting, looked after the players' contracts, negotiated with agents, went to board meetings, discussed everything with the chairman – the list is probably endless. Those days, probably prior to maybe 2002, were a wonderful and unbelievable time to be a football manager. Although there were an awful lot of things for me to learn, being at 'Boro working under Bruce, I was in good hands.

Following the 1986–1987 season, the club gained promotion into the Second Division by coming second in the league. 'Boro had completed a remarkable comeback from being homeless and on the brink of oblivion to winning promotion from the Third Division at the first attempt. The amazing revival continued with a second successive promotion taking the club back to the First Division. Promotion was achieved with wins over Bradford City and Chelsea in the playoffs as 'Boro's youthful side, comprising of a number of homegrown players, marched onwards and upwards under Bruce's guidance. However, the club still wasn't in great nick financially. Although Bruce and Colin had led the club to unbelievable glory during those three seasons, the very next season, they came straight back down to the Second Division, and with it came the then British transfer record move of Gary Pallister to Manchester United for £2.3 million in 1989.

It was around that time that Bruce approached me one day saying the club was developing and they needed some more help with the coaching side. He basically gave me a choice of being the reserve team coach or a youth team coach. It wasn't a simple question because I had to stop and think about it so I told Bruce I'd give him my answer the following morning. I remember going home that day and thinking, "I want to get closer to first-team football; I need to get closer to it." However, the next day I surprisingly told Bruce I wanted to become the reserve team coach. David Nish then took over my role and was appointed the youth team coach.

In hindsight, I'd made the wrong choice, because even though it was a step closer to first team football, or so I thought, as it turned out, it meant I had less responsibility. It was a million miles away from responsibility. Bruce would pick his first team and I'd be left with the remainder of the squad, which sometimes amounted to five or six players, which was similar to the problems Bill Shorthouse faced at Villa. I wasn't able to pick my own team for a start as the youth team coach I was in control of everything, but as the reserve team coach I was left with what was left and lacked selection choices.

It was frustrating to say the least and I had to get out of it. I needed to get a job as a first-team coach, so I could pick my own team, a team to win football matches. I wanted to watch players so I could sign them. The three and half years working close to Bruce and Colin, watching them work with the players, gave me a massive desire to want to try it for myself. It had given me that motivation to try it and it had given me that incentive to be able to feel that way. It gave me the confidence in myself that I could do it and be good at it.

There often comes a time in life when you need to be set free to make your own way, so one day I went into to see Bruce, and said to him straight up, "Look Bruce, I want to be a football manager, and to be honest, I want to become a football manager now, and because of that, I don't want to go and look for jobs

Being presented a trophy for services to Midlands
football by Ron Saunders in 1981

In the 1975 League Cup Final against Norwich
City, with their defender, Dave Stringer

My strike partner at Villa, Andy Gray

Taking on the Everton defence during the
1977 League Cup Final for Villa

In my early days as a player, slapping Coventry's Mick Coop

Meeting Vic Crowe (right) for the first time, with Roy Stark (middle)

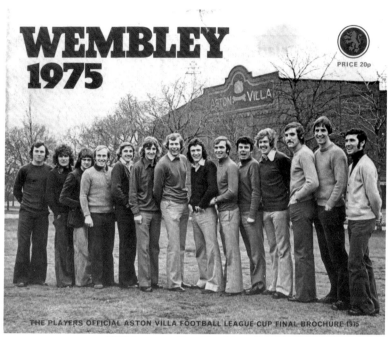

1975 League Cup Final brochure

Holding up three Champagne bottles after scoring a hat-trick in
the semi-final of the 1977 League Cup against QPR at Highbury

Me with my two lovely dogs at the time, Tessa the
Border Collie and Leyla the German Shepherd

The Villa squad returning from our post-season trip to Martinique

Relaxing at my house in Sutton Coldfield in the 1970s

I still can't work out how we won games with two goalkeepers - a random Villa team picture with an outfield player missing. Can you spot who it is?

Me with the matchball after scoring a hat-trick against
QPR in the semi-final of the 1977 League Cup

Just about to celebrate my first championship as a
manager for Darlington with my physio, Ron Lamprell

behind your back." He understood my stance. I went on, "I don't feel right doing a reserve team job and looking for work. I don't want to walk in one day and say I'm going, and for you not to be able to get the sort of people you want in and you may miss out on someone, so if you can tell me if you can find the right person for my job, then I'll happily move on and try and find myself a job in football management." I effectively gave Bruce two weeks notice to find someone to replace me, otherwise I'd walk away from my job. Bruce thought I was being daft because it may have meant I would be without a job, but I reiterated that I couldn't bear walking out on him when he wasn't ready for it. I just felt I owed it to him to find somebody else before I left. Bruce listened to what I had to say and we shook hands. He was brilliant, as he always was with me. It was because of the respect I had for him that I said what I did.

The way I did things back then would probably be considered a bit strange to some. I didn't really think about what would happen if I didn't find another job. I didn't think too much about how much my next job would pay. I was driven by an "I'm going to get a job" attitude, and thinking a door would open somewhere and at some stage. In hindsight, Bruce was right, it was stupid, but it was my own personal mentality.

I left 'Boro in the February 1989 and lo and behold, within no time at all Bruce found the people he wanted. Luckily for me, my thinking mechanism proved right and I soon found myself another job, my first in football management   the door opened for me at Darlington.

Chapter 6

THE GAFFER
Darlington manager: February 1989–May 1991

"The recommendation I've had is that you're
the type of person we need at this club."
Richard Cordon, former chairman of Darlington FC

In February 1989, I left the Ayresome Park coaching staff, determined to become a first-team coach or manager. My experience at Wolves, where I'd been in charge for seven games, winning the last two and ending up with the sack, didn't put me off, as I always wanted to try it again. I'd spent three years at Middlesbrough, but the last few months dealing with the reserve team wasn't enjoyable, I have to say, not for any disrespect for Bruce, but because some days I'd only coach five or six people if the first team took 20 with them and the situation got a bit messy, so I foolishly walked out of a good job, with nowhere to go.

Within a week, I had a call from a guy called Richard Cordon, who was on the board of Darlington. He was a good friend of the Hatfield family, who were massive fans of Middlesbrough and had sports shops in the area. All the Middlesbrough players collected their gear from their shops and I had called in there with the youth players and met the family a few times. Richard was also a Middlesbrough fan and was in the steel business, but was on the board at Darlington. I think he had been speaking to the Hatfields' about me, and the work I'd done so he had decided to contact me out of the blue.

Darlington had just sacked their manager, Dave Booth, and were rock bottom of the old Fourth Division. It was February time and Darlington hadn't won a home game all season, and were really struggling. When Richard contacted me, I had second thoughts because of the situation the team were in. However, I thought again and warmed to the idea. The club were situated 10 miles from Middlesbrough and I lived in an area where I could get to Darlington easily, so I agreed to meet the chairman, a gentleman by the name of Archie Heaton.

We met at the Blackwell Grange Hotel, a place where lots of teams stayed when they played Middlesbrough. Richard and a few of the board members were also present. I talked to the chairman about the work I'd done at Middlesbrough, about the impression Bruce Rioch and Colin Todd had on me and how I'd worked hard with a group of players who worked hard on a daily basis at a football club who were focused, organised and disciplined. I told Archie that all of those things added to the experience I'd gained coaching youth team players over the previous six years. I also said that I was ready to do a job as a first-team coach, but accepted the fact that Darlington would be a difficult job. At the end of the conversation, Archie turned round to me and said, "Right Brian, we've a game on Saturday and I think we've got a game in midweek, so I'll give you two games and see how you do." Having talked to the chairman for over an hour, I politely decided to turn the job down. I thanked him for meeting and listening to me, shook his hand and left. Under those circumstances I wasn't going to take the job. Whether you're desperate or not in life, the last thing you want to do is to walk into a football club, be there for seven days and get sacked, so that's why I decided there and then to politely decline their offer.

I was just about to get into my car and drive off when Richard came running towards me and said, "Brian, stop. Please could you come back in? I've just had a bit of a shout at the chairman. There's no way we're going to get anyone in under those circumstances unless they're given the job until the end of the season. The recommendation I've had is that you're the type of person we need at this club, so would you come back in and sit down with the chairman again?" So, I did just that, and I was proud of the fact that I had stuck to my guns and I was proud of the fact that I wasn't desperate enough to say "Yes" to something so pathetic. I went back inside, sat down and had a good half an hour talk about what was required and I said that I wanted to know everything about the club. I also wanted to know if I would be able to bring players in. Even though it was February we could have had a look at loan signings. Having said that, we weren't the most attractive club in the country; we were in the North East and bottom of the fourth tier of English football.

So, after the initial setback, I became manager of Darlington until the end of the season.

On the first day, a Monday, I was given a car by the club, but when I got into it all I saw was the car covered by dog hairs. I'd never seen so many dog hairs in all my life. I was a dog owner at the time but whoever had been using the car before me obviously took his dog to training every single day and never bothered to clean the car out. I'm quite anal about my cars and keeping them clean and tidy is a big thing, but I just remembered how filthy that car was and how it smelt inside. It was that bad I got it cleaned straight away. After a few days, I got in contact with the car supplier and asked him to get it valeted, which they did do straight away. That sloppiness made an immediate impression on me and I thought to myself, if that's how things are on the outside, then things must be bad on the inside of the club. First impressions are quite important to me.

I walked into the Darlington ground on the Tuesday morning, met the players and the assistant manager, Phil Bonnyman, who I was told had left the club, but obviously he hadn't. I had mapped out my plans for the team and told the players that anything that had gone on in the past was irrelevant. "Today is a new day and a start of a new way." I wasn't interested in the previous regime or what they did. I wanted to wipe the slate clean. At that point in time, I couldn't answer any questions on the type of training I'd be giving, but I stressed to them that I expected full cooperation, which included being on time to training – all the little things which I'd learnt from Bruce Rioch and which were important to me. I wanted the players to know who I was and what I was as a person, together with the rules and regulations that I wanted to implement that were important for discipline and organisation. I wasn't being critical of the previous regime, but I wanted to get across to the lads the way I did things. It was quite a lengthy meeting, but it was massively important for a team that was bottom of the league.

We trained in the afternoon following our meeting, and until the Friday we worked on shape and pattern of the team, how we set up against the opposition, giving the opposition the ball, taking the ball off them, and preventing them from scoring. It was all about how we would work against the opposition when they had the ball and how we'd get the ball off them. The good thing about the first week was every single player was out there training. I adopted the 4-4-2 formation at first, and everything I did coaching-wise during that week I'd learned it from Bruce and Colin Todd during those three years.

We worked morning and afternoon all that week until our first game, away at Rotherham, who were top of the league. It was quite a daunting prospect, indeed. The beauty of it was we went to Rotherham on the Saturday and won 2-1. What an incredible feeling that was and what a response we got from the boardroom and from the fans. It was a great start to a situation that was deemed difficult.

Everybody at the club was jumping up and down with joy, and the lads were happy going into training on the following Monday, after having the Sunday off, as most teams did in those days. We'd had four days of intense training and all of a sudden we got a result; however, it was that day I learned what was wrong with Darlington. Within ten minutes of the start of my second week I knew they didn't have the stomach for it. That sounds harsh, but it was the truth. I can guarantee that 50% of the players didn't want to or couldn't train on the Monday, and I picked up on another side of football, a side that I'd always had a soft spot for – the treatment room. I wanted to find out who was in charge of the treatment room, and how strong the physio was, and in those days they had to be strong.

So, I'd learnt a harsh lesson that the players had proved they could do it, but at the same time they didn't really want to do it. It's something that I've looked at very closely over the years from that one little lesson. The question was why is the team I've taken over struggling so much, when they could perform if they put their minds to it? Was it their mentality, attitude, belief or desire? All of those things come in to it when you have to practise what you preach on a training ground, and if you don't get to do that then it will nearly always go wrong. There are always exceptions to the rule. If you've got one player who you genuinely know is better off having a breather here and there, as a manager you take up that option.

I saw very quickly the problems I was about to have and what the previous regime had, irrespective of whether they had any responsibility for the problems or not. As the second week went on, we had pretty much a full squad back by the Friday so I had a chance to practise with the first team. However, on the Saturday lunchtime, I received two phone calls from players who would have been in the team, and they told me they were sick and couldn't play. Although I was the new manager, the situation hadn't changed and I was always going to battle against their mentality more than anything else.

One of the first signings I made was to bring in my old team-mate John Gidman to help me out as a player/coach until the end of the first season. It was an arrangement where I was doing him a favour, and he was doing me a favour. In all fairness, watching him, I knew he'd lost the enthusiasm to play, which was not like Giddy, but he was probably better than most of the lads in the team. In all of my playing days, I've never met anyone so enthusiastic as Giddy, but in his mid-30s he'd lost that vital ingredient. If anybody ever saw Giddy play in his heyday, energy, athleticism and enthusiasm were top of his tree. That's not to say he couldn't play back then, he probably could, and still put his foot on the ball, but back then I had him in the middle of the park, just sitting there passing the ball around for us. I think he would agree, at the time I signed him, his football days were probably over, but he came to help me, tried his best and often kept me smiling in some troubled times. However, it was good to have him around the place, but it was a shame there wasn't a bit more he could have done on the pitch. It told me that doing each other favours wasn't going to win us anything, and maybe there was a lesson learned from that. It's OK having a great pal with you, but in football management, you have to be ruthless and selfish at times and it has to be done for the right reasons, not that I did it for the wrong reasons, but it just never worked out, and for that I was gutted. Although we never fell out over it, I realised that I needed to do things my own way and I needed people I trusted around me, so I thanked Giddy for the time he spent with me during those few months and we parted company.

As the season went on, we did OK and of the 18 games I managed the team, we won six, drew four and lost eight and collected 22 points despite having what I call a messy group of players. There were some very important games and I especially remember playing Colchester, who were one place above us in the league. If there was ever a game that was win at all cost, then that was the game. We lost 2-1 and that was the day we realised we were going to be relegated. Jock Wallace, who was a big name in that level of football, managed Colchester, and on that day he was up against a rookie in me, trying to keep my team up, and on that occasion I lost out to a more experienced coach. Whether you put that down to experience or not, I don't know, but on the day I thought we were the better team and had our chances. That defeat really knocked the stuffing out of us and from there on in we lost our last four games.

I still think if we'd won the Colchester game we could have stayed up. We were very close and we were in a fairly strong position until the last four games right at the end of the season that we lost. The day we went down officially was a day I'll easily remember. In fact, it started with the news that Archie Heaton had resigned as chairman of Darlington. Richard Cordon had stepped up to become chairman and it came as no surprise really, given the amount of flak Archie had received. That news emerged and filtered through the day before we were due to play at Scunthorpe United, a place where I had previous history during my Wolves caretaker manager days. Wolves beat Scunthorpe, but I got the sack the following day, so before the game, I had that very memory in my head. However, on this occasion, we got battered 5-1. They were a good side, but we were down in the dumps on the day, and it was evident the players had lost much of their desire and belief. Everybody at the club was completely gutted, especially myself – I was really devastated. I will always stick by my record at Darlington, which wasn't bad, but we had a poor group of players that season, if truth were told.

Twenty minutes after that final game, we were all still in the dressing room; everybody was quiet and I was walking around a bit until the dressing room door opened and Richard Cordon popped his head around the door to ask to speak to me. Straight away, I got the feeling my time was up and the end of another football dream. However, I knew Richard wanted to do well by the club, but I was convinced that my fate was going to be spelt out. As we walked away from the dressing room, and away from the press guys, Richard led me into the empty stand and into the terraces. We found two seats, sat down and started chatting. I have to say, in the many years I've been in football Richard delivered the greatest sentence anybody has ever said, "Well, Brian if you're packing it in today, then I'm packing in today, too."

I looked at him and said, "Sorry?" Richard repeated, "If you leave this club, then I leave this club." To that I replied, "Well, you've only been chairman for one day." Richard told me he wanted me to stay and give me a two-year contract. He continued, "Listen to me Brian, in two years, if you don't get this club back into the Football League, we'll go bust." Such was the drop in revenue the financial burden and the stigma of it would have been unreal.

So, we had been relegated to the Conference and in those days it was like falling off the end of the earth. It also meant was we would have no reserve team to play in the Central League, so we'd have no league for our second team to play in. The Conference was a completely different setup and we had to plan for that.

During that 20-minute conversation after the Scunthorpe game, Richard laid out his proposal for me remaining as manager for the next two years. He said we had a lot of players out of contract, so I had the freedom to change it around on the pitch as I wished. We needed to bring in a new and fresher mentality into the club; we needed to bring in reasonable players on free transfers and he also hinted we might have been able to buy a couple of players. He'd been thinking about it all week so it wasn't an off-the-cuff statement, and I knew he was being genuine. After he'd explained what he wanted, I looked at him, shook his hand and said, "Yeah, I'll come in on Monday and we'll talk about it and have a proper sit down and we'll go from there."

Without a doubt, that was the best thing anybody has ever said to me in football; I put it above anything else, for someone to have so much belief in me and for that, I hold Richard Cordon is high regard and have much respect for him. It was a great day in that respect, even though we'd just been relegated.

We still had one game left, against Carlisle United at home and we lost that 3-0, but it wasn't an issue really, because our fate had already been confirmed. Our fans came out in the thousands to watch us, mainly because it was the last time they'd see us play in the Football League for a while at least. It was one of those things, really and the result didn't matter.

Within 20 minutes of the end of the game, I told every single player on the books that they had an appointment to see me on the following Monday. I'd planned it so that every one of the 25 players had a 15-minute slot throughout the day, but typical of footballers everybody turned up at the same time. Irrespective of what happened in their meeting, the players had obviously decided they'd go for a drink afterwards – to drown their sorrows or to wish each other well, whichever one applied to them.

The first two meetings took 20 minutes each and the players were both released. I was trying to explain everything to them, about my thoughts and why it was happening, but as soon as I said they had been released, they just got up and walked out. Before I called the third person in, I stopped for a few minutes and thought to myself, "Why am I doing this?" For me, I wanted to be polite and pleasant, and explain to the players what I was trying to do, but I ended up telling most of them they were not being retained and that was it. Ultimately, they weren't listening to me because all they wanted to find out was if they were going to be staying or going. With that in mind, I released another 18 players in the space of 20 minutes. On top of that, another two players were told they could leave once they found another club, which they didn't do because they were contracted. In the end, I only retained four players: Paul Emson, Jimmy Willis, Mark Hine and Mark Prudhoe. There were also a few young lads who were on the periphery of the first-team and they were retained too.

In the space of an hour I'd sacked 20 players and most of them had been out of contract anyway. It spelt the end of an incredible education, but it was also the start of a new journey. My next task was to put together a new team that would be competitive in a division that I knew absolutely nothing about; in a division none of us knew anything about. Added to that, Richard and I knew we needed a younger player/coach to replace Giddy, so he took that decision off my hands. That was the toughest thing in that whole process, talking to Giddy and to tell him exactly what I wanted. Over the years I've always stuck up for people because they were the right people, but in the case of a player/coach it was imperative that I got the right person, and I'd already had a few ideas who that person was. I'd heard a few shouts about Frank Gray, a former Scottish international who was at Sunderland and wanted to get into coaching. I was trying to replicate what Giddy gave me, but Frank was younger and a lot fitter. One of the problems with Giddy was that he lived in Liverpool, but Frank lived in Harrogate, about 45 minutes away and he was the ideal guy to replace Giddy.

I could see a group of players I wanted in my head, but it was all about convincing them to come to Darlington. If you look back at the group of lads I brought in, I tried to recruit northern-based players – no way could I have had people travelling long distances. I also had the criteria of wanting lads who had played in the Football League and were in their mid-20s, had got a family and who were hungry to play. I had people like David Corner, a big centre-half who had been at Sunderland and Barnsley and I knew he could play at our level. I'd already signed Mark Prudhoe as a goalkeeper and he was a different class. The one I wanted most of all was a lad called Kevin Smith, who had played at Darlington before, but moved to Coventry City in the First Division. He'd had a few injuries and found himself at York, where my brother Alan was the assistant manager. Alan had a word with Kevin to see if he was interested in a move, but the first impression was that he wasn't interested. He didn't really want to play at a lower level. I tried to get Alan to convince Kevin to meet me, which he eventually did. I met with Kevin and although he didn't want to drop down a level he immediately sensed we could match the money he was on and there was the ambition to get back into the Football League. Kevin finally agreed to come, and although he didn't come for the money, we made sure he wasn't worse off. We were willing to pay a bit more for quality and a player whom the fans had loved before; I think we paid around £10,000 for Kevin. He was in his late 20s, a centre-half, but more importantly he was a leader and I realised that when I first met him. He loved organising and loved being the centre of conversations in the dressing room. It was a fantastic signing for me and on the back of that, we got the likes of Archie Stevens, an experienced, hard-as-nails centre-forward from Middlesbrough. We also got young Drew Coverdale and Gary Gill from Middlesbrough and raided Hartlepool for John Borthwick and Andy Toman at a cost of £40,000 and I also brought in David Cork from Huddersfield in the Second Division.

Within no time, I'd established a group of players I felt happy with and who could compete in the Conference. It would all be about mentality and how we adjusted to the Conference. I've mentioned before that the one thing that concerned me before I became manager was the treatment room, so I needed someone on my side so to speak, someone who I could influence and would report to me, as I felt a lot of the players got away with murder. I'd met a local guy called Ron Lamprell when I was at Middlesbrough and he came to all my youth team games. Ronnie was part of the St John's Ambulance team and did a bit of physiotherapy work and we'd kept in touch. He was a big Sergeant Major type character, a funny fella and the type of person I wanted in the ranks. When I spoke to Ron about the position, he jumped at the chance and couldn't get there quickly enough. I knew he was the type of person who could handle footballers and they would love him, too. He loved telling stories, joking and messing around, but at the same time, he had that other super-serious side to him.

If you didn't know it, the configuration of the Darlington foot-ball ground would take some imagination to picture. There was a cricket ground next to it, so to get into the football ground you'd have to enter the cricket ground and drive around the outside into the football stadium. The main stadium was old-fashioned and there were entrances into the ground from the main road that goes around the ground. There was even an entrance into the treatment room and the coach's room from the road. That meant that anybody could knock on the door and walk in. I remember during the pre-season, I'd see Ron in the dressing room for a lot of the time. Ron loved being around the players, and if he weren't in the treatment room you'd find him in the dressing room.

What I had now was a complete contrast to what was there before because the players were no longer hiding and sitting in the treatment room, having a laugh and a giggle, or skiving from training, but the physio like them would now be found joining in the banter, telling stories and having a laugh and a joke in the dressing room. It was funny because I'd have to jokingly tell Ron to go back to his treatment room because he tended to spend a lot of time there, "Ron, I'll send the players to you when they need treatment." I said the same thing day in, day out to Ron, and although I had a bit of devilment in me sometimes, it was usually all harmless fun. One day, I went into his treatment room, which led onto the car park, gathered all of his physiotherapy equipment, opened up my car and put it all in the boot. I then went back inside and back to my room. Lo and behold, half an hour later, Ron came into my room and said, "Gaffer, we've had a robbery. Somebody's been in my room and I'm afraid a lot of the equipment has disappeared." I suggested Ron must have been in his room all the time, but Ron replied, "Well, I just popped into the dressing room for a minute or two to see if the lads were alright." I was trying to keep a straight face and said, "Ron, if you're out of your room, then you're technically responsible for making sure the door leading into the car park is locked and looking after your gear." Ron agreed, "Yeah, I think it must be one of the lads, gaffer. I'll sort it out". He hadn't a clue that it was me who'd pinched his gear. I left it in the back of my car for two days and in the end he came to me and said, "Are the club insured for this stuff?" Altough we were, I told him the club weren't insured and Ron's tone dropped and said, "Ah, well I'll go to the bank and get a loan and buy the gear I lost as it's my fault."

I let the joke run for two more days, and when Ron went home at the end of the second day I put all the equipment back in his room, together will a little note from myself saying it was imperative for him to do his job properly. While I understood it's an integral part of his job to be part of the fun and games with the lads, but only at the right time. He took it all in good spirit and I played a few more jokes on him during my time there.

We played some big games during the pre-season. We had a match against Sunderland and did really well and we played a lot of lower league teams too. The favourites for the league were Boston United so we decided to watch them play. I think we went to see them play a team in Lincolnshire and after watching them we knew we'd be good enough to win the league. During that game we didn't see anything to frighten us and took that back to the players during a meeting the following day. I told the players that if we trained properly, looked after ourselves and were focused as a group we'd win the title.

One thing that not many people know, is that I actually scored for another team other than Aston Villa. I actually selected myself as a substitute during a pre-season game at Feethams, came on and scored for Darlington. I don't know why I did it, but I did; maybe I just felt good that day. I used to train as much as I could with the players and it gave me a feeling that I might just join in one of the league games at some stage during the season. I actually went as far as checking with my insurance and that was fine. I'd have played as a non-contract player. I really enjoyed coming on and playing in that game, so I was happy to have contributed. What put me off though, was during pre-season training a week or so later, we were doing some hill running and I felt a bit light-headed. I hadn't had anything to eat in the morning and felt hungry and my blood sugar must have been low, but the next thing I knew was that I was spark out on the floor. I'd obviously fainted so was taken to hospital to get checked out. I was fine, but that probably put an end to my plan of joining in one of the games during the season. Although it may have put me off playing and hill work, which I didn't like doing anyway, it didnt put me off training. As a manager you see everybody else doing it, you think you can do the same. I'd always been fit as a young player, but there comes a time when you have to draw a line under some things. Having said that, towards the end of the season, I did actually name myself as a substitute in a GM Vauxhall Conference League fixture, away at Stafford Rangers. It's in fact my local team now, believe it or not and so how ironic is that? We were winning 4-0 and the lads were egging me to get up and go on for the last 10 minutes, and you know what, I'm not saying I bottled it, but I just didn't fancy it and missed my opportunity. To a degree, I regret that decision to this day; it would have been nice to have been involved, especially as, a yet unknown, Stan Collymore played for Stafford Rangers in that game.

We had about 20 senior players in the squad that season and I told them everybody would receive a full bonus, regardless of whether they were playing or on the bench, and for every game we played in, everybody would travel. I wanted everybody to feel part of the team; everybody had a club tracksuit or rather more of a shellsuit; everybody had a club blazer, shirt, tie and flannels to travel in. We looked a million dollars and very professional. I even went to the local market to buy black and white bath towels for everyone in the squad. We didn't have the privilege of having everything provided for us. We had nobody backing us at all. As it happened, I actually designed the black and white hooped home kit with yellow trim for that season; it actually fitted in well with the chairman's company logo and colours, so the kit went down well with him at least. I also designed the yellow away kit, too. I don't know if anybody was aware of that at the time, so maybe that is a hidden secret I've just revealed.

I was involved with just about everything that went on at the club. On matchdays, I would get to the ground early, before everyone else and I even manned the phones at times, as we only had one receptionist at the club. There was a little bed and breakfast in the town and the owners were Darlington fans so we used to go there for our pre-match meals; eggs on toast or beans on toast was the usual fare. The players loved the homely feel and they responded well to going there.

There was one drawback about being relegated out of the Football League. Although we were a full-time football club, the one thing we had to do during that season was to join the Durham and District Sunday League because we were no longer part of the Central League (the reserve league). Some of the lads used to have to play on a Sunday morning, and that included Tony McAndrew, our youth team coach. The club secretary, Brian Anderson, had a mate who had a team and were struggling to get players and he suggested some of our lads join the team.

Looking back, playing in that league was rough as hell, and some of the lads we were playing against stunk of alcohol and had probably just come from the pubs and clubs for the 11am kick-off. We all had a good laugh, even if some of the lads were that wound up it sometimes got a bit feisty. My two boys came to watch the games and they thought Tony McAndrew was our goalkeeper, because we didn't have a full-time one, so he would put the gloves on, even though he'd played as a centre-back all of his career. In one game, the first tackle of the game was a blatant foul. You could see the opposition goalkeeper was wound up and angry and he ran 40 yards, pushed one of our players down and got sent off within the first 15 seconds of the game. In another game, against a team from Newcastle, their players all had short-sleeved Newcastle shirts on and every one of the lads had the same tattoos on their arms. Those were the days and I often wondered what I was doing there.

It was a very grounding experience working at a club like Darlington. For instance, we didn't have our own training ground. We had to use council pitches in the suburbs of the town to train on and guess whose job it was to go round making sure there was no dog's muck on the pitches and make sure the pitch was as clean as it could be? It was a job somebody had to do, so Tony McAndrew and I took it upon myself to do it. It wasn't ideal, being a public area, very often some dog would run onto the pitch to fetch its ball or chase ours around the pitch during training. Having said that, it was fine by me. You had to have a strong mentality and we used to have lots of laughs whilst we were training.

One of the first things I introduced when I went to Darlington was a fining system. Bear in mind, some were on reasonable money, but some of the lads were on peanuts, so the most I ever fined anybody was £5, and then it didn't cost them a fortune. It was just the principle of it that I wanted to instil into the players. Some of the things I'd fine the lads for included: not wearing flip-slops in the shower, late for training, getting booked and lots of other little things. However, every time I fined somebody I used to write a poem to him, about why he'd got fined. I had to listen to so many bizarre stories the players came out with I thought I'd make a light-hearted joke about them. For example, if somebody got fined for walking in the shower without flip-flops or had worn the wrong tracksuit because the other one was in the wash, I'd make a little joke about it and make the poem rhyme. Then I said the poem would cost the player £5. I think it went down quite well, even though it was a bit quirky. I bet the lads didn't keep a copy of the poems I wrote – I wished I had.

All the money collected at the end of the year was donated to the local hospice or children's hospital, so I think that made the lads accept their fines even more. However, one or two of the players asked me if we could use the money collected from the fines for an end of year party and my response to that was, "No chance!"

When I talk about going out of the Football League and being thrust into things that were unreal and alien to us, we had to do all of that and more. I had lads who were on professional contracts, playing on a Sunday morning but they loved it and we won a lot of games. We managed to win the Durham and District Cup, and if I'm correct I scored in the final and that made it all the more worthwhile. It was a great experience.

Our first game in the Conference was at home against Kidderminster Harriers. They played really well against us. Boston were supposed to be the best team in the league, but Kidderminster were miles better, even though we beat them 3-0. It was a great start to the season. We got a load of good publicity from it and it was a step in the right direction to get the fans back on side. The fans enjoyed that opening game and from then on, they followed us in big numbers.

The biggest game we had that season was against Barry Fry's Barnet. They were pressing us all season for the top spot and when we met them away from home, we played with a 3-5-2 formation. We had the perfect team for that system, with three big centre-backs and wing backs who could run all day. We had a strong all round team but I knew that particular game would be hard, so I did something quite random. I changed the system completely, and went for man-for-man marking. My thinking about the systems was based on the fact we were individually much better than them. We went there with the mindset that if they play the way they could play and we play our style of football we could have easily lost, so basically I gave everybody a job on their opposing player. We had a meeting about it the day before and I wrote on the board whom each player was marking. They played a 4-3-3 formation, which we normally played. Some teams, like Runcorn, had given us problems when we used a 4-3-3 system, so my philosophy going into the Barnet game was, if we were to play a tactical game it was likely that we'd get beaten. So changing the system was a way of spelling out that we were better than them. I remember when the team meeting finished, everybody stood up in anticipation, ready for the game. If it wasn't for the fact that we had to travel down to Barnet, they could have played there and then, they were so pumped up.

Not only had the meeting gone down well when I spelt out that each of our lads was better than each one of their players, but in reality it proved the correct assumption – we beat Barnet 2-0 and it felt fantastic.

I also remember going to the Macclesfield v Barnet game as a spectator. It was the second from last game of the season and Barnet had to win to keep us on our toes and extend the chase for the Conference championship into the last week of the season. If they didn't win, we would be promoted. It was the most boring game ever but I couldn't leave because our whole season hung on the result. The frustration lasted right up until the 87th minute when Macclesfield won a corner. and every single one of their players went up into the box. Barnet left just one player to play outside the box. The ball was headed out and the Barnet centre forward collected it. He ran the length of the pitch and pushed the ball past the 'keeper to give them a 1-0 victory. Frank Gray and I sat there totally stunned by the goal they had scored. We couldn't believe the tactics of gambling to win a game knowing that when the biggest chance came up, you could equally lose it. It was truly ridiculous and I could have cried. Even now, after all those years, I still can't get my head around that particular game. It will probably live with me forever.

CHAPTER 6: THE GAFFER

We went home gutted, but in a way glad we saw the goal. Anyway, our penultimate game was away at Kidderminster, a game in which a win would secure the title, and meaning we would not have to rely on wining our last game of the season, away at Welling. We lost 3-2 at Kidderminster, who were incredible on the day. They had nothing to play for, but they fought like lions. They were unbelievable. So, it was all down to the last game at Welling and we needed to win. Anyone who follows Darlington will tell you we won 1-0 from a Gary Coatesworth goal from the edge of the box. All of a sudden, that goal sent me from zero to hero; from nearly getting the sack to winning the Conference league in my first season. If I look back at that season, we won 26 games and only lost seven throughout the campaign. Attendances at Feethams were up by 55% and every away ground we travelled to enjoyed their highest gate of the season. I'd spent £100,000 on new players, recouping £60,000 in sales. I think I'd done a pretty good job for a rookie.

After that game at Welling, we all stayed down in London for the night. The club paid for us to have a night out, which was brilliant. A few weeks afterwards, I was voted Conference Manager of the Year.

We were back in the Football League and it was absolutely incredible, worth its weight in gold and it saved my job. It was the end of an incredible season and one that I will remember for many years.

****

We were back in the Football League after just a season and one of the first things I did was to ask Allan Evans (Evo) to join me. Evo had taken a year out with his family and travelled to some far-flung places and ended up playing football in Australia. He actually rang me from Australia and said he wasn't settled and wanted to come back home. I said he could come and play for me, although I stressed the money wouldn't be great, but as he could help with a bit of coaching, so he jumped at the chance.

I remember that year more than most because I'm convinced it was the first year that the back-pass rule was changed, where the goalkeeper couldn't pick up the ball if the player passed back. It has to be said, I reckon my team were experts at it once we went 1-0 up, with the 'keeper rolling it back out to the centre-back and him passing back to the 'keeper. In that era, all the best teams, once they went 1-0 up were hard to score against because they just kept the ball. The rule changed the game significantly and in the years that followed, it's possibly the reason why centre-backs became better in possession of the ball and better than some of the midfield or forward players in some cases. In the early days of the rule change, it made things really difficult and especially so for Evo, who was used to passing back to the 'keeper. We had won the Conference based on winning games and being hard to beat so the rule change was a massive game-changer, not just for us, but for every team.

I also signed a lad called Mick Tait, who had hundreds of games under his belt. He was a genius and hard as nails and was a brilliant acquisition. He was what you'd call a 'man's man' as he was loved and respected everywhere he went.

Our first game was away at Gillingham; we'd have loved a home game to kick-off our season, but it wasn't to be. It was a hard place to go to and we lost the game 1-0, but we put up a decent performance. I think it was a bit of a reality check. It's amazing how things change so quickly and how football goes in cycles. We beat Burnley 3-1 and they are now an established Premier League club. Carlisle beat us 3-0 in the year we went down, but two years later we beat them home and away. That tells you the progress the club had made in those two years.

We won the Fourth Division Championship in our first season back in the Football League. It was an immense achievement. We had built a great group of players and we kept building season on season. From a team that had been relegated, we had turned into a team who in those two seasons were unbeaten in about 84% of our games, had won two championships in a row and on a personal note, had presented me with the manager of the year award two years in a row. We were a team and a club who were progressing. Our fans had come back in their droves to support us. We had over 9,000 people at our ground on a couple of occasions. It was another marvellous campaign and a wonderful two seasons.

It helps a manager to have a chairman who backs you to the hilt and in Richard Cordon I had the best; he was brilliant with me. However, everything comes to an end and there were several occasions when clubs had spoken to Richard about me and every time they came knocking, Richard would come to see me. Every time that happened, I said the same thing, "There may be a right time to go, but the right time isn't in the middle of a season." I was enjoying it and I didn't want to leave. I constantly got asked the same question by fans, "Are you leaving?"

However, I was preparing to go to the Town Hall in Darlington to accept the Fourth Division trophy when Richard called me. We were always straight with each other so I asked him what it was and he said, "Leicester City would like to talk to you." Richard didn't hesitate and said he would give me permission to talk to them, but he also said, "I'm going to tell you straight, I don't want you to go. Obviously, I don't want you to speak to them, but at the same time I think it's a good club. I know you've worked in the Midlands most of your career, so I would understand it if you wanted to speak to them". Richard continued, "I've got a sneaky feeling this might be the call I'm going to regret having, but as ever, I realise the way things are going somebody, somewhere along the line may well take you. I've passed your number onto their chairman. He will ring you within the hour, and he'd like to see you." I agreed to take the call, and assured him if it wasn't right it wouldn't happen, but I had to be interested in a club of the magnitude of Leicester City. They were one of the many clubs who had come calling, but they were the one that made me sit up and think. There were others that I just wasn't inter-ested in. Richard said he'd call me after the meeting to see how things went, but after I put the phone down to Richard, I began to think, "Wow, this is becoming a bit real,"and thought that Leicester might be the club I'd like to talk to. I'd played against them for Villa and I knew the area reasonably well, so I started to think about it seriously.

Within the hour of speaking to Richard Cordon, Martin George, the chairman of Leicester City called me and intro-duced himself. We had a typical first conversation, but he also asked me if I was interested in having a chat in person about the job. Bearing in mind I was preparing to go to the reception at the Town Hall that very day, I though it would be a bit of a rush. However, what surprised me most, and impressed me, was that he wanted to talk to me before I went to the Town Hall and offered to come and see me within a couple of hours of that phone call. He asked me to meet him at Teeside Airport and told me he was flying there in his own helicopter. Hearing someone say he was going to jump in his own helicopter and fly 150 miles to meet me was astonishing to say the least. Martin had obviously done his homework and knew exactly where he wanted to meet me. It was another world and a different league altogether from what I'd been used to at Darlington. At the end of the brief call, I agreed to meet him at the airport.

I felt excited by the conversation with Martin; I felt he was very interested in me; he was very impressed with what I'd done in the past, and that was that; I went off to the airport to meet him.

Leicester had just been through a really rough season and had just escaped relegation from the old Second Division (second tier) by two points. They'd already had two managers that season in David Pleat and Gordon Lee (as caretaker manager) so they wanted to employ a new manager. They had spoken to other people, but for whatever reason, they hadn't found what they were looking for and that's why he wanted to speak to me.

At the meeting, we chatted about the job; we chatted about the way I played; we chatted about the way I trained the players; we chatted about the job I'd done at Darlington, and also what they wanted from me. I knew Leicester had a traditional way of doing things, but I stated that if he wanted me to come, then I'd have to do it my way. However, I got the feeling that Martin George was quite impressed with me and the fact that I told him how I played, with three centre-backs and that I wouldn't change from that formation. I told Martin that it wasn't about money, more about my progression, although I did say any contract would have to be an improvement of my current salary. My philosophy was that if I proved to be doing a good job, the club would soon come to me with an improved contract. I wanted to show people I was better than the contract I was being offered. In those days I didn't have an agent or anybody representing me, but I knew exactly what I wanted and didn't want from a contract. I was a very hands-on manager, and I could tell he would want to work very closely with me, if I was to be offered the job. We also touched on contractual terms and other things and at the end of the talks Martin suggested he went away to think about things.

It was a good hour's meeting and after it I honestly felt it could be the club for me. If they came back to me in the morning and if they were prepared to offer me the type of contract I was looking for, then I'd have to think about it. We shook hands and he flew himself back to the Midlands and I prepared to go to Darlington Town Hall.

So, as I arrived at the Town Hall there was still an air of uncertainty about whether I'd be at Darlington next season, or not. I wasn't shy to share my news and spoke openly to my players and staff about my position during my speech. Some of the lads told me it was one of the nicest speeches they'd heard and it sounded like a farewell speech, without it being a farewell speech. Some of the lads asked me if I was leaving as there were one or two things brewing. I spoke privately to Allan Evans, who was one of my coaches and Frank Gray, my assistant manager, and I had mixed responses from them. Allan, as an ex-Leicester player himself, couldn't speak highly enough of the club, yet Frank, who had expressed an interest in becoming a manager himself, seemed less interested.

The very next day, it happened. Martin rang me and he'd spoken to his board members and he was tremendously impressed with me. He suggested there wouldn't be a problem with the contract and duly offered me the job. Not surprisingly, I said, "Yes". I then asked to see him in person so I drove to his home in Leicestershire where we had a bit of dinner and sorted out a salary and a three-year contract. I stayed at Martin's house and the next day, Martin flew us to Filbert Street for a press conference, where I was announced as the new manager of Leicester City. The press conference was a little testing. I think one of the press lads asked me, "What's it like to be sixth choice?" So I replied, "Well, it's better than being 60th choice." That question threw me a bit because I was under the impression at the time that I was first choice. However, for me to be considered for a club like Leicester was a massive step in the right direction, so I wasn't fussed. I was very much up for the challenge. I also had a question about the style of football I was going to get the lads to play, and that was an easy reply. I suggested they should look at how Darlington played to find the answer. There was a misinterpretation by some quarters of the media that playing with three centre-backs was a bit 'long ball' and a bit defensive, but I threw it back to them and said I would prove them wrong. I was well aware of all the goals they had conceded from the previous season, having watched all the games on video so that would be the first thing I'd try and sort out. In fact, I threw it out there about all the goals conceded and said, "To score four goals every week to win football matches is not the easiest thing in the world to do." I suggested the team needed strengthening to make them more defensively solid. To say the press conference was a little bit frosty is probably fair, but there was nothing I couldn't handle.

So, it was happening: I was off and about to take on a challenge at Leicester City in the Second Division.

After that press conference, I jumped back into my car and was off back to Darlington. Having agreed to take the Leicester job, the next thing I had to do was to speak to Richard Cordon. Obviously he was gutted, but not surprised. Richard and I met at Feethams to do a farewell press conference, and in it he said he'd agreed to the move, but he wanted compensation for me from Leicester City. However, he also said, "If they gave me £1m today, I wouldn't want it. I'd rather have Brian." It was an incredible compliment to get. While Richard was great with me, the Vice-Chairman appeared a bit frosty and was a bit disappointed I was leaving. In my eyes, now the deal had been done, if the club was given an amount of compensation, it was the right time for me to move on.

Richard remains the one person who was incredibly kind to me at Darlington, and said the sort of things that would make anybody say, "Crikey, this is a decent bloke." Richard Cordon goes right to the top of the list. I have total respect for Richard for letting me leave and for the way he handled my two years there. He was miles better than anybody else I have ever dealt with, previously or subsequently.

Looking back at my time at Darlington, I will always remember the late Cyril Knowles, one of Darlington's greatest managers saying to me, "You're doing a great job here, Brian. When I was here I did a good job, a similar job and I was offered a couple of jobs elsewhere, but I thought, 'Nah, I'm not leaving Darlington I'm comfortable here.' I had a good job, but I've regretted that decision every since." That stuck with me and made me think. If you can leave at a right time, a time when everybody stands up and pats you on your back and is so appreciative of your efforts, then do it.

In the end, Frank Gray didn't want to come to Leicester with me; he only had eyes for the job at Darlington, which he duly got, deservedly so and I backed him to do well.

It was the end of an incredible two-year period, both for me personally and for the club as a whole. My next priority, with all the contract negotiations and press conferences out of the way was to book a two-week holiday away, so I could recharge the batteries and prepare for the season ahead.

Chapter 7

OUTFOXED
Leicester City Manager: May 1991–November 1994

"I've come here to win things"

I **was appointed Leicester City manager in May 1991 as a**
replacement for Gordon Lee. The Foxes had just avoided rel-
egation to the third tier of English football and I was seen as
the right man to turn the club's fortunes around. My job was
to get us into the playoffs, simple as that.

Leicester City have had their fair share of great players, with
the likes of Frank Worthington in the 1970s and Gary Lineker in
the early 1980s and when I become manager there, I was asked if
my team was going to play attractive, free-flowing football, and I
said, "No, I've come here to win things." I knew how I going to set
out my side, but the only thing on my mind was to get the side
winning games. They had a reputation of being an open, attractive side in the past, but I knew I was going to play my proven
formation, which was: three centre backs, two wing backs, three
midfielders and two strikers. Some fans and the local press were
up in arms for weeks and weeks with my statement, but I had a
system that worked so why would I play another way?

Just like I did in my job at Darlington, I knew I'd have to piece
the jigsaw together and that would take some time. My role was
to get the right playing staff and backroom team in to do the job
I wanted them to. The first thing I had to do was to sort out the
staffing side, and the first request I had was for Evo to join me. I
had a free rein in that, because the previous backroom staff had
all run out of contract. I'd received lots of messages of congratulations and one of them was from John Gregory, who had done
a little spell at Portsmouth, but it hadn't worked out for him so I
had no hesitation to get him back in as another assistant. John
was desperate to get back into football so it was a no-brainer.

While I knew there were differences in the way John and Allan did things, I felt that was needed. John gave a whole new way of going into a dressing room and another edge to Allan and myself. We all had our strengths and weaknesses, but I knew we could all work together. Another ex-Villa man was mentioned to me in Steve Hunt, who had been coaching at Port Vale and was looking for a new challenge. I'd known Steve as a young lad at Villa so I spoke to him about being an assistant. My thinking was Steve could also offer something different. Then I looked to David Nish, who I'd worked with at Middlesbrough. He was a Leicester City legend during the late 1960s and I wanted him to work with us in some capacity. I believe he wanted to come back to the Leicestershire area anyway, so it was an opportunity for him to come back to the area he'd played a lot of his football in. So, I'd quickly put together my backroom staff before anything else happened. Putting in place a framework, which was a very important thing for me to do.

With my staff in place, we spent a couple of weeks together talking about things and looking at how we were about to take on the challenge. The main priority was to take the club away from the bottom half of the league so we sat together plotting things prior to the start of pre-season.

When you take any manager's role, the first job is to analyse the backroom staff, then look at the playing staff. A change of system always makes a difference to the playing staff you keep or move on. I knew that by looking at the squad we had, the style of play would help it move forward and change the dynamics of the team. From my initial assessment, I saw a few players who could fit into the style of play. I needed the right type of player and ones who could fit into the role in my formation. Just like at Darlington, I didn't have much money to spend in the first season. The first player I earmarked was Nicky Platanal and I signed him as my left wing back. I already had Gary Mills at the club and he was pencilled in as my right wing back. Another player I wanted was Ashley Ward, who was at Manchester City at the time and only a young lad, maybe 19 years old. We paid £80,000 for Ash to be part of the group, and Kevin Poole was drafted in as another goalkeeper. We only made three or four signings and a number of players were released, so there wasn't a great deal of movement either way, but it was enough that I thought could make a difference. We already had a fairly strong group, including the likes of Steve Walsh, and in time, I could further improve the squad throughout the season.

We went off to Ireland for our pre-season tour to play four games in seven days and we had to stay in a university complex of all places. It was a bizarre situation because we had to give the players money to buy their own food; the complex was closed, and we had to stay in self-catering units with each room having cooking facilities, so it wasn't ideal at all. The first thing I had to do was to switch myself off from the moans and groans about the facilities, reminding them that it wasn't my idea; it was a plan that had already been put into place and I had to fulfil it. I wasn't going to listen to anyone moaning about it; we were there as a group; we would bond as a group; we would work as a group and people would help each other.

Colin Gibson (Gibbo) was already part of the squad at Leicester, and I'd played with him at Villa, and him calling me "gaffer' was a bit awkward for us both at first, to the point where he got flak from the players because he'd often shout "Brian". Having said that, Gibbo's room was probably the best room to be in. Given the fact he was probably the only player who could cook there were queues outside his little apartment at times because everybody knew his food was the best. It all added to a bit of fun, frivolity and laughter.

It wasn't a great pre-season it has to be said, and it was one that tested us all to a certain degree. During that tour, we played in some of the most out-of-the-way places you could think of, to a point there were probably more cattle around watching the games than supporters. It wasn't an ideal environment, but I guess you'd call it an experience. In no time at all, I sensed we'd built some sort of a relationship between us all, and that was important. It was vital we used the poor facilities and poor venues to our advantage and not to pull us down. It was important it pulled us together and that's what it did. With our enthusiasm, Allan, John and myself as leaders of the group also joined in. We had the same sort of facilities as the players and we had to look after each other and cook for each other.

We had drawn a few and won a few by the odd goal during pre-season and questions had been asked about the system already. The season started with an away game against Swindon, which we drew 0-0, and could be described as 'solid' without being open and exciting. We managed to win three games without conceding; one a 3-0 home win against Maidstone in the League Cup, a 2-0 win against Plymouth in the league and a 1-0 away win against Maidstone in the second leg of the League Cup. That good streak continued with another three back to back wins in the league and only two goals conceded. People started to warm to our style of play, saying things like, "It's not that bad after all". Our wing backs were brilliant and the centre-backs were looking strong. We felt we'd started something, and started it very quickly and it was explosive; six wins out of the first seven games was excellent form. However, we hit the deck with a 3-0 defeat at Middlesbrough.

We managed to bounce back and introduced Paul Kitson into the team soon afterwards. He was a player who was labelled 'the next Gary Lineker', and he made quite an impression. We also brought in Colin Gordon as a centre forward, mainly because we were under pressure from teams interested in Dave 'Ned' Kelly. By the time we had got to December, we had fixed up a deal for him to go to Newcastle. Although we'd had a few dust-ups, mainly due to our similar temperaments, it was a little unfortunate to have to let him go, because I warmed to him as a person and a player: he was a super player. It was a great move for him though, and it meant I had a chance to bring in a couple of players. I was always on the lookout for more players. I'd created a bit of money through the outgoings, and it was my job to consolidate, which was part and parcel of my job in the first year. I brought in players like Paul Fitzpatrick, a six-foot-four-inch versatile player from Carlisle. Technically, Paul was brilliant for a big lad, although he wasn't that mobile his ball passing was wonderful. He was also a great lad to have around the dressing room, which was important. We also brought in Simon (Larry) Grayson from Leeds. I'd watched him years before, playing for Leeds youth team when I was coaching at Middlesbrough. I always felt that one day I'd sign Larry, and that day came while I was at Leicester. He wasn't breaking into the Leeds first-team as quickly as he had wished, so we snapped him up in the March of 1992 for around £50,000, which was a brilliant bit of business. Larry could play in any position. He had tremendous enthusiasm for the game. He was a brilliant talker on the field of play, and I'm not surprised he became a manager himself in later life. I believe players who can talk on the field improve their own game by up to 15%, and Larry was one of those who, when he released the ball would instruct the recipient what to do with it. Those type of players are a fantastic help to your team. Lots of people play football very quietly. One of my pet hates is when players come into the dressing room and say, "Remember that ball I passed to you? I thought you were going to do this or that..." That's where the talker will give an instruction what to do with the ball, although lots of people find that very difficult, including lots of senior players. My ideal is pass, move and talk, and Larry was excellent at all three.

During that first season, the biggest decision I had to make was what to do with Paul Kitson. He had become a hero among the fans, but we were constantly being asked about him by Derby County. The whole of the East Midlands knew about Kitson, but it was Arthur Cox, the Derby manager, who called me one day and said he wanted to buy Paul Kitson because he fitted the bill. At that time, I didn't want to sell him and told Arthur that. Derby were our nearest rivals and were above us in the league, so it didn't make sense to sell at that time. While I knew our team had to change and I had to sell some players in order to buy players, I wasn't about to give Paul away for peanuts. I said to Arthur he had to "Make me an offer I can't refuse," and even then, I'd have to speak to my chairman and see if we dare do the deal. Paul was our brightest prospect and our biggest asset, so I wasn't going to allow him to leave on the cheap. A conversation started and as it turned out, Arthur was prepared to include players as well as cash in exchange for Paul. That sort of deal began to interest me so I began to look around at the transfer market in order to see who was available. Eventually, Arthur and I met face-to-face at the Baseball Ground and talked about it in his office.

The old football grounds like the Baseball Ground were great in that you could actually park outside the ground and walk into the office, which very often opened out onto the street. When I parked my car outside the ground I noticed Arthur waving at the door, so when I got out of my car, I made sure nobody saw me and quietly slipped into the building. Even in the corridor on the way to his office, he walked in front of me and checked every room to make sure nobody saw us. While we were talking about the deal, if he heard any movement from outside his office, he'd shush me and we'd stop talking, "I thought I'd heard something there, Brian..." It was a bit cloak and dagger and a bit comical if I'm honest. Arthur was quite serious about our privacy, but I was almost in stitches.

I managed to get away from our meeting without being spotted and drove back to Leicestershire laughing all the way home. On the back of that meeting I had to report back to my chairman about a deal worth £1.3m and for me to be able to sign Ian Ormondroyd, Phil Gee and a sum of money.

That deal came to fruition before the transfer deadline, but I think it was the weirdest meeting I've ever had with another football manager.

We had stayed around the top six most of the season and during the March time, we lost a few games on the bounce and I felt we were falling out of the potential promotion places. It was a crucial period as the transfer window was about to shut at the end of the third Thursday in March. I was confident enough to spend that sort of money because I really thought we were at a point where we could start doing things, although I felt I had to do something special to save our season. Leeds were a good club at that time and they were progressing well under Howard Wilkinson. They had brought in some good, young lads and had a wonderful reputation of being very competitive. One of those talented lads was Michael Whitlow, who was a wonderful player, had a great left foot and could play in many different positions. When the opportunity arose that he might become available, I made an enquiry and managed to sign him up for £250,000. It was a big sum of money for me to spend, but I had to be proactive if we wanted to get a sniff of the playoffs. During my short managerial career, I'd never spent that sort of money, and what money I had, I spent it wisely, but in this case, I'd just brought in a large amount of money from the proceeds of the Kitson deal in order to make my team stronger.

My team had been revamped with the three incoming players on the back of the Paul Kitson deal. Selling our prized asset for a relatively large amount of money was something I hadn't done before, and it caused uproar with the fans' as you'd probably expect. People were also critical of the Ormondroyd signing, thinking I was going long ball, but he was a better player than most people gave him credit for, because if I didn't want to play him centre-forward, he could play on the left side. I was paid to do the job my way and I needed to be brave in my decisions and actions, so I had to sacrifice something to make the side stronger. It was no good just selling Kitson then putting the money in the bank. I had a plan and I had to justify my actions.

In any case, the club trusted me to do just that. The role I had at Darlington was about moving people out and bringing in fresh faces and the task at Leicester was basically no different, other than a few slight variations on what I'd done previously.

As it turned out, we managed to get into the playoffs with a string of wins at the back end of March and into April. It was a great achievement in my first year at the club. However, one of the standout games of my entire management career was in the playoff semi-final, when we faced Cambridge United, who actually had given me my worst nightmare earlier in the season. We went to their place in the September and got hammered 5-1. They had a really good team and well organised under John Beck, with the likes of Dion Dublin, Alan Kimble, Lee Philpott and Steve Claridge in the side. They were what some people call a direct or a long ball team; long balls into the channel; long throws into the box; the pitch was fully sanded so the ball stopped in the channel, and they were unbelievably competitive too. Coincidentally, John Beck had been interviewed for the Leicester job before I was offered it, and after our drumming by his side I got butchered by our own fans, and they even surrounded the team bus – our fans were awful towards me on that day.

Fast-forward eight months and we got Cambridge in the playoffs. We drew the game 1-1 in the first leg, but in the return leg at Filbert Street we turned on the style big time. I can't remember the number of times I've watched the game on play-back, with Jimmy Greaves doing the co-commentary, but every time I watch it I always recall how good we were. We absolutely battered Cambridge 5-1 on the night; the crowd were incredible; the atmosphere was incredible; the performance was incredible; the team was brilliant, and the ironic thing was, all that wouldn't have happened if I hadn't have sold Paul Kitson and brought in those three lads. That team I sent out against Cambridge was organised, well balanced and well drilled to play my formation and we set Filbert Street alight that night. The team I sent out was: Carl Muggleton in goal, Michael Whitlow and Gary Mills as wing-backs, Tony James, Colin Hill and Steve Walsh as centre-backs, Larry Grayson and Steve Thompson in midfield, Kevin Russell, Tommy Wright and Ian Ormondroyd up top.

The game started at a frightening pace; Cambridge were really good at squeezing down, putting you under pressure and working the ball into your areas. Early on, Dion Dublin rose above everyone at a corner and hit the bar. It was as big a scramble as you'll ever see in a football game. Bodies were flying everywhere. From that point, I knew we were up for the game and the crowd started to get going and got behind the team. The game was all about set pieces, long throws and corners. It was a very physical encounter, and our first goal came from a corner on the right and it was pumped towards our big lads, but it bounced close to the near post, where Tommy Wright was standing by the 'keeper and he jumped in front of him and toe-poked the ball into the net. It was a set piece we hadn't rehearsed, but it worked all the same and that was the start of the onslaught. While the first goal was probably a bit of a fluke, the second was magnificent. The ball was bobbling outside the box before Larry got hold of it, dribbled past two players and overran it a bit, then the 'keeper came out to meet the ball, but it bounced off him into the path of Steve Thompson who put the ball away. Stevie always tells me, "I was your greatest ever signing, wasn't I?" and I'd probably have to agree. The third goal was a classic counter-attack with the ball falling to Stevie Thompson who put a lovely ball into the path of Kevin Russell in our own half. Kevin then played an incredible ball to Tommy Wright and suddenly, he was off and ran 50 or 60 yards; Tommy was a machine. He could really shift. Suddenly, we had people arriving in the box from nowhere. Tommy arrived on a one-on-one and then shot into the keeper, but it fell to Kevin Russell who headed it into the net. Kevin, also known as 'Rooster' was a good player. He was talented; he loved football and he's a coach now, maybe something not a lot of people would have thought back then. Our fourth goal came quickly; it was all happening all of a sudden, and when Muggleton cleared the ball right up the pitch, within three seconds we scored again. It was pure route one football. The whole team were hyped up. The fans were in dreamland and we were thinking about the final. We ended the game with big Ian Ormondroyd scoring with his right foot, would you believe and that really did put the icing on the cake. By then, Cambridge were all over the place, but we were just on a different planet all together.

As a player, coach or a manager, you can't understand why those sorts of nights don't happen all the time, but when they do happen, everybody is so up for it. You know, if Dion Dublin had converted that chance before we even scored our first goal, it could well have been a different game and who knows what would have happened. It definitely changed the game and our lads were whipped up into a frenzy after that chance went begging. I couldn't believe the energy levels of those lads on that night, and that's probably why it remains one of my favourite games as a manager or player, for that matter.

We were at Wembley to face Blackburn Rovers in the playoff final. It was around the time that Blackburn were being funded by Jack Walker's millions and they were odds-on favourites to win the game and indeed they did win, by 1-0 through a Mike Newell penalty. It was a controversial goal too. Some say David Speedie dived and went down under a challenge, but the referee awarded a penalty, and he converted it. We were gutted to have lost, but travelling back to Leicestershire that evening, the fans were right behind us because they all knew we'd over-achieved by getting that far.

The playoff final wasn't the only final we played in that season. We entered the Zenith Data Systems Cup (Northern Section), beating teams like Barnsley (4-3), Port Vale (4-0), Everton (2-1), and Notts County (2-1) on the wettest night I've ever known in football. I remember John Allen and myself didn't sit in the dugout, but chose to stand on the touchline like drowned rats. The players were soaked to their skins. Even though it was early January I've never seen a storm like it, yet we played through it. By beating Notts County, we'd reached the Northern Final and we played Nottingham Forest at the City Ground in the first leg, where we drew 1-1. In the second leg, we lost at home, 2-1. That night was one of the saddest nights of my life if I'm honest, and that's not really an overstatement – and it's not because we lost.

I, like everybody else, was a massive admirer of Brian Clough. He was brilliant to me and always called me, "Young Brian". I once got told off while playing for Villa when he shouted at me for having my socks round my ankles, which is what I often did. "Pull your socks up young Brian," he said. I replied, "I don't want to pull me socks up, Mr Clough." To most people, he would have probably gone off on one of his rants, but on that occasion he just looked at me and stood there speechless. I think he was amazed some youngster had spoken back at him. I met him many times after that, as a young coach, and he'd come up to me and ask, "How are you young Brian? Are you all right?" I used to say, "Yes, I'm brilliant thank you, Mr Clough. How are you?" He was just someone I admired and because I stood up to him well and answered him back politely, I think he took notice of me, and I felt so honoured. Every time he saw me, he'd go so far as to walk across the car park and say, "Hello," and have a chat with me.

So, after the second leg of that final at Filbert Street, Brian just wasn't himself and he looked a little bit worse for wear and under the influence, which was so sad because I loved him to bits. In a way, I was chuffed Forest beat us, because I just wanted him to be in better health. It was the start of his decline. I think he went on another season as manager of Forest, but that season ended in relegation and I was gutted for him because of the way it turned out in the end as he was a brilliant, brilliant man. Brian is one of the only men I've ever met, that when he walked into a room the hairs on the back of your neck stood up, because of who he was and everybody in that room knew they were in the presence of a great man. Everybody knew they should look out when Brian entered a room, virtually everyone stood to attention. He was a class act and very much a genius of his profession.

So, what a brilliant opening season it was, finishing fourth off top in the league, above Blackburn, who beat us in the playoff final and who were promoted to the new Premier League, which started in the 1992–1993 season. We'd come through a lot together and for me, it was a wonderful place to be.

****

It was a massive disappointment losing at Wembley, but at the same time it was a triumph in a way, given where the club had come from in the previous season. During the pre-season, Allan, John and myself set about planning for the season and the main question we had to ask was, "Where do we go from here?" A lot of teams don't do so well after they lose in a playoff final and disappointment sets in during the following season. In that era, there were no physios or sports scientists helping the players prepare; it was down to the coaches who had to lift the players and decide what we needed to do. Getting to the playoff final brings its downside, in that you have less time to prepare for the next season as the finals come at the end of May and everybody else is on the beach. Instead of seven-week break, you only get about four weeks off. Players did look after themselves, even in the early 1990s, as they began to realise how important it was to do so. The question was, would the players who had a seven-week break be any better off than our lads, who only had four weeks off, or should we give them an extra week? We needed to answer the questions and pretty quickly, too.

We decided to get the players to report back on July 1st. We felt four weeks was enough and there was no messing around. We told the players they needed to work, and they needed to work with us. It was all about positive thinking, rather than letting the players take another week off just because they had worked hard during the last season. The first thing we did was to sit them all down and talk about the playoff final. We didn't want anyone coming in feeling sorry for themselves, and we wanted them to continue the momentum. We also wanted to get it out of the way and move on. I know some sports scientists these days may look at that as being the wrong approach. They may consider it the right decision mentally, but physically it might not be the best thing for the players. Back then there were no stats to back these ideas up, but we just felt they were a good group of players who got on well, and a group of lads we believed in and who, given a bit of fine-tuning had the potential to do really well.

Every season sees comings and goings at a football club, and inevitably, we knew we'd have to do some business, but we wanted to do it in a time frame that gave us enough space to prepare for the next season. We didn't want to start poorly. We needed to start the season on the front foot.

It was always Allan, John and myself who took the training, and we even took part in the fitness work and the running, even if we finished at the back. We were all involved in the team and the fact that we were up for it, ready to do our best, I feel led the players on and inspired them to do their best, as well.

One of the jewels in our crown during the previous season was Julian Joachim. He was a young lad who was still raw, and even though he was still an apprentice, we felt he was good enough to be introduced into the first team. Rather than alienate him from his pals, what we did was to bring someone else with him into the first-team environment on different days of the week. By doing that, it made it look as though we were watching different people, while at the same time, making Julian feel at home, knowing someone of his own age was around him. We also encouraged Julian to still do his jobs as an apprentice, even though he had started to play in the first team. It was a situation

I thought we handled quite well. As I've said before, I remember when I was an apprentice at Villa, we had a young player called Jimmy Brown who made his first-team debut at the age of 15 and he stopped doing his jobs, and that didn't go down too well with the other lads. That situation with Jimmy stuck in my mind and I used it to make sure we didn't get the same outcome with Julian, and more importantly, I wanted to keep him grounded, so grounded in fact that we even got him to make the tea on occasions.

Julian became very close to me and we always had time to have a chat and so I kept an eye on him. He was a massive talent and everybody at the club knew that. The one thing I liked about Julian was he always kept his feet on the ground. He loved being in the first-team, but he also loved being with his mates in the youth team set up.

We continued to change the squad around, with people like David Lowe, Bobby Davidson, Steve Agnew and Steve Thompson coming into the fold. Most of those guys were in their mid-20s, and they were all in their prime. I tend to follow the careers of most of the players I brought into a football club and being at a club like Leicester, it was an ideal opportunity for them all to come together. In the case of Bobby Davidson, he was more of a senior player, but had been a great pro and was brilliant in the dressing room, although it didn't go quite as well as I'd have liked on the pitch for him. However, we had gathered together what I thought was a really strong squad for the 1992–1993 season. It was important to be competitive in the league and it was imperative we didn't fall out of that top six.

We got off to a flyer with a win at home to Luton, but away at Wolves we got battered 3-0; it was a typical Steve Walsh v Steve Bull confrontation, and although not many people got the better of Walshy I have to say, most of the time Bully came out on top. He was so wound up every time he played against Bully it was untrue, and more often than not, he got himself into trouble. The game was billed as those two playing against each other, rather than Wolves v Leicester, and we received a bit of an early season lesson.

As the season went on we were pretty consistent; when we lost we didn't lose by many goals. Little Julian Joachim set the world alight that season. Some of his goals were fantastic. There was a goal against Barnsley that was incredible. I remember getting to the end of the season and the playoffs, and then I look back at the league table and I ask myself, "Are the playoffs fair?" Take Portsmouth for instance, who we actually beat once and drew with once, in the league, but they finished 12 points ahead of us and 10 points ahead of Tranmere who were fourth. We met them in the semi-final of the playoffs, but as Filbert Street was being knocked about, we had to play the first leg at the City Ground, Nottingham, so it was like playing two away games for us. Julian Joachim scored one of the best goals I've ever seen. It was an individual effort. He burst past players with pace and power as if they weren't there, and he ended up putting the ball in the back of the net, and we beat Portsmouth 1-0. In all fairness, Portsmouth were the better team in the second leg, but we ended up going through to the final, for the second year in a row.

It was an incredible thing to do, to go to Wembley two seasons in a row. We went on to play Swindon in the final, and again, we were unbeaten against them in the league that season. We felt both times we were a much better team than Swindon so we were happy to play them again. Swindon were a good footballing side back then, with Glenn Hoddle being their player-manager, so you'd expect as much. Glenn was a magnificent footballer in his day, but leading up to the game at Wembley, there were so many rumours around about Glenn's future with Swindon. Stories were flying around that he was to become the manager of Chelsea. In a strange sort of a way, you'd look at that and think that wasn't healthy for them, and it must have unsettled the team. He'd done a great job at Swindon, to get them to the playoff final, but people were doubting their chances of being promoted into the Premier League. We were favourites and that was clear, and we were positive we could do it.

We went into the final with a completely different mindset from the previous season, which we considered to be more of a day out and didn't expect to win in all honestly. Our focus going into the Swindon match was purely on that game. It wasn't a learning trip out. It was down to business and focus on winning. We wanted to be ready.

However, on the day, Glenn turned in an incredible masterclass display on the pitch and before we knew it, we were 3-0 down. It was just unjust in many ways because we weren't playing that badly. It was just his team were playing magnificently well. Some of his passing was immaculate, and we were sitting on the touchline thinking, "His team's going to the Premier League and he's going to leave them." Football, being the great game it is, always throws up surprises and all of a sudden, there was an incredible turnaround after half time. Once Julian scored our first in the 57th minute it gave our fans some hope, but after 83 minutes it was 3-3 and all we could see was extra-time. We had Swindon under some severe pressure, but nearing the end of the game, in the 84th minute, we switched off. They were awarded a penalty and scored from it. It was 4-3 and we were utterly shattered. It even felt different at the end of the game. Last season we were just happy to have played at Wembley, but against Swindon, we honestly thought we were going to do it. On that occasion, the momentum we had just wasn't enough.

So, it was two defeats in two seasons at Wembley, and the dressing room was a sad place compared to the previous season. I remember Stevie Thompson breaking down after the game and I had to console him on the halfway line. Wow, it was hard to take and if there was ever a game of football that I felt gutted, it was after that one. You lose loads of games, as a player or a manager and you feel devastated, but the feeling we all had after that final was something that was hard to describe.

We were almost there, but we were kicked right where it hurt in the dying minutes of the game. Wow! It was horrible and it hurt like hell! It was at Wembley and we missed out on promotion to the Premier League again in probably the worst game in football to lose.

After the game, it was the same as the previous season; we sat in the dressing room and talked to the players, trying to lift them up a little bit, but not too much as it wasn't the time or the place. On that bus back to Leicester, Allan, John and I sat there thinking, "What are we going to do this time?" We were almost in June again, and the pre-season was just around the corner. We asked ourselves, whether it was wise to push them again. We'd been to Wembley twice and failed, could we pick the players up enough to push on the next season? The Premier League was in our minds at the start of the play off final, but now it had clearly disappeared. However, it wasn't as though we hadn't contemplated being in Division One, but even with the different mindset, it hadn't worked for us. We had to think of a new strategy for the new season.

We, as a management team, had to be really strong. We believed in all the hard work we'd put in; we believed in the regime; we believed in the group, so we all decided it wasn't right to change. We decided to look at all the ingredients that we could work with; we looked at the hard work we'd put in during the season; we looked at possible improvements in certain areas we could make; we looked at the mentality that got us so far. What we couldn't do was let them have more time off. We didn't want them to stew on the defeat and come back even more gutted, so we made the exact same decision again, even though the context was different. We told the players we'd be strong, so they should be strong too, and that they were coming back to training on July 1st. We didn't want anybody moaning and if they did, we'd move them on.

Here we go again. Season three at Leicester and pre-season training was more-or-less the same. However, I decided to do something slightly different by planning a pre-season trip to Norway. Well, I say planned. I had a call from an agent who offered me a trip to Norway for nothing. What had happened was a team had pulled out of the trip. It was all paid for and he asked me if I'd like to bring my team to Norway for 10 days and play three or four games there. I must admit I had to think about the offer, only because I always enjoyed being closer to home for pre-season, and thinking back to the previous season, where we went to Dublin and that was a waste of time, apart from building a bit of team spirit. Did I want to go to Norway? Well, not really but I accepted the offer without thinking about it first. I never really did any great homework on it, but I knew it would be a difficult place to go and play.

So we were off to Trondheim in central Norway. Boy, what a tiring trip that turned out to be. We spent hours travelling there, and we spent hours and hours travelling in between games. One game was a nine-hour bus journey and we stayed after the game and then returned to our base in Trondheim. The journey to play in the last game was every bit as long, but after the overnight stay, we had an almighty journey to the airport to catch our flight back to the UK. It was horrendous.

Apart from the travelling, I must say the training facilities were good and we did all sorts of recreational things to keep us occupied during the day. We went clay pigeon shooting; we went kayaking; we walked up mountains with a guide; we did anything to entertain the lads while we weren't training, travelling or playing.

The downside was we could only take about 18 players and staff, so I asked John to come with us and also asked Allan to stay at home to look after the remaining lads. He was gutted at first. However, I think Allan was laughing at us in the end, as we were bored out of our brains most of the time. It was a hard trip, but we managed to get some good work in. However, we made some great friends and the hosts loved having us there. Before we left, our host wanted to give us some good luck for the season ahead. He suggested we go to a place that he reckoned was lucky and have a photograph of the team taken there. So, we all went off to this place and had a group photo taken, in the hope it would bring us good luck for the new season. Now, as you know, I'm not superstitious or anything, but I agreed to travel half an hour away to this place called Hell Station. Our host grouped us all together underneath a sign saying, "Welcome to Hell" behind us. Still to this day I have the photograph. Was it lucky? Well, you'll need to read on to find out.

So, what did we do when we returned from our pre-season tour? Well, I probably did the most controversial thing I could have done when I signed David Speedie from West Ham during the pre-season, as he hadn't been offered a permanent contract at Upton Park. Two seasons previously, Speedie had 'fallen over' in the box to earn Blackburn a penalty against us in the playoff final, which resulted in his team getting promoted. Although he probably wasn't the usual type of player I'd sign, I thought I'd rather have him on my team than playing against him. From a manager's point of view, he was a nightmare, because he'd argue with everything you said to him anyway and wind everybody up, even his teammates, but after watching him play so many times, I realised I didn't want him against me. It was a case of putting up with him and dealing with him in my own way, which would mean leaving him out of some games. It was a big decision for me to sign that sort of player and it didn't go down well at first with the fans.

Still to this day, David Speedie is the most awkward so-and-so you can ever come across both on and off the pitch. He'd always argue his corner. Even knowing he was wrong, he'd still argue he wass right and he'd probably argue with himself, too. It was a real test of my man-management skills looking after Speedie. He and

Walshy in the same side was a nightmare scenario. They could be best of mates one minute, then the next the pair of them would be hitting each other with anything and everything they could get hold of. The pair of them could start a fight over nothing, and Speedie would never back down, and Walshy wouldn't back down either and at times there was a bit of friction in there, but I'd like to think I held it together, so it didn't get out of hand.

We also signed Lee Philpott from Cambridge, a left-sided player who had a great ability to cross the ball and could play in midfield or left wing back. Another great signing was Iwan Roberts, another centre-forward option, who I'd looked at for several years previously and said to myself, "I'm going to sign him one day." I looked at my Leicester side and just thought it was the right time for him. Iwan was a terrific target man, not the most mobile in the world, but he loved scoring goals, and all types of goals.

We'd only changed the group slightly with the additions, and we were ready for another onslaught for promotion and another test of our character. We just had to do it that season. It was so massive for us it was untrue. There was no way we could sustain a promotion charge season after season.

Someone once asked me, "Was there a particular game that justified the signing of Speedie?" My answer was, "Yes, the Tranmere Rovers playoff semi-final, second leg, without a doubt." In those days, having someone like David Speedie in your side, who was a thorn in the side of the opposition, was a big advantage. He was a thorn in our side on that day, so much so their goalkeeper, Eric Nixon saw Speedie tangle with one of their defenders and got so wound up that he actually ran out of his area and literally picked little Speedie up as if he was about to shake him. It ended up with the two of them having a bit of a tussle together and they both got sent off. That incident changed the shape of the game and rattled Tranmere. We ended up winning the game 2-1 and for me, that performance justified signing him, because it got us to Wembley for the third time.

Having said all that, I very much think that the David Speedie signing was the main reason why we did well that season. We scored another 70-odd goals, something we did over each of the three seasons that we reached the playoff finals. We also made ourselves harder to beat and we were involved in some great games.

However, Speedie was banned for the final, and that gave us a different test in itself, because we were facing a Derby County side managed by Roy McFarland, and of course we were facing Paul Kitson, who I'd sold to them for good money. They had a good side, with the likes of Gary Charles, Gordon Cowans, Paul Simpson, Marco Gabbiadini and Tommy Johnson. They finished beneath us that season, but they were the best footballing side in the league. I liked their side and had a lot of respect for them. Without Speedie though, I had to think carefully how I chose the team. I wasn't prepared to lose three games in a row at Wembley, that wasn't going to happen. Looking back, I think I picked the most controversial team that I'd ever picked for a game of football. I didn't name the team until the morning of the final, mainly because I sat and stewed on it for days; about how to play the match; about how was I going to beat Derby; about how was I going to compete with their passing game. There was a very slim chance of us winning if we played a passing game, so I went into controversial mode and made all my plans for the play off final.

Wembley had become a familiar sight for us, but at the same time we couldn't believe we were there again. There were a couple of things that were important to me that day. Gary Mills had been injured for weeks, but carried on playing with a swollen toe and it got to the stage where he couldn't play another game. I was gutted he couldn't play at Wembley so I made the decision he would march the team out onto the pitch, a role normally given to the manager. I felt that was an important thing for me to do because he was a leader and had played his part in getting us there. Some people may wonder about whether that was a big decision to make, but I considered it a huge thing to decide on. It was important to me that a player who I'd had for three years and had been outstanding would lead the team out. When I told him the news, he just said, "Wow. Thank you. That's brilliant."

The second big decision was obviously team selection. When I actually decided on the team, I can look back and think that it was a one-off. You get moments in football when you make decisions that may backfire and you'll be under pressure for sure if they fail, but if they work, people will praise you (hopefully). That team I selected for the final was one of those moments. If we hadn't have gone up with that team, people would have said I'd lost the plot.

Allan, John and myself had geared everything up and prepared as best we could for that game. We had planned for everything being 100% right on the day, and we approached it in a very professional manner because we didn't want to lose the match. It was a big decision for me, to tell the team I was going to play a different system, which included three big lads upfront, and it was a defining moment in my managerial career. Even though I had faith in my selection, as a manager I was not quite sure how they were going to respond. This was the controversial team I selected:

Goalkeeper, Gavin Ward (six-foot-four), Gary Coatesworth, Brian Carey, Jim Willis (all six-foot, three centre-backs), Simon Grayson (right-back), Mike Whitlow (six-foot plus left-back), Mark Blake and Colin Gibson in midfield, Steve Walsh, Iwan Roberts and Ian Ormondroyd up front.

How often would that combination win you a game of football, with seven, six-foot plus, strong players in the side? We had to have a team who could put balls into the box. I had been labelled a few times as a 'long ball' manager, but when I look at that team now, I think, Wow! I couldn't get out of my head we had to play a certain way, even though it was a massive gamble. I felt we could win the game from set pieces, but in open play, we needed to have a bit of good fortune. It's like saying to your team who are 2-0 down and you've got to gamble by bringing on two big centre-forwards, "Go on, just lump it up to the big men." The reason for playing Walshy up front was that it gave him the incentive to play. He was one of those adrenalin junkies who would play anywhere he could, just as long as he was in the side.

They say it's all in the preparation, and it almost certainly had a lot to do with the result on the pitch. It was very much a 'no-thrills' visit. We went down the night before and went home straight after the game. We didn't have three or four days as we had done on the previous two occasions. It was very much get there, do the business and go home.

The game itself didn't start too brightly for us and probably didn't go to plan, because we did what I didn't want us to do and that was get amongst them. Their two strikers, Marco Gabbiadini and Tommy Johnson were causing us all sorts of problems, and we went a goal down through Tommy Johnson. He could have had a hat-tick before he scored that day. We were also lucky that Larry Grayson got away with a few touch-and-go decisions against Tommy. The referee was a little bit too kind on the day, if it hadn't been a final, Larry could easily have been sent off.

After two finals where we'd had no luck at all, we were eventually compensated with a touch of good fortune. Our break came just before half time, and it was a massive bonus for us. A cross came into the box and Walshy out-jumped their keeper, Martin Taylor to score. How Paul Williams, standing on the line didn't clear it, I will never know. With the ball spinning a lot, it was probably easier to boot the ball out with his foot rather than clearing it with his head. It was a fortunate goal for us, but in those situations you'd take them all day long. We rode our luck in the second half too, when their American international, John Harkes missed a great opportunity late on in the game. We had decided to go for broke just before then, when I brought off Roberts and Coatesworth, and changed the formation slightly. We started to play a bit more adventurously, with Whitlow playing as a centre-back and Gibson at left back, and I played Larry as a right wing-back, where he was more productive and of course, I brought on Julian Joachim to play on the right. JJ was completely different from Iwan and was probably unlucky not to start, but when he came on he was always a threat to them with his pace and power. I also stuck Walshy up front and Ormondroyd on the left hand side. Suddenly, Derby had several different threats to contend with and we could go from A to B very quickly.

In terms of a game plan, our 'Plan B' had been put into force around the 60th minute and we had a chance for it to come into play in the 84th minute. That chance came when JJ received the ball 20 yards outside their box in a central area, he spun on the ball and passed it to Larry, who put an incredible ball into the box. Ormondroyd had made a great run from the left and got a brilliant header in at from front post, but unbelievably, Martin Taylor saved it. The good thing about having a centre-half playing as a centre-forward is generally they run off the ball and they don't stand still off the ball in the box. Some forwards tend to stand in the box waiting for the ball, but defenders tend to be on the move and Walshy had an uncanny knack of being in the right place at the right time, so he found himself on the end of that save from Martin Taylor and shuffled it into the net. We were suddenly in dreamland.

At that point, there was an unbelievable determination to hang in there. We had one or two nervy moments and we had one or two moments that put pressure on them. Late in the game, Paul Kitson came on for them to try and rescue something; he had one effort that flew over the bar, but it all came to no avail and we hung on to win 2-1. When the final whistle blew it was more a sense of relief that we'd won what had been our third final in a row. It was a crazy, crazy day in the life of a football manager, but fortunately it worked for me. Was there a 'Plan B'? I'm not sure there was. If 'Plan A' hadn't have worked, well I'm not sure what I'd have done, but as history tells you now, we beat Derby County in the 1994 Division One playoff final.

I'm not sure how many people have actually looked at that team, and considered how controversial it was with the formation of three big centre-backs, two wing-backs, two holding midfielders and three six-foot something strikers, who weren't the most athletic in the world, yet we beat the best footballing team in that league.

Looking back at that pre-season tour to Norway and remembering the photograph we had at the lucky 'Hell's Station', back in the July, it could be said that it gave us a bit of luck because we won the playoff final – even if it was third time lucky? So, if anybody wants a bit of luck, get yourself to Norway and get your photograph taken at 'Hell's Station', because it worked for us in 1994. Leicester City were in the Premier League after three years of constant decision-making, trying to revamp a team in order to gain promotion. It was a brilliant achievement for a fantastic football club with a great set of fans. However, nothing lasts forever.

****

I'd had a back problem for a long time. They called it a congenital abnormality of the vertebrae. I've mentioned before that it prevented my potential move from Aston Villa to Birmingham City when I was a player during the 1979–1980 season. Towards the end of the 1993–1994 season I was really struggling, and it even prevented me from driving. I was on painkillers so a good friend of mine, Malcolm Beard used to drive me all over the place. Malcolm and I played together at Villa and he now worked for me at Leicester as a scout, so we knew each other pretty well. However, the win at Wembley eased a lot of the pain as the adrenalin was flowing, but I was soon struggling again and one of the things I'd decided on was to have a couple of weeks away, regardless of whether we won or lost the final. I had been having treatment, but it hadn't been looked into in any great detail, other than the fact that I had a back problem.

As it turned out, Martin George had a beautiful property in Majorca and he suggested I could go and stay there for a couple of weeks, which was a lovely gesture on his part. However, it was there that I had a complete breakdown in terms of painful back spasms and it got to the point that I could hardly walk or do anything really. I couldn't sit down in the sun and relax and I was in complete agony, so there was no real point in my being in Spain. It was at that point that I decided to cut my holiday short and managed somehow to sort flights back and get home. It was unbelievably painful, especially getting on and off the plane.

When I arrived back, I was taken to hospital in Leicester, saw a back specialist and had a set of tests and scans done. The prognosis was that I needed an operation and that was arranged very quickly. So, in the summer of 1994 I had a disc removed and a spine fusion operation, which was awful and kept me lying on my back at home for a month or so.

Before the start of the next season, I was rewarded with a new contract, and the future looked good for me personally. However, my health was suffering and after my convalescence, I still couldn't drive but I did report back for pre-season. However, rather than taking training, I sat there watching John and Allan doing the work on the training field. I wasn't allowed to take part in anything. I was zonked as I was still in rehab and on painkillers. It was very frustrating.

We did a bit of business pre-season (and during the season) and signed a young lad called Lee Ellison from Darlington on a free; Franz Karr from Sheffield United for £100,000; Nicky Mohan, who was one of my apprentices at Middlesbrough, was signed for £300,000 and Mark Draper (Drapes) for £1.25m from Notts County. We hadn't spent big money and the cracks were beginning to show, and I was struggling personally during the first few months of the season. It was a tough period and proved how big a step up it was.

When the new season started I still wasn't in the best of health, having spent several weeks in rehab, trying to get fit and healthy. We were in the Premier League, but nothing in the early part of the season helped my health improve. We kicked off the season with a home game against Kevin Keegan's Newcastle United. I'd always got on well with Kevin and we had a chat and he was very complimentary on what I'd achieved at Leicester. However, on the pitch, his team taught us a lesson and battered us 3-1. We actually played OK, but the difference between a Division One club and a Premier League team stuck out like a sore thumb in that first game.

Our second game was against Blackburn Rovers (who incidentally became champions that season) and we were battered again, 3-0. In fact we lost our first three games, and that wasn't something I was used to. It wasn't until the fourth game of the season that we got our first point on the board. It didn't get much better either; in our first 14 games, we only won two and lost nine. It was a huge eye-opener. Welcome to the Premier League, I thought. We continued to struggle in the Premier League and by the beginning of November we were near the foot of the table.

There were some highlights though; we beat Spurs 3-1 at Filbert Street and we were 4-1 up against Southampton, but had to hang on for dear life to win 4-3. All the other games I can remember were intense and very often we ended up with nothing. We were in the bottom three, but the fans were still with us, which was important. I must point out here that Aston Villa were only one point above us at that time, which was quite significant.

It was at that point that I began to be linked with the Aston Villa vacancy, vacated by Ron Atkinson in the November of 1994. There were lots of speculation about the Villa job and people were asking me all sorts of questions. Was I up for it? Was I ready for it? Did I want it? Other names were in the frame, like Graeme Souness, Steve Coppell, Bruce Rioch and David Pleat. My chairman at Leicester, Martin George, had been asked about the situation too, and he said some nice things about me, saying he was happy with me and didn't want to lose me. I hastily made arrangements to meet Martin to speak about the situation.

I can honestly say, I wasn't unhappy at Filbert Street, and at the same time, I wasn't 100% sure Aston Villa wanted me to be their new manager. Initially, there was no contact between us, none whatsoever. Obviously, I had media people ringing me left, right and centre and there were articles in newspapers here, there and everywhere. Sometimes, deep down, you have to say what you've got to say, as opposed to what you believe as being the truth. I had tried on several occasions to speak to Martin on a one-on-one basis, in an open and honest discussion on how I felt at the time. I remember having a meeting with him and telling him about my past connections with Aston Villa, just in case he wasn't aware of the facts. There was one particular meeting that ended up in me getting to the point where I actually said, "Look, if there is a chance of me going to Aston Villa, and if you refuse me permission to go there, I genuinely wouldn't want to stay on as manager of Leicester City." It was quite a significant moment for me, because it basically pointed out to him, if there was contact, he needed to let me know. I had got to the point where I just needed to know IF there was a chance. I know that sounds a bit one-sided, but it gets you like that sometimes and you feel you have to say something like that. By saying that, I'd laid it exactly on the line, and I'm sure Martin knew how I felt.

It all came to a head after the game with Manchester City on 19th November 1994, which was live on TV. There was continued speculation and before the game kicked off, Martin was interviewed by Sky TV and asked questions about my position. In his interview, he made comments that made it very obvious that I hadn't got through to him. He made it quite clear, he would NOT give me permission to talk to Villa and that I would NOT be leaving Leicester City. After I'd tried to speak to him in a one-on-one situation and I had begun to think, "Right, he understands where I'm coming from", and for him then to come out to publically and deny an opportunity for me to move on (if that was the case), I felt very let down and disappointed. Incidentally, we lost the game against Manchester City and I wasn't too surprised because my mind wasn't totally there that night. I'd had three successful years at Leicester City and everybody who knew me and knew how I approached things could tell it wasn't the same.

Initially, Martin denied that I would be leaving Leicester, but after that game, my departure looked more likely. Villa chairman, Doug Ellis was quoted as saying: "Let me assure you I have abided by the code of conduct that is not legal, yet that ensures there is no poaching between clubs. We have not contacted Brian and he has not contacted us and will not if he has not resigned and is not free to do so." Although I had committed myself to Leicester a few days, Martin was also quoted as saying, "If he now says he has changed his mind, I will say, 'Tough'. I don't see why any big club feels entitled to just come in and take a manager from someone else if they feel like it. It's a nonsense." Martin also denied that a compensation figure of £1.5million pounds had been accepted.

However, all doubts were cleared up the next day.

The next morning, I went into work as normal, and headed straight to Martin's office, handed my car keys to him and said, "As far as I'm concerned, I'm resigning". He looked at me and said, "Look, I'll tell you what. I need you to tell the board that." I agreed, without hesitation, so the following day I went to the board meeting and met the directors, some privately, and told them how I felt. I'd written a letter of resignation in my pocket, which wasn't as well written as it should have been as there was a line in there which basically said if they refused me permission to go to Villa, I'd pack in football and I wouldn't even apply for the job. I was that disappointed that people couldn't understand my career aspirations. However, the board accepted my resignation and I was ready to move on. There were certain compromises made and agreed and I left the board the resignation letter

Unusually, the Leicester Mercury newspaper put a football story on the front page, with a huge banner headline that read: "LITTLE OUT". It went on to say that I had quit citing 'personal reasons' and that I had refused to link this decision with the Aston Villa vacancy.

Shortly after I resigned, I had to sit alongside Martin George at a press conference and I said, "I felt it was time to do something else. Football is my life and I would hope to get another job at some stage. I just feel that at this stage of my life I have to do something else." The Leicester City board then issued a statement accepting my decision "with much regret". They recorded their "sincere thanks for the immense contribution made by Mr Little to the Football Club since the summer of 1991". Martin George was then quoted as saying: "The board received a categorical written assurance from Brian Little that he would not be the next manager of Aston Villa. As a result, urgent instructions have now been issued to our legal advisors to proceed forthwith."

Allan Evans was put in temporary charge of the team, but John Gregory also resigned with me. Ironically, the day after my departure, Evo steered Leicester City to a 2-1 against Arsenal in front of a capacity crowd at Filbert Street.

It seemed like déjà vu; I'd previously walked out of a perfectly good job as youth team coach at Aston Villa because I really disagreed with one or two things the then manager was doing and I felt I didn't want to be part of it. I can't pretend to do something I don't really believe in or don't really enjoy. There were also times when I walked out of jobs after informing my manager because I wanted to pursue something else, so this wasn't a one-off for me; it was the type of person I am, that I couldn't go behind someone's back in my pursuit of something better. At the same time, it wasn't anything to do with me wanting a quick exit and it wasn't anything to do with money. The crux of the matter was it was something I wanted to do and someone was denying me that opportunity. I would never deny anybody another opportunity if they genuinely wanted to go elsewhere or better themselves. I would do nothing other than help them shape that direction.

Looking back, I was totally gutted at the way I left Leicester; I was gutted that I couldn't leave on a good note, with my hands in the air, waving to the fans who had supported me for those three great years; I was gutted that I had fallen out with the chairman – it wasn't right. There's nearly always some good that comes out of bad situations, and I do believe my case was very influential in changing the contractual agreements managers are given. I'm so glad the modern managers now have compensation clauses in their contract; that everything is mapped out and everything is sorted out in black and white. As a manager now, you know exactly where you stand and how much the club pays you if you're not doing what the owners want you to do; the manager knows exactly how much they're entitled to if another club comes in and takes you.

There are now clauses in a football manager's contract that eliminate any of this falling out with each other; any of the game playing; any of the going behind people's backs, so if I helped that situation, then all well and good. I believe my case at Leicester played a major part in influencing a change in the compensation rules governing football managers' contracts. My case was a prime example of a young manager at a great club who had done a great job, but was wanted by another club. In that case, there is a simple answer to it: if that club wants to speak to that manager, there ought to be a compensation clause in his contract, and if that clause is reached, then he's given the opportunity to move on. It's the same with sacking managers. People used to be put on 'gardening leave' left, right and centre, with the club knowing they couldn't move anywhere else and it used to be a real mess in those days. My contract was no different. I had a good contract at Leicester City and I was happy there, but something was going on that was about to change my mindset and my belief in what I wanted to do. It was a very tricky period for me and it ended up with meetings after meetings, almost daily and they became monotonous and each day, the board moved a bit further in the other direction or someone would say something to upset the chairman. You end up with a real mish-mash of ideas of who's saying what, and you end up not singing from the same hymn sheet, even though deep down, you want to. You could say it all got very 'messy'.

That season was so different for me as a person – it was a massive test of my mentality. It was the first season as a manager that I'd faced any degree of criticism, but I was suddenly hit with a season that didn't go to plan. Did I doubt myself? I guess I did to a degree. When is the best time for a manager to leave a football club once things turn against you? That is a very hard question to answer, but one thing that stands out in my mind was the amount of criticism I received during the last few months as Leicester City manager. No matter how much time you spend trying to improve your team if you're not doing very well you just get absolutely pummelled by people – the media, the fans and everyone else. It startled me, I don't deny that and it had an effect on lots of things in my life. If I had stayed as Leicester manager for the whole season, would we have been relegated? That's the unanswered question, but the fact is, that's exactly what happened to my replacement, Mark McGee.

Chapter 8

RETURN OF THE PRODIGAL SON
Aston Villa manager: November 1994–February 1998

"Do you like this tie, Brian? It's a Helsingborgs tie. It's very expensive, is this tie, because it cost me nearly £1m, because they knocked us out of the UEFA Cup, and that's how much money I lost with going out of the European competition"
Sir Doug Ellis, former Aston Villa Owner and Chairman

While I was Darlington manager, I'd been mentioned in the media about becoming Villa manager, probably as far back as 1990, but I knew I wasn't quite ready for that sort of challenge; however, fast forward three or four years and several playoff finals later with Leicester City, I was totally ready for such a massive club; I knew then, I could take anything on. Having said that, I did stop for a few minutes and think to myself, "I wonder if...", but, I didn't get too excited.

Three days after quitting Leicester City in controversial circumstances, I applied for the Villa job, vacated by Ron Atkinson. I was given an appointment to meet Mr Ellis at his home, along with Steve Stride, Villa's Operations Director. Word had obviously got round that I was being interviewed because the street outside his house in the quiet village of Little Aston in Sutton Coldfield was rammed with media men. I remember the last time I met Mr Ellis in such a formal way was as a 15-year-old apprentice, but now I was meeting him to become Aston Villa manager. I'd gone full circle – the prodigal son had returned. However, I was now a completely different person. I was an adult for a start and I was hopefully about to take on one of the biggest jobs in English football.

I had a brilliant meeting with both Mr Ellis and Steve Stride, where they laid out the concerns they had with the team. They had only won a handful of games at that stage in the season (November), and they told me there was some money to spend on players if I so wished. I also made it clear to them that it wasn't money that was motivating me and told them it was the right time for me to do this job. I felt right for the job, based on my previous management career with Darlington and Leicester. I'd just taken Leicester City to the Premier League and had won back-to-back championships with Darlington, so I firmly believed in myself. Obviously, it was a massive step up, but I stressed to Mr Ellis that I had a different way of playing which could benefit the Villa team and it was a system I believed 100% in. I was also aware that I was going into a different type of environment from what I'd been used to before. I would be going into an experienced dressing room and would have to change the whole dimension of how the team prepared and played in football matches. I was under no illusion that I'd have to change certain players' mindsets, but it was a challenge I would willingly take on. I was also aware that I couldn't just change the system overnight, bearing in mind we were mid-season, so I knew I would probably have to watch a few games first, before pushing on the system I wanted to play. The main short-term aim was to push Villa up the league and away from the danger zone. All of those things were discussed at the meeting and my ideas went down well.

Following in the footsteps of one of the most flamboyant personalities in the game (Ron Atkinson) was no mean feat. I'd always had a great respect for Ron, how he dealt with his players and how his teams played, but we were poles apart in some respects; in terms of how my teams played, how I organised my teams and my mentality as a football manager.

I so wanted to do the job and I wanted to keep the club in the Premier League. I sensed how worried they were about the position the team were in. I didn't ask for a bonus; I didn't ask for a huge salary, in fact, I remember saying to Steve Stride that we would talk about my contract when the season ended in May. The salary on offer was only slightly more than what I was earning at Leicester, but that wasn't an issue. It was more than enough for me. I just wanted to prove to them I could do the job.

The job was offered to me there and then and I was announced to the media on 25th November 1994, my 41st birthday. I hadn't even realised the significance of the date, to be honest. I knew I had a hell of a squad to work with; I knew the job came with an impressive stadium; I knew I had money to spend, but the only drawback was that the shelf life of Villa managers started to run out after three years, with Mr Ellis in charge.

John Gregory phoned me and he asked me if there was anything doing at Villa, so he joined me from day one. We go back a long way; we played together for Villa lots of times, including up front on the odd occasion. In fact, John and I played there against Spurs in a 4-1 win – the game where Ozzie Ardiles and Ricky Villa made their debuts. So, we knew each other well enough for me not to think twice about bringing him back as my first-team coach. Allan Evans also followed me out of the door at Leicester and he became my Assistant Coach.

My life had been a series of challenges and this was simply the latest of them. I wasn't coming to Villa simply to be a manager; I wanted to be a successful manager, winning honours. I had been successful for the last five years and that was the way I wanted it to continue to be. I didn't have any problems getting on with the big name players and I wasn't going there to be awkward. I wanted to be creative. There wouldn't be any great changes in style. I wanted a winning team, but I wasn't going ask players to perform in a way that was foreign to them.

****

I still wasn't 100% fit and well following my back surgery, but I was fit enough to take my first training session at the club's Bodymoor Heath training ground. First impressions are always important for people like myself and I remember how jovial the lads were when I took my first session; how energetic they were; how much banter was around the place, so I didn't need worry about that side of things; however, day one was very much an eye-opener. The group seemed happy enough and because of that, you sometimes wonder whether they're a little too happy. I could see immediately, there were some decent players, some good players and some great players in the group. Sometimes, when a new manager arrives, players can be quiet but that group of lads were buzzing. With that in mind, I decided to set them a little challenge, which would basically allow them to be loud and experimental. I set the lads up on a pitch, 10 outfield players and a goalkeeper, told them they weren't playing against anybody, but the maximum they could have was two touches.

I wanted them to re-enact a football game. They had to move and pretend they had someone marking them, communicate with their teammates at all times and generally, act out a game situation. It turned out to be the quietest session I've ever seen. There's a lot to be said about shadow football; you have to be able to show off on the football field; you have to be communicative; you have to move around. That told me that the session was almost beneath that group of players. It was the worst session I've seen. Yes, they were a group of experienced, international players who knew how to play football, but I just wanted them to act out a situation without an opposition in one and two-touch football. I'd done that session loads of times before that day, and I've done it loads of times since and I'd do it today, if I was still managing. Sometimes, as a coach, I would step in and suggest a player did something different to create movement. I hate my teams playing in straight lines, the way a 4-4-2 formation is set up; two wide players running up and down in straight lines; two midfielders run straight through the middle; two strikers up top occasionally change position with each other. It's a very basic, but disciplined approach, but for me, an unattractive way of playing football.

Funnily enough, in the canteen after that session, that same group of lads were as loud and leery as they were before the re-enactment. I knew then, they were a good group of players. However, I also ascertained that they wanted to do it the way they wanted to do it, and that meant I had a big decision on my plate. I had to win this lot over or make a lot of changes.

It was clear that it was time for me to make some changes and I was determined to do it from day one. I was absolutely determined to change the ways and means of what was going on at the club. When you go to the training ground, put your gear on and walk onto the training pitch, that is work; being in the canteen afterwards, jumping up and down and being loud is not work. The training ground is a place where players try to improve themselves and try to prove how good they are. It's a place to learn and to work, no matter how good they are. I just felt that work ethic wasn't there at that time.

It's easy to remember my first game in charge at Villa because it was on day three, a home game against home Sheffield Wednesday in the Premier League, with Trevor Francis their manager. A lot of people were delighted to see me in the dugout and I received an incredible reception from the 25,000 fans. I was looking forward to the game, even though I was a little bit nervous. We were at the wrong end of the table so I was looking for a reaction from the lads. It was important to start winning games.

We played well but drew the game 1-1, our goal coming from Dalian Atkinson. When you're down at the wrong end of the table, you can play well and not get the result you need. I learned a lot more about the group, which was a positive, after the first game.

In the next game, we played away against Crystal Palace in the League Cup and we lost 4-1 on a night everything seemed to go wrong; Kevin Richardson was injured just before the game. It got worse when Ugo Ehiogu got sent off, but there were other things that added to the result. I knew as a football person that the little things didn't happen that night; players were getting into the wrong positions; certain players didn't need to do this or that, so it was an opportunity for me to step in after the game and say, "Look fellas, I'm manager here. Like it or lump it and what I've seen in the first week isn't what I want to see, and we will do it my way. It will be done the way I want it to be done."

After that game at Selhurst Park it was the time I started to implement my system using three centre-backs. I looked at the group and decided not to play that way at first, but the defeat at Palace set the tone for me to try one or two things out, maybe earlier than I'd anticipated. We then went on a bit of a run, losing only two of 15 games in the league. My first three league games were all draws. The game following the Palace defeat was interesting: a visit to Filbert Street. The Sun newspaper had printed the headline, "JUDAS" on the front page. I remember receiving a phone call from a friend of mine at 7:30am, "Have you seen the headlines in the newspaper? I think you should nip out and get one." So I did, and you can imagine how I was confronted with that when our team bus arrived at the Leicester City ground. I'd only been gone a few weeks and every single Leicester fan was butchering me, shouting obscenities at me from start of the game to the end, as I stood in the opposition dugout. We drew 1-1 and it was awful. It was the first time in my life that I'd been hammered by opposing fans. I experienced the other side of football that day. The worst side of football, that's for sure. The only order of the day for me was to get there and then get out of Filbert Street (in one piece).

During that spell, we had some great results, notably a 3-0 home win against Chelsea and a 0-0 draw at Highbury. I also signed Ian Taylor from Sheffield Wednesday after doing a deal with their manager, Trevor Francis. Tayls was an interesting story, because I was advised to sign him when I was manager of Leicester, and he was playing for non-League outfit, Moor Green. However, Port Vale signed him in 1992, and then he went to Sheffield Wednesday two years later. When we played Wednesday at Villa Park, in my first game as Villa manager, Tayls played on the right of midfield in a 4-4-2 formation as an out-and-out wide player. He wasn't the quickest in the world, but he could run all day long at good pace. He had outstanding energy and I remember looking at him then, thinking, "Crikey, that's the lad I'd been recommended; I should have done something about it." In my Villa team, I was looking for energy in the middle of the park so I spoke to Trevor about a £1m deal plus Guy Wittingham. Lo and behold, Tayls was a massive Aston Villa fan so for him, it was a no-brainer to sign for us. He said to me, he only wanted to sign for Villa. It's very difficult turn a club like Villa down if you've got some affection for it. Tayls went straight into that three-man midfield formation, where he could run up and down the field and show his energy and enthusiasm all day long. As it happened, Tayls scored his first goal in that game against Chelsea, which was my first win as manager.

Things were beginning to pick up and people were warming to the new system; we weren't pulling up any trees, but we certainly weren't being battered by anyone. We were solid and closer to winning games than losing them. I felt the system was working; the lads were beginning to adapt to the way I wanted them to, and it gave me the confidence to try a couple of transfers. I always liked the thought of signing ex-Under 21 internationals who were playing league football, perhaps not necessarily in the top flight, but probably playing in the second tier. The two players I was looking at were Tommy Johnson and Gary Charles, who were playing for Derby County at the time and I thought they were the best players in Division One. I quickly struck a deal to bring both those players in and all of a sudden, people began to sit up and take notice of us. The team, too, knew I wanted to change things around and I'd brought in three new players in the space of no time. Some of the older players like

Guy Wittingham for instance, left the club, as I've mentioned and also Kevin Richardson.

In January, we won four and lost one in the league and FA Cup games and that golden spell won me the Manager of the Month award. As most managers will testify, it was probably the worst thing that could happen, because it very often signals a defeat in the next game, and lo and behold, we lost the next league game to Manchester United at Old Trafford. However, in the following game, we went 1-0 down to a Warren Barton goal at home to Wimbledon, but ended up putting seven past them, which was unreal. Dean Saunders (Deano) scored a truly fantastic individual goal from outside the box that day. Deano was a really good player and I was getting him and Yorkie to play together, which I liked as a partnership. Scoring seven goals against a team like Wimbledon was a fantastic performance because they were a side that didn't give much away.

That Wimbledon game may not be considered a classic to most fans, but for me it was a brilliant day, and to win 7-1 against any team is immense. You don't score seven goals in many Premier League games. We played at an unbelievable tempo and worked hard to get back into the game. I had a theory whenever we played Wimbledon that we should keep the ball on the pitch; not to give free kicks away; not to give silly fouls away and not to let them have any long throw-ins. It was as though we would allow them to have the ball and their game was all about getting involved with the opposition. If you let them play, they actually gave the ball away to you. That was the game when the three at the back formation was firmly established, the start of things to come, with Shaun Teale, Paul McGrath and Steve Staunton (Stan), with Gary Charles and Bryan Small as wing-backs, Tayls and Townsend in the middle and a front three of Yorke, Saunders and Johnson.

Tommy Johnson scored our second and third goals to open his account for us; he showed what he had to offer that day. He was one of the best in a one-on-one situation as I've said before, and he's absolutely lethal, even though you wouldn't think it looking at him before any game, where he was the most nervous character you could imagine. It's well documented that he was very often sick before a game, but once he got onto the pitch, my word he was an absolute livewire. With the score at 3-1, a Steve Staunton corner rifled into the box found the feet of Shaun Teale, but his shot was blocked but it only found Tommy who side footed it into the net for his hat trick. From being 1-0 down, we went into the break 4-1 up. I was telling the lads at half time just to keep the ball on the ground and don't give too much away, and if we could get one more it would finish the game. Against a team like Wimbledon, if you start changing your game you could get caught out, but we didn't that night. With Tommy and Yorkie playing well, it was only a matter of time before Deano stepped into the action – and he certainly did. There was a mix-up in the middle of the park with Tayls and Steve Staunton, but the ball landed in the path of Deano, 35 yards out, and he half turned; you don't normally expect him to shoot from that distance but he absolutely rifled one in to the top corner. We were flying, and then we were awarded a penalty in the 66th minute when their goalkeeper brought down Tayls and Deano converted the kick and it was six. I think Yorkie got our seventh right at the end to top it all off.

After that game, I sold Bryan Small to Bolton; he was a great lad, but I wanted him to play a lot of football and we'd already had Steve Staunton in that position. He played really well in that Wimbledon game and I wanted to reward him for his honesty and loyalty.

The victory over Wimbledon gave signs of us being able to continue for the rest of the season along the same road; that result occurred during a period when we'd started to play really well in the league; we'd had a good January and first part of February, but we needed to continue the form. It also gave me signs of what Yorkie could be capable of doing for us, and that he had to play up top. Although it wasn't that game that made my mind up about where to play Yorkie he had really impressed me, by the way he took his goal. He was set up in a one-on-one situation with the goalkeeper after Deano played the ball to him. He dummied the 'keeper and chipped it over him. For most of the game he played out on the right and kept darting in and out, and that had an impact on me.

It was really a defining game for me, not only because it showed me what Yorkie could do, but it also told me how important players like Taylor, Townsend, Charles and Johnson could be for me and the team. The whole team played the way I wanted them to play during the Wimbledon game, and for me that was crucial for my future management career at Villa.

However, shortly after that game, the wheels came off and it seemed everybody switched off because we only won a few games until the end of the season. I don't know why, because we weren't safe in the league by any stretch of the imagination. Then I had the biggest wake-up call in my managerial career, in a game that sticks out in my mind still to this day. We played Leicester City at home on 22nd February 1995 and I genuinely wanted to beat them for lots of reasons. We'd just signed Franz Carr from them, as a squad player more than anything else. Franz was ideal as a substitute; he was good to have around the squad; he was quick and could play in different positions; he did a good job for me when I was at Leicester, so I knew him inside out. I was beginning to build a bit of my own territory in the ranks of how things were going to be and I was feeling good about things. However, we were 4-1 up with about 10 minutes to go and I thought I'd give Franz a run out, and also give Dalian Atkinson 10 minutes. Dalian had been hit with a few injuries and Dwight had been playing with Deano, so it was the right time to give him a run out to test his fitness.

Well, things didn't turn out the way I'd expected, because that final 10 minutes was the worst 10 minutes of football I have ever encountered. We ended up drawing the game 4-4 and it hurt me, and the 30,000 Villa fans in the stadium that evening, so much. It was an unbelievable game, not just because it was Leicester City, but the fact that I had taken my eye off the ball and I was in a situation where I'd won Manager of the Month and we'd gone on a great run, losing only to Manchester United and we'd climbed to 10th in the league. At 4-1, we completely relaxed and ended up giving away three cheap goals. It felt like a defeat after having been in control of the game.

That so called 'defeat' against Leicester signalled a downturn in form, so much so we lost three out of the next four games. We looked as though we were safe in the league, but all of a sudden, I could sense there was something not right. I'd signed some younger players and some of the older players probably thought it was time for change. We had slipped a bit, so much so we drew 0-0 at home to Coventry City and normally we'd have beaten them. We played West Ham in the next game at home, and lost and I remember a young Rio Ferdinand playing in mid-field and he was outstanding, leaving Harry Redknapp gloating about him. All of a sudden, we'd been dragged back into a scrap, until we won our game away at Ipswich and drew at Palace, to ease some pressure. However, our next three games all ended in defeat, against Chelsea, Arsenal and Leeds.

Towards the end of that season, Dwight really started to shine, and at Leeds, he played so, so well on that day, but we ended up losing to a Carlton Palmer goal. I thought to myself after that game that I saw something for the future and hoped I could get the chance to put it into practice. Deano was a great player, but there were a few rumblings from his agent that it was time for him to move on and there were a couple of teams interested in him. I initially said I couldn't move Deano on during the season, and I told his agent I was open to a move after the season had finished. However, Dwight had played magnificently at Leeds alongside Deano, and that told me Dwight was good enough for that role in the formation we played, so in the end I decided to move Deano on before the end of the season. Dalian was another striker I liked, and he used the same agent as Deano, and there were moves afoot for him, too. Of course, selling those two lads meant looking for replacements, but with three games left I couldn't bring in reinforcements until the summer; we needed to stay in the Premier League and we weren't quite safe at that stage.

Those last three games were massively important to us, and our season. We drew 1-1 with Manchester City at home; we beat Liverpool 2-0 at home, with Yorkie scoring a brace, and almost securing our position in the league. We needed to go to Norwich for a draw or win, and Steve Staunton scored in the first 10 minutes and we managed to draw that game, but more importantly, our main relegation rivals, Crystal Palace were 4-0 down in no time and we were virtually safe at half-time. It could be said that the last dozen games of the season proved to be a testing time for me as manager of Aston Villa.

Straight after the game at Norwich, I drove home and immediately started to think about the next season; thinking about the highs and lows of the season just gone; thinking about the sort of things I needed to do; thinking about the type of players I required; thinking about which of the senior fellas I wanted to move on. I had so many thoughts going through my head on that long drive back to the Midlands. All the lads I'd inherited and brought in were good players in their own right, and they all had agents who were capable and competent enough to look after them. There were some great characters in that dressing room when I took charge, the likes of: John Fashanu, Deano, Steve Staunton, Paul McGrath, Andy Townsend, all unbelievable characters and players, but I knew it needed freshening up for the next season. I needed to mix it up a bit but I had to find a balance in there. I knew I wanted to keep Mark Bosnich (Bozzy) in goal; I wanted to keep McGrath, Staunton and I wanted to make Townsend captain. I saw that in him from day one. By the end of the season, I'd changed the vibe of the dressing room in such a short space of time. I'd brought in some young, vibrant players, energetic and all keen and they were the immediate future of Aston Villa. Another thing that went through my head was the fact that I'd survived my first season and it was a massive test of my management skills, but more to the point, it was a great sense of achievement for me personally. The period between January and mid-February convinced me I was getting close to something special.

It had been a hard 12 months for me personally, following on from the Leicester episode to guiding Villa to safety at the end of that 1994–1995 season. I was happy to have a smile on my face at last. I was determined throughout that first summer to revamp the group even more. I didn't want a massive squad, but I did want to tinker with it. I knew I could rely on the senior lads, but I just needed to find another three or four younger players to complement the group and that would be a squad that would suit me and a squad that would be energetic and enthusiastic enough to challenge.

****

I was desperately determined to resurrect the fortunes of this incredible football club, following the dismal first season, which saw us narrowly survive in the Premier League. We lost some big senior players, the likes of Earl Barrett to Everton, Dean Saunders to Galatasaray, Graham Fenton to Blackburn, Guy Wittingham to Sheffield Wednesday, Dalian went off to Fenerbahçe, Fash retired due to injury, Shaun Teale went to Tranmere, Kevin Richardson went to Coventry and Ray Haughton went to Palace. Also, Nigel Spink, who'd incredibly been at the club since 1977 when I was a player at Villa, went across to West Brom, having served the club for nearly 20 years. There were some younger players that we lost too, people like Bryan Small, who probably wouldn't have got a game in the first-team anyway.

Talking of Graham Fenton, he was also known as 'Rab' or 'Rab C Nesbitt', because he was the scruffiest little so-and-so at the club. Graham came to me a few times about not being in the first team. He'd played a lot under Ron Atkinson, so in the end we fixed up a move to Blackburn Rovers for £1.5m and told him to speak to his agent to sort the deal out. However, some hours later I received a phone call from someone at Blackburn saying the deal was off and they couldn't sign him because of his attire. "We expect the lad if he's going to turn up to sign for us to be, well looking a bit better than Graham looked." said the Blackburn representative. Apparently, when Graham went for his interview at Ewood Park, he hadn't had a shave for five days, wore a baggy pair of shorts, no socks, a pair of flip-flops and a scraggy tee shirt. To be honest, they must have taken one look at him and thought, "No, no this isn't what we want." I called his agent shortly after hearing the deal had fallen through and asked him if he'd gone up to Blackburn with him, but apparently he couldn't go for whatever reason, so Graham had gone on his own as the deal had been agreed by his agent. I told him he was in danger of losing the sale purely based on his attire, and Blackburn weren't happy. The agent then got onto the club and made all the excuses under the sun on behalf of Graham and proposed another date for them to meet him. The agent got to Graham, told him to tidy himself up and took him to Blackburn a couple of days later, when the deal finally went through.

The summer of 1995 saw a massive turnaround of players, incoming and outgoing. Most of the players that left were big players, and exceptionally good players from the Ron Atkinson era. I've already mentioned some of the outgoings. Of course, with departures at any club, it usually means new faces coming in. We brought in the likes of Gareth Southgate from Palace and Mark Draper from Leicester; we'd already brought in Gary Charles and Alan Wright, amongst others. Gareth was a player who I spotted at Palace; he was a versatile player, and the right age for my team. He had a good pedigree, having played a lot for Palace (152 games) and he was one of those players I wanted to put on my list to enquire about. I think Ron Noades was the chairman of Crystal Palace at the time, and I asked Mr Ellis to enquire about the availability of Gareth. Listening to Mr Ellis and

Ron deal over a football player was just incredible. It was like dealing on the stock market; every time Ron put a few quid on, Mr Ellis would take a few quid off because he didn't agree with him – and vice-versa. They laughed and messed around with each other over the phone for hours until a deal was struck. It was like, "You should pay more because of...", and Mr Ellis would respond in kind, "You should get less because..." In the end, the two chairmen came to an agreement and a £2.25m deal for Gareth was reached, which was perfect for me.

We bought Drapes for £3.25m. I'd always thought he was a Premier League player and he was one of the loveliest lads I've come across in football. He was a big asset to the younger looking dressing room. People like Julian Joachim came into the club from Leicester as well. I'd always wanted to sign him, as I'd given him his debut as a young kid at Leicester. He was an unbelievably explosive player who struck the ball so well it was untrue. Technically at times he wasn't the greatest, but in a one-on-one situation with goalkeepers, he was in his element. He and Tommy Johnson were ruthless in those circumstances.

Aston Villa have always had a reputation for trying to sign talented players, and one of the most enigmatic characters and one of the finest ever English players in the modern game almost signed for the club during the summer of 1995, well I say 'almost', in truth he was nowhere near signing, but we tried. Paul Gascgoine (Gazza) was at Lazio and their were rumours he wanted to leave, so Mr Ellis and our Club Secretary, Steve Stride, went to see him in Rome, even though everybody knew he wouldn't come to us. I think Mr Ellis and Steve had a dinner meeting arranged one day, but Gazza couldn't make it. However, he turned up for breakfast the next morning. As the story goes, Mr Ellis had left half his breakfast and when Gazza came down, he finished off Mr Ellis's meal. Gazza didn't really take the meeting seriously, as he and his mate, Jimmy 'Five Bellies' were messing around and started calling Mr Ellis "Dougie". Mr Ellis took it all in good spirits, though. Gazza eventually signed for Rangers in the summer of 1995.

Talking of Gazza, I did get to manage him later on in my career, be it in Steve Walsh's testimonial game. Gazza came along with DJ Chris Evans, who was a good friend and part of a 'double act' if you like. Gazza was an incredible character and was fantastic in the dressing room. However, I was concerned for him because he was drinking Red Bull and Brandy in the dressing room, and I kept asking him if he was OK. Gazza kept saying he would be fine, and in the game he was fantastic, captaining our team and doing his usual bits of brilliance on the ball and generally entertaining the crowd who had come to see him. How he performed like he did after drinking Red Bull and Brandy (not just one, mind) I just don't know. There was one instance where Steve Walsh's All-Star team were awarded a penalty and the next thing we knew, Gazza's in goal, trying to stop it. When we get back into the dressing room at half-time, I looked at Gazza and was really worried about him, and said to him, "Look Paul, I think it's a good idea if you have a rest now; you've done fantastically well, but we've got a lot of people here and I think everybody needs to have a game." I said it only out of concern, and I knew I had upset him because his face suddenly dropped to the floor. I then had a chat with the other lads, and by the time I turned back round to speak to Gazza again, he'd disappeared. I was thinking, "Oh my God, what have I done?" When I asked somebody if they'd seen Gazza, he said he'd walked out of the dressing room door. I thought the worst and that I'd really upset the lad. When we all went out for the second-half, lo and behold he was in the other team. So, he walked out of our dressing room into the Leicester dressing room, put a Leicester shirt on and walked out and played the full second-half. I have to say it was a classic day, and just about summed Gazza up. I think by then he'd retired, but by God, what a talent he was.

In fact that wasn't the only time I managed Gazza. He had also played in a game for me when I was at Darlington. It was a charity match just after we moved into the new stadium. Again, before the match he was in the dressing room drinking his Red Bull and Brandy, but as he ran out onto the pitch, he'd had so much booze that he tripped over as he stepped onto the grass and just laid there for 15 seconds. It was very comical.

I often wonder what would have happened if we'd signed him at Villa; those antics on and off the pitch at those two games reminded me that I might actually have had a lucky escape in not signing him. However, in his heyday and at his best, he would have been absolutely fantastic for us and the Villa fans would have loved him.

However, the talking point of the summer was a young 21-year-old from the former Yugoslavia called Savo Milošević.

He was a player whom I had been keenly interested in for some time as a proven goalscorer in his native Yugoslavia (now Serbia). He made his name at Partizan Belgrade, scoring 65 goals in 98 appearances, and had broken into the Serbian national side. I'd studied lots of videos of him and spoken to other managers about Savo, and I liked what I saw. He was a left-sided centre forward who had a tremendous touch for a kid and probably should have scored more goals than he did. I thought he would be ideal for us, playing alongside Dwight; I couldn't get the pair out of my head – that was the partnership I wanted to form.

I'd been informed that Savo was available for transfer. The agent was a well-known agent whom I'd had dealings with before, so it was a no-brainer, at least to meet him in person, and a meeting was arranged in Belgrade.

There's a funny story when I flew out to Belgrade with Mr Ellis to talk to Savo. We were in the air and Mr Ellis told me, out of the blue, "Brian, I suppose you know you're taking me into a war zone, don't you?" Of course, I didn't realise at the time, not having read the newspapers for some time, so it came as a bit of a shock. When we landed in Belgrade, we were ushered through security as there was a massive queue and as we were going to the football ground, we had an escort and were given special permission to get past security. Once we got to the ground, we started contract negotiations and they lasted the whole day. Outside it was a very strange and eerie atmosphere, but once we got inside the club, there were things going on and it seemed like any other football club. His club wanted to sell Savo, but also wanted a sell-on clause built into the transfer. Money was king in a place like Serbia at that time. Partizan wanted it and we had it, and they made no bones about it, and tried to squeeze even more money out of us. In fairness to Mr Ellis, he didn't give in very easily and gave as good as he got; he was in his element, even in that environment; he knew exactly what he wanted and knew his financial parameters. Mr Ellis wouldn't budge and would not go over his limit – and fair play to him that he didn't.

Of course, when you sign a foreign player, the communication side of the negotiations is sometimes an issue and can be a little bit awkward. Although Savo didn't speak English, his representative did, but as ever they very often spoke in their native tongue in front of us and you began to think, "I wish I knew what they were saying". For me, it was a big learning curve. While I'd

As Villa manager at Norwich in the last game of the 1994–1995 season - we managed to cling on to survive in the Premier League

DARLINGTON F.C.

1990 ——— "the family club" ———

Back row, left to right: GARY HYDE, PAUL EMSON, KEVAN SMITH, JIM WILLIS, JOHN BORTHWICK, GARY COATSWORTH.
Middle row, left to right: DREW COVERDALE, DALE ANDERSON, KEITH GRANGER, NIGEL GRANGER, NIGEL BATCH, MARK PRUDHOE, PAUL WILLIS, DAVID CORK.
Front row, left to right: LES McJANNET, NEIL ROBINSON, ARCHIE STEPHENS, FRANK GRAY, RICHARD CORDEN (Chairman), BRIAN LITTLE, ANDY TOMAN, MARK HINE, DAVID CORNER.

FOUNDED 1883

I designed the Darlington kit for the 1990–1991 season

Celebrating promotion to the Premier League with Leicester City

Ian Taylor – my first signing at Villa

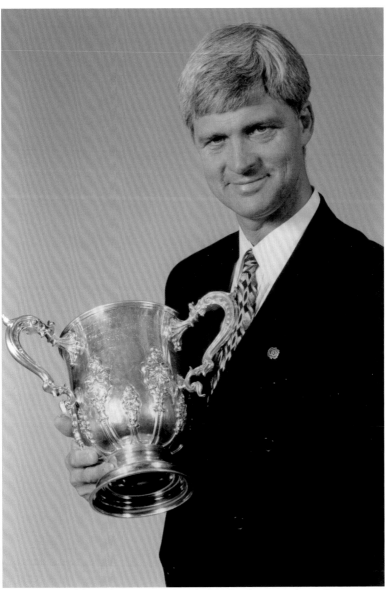

Holding the League Cup in 1996 – the proudest of
the three cups I won as a player or a manager

After the 1977 League Cup Final with 'Budgie' at Old Trafford

Scoring an overhead kick – I always liked to show off in
front of Ron Saunders because it wound him up

Celebrating with the Gaffer, Ron Saunders
after the 1977 League Cup Final

Celebrating victory after the 1977 League Cup Final

"Leave me a lone – I've had enough. I'll do it my way"

I was recovering from a back operation but still lead the
training – at the Leicester City training ground

One of the most iconic pictures of the me scoring
a goal against Bristol City for Villa in 1977

The late Sir Doug Ellis with myself and John Gregory.
I was proud as punch on my 41st birthday

Paul McGrath (AKA God) with Bryan Small
and myself at a reunion at Villa Park

played football in Europe for Villa, I'd only managed Darlington and Leicester previously, so this was a massive step up for me. I'd always signed players I'd had personal contact with, even if was just by shaking their hands as they walked off a football field, but I'd never signed a player from video evidence before. Now, here I was in Belgrade, a war zone, trying to sign a young player who couldn't speak a word of English and I hadn't even seen him play in the flesh.

Savo seemed nervous and you could see that in him. He must have been thinking, "Where am I going? What am I going to do there?" Having said that, we gathered from the club representative he genuinely fancied the challenge of playing in an ever popular and ever growing Premier League, which was still in its infancy. However, I wasn't even sure he knew who Aston Villa were, but that didn't matter to us.

At the end of those talks, which took all day, our hosts said they were going to take us out for a drink and something to eat. It was about 10:00pm and everyone had had enough by that time. So, bearing in mind everything was blacked out because of the troubles, we got in a taxi and drove around with no lights on, and there were no streetlights on, either. We had no idea where we were, or where we were going. Most shops were boarded up and the streets were deserted. It was like a ghost town. There we all were, sitting in the taxi and Mr Ellis was laughing and joking saying how excited he was, whereas, I was thinking it could be my last day on earth. After driving around the streets for an hour, we finally arrived at a big farmhouse. When we entered the building we were greeted by probably the biggest party I've ever seen taking place, in my life. There must have been about 200 people in the farmhouse, all having a good time. We'd been invited to the party just because we'd signed Savo. It was all very strange. You couldn't really write the script, it was so incredible. We stayed at the party for two or three hours, until the very early hours of the next morning. Mr Ellis and I didn't go mad, we just had a couple of drinks and tried to relax, and celebrate the fact we'd just signed a very talented striker.

When we eventually left the party, we were taken back to our hotel and then flew back to Birmingham later that day. I would imagine that day just sums up the whole of Mr Ellis's life. I bet he's had some incredible adventures during his time. A lot of chairmen wouldn't have gone to a war zone to sign a footballer, but Mr Ellis didn't bat an eyelid at the thought of it, all because I explained Savo was the right player and I wanted Savo to join Villa, and for that, I was truly grateful to him. Signing Savo in the summer of 1995 for £3.5m was a tremendous coup for us, and it was an incredible experience for me personally, one that I will never forget, and one that Savo won't forget either.

So, Savo arrived along with his girlfriend Vesna in Birmingham during the summer, shortly after we'd signed him and he was given a three-bedroomed furnished house in Sutton Coldfield. He was also given a car by the club. As he lived in an area where some of the other players lived, we alerted them to show Savo where the training ground was. That's how it was back then. Things weren't organised like they are now, and I don't think Savo had anybody from the club to look after him. When I look back at how little help there was from the club for Savo and his girlfriend at that time, and compare it to how it is now, and how much help foreign players get, we were miles behind the times back then. We'd signed a young lad who spoke no English and basically dropped him in a house with a car and told him to get on with it. We also expected him to be exactly where he needed to be for training at the right time. Incredible! How well that lad did in those circumstances is beyond amazing.

Savo was a character and it started off with the famous red bandana tied around his head. Mr Ellis, in all his innocence, assumed (wrongly) that he'd always played with the bandana around his head, but it started when Savo cut his head during a training game and the physio covered his head with a bandana to protect the cut, then he decided to play the first game of the season against Manchester City with the bandana on his head. That started a trend with Villa fans, and they started to buy bandanas from the club shop.

At last, I'd got together a very talented squad, not a massive squad, but the one that I wanted and one I thought could cause teams damage. We kept the pre-season very low-key; we didn't want to show off what we were doing; we didn't want to show-off our system; we didn't want to show-off our players. In fact, I think most of the pre-season took place at the training ground, behind closed doors. I never opened up to the public what the full team would look like. I wanted to keep things under wraps and surprise our opposition in the new season. We worked hard at the training ground and discovered Gareth Southgate was an excellent centre-back. While I'd signed him as a holding mid-fielder, alongside Andy Townsend and Mark Draper or Ian Taylor, as it transpired Gareth had performed well playing alongside Ugo and Paul McGrath. Looking back, I still say, "Wow!" because it was an incredible combination. Both Ugo and Gareth were both competent at stepping out with the ball; Paul was less comfortable on the ball, but was a powerhouse at the back; if he stepped out with the ball in the midfield area, he used to burst past players. Gareth was the same; he'd come out with the ball and use it in good positions and then get back into a defensive position.

I felt the balance of the side was great and I really fancied our chances for the new season. Andy Townsend was the captain, Tayls was a grafter and Drapes was a fantastic player who didn't realise how good he was. On the opening day of the season, we played Manchester United at Villa Park and we beat them 3-1, with goals from Taylor, Draper and Yorke in the first half and everybody could see what we were all about. United must have done some homework on us as they played three centre-backs to match our setup, but we absolutely hammered them in the first half. In the second half they switched to a four at the back and we saw how good a team they were. Believe me, they were a good team. They were young, hungry, enthusiastic and brilliantly talented. I remember saying after that game, "Man United will do well this season – you mark my words." Famously, a certain TV pundit didn't agree and wrote them off after that game as being too young, "They'll win nothing with kids..." I guess that was a compliment on how well we played, especially in the first half. We then travelled to White Hart Lane and beat Spurs 1-0, but then had a poor result at Leeds. We then went on a little unbeaten run until mid-October, including Savo's first goal for the club against Blackburn. That was the game he actually ran the full length of the pitch, then he slid down on his knees to celebrate with the travelling Villa fans. I think that was the day Savo endeared himself to the Villa faithful. I can still see that now. It was a special day for him.

We were up and running. We were flying in the league with only one defeat in nine games. We were beginning to show people that we were a 'different' team. an energetic team and a hard team to play against. The system worked for us magnificently well. Dwight Yorke was coming into his own and was showing the world he was a quality player. Savo and Yorke had

struck up a great partnership. At times, Savo was often criticised for missing chances, but his deft touches were sometimes
sublime. Ian Taylor's runs from box to box were causing teams
problems – he never stopped running. Most importantly, we had
a TEAM.

There were so many highlights during that season. We had a
game plan for every team we played against. The League Cup run
was special, starting in the second round against Peterborough,
and unlike today, where managers swap and change teams for
the lesser competitions, I fielded our usual first team. We wanted
to do well in the competition, so I fielded a full-strength team. We
won the game convincingly 6-0 at home in the first-leg, so that
gave me licence to do what I wanted in the second leg. I made a
few changes, but it was close to our first team and we drew that
1-1, and we were on our way. To win 7-1 on aggregate, you can't
ask any more than that. In the next round, we played Stockport
at home and just did enough to beat them 2-0. I rested Paul
McGrath and brought in Ricky Scimeca for a run out, but apart
from that, I again fielded a full-strength side. My way of thinking
was that we had to build up a desire to win the competition, so
I didn't often make too many changes. In the fourth round we
beat Queens Park Rangers 1-0 at Villa Park; again, my team was
at full strength. The Rangers team was strong too, with the likes
of Trevor Sinclair, Ray Wilkins, Kevin Gallen and David Bardsley.
The next game, the quarter-final, made us think a bit: Wolves at
home was a local derby, so it had a bit extra, a bit of an edge. We
now started to believe. It was the serious end of the competition with a potential semi-final on the horizon and nearly 40,000
fans thought the same. Tommy Johnson scored the only goal to
see us through a very tight game. Wolves had a good side, with
Steve Bull, Mark Rankine, Don Goodman, Mark Atkins and Dean
Richards. All of a sudden we're in the semi-final.

Now, several games stick out that season and the semi-final
against Arsenal was one of them. It was one of those special
games because of who my opposite number was. I've mentioned
Bruce Rioch many times so far; he had mentored and influenced
me for many years, both as player and as a coach and he was a
person whom I looked up to tremendously. It was really important for me to pit my wits against Bruce and it was an important
step in my football management career. Now, here I was about
to put my Villa side out against a very good Arsenal side that had

the likes of Seaman, Dixon, Keown, Winterburn, Merson, Parlour, Bergkamp and Wright. Wow!

In the first leg at Highbury, we were 2-0 down, but managed to claw back into it, with two goals from Yorkie cancelling out Bergkamp's brace. I think we were a little bit lucky to get back in the game, but having come away with a draw, we still had a chance and it was a brilliant result in the end. This may seem double Dutch, but that result saw us through to the final, because we had only to draw 0-0, or win the tie to get through, and we were at home. We certainly didn't play for a draw and we certainly didn't expect a 0-0, but in the end, those two away goals were just enough to get us through to the final, after the game remained goalless. That second-leg tie was probably one of the tensest games I've ever sat through as a manager. It was like watching a game of chess. However, from our point of view, our lads grew in stature that night. We were excellent. With the exception of Paul McGrath, who was injured, it was our strongest side. Stan Staunton stepped in to fill Paul's boots and he was outstanding.

Not only had we beaten Arsenal, we had also beaten a manager who taught me how to manage.

One other game that sticks out from that season was the League Cup Final against a decent Leeds side, on 24th March 1996. It was my fourth trip to Wembley in five years as a manager, and my third League Cup Final as a player or a manager, but it was probably my favourite final, given the fact I managed that Villa side. It was my first full season at the helm and I was about to embark on a League Cup final, although by that time, the competition had taken a back seat to the Premier League and the FA Cup.

I've said it was a decent Leeds team and it was, managed by Howard Wilkinson, but with names like Gary McAllister, Gary Kelly, Lucas Radebe, Gary Speed and Tony Yeboah, they were a side full of international players. It was a side that also included Andy D Gray, son of Frank Gray who was my assistant at Darlington. I'd known Andy since he was 10 years old, and for him to play in the final against my team, sticks out more than anything else.

The game itself went precisely to plan. If there was ever a perfect performance, then that was it. If I look back at the two finals I'd played in against Norwich and Everton, there was nothing between the teams on those days, but Aston Villa v Leeds United in 1996, in terms of the performance there was a gulf so big it was untrue. It was the most comprehensive and professional performance I've ever seen from a team of mine. I loved that team I sent out on that spring day in March 1996:

Bozzy in goal; Gary Charles and Alan Wright as wing backs; Ugo, Gareth Southgate and Paul McGrath in defence; Mark Draper, Ian Taylor and Andy Townsend in midfield; Savo and Yorkie up top.

I look at that team, not forgetting some of the lads I'd inherited, and it was my perfect selection; there were better players around, but the balance of that team was superb. To think I couldn't find places for Tommy Johnson and Steve Staunton tells you we had a very strong squad too.

Before the game, we were very relaxed; our preparation was fantastic; our commitment on the day was outstanding, and most importantly, the result was amazing. I was very proud of that team, and over 20 years later, I'm still proud of each and every one of those lads; I am still proud and privileged to have managed them. To win 3-0 the way we did, with goals from Tayls, Savo and Yorkie and to win a cup at Wembley was a brilliant feeling. I couldn't praise those lads enough after that performance and I was chuffed to bits. It certainly was a big feather in my cap.

So, we won the cup and Mr Ellis was beside himself, jumping up and down like a two-year-old. After the game, he walked into the dressing room at Wembley and stood there waiting to be showered with beer and Champagne by all the players (which he was). He then opened his mouth and said, "Right fellas, we're going on holiday. You can go anywhere you want to go to," and the unanimous response from the lads was, "Magaluf". Now, I've spoken to Ian Taylor about this since, and he reckons the lads didn't say that, but believe me, Tayls, they (you) did. If my chin could have dropped any further towards the floor, then it would have. Magaluf!

Well, we did all end up in Magaluf of all places at the end of the season, and it was carnage, but we did all have a great time. I still remember some of our players walking around the hotel in the middle of the night and telling them to go to bed. I couldn't help myself. There are still a few stories that will stay in Magaluf. However, seeing those lads enjoy themselves as much as they did was pleasing for me, especially after the season we'd just had, and they all deserved it – but Magaluf? Dear oh, dear. There were lots of places in the world I'd like to have gone and they chose Magaluf. All of those lads have grown up considerably since then, and they will look back at that decision and say, "Magaluf? Why did we say Magaluf?" They were young and daft at the time and we did it all the same. I can't believe I actually went there myself, but I did. Personally, I didn't really enjoy it, but it was a kind gesture from Mr Ellis for the lads more than anything.

Talking about Mr Ellis and all things Spanish, he'd very often slip in some Spanish words or phrases in conversations. Midway through any conversation with people, he'd come out with little words that made me laugh. Very often we'd be in a conversation and Mr Ellis would say something like, "Joan Gaspart is a very good friend of mine; he's the el Presidente of Barcelona Football Club, you know?" He'd continue with the conversation, then say something like, "When I'm with Joan Gaspart, I'd generally order lots of things; I could say, "un poco de mantequilla por favor", which actually means, "Some butter please?" Another classic would be when we'd board an aeroplane, and it didn't matter what airline it was, he'd say something like, "Tienes cacahuates maní por favor?" and that means, "Have you any peanuts, please?" It would always be totally random, and would happen especially when we were sitting in a restaurant. He'd think he was saying something really important but he'd say something completely rubbish. It really sums him up, because he wanted to make everybody believe he could speak Spanish – but, I'm not so sure he could, to be perfectly honest.

****

I really think teams that you manage are relevant to the divisions you're in; my Darlington team that won two championships in a row were by far the best team in the particular leagues during those seasons and I still have loads of affection for those lads; the Leicester team that I swapped and changed, built and rebuilt to get them into the Premier League were a great bunch of lads. We had a great team in 1977–1978 with the likes of Andy Gray, Gordon Cowans and John Deehan, and that was my favourite team that I played in, for sure; however, my 1995–1996 Villa team, without a doubt, even surpasses any of those teams I've mentioned.

It was just a fantastic year for us, one we all thoroughly enjoyed. I still pinch myself from time to time, thinking I took a team who had just survived relegation on the last day of the 1994–1995 season to fourth in the Premier League within a season. Not only that, but we won the League Cup and got to the semi-final of the FA Cup. Losing that semi-final was a major blow for me. We'd won the League Cup on the Saturday and went straight into an international break, with the team on a massive high. A lot of our squad went off on international duty; it would have been great if I could have kept the players at home; we could have settled the lads down and prepared for the Liverpool semi-final properly. Having said that, Liverpool were more experienced than us and we weren't as organised and as prepared as they were. It was no surprise we lost to Liverpool by 3-0 as they were one of my bogey teams. However, we played well and pressurised them for long periods, and for me, the scoreline flattered them a bit.

We had made huge progress in our first full season under my management. We'd also qualified for the UEFA Cup; fourth place would now have guaranteed us Champions League qualification, but in those days, it didn't. The season went well beyond our expectations, and everyone else's expectations for that matter. Big things were expected of us for the next season, 1996–1997.

We were always trying to improve and I felt we weren't quite right in our set-up going into the new season. The first question I had to ask myself was, "How do we follow that season?" I also asked myself, "What do we do different?" However, we had a few major blows towards the end of the previous season, with Gary Charles picking up a nasty injury for a start. We also let Paul McGrath go at the age of 36 in the autumn of 1996, after making 253 appearances for the club. I knew we had a number of players at the club who could play that role – younger players in Gareth Southgate, Steve Staunton, Ugo Ehiogu, Riccardo Scimeca and even a young Gareth Barry, who was coming through the ranks. Those guys were younger, fitter and trained every day, and sometimes they'd be knocking on my door asking to be in the team, which is just what you want as a manager.

Paul was known (and still is) as 'God' at Villa Park so it was a big shout for me to let him move on to Derby, but it was right for him, in all fairness. My thoughts were, he'd played the whole season before, helped us win the League Cup, but I could sense time was running out and the opportunity for him to play week in, week out somewhere else would have been a better one for him. The last time he played for us was in the September and four weeks on I think he knew he wouldn't be playing for us again. While I know he was bitterly disappointed, I needed to think about how many games would Paul realistically play in. The less games he played, the less chance I would have had in playing him in a long run of games if I needed him. Given the fact he never trained, he was nothing short of a phenomenon. Paul McGrath was a special player, but I made a decision that wasn't the easiest one I've ever made, or the most popular, and it's not one I live with easily now. Paul needed a focus and if he wasn't playing it was no good for him, and that would have possibly have brought more temptation into his life.

As a manager, you need to keep moving around and searching for different things if issues arise and you feel it needs to be done. I genuinely feel I did it all for his own benefit, and I would say that about anybody I've sold in my entire time as a manager. However, sometimes people rock the boat from time to time and you get the odd troublemaker you need to move out, but Paul wasn't one of those in any way, shape or form. I was once told never to brush things under the carpet – if you've got an issue you should deal with it now, not wait until next week or a fortnight or a year. That way, you do what you think is the right thing, and don't just wait for something to happen; you make it happen, and that's just what I did with Paul.

I look back and I know what a great player he'd been, but I think sometimes in management you have to make a decision that isn't going to be popular. I'm afraid it's the story of being a football manager: you'll never get the full blessing of everybody, but it was a decision I had to make for better or for worse. At the end of the day, I was trying to do the best thing for him, as well as the team, and that's what I tried to do for every player that I moved on. I ended up thinking to myself, "If he's not going to be in my team, he's going to be in a better place somewhere else." Given there was still an open transfer market (until the third Thursday in March) in place back then, you as a manager could effectively look after a player who had been out of the team for a while. Managers knew they could sell players on, but they also knew they could replace players, too. There was a lot more fairness and fair reasoning in the transfer market, back in those days, even though it wasn't perfect. However, nowadays the marketplace is different. January becomes such an outrageous period: managers have one month to get players out of the club, and then get players in and it ends up with managers signing players who expect to be in the team but aren't.

Any football fan can see an issue with any player, but will never know all of the things that go on behind the scenes. The football manager's door is the one the players knock on (or they did in those days) and he's the one who has the conversations with the players, and with Paul, it was an issue I dealt with in my own way. If I hadn't have sold him and he didn't play, it would have been worse for him, because he needed to play; it was getting harder and harder for him to play with the way the club was going, with us bringing in younger players, and Paul was 'old' for his age.

However, I will go on record here and now by saying Paul was the most talented player I have ever managed, based the fact he was in his 30s, had dodgy knees, didn't train and had problems off the field. For him to be able to perform the way he did was quite staggering. When you talk about Paul McGrath as a player, I think of words like 'brave', but I don't think people talk about him in that way very often. The amount of times there were boots flying around and you'd see his head in the middle of them all, heading the ball away showed he was unbelievably brave. He was also brave because, for someone to play with the pain he was in, must have been incredibly difficult. He defied the physics of a human body, and he was a genius on the field too. He read the game really well and was unbelievably quick for somebody who couldn't walk during the week; he had a football brain, if that makes sense. On a Saturday he would sprint 30 yards to get a flying tackle in, or put his head somewhere you wouldn't expect; he was just on a different planet. He was a major talent who had amazing technique; he could back heel a ball further than I could kick it forwards – it was all part of his repertoire.

Even though Paul lived in the North West, I made Paul come into training every day. It was my way of making sure he was looking after himself. He didn't train as such, but he kept himself in shape. We'd often let him join in an eight-a-side just to get his adrenalin going, but we didn't let him do it for very long. We knew all about his problems off the field with alcohol, and even during my time we'd 'lose' him for a day or so when he'd get himself into bother and fall off the wagon. It wasn't easy for me as his manager when that happened, because he'd have to sit in front of me, and his carers, to apologise for having a bad day. Watching someone who's an iconic figure and a great footballer, coming in to the office because the people who looked after him and trying to rehabilitate him were making him apologise for having a drink or two was not something I enjoyed It was quite a bizarre and uneasy situation.

You can't help but admire Paul. I'm one of his biggest fans and in the end, Paul got another 18 months or so out of football, and played a lot for Derby, in a team who struggled that season. As I said, it wasn't an easy decision to make. Was it time for Paul to leave Villa? Could I have kept him for another season? I'd never win those arguments with the fans, for sure, and in fact I don't want to win that argument, if I'm honest. I've bumped into Paul many times since and he's been great with me, so there were no sour grapes on his part.

It was a time of transition; you have to have those periods where people come and go; at some stage you have to turn your team around in order to improve.

Talking about people leaving, we also lost my first-team coach, John Gregory, shortly after Paul left for Derby. John had been with me for five years, and was at Leicester before joining me at Villa, so he was a big loss to me. I'd always told both John and Evo that I didn't want them to be my assistants or coaches forever, because at the end of the day, if they had any aspirations of becoming a manager I'd understand and wouldn't stand in their way. If I ever wanted to do something and someone stood in my way, I'd be gutted and I'd fight it. John had a similar background to me in many respects, because he had a spell at Portsmouth that didn't work for him, just like my spell at Wolves didn't work for me. So, I always felt John had something in sync with me, in that he had had a go at being a football manager and didn't get it right, but when that happens, deep down you will more often than not want to have a proper go at it. I always felt he'd want to be a football manager and I never had a problem with that. So when John came to me, around October 1996, and said he'd had an offer to be the manager of Wycombe Wanderers, I was obviously gutted, but I knew it would be the right fit for him. For a start, he lived in that neck of the woods and he knew people connected with the club. I'd always promised him that he if he ever wanted to go I'd do my best to see it worked out for him, so from my end, I had no problems with him taking the post. However, looking at it selfishly, I knew by losing John it would change the dynamics of what we were doing. We had a great three-pronged attack, which for five years together had worked and had been successful.

Whilst we were all completely different characters, and to be frank, I don't even think we've even been out at night together, we all knew our roles and it was all going swimmingly. As the manager, I obviously dictated what the roles were, decided on the systems, who was playing and the formation of the side. John was the one who dealt with the group for the day-to-day coaching and was close to the players, while Allan would mainly coach the defenders. John was very important for me because he was the life and soul of the group, but had a streak in him and could be 'Mr Bad Guy' or 'Mr Angry' when he wanted to be, which was funny to see. Most of the time he was great around the dressing room for lots of different reasons. I'd call him Peter Pan because he thought he was still 20, because he had so much energy. I remember John would come out into the tunnel area, stand with the door half open, and he'd be in there shouting things out to wind up the opposition, and then he'd shut the door and run back, so they wouldn't know who'd done it. He was forever shouting abuse at people, not in a nasty way mind, and it was so funny, but those were the sort of things I could never replicate, and nor could Allan. Then he'd have his tantrums on the sidelines; there was always a bucket of water or a drinks bottle at the side of dugout and on a number of occasions he kicked the bucket or bottle onto the pitch, over the subs or into the fans behind the dugout. I always ended up apologising to the poor fan that ended up soaking wet. Then there was the other side of him, after games, if we'd lost. John would sit in the corner and everybody would avoid him – nobody would dare speak to 'Mr Angry'. It was brilliant and very funny to watch. Everyone would come to me and ask, "Is Greggo ok? Can we go and speak to him, yet?"

Losing John was a massive blow to me and left a gaping hole. I've not known many (if any) John Gregory-type of characters. I knew I wouldn't find a like-for-like replacement for him. I didn't try and persuade him not to go; there was no argument about it at all because I didn't want to stop him, to be honest.

When John left, Allan Evans stayed on and Tony McAndrew and Kevin McDonald filled in the coaching roles. Kevin had unbelievable strengths as a football coach; he's probably one of the technically best coaches I've ever come across, especially with development coaching. However, he didn't have the same personality as John, but who had? Kevin did it his way, but I didn't expect him to do it John's way, or anyone else's way. In fact, Kevin set up training sessions in every way as well as John did, if not more so. Tony had worked with me at Darlington and Leicester so I knew his strengths inside out, too.

However, it just wasn't the same without John, which doesn't mean to say it was bad, but it was different. It was his personality that changed the whole dynamics of the set up. However as a team we still put in some great performances and by the end of that season we finished 5th in the Premier League.

As a manager, it's important to get good players in who have the right temperament. I felt pretty invincible at that time, being into my eighth season in football management and I was at the top of my game. The season before (1995–1996) I hadn't done much wrong in terms of the players I'd brought in. The likes of Ian Taylor, Gary Charles and Tommy Johnson, had all just moulded in very easily. We played a system with Savo and Dwight up top and in midfield we had Ian Taylor, Mark Draper and Andy Townsend as a three, but if one of them wasn't fit Tommy Johnson would slot in, although we'd change the system slightly, playing with two holding midfielders and then a 'diamond' up top, with a player, usually Tommy, playing in a number 10 role.

In fairness to Tommy, he was really good in his role, but he needed to play every week. It was still that era where players wanted to play every game, not that they don't want to play today, but I think they are more aware of squad rotation now than they ever were in the past, and the money thing has a lot to do with it now. Not only that, our squads were smaller in the 1990s, but even then, people were talking to me about expanding that squad and having more depth. As a manager in those days, every time you picked a team there were players who were unhappy. What I found was that people like Tommy Johnson were getting a little bit frustrated at being on the bench, especially if he'd scored the week before. Bear in mind we were still in an era of appearance money as well, and players like Tommy had more incentive to play week in, week out. Players who weren't playing had a double whammy, if you like; number one, they weren't in the team and wanted to play and number two, they didn't earn the same money as the players who were in the team. In short, players at Aston Villa were told how much they would get if they played, and told how much they would get if they didn't play, and in some cases it was almost double if they played. It wasn't like it is now, when most players receive a salary and are paid for being in a squad regardless. There seems to be more of an acceptance of not playing every game and of squad rotation because the player won't lose out because he's still picking up his salary.

I'd been alerted to a player called Saša Ćurčić and I'd watched him play a few times for Bolton and I thought he was outstanding in the number 10 role. I thought if we signed him he would give me a different option from Tommy Johnson, who was left footed and very direct, whereas, Saša was a dribbler and loved to come into the game from that number 10 role.

There were a few rumours flying around about Saša, mainly about his social life. He was, shall we say, a bit of a lad and maybe a bit of an eccentric who liked a night out and a bit of fun. Some people told me to be careful with him. However, that didn't deter me and I decided to run with it. I was right on board and felt I could handle him so we ended up signing Saša for £3.5m from Bolton Wanderers, who were managed by Colin Todd. Sasa was joining his former Partizan teammate, Savo Milošević. At the time, it was a massive signing for us and he was on good wages. He was a talented individual and we wanted to try and get another bit of quality into the side – something a bit different. I also thought it would help Savo settle in better.

At his first training session, I think everyone sat up and was taken aback a bit with Saša. He'd taken the ball and dribbled past a few people and hit it into the bottom corner of the net, which was absolutely brilliant. However, just as everyone was about to clap him and say "Well done", he jumped up, put his arms in the air, looked around at everyone and said, "3.5 million for me!" This was a player who marketed himself as 'the Yugoslavian George Best' so I guess that didn't come as a surprise. It was a lot of money in those days, but what he said probably made him look slightly big headed, arrogant and self-confident. I think his cards were marked with the lads from then on, because for the next 20 minutes I was trying to stop everyone kicking lumps out of him. I think it was his way of saying, "Look what you've bought.," but, although he showed what he had, it didn't go down with the players that way at all. From that day on, I told myself to keep an eye on that situation.

While I'm on the subject of Saša Ćurčić, there is a wonderful story I'd like to share. He'd been part of the group for a few months, in and out of the team and had played some great games for me. My physio at the time was a lad called Jim Williams, and players like Paul McGrath had leant on him for years. Jim was the 'go-to guy' for the players and he'd often ring me and let me know if anyone wasn't well or injured. In fact, Jim was usually the one person I'd answer the phone to late at night, after an issue I had with a player, but more about that later. Having said that, Jim would always pick the right time to ring me, but if it was urgent it didn't matter what time of night it was, I would take his call. It was a Friday night before a game and we'd had a great training session, everybody looked bright and I'd selected the team. However, Jim rang me very late at night to say there was a problem with Saša, even though he looked fine in training. I quizzed Jim, "Has he gone down with a sickness bug or something?" Jim's reply was a bit sheepish and I could tell by his voice it was going to be something ridiculous, "Err, nooo, Saša's actually in London," and there was a pause, then I replied, "Well, what's he doing in London? We've got a game at home tomorrow." Jim then said, "Yeah, I know. He's booked into a clinic in London and he's having his nose done tomorrow morning. He's having a nose job." I just couldn't believe what I was hearing; I thought Jim was having a laugh, but he carried on, "He's done it himself and he admits it, but he's having an operation on his nose. He's having his nose changed by cosmetic surgery." I paused to take the information in for a few seconds and said, "No? Seriously?" Jim was right to tell me, but I just couldn't take it in. But that wasn't the worst of it. So, I have a player the club spent nearly £4m on and the bottom line from Jim was, he wasn't going to be able to play for eight weeks because he's had a nose job. Brilliant!!

Certain things were going through my head at that stage, things like, how am I going to explain this to the Chairman? It was incredible and still to this day I can't get my head around it. I had two choices; number one, I sack him, or number two, I fine him two weeks money (which was the maximum you can fine a player) and we carry on from there. At the end of the day, the club had £4m invested in him so we chose to swallow the news and kept it as quiet as possible, within the club. I don't think that story ever hit the headlines and got out into the media even though when he came back he looked a completely different person. I'm not sure how many of his teammates noticed though.

Let's just say, Saša was hard work and we had to 'mop up' after him, several times in fact. After that episode, I don't think things were ever the same and we were looking for opportunities to move the player on.

We knew Gary Charles would be out for a long time after he broke his ankle towards the end of the 1995–1996 season so I had to replace him and had been alerted by an agent to a fella called Fernando Nélson Jesus Vieira Alves – imagine trying to put all of that on the back of his shirt, so we called him simply Nélson. He was playing for Sporting Lisbon at the time and I'd done my homework on him. According to the information I had on him, he was a nice, quiet person, very religious and who spoke perfect English. More importantly, Fernando was a good footballer who could play right back or left back, had played a lot of league football and had played at Under-23 level and full international for Portugal, so he fitted the bill as the perfect wing-back for me. I always liked to buy players who had played around 150 league games and had broken into the Under-21s of their country but hadn't got the break they wanted, so Fernando fell right into the niche of players I was looking for, and he was just the type of player I wanted to fill the gap left by Gary Charles.

Some of the information on players we receive as managers can be quite detailed, and some can be sketchy. For example, it may state whether the person likes a night out and a few beers, but in the information on Fernando was all very positive. I met him for the first time at The Belfry, before he signed, and I have to say the information I'd been given was spot on. He was a lovely lad with a good temperament and could speak quite a few different languages. However, when I signed Fernando, I realised just how needy European players can be. He was very meticulous and had to have people do things for him. He was a funny lad in a way, because as I got to know him, I found out he prayed before he went out onto the pitch and his kit had 'Jesus' written on. Even his playing shirt had 'I love Jesus' on it. While there's nothing wrong with that, it was different, but I have to say he was a really super lad.

CHAPTER 8: RETURN OF THE PRODIGAL SON

Even in 1996, the Premier League was big, although in its infancy, but there were more and more foreign players coming into the game, and Fernando was one of those who wanted to get into English football. I knew there would be no problem him fitting in. He knew Kevin Mason, who had also recommended a few of the other lads I'd signed, namely Tommy Johnson and Gary Charles, so Kevin would make sure his players would look after Fernando. All in all it just seemed an ideal signing for us at that time.

Having said all that about Fernando, there was one time, later in the season, that he did upset me. We were having some bad weather around the Christmas period, and it was chucking it down with rain and very windy, and I was fast asleep at 3:00am when my phone rang. It was Fernando and he said, "Gaffer, gaffer, my gate outside is banging against the house at night time. It's really windy and the gate is broken. Can someone come and fix it for me." I'm not going to repeat the exact words I replied to him, but the second word was 'off' and I slammed the phone down on him. It seemed that every time the foreign lads had a problem, they went straight to the top, and in this case it was me, whereas the British lads would know not to have phoned me and would have spoken to Ted Small in the morning. It was a phone call about the most ridiculous thing ever, and after that I started to switch my phone off at night. Incidentally, the lads ribbed him for weeks and weeks after that. As I've said before, I didn't usually pick up the phone late at night and after Fernando's request that night, Jim Williams became the only exception.

Outside of that one night when he got my wrath over the phone, he was never a problem. Another time, I remember Fernando was sitting next to Saša Ćurčić on the team bus and he was talking to him about how important Jesus was to him, and poor Saša was sitting there listening to him, uninterested. Fernando loved an audience when he was talking about his Godly thoughts and how he loved his religion, but he lost most of the other lads and I think he lost poor Saša that day.

The one thing that is always true about being a football manager is that things constantly change around you. Towards the end of the 1997 transfer window, we received an offer for Tommy Johnson from Celtic. Although the bubbliness in the dressing room was important to me, and the team, Tommy had got to the point that he wanted to play every game, but with Saša Ćurčić being around, he wasn't getting a start all the time, especially with Savo playing the role with Mark Draper behind him. To be fair to Tommy, he never moaned once, but had asked me about moving on. I'd always said to him if I ever got the right sort of offer, I would speak to him about it. It was late one night, I may have been in bed even, and I received a call from someone at Celtic saying they were very keen in talking to Tommy and they were prepared to offer £2.4m. I knew there and then that I'd just had the call I didn't really want. I didn't want to sell Tommy if I'm perfectly honest. As it was late at night I asked the guy from Celtic to call me back in the morning, which he did and we had a chat about him.

Tommy was probably the best finisher at the club. He hardly ever missed one-on-one chances, even in training. He had a wonderful left foot and a brilliant technique at finishing. He was massively important to me on and off the pitch. He's just a brilliant lad and for me, probably one of the best players to deal with. I didn't want to sell Tommy, but at the same time, it was Celtic, a massive club and I thought it would be a great opportunity for him. He'd win trophies and he'd play in a successful team; he'd be part of that team and I think he knew he'd go there and score goals. I always put myself in other people's position in times like that and I fully understood Tommy's view, and like all players back then, Tommy had to play to earn a decent amount of money and that was another factor in letting him move on. I wasn't the type of manager who would deny a player a chance to move on, so I owed Tommy the chance to join Celtic.

On the back of that conversation with the club, I had to call Tommy and tell him of Celtic's interest in him. The move happened and Tommy went to Celtic for just over £3m so it was a lot of money for Villa to turn away.

****

Winning the Coca-Cola League Cup in the previous season (1995–1996) gave us qualification to the UEFA Cup (now Europa League) and our first round tie was against a little known Swedish team called Helsingborgs IF. Truth be known, this is where I had a big learning curve, and I didn't think we were as ready as we needed to be. I remember going into the tie, not feeling 100% sure about things like the away goals rule, the extra-time rule and how European teams play.

Even though we must have had about 80% of the possession in the first-leg and drew 1-1 at Villa Park, we only had one shot on target (and scored through Tommy Johnson), and it has to be said we went into the return leg a little bit blind. It was a poor home result, but it was a result we should have got over. Unlike today, where most European football is on TV and every team knows every other team, playing away at Helsingborgs was a step into the unknown, that's for sure. We had prepared to the best of our ability, had them watched, but we really didn't know a lot about them, apart from obtaining a written syopsis of how they supposedly played. We tried to watch them at least seven times, but in reality we had only seen them play live once.

Having drawn the first game, I wasn't sure how to approach the second leg. I was asking questions of myself. Was there something I needed to do differently? Did I need to play a different system? I was set in my ways of playing three centre-backs and my team played in a set way and in general, it worked in the Premier League. We went there and played on the smallest pitch I can ever remember, a tactic a lot of teams used, but we just weren't used to it. We knew from the size of the pitch that they were playing for a draw and hoping to go through on the away goals rule. On the night we dominated the game, but we were up against a well-organised, strong, typically Scandinavian defence, with lots of people behind the ball. We were playing catch-up the whole game because of their away goal, but we couldn't score against them. Having previously only managed at Darlington and Leicester, I didn't know European football so I clearly wasn't ready for it and neither were the team. I think that shone through on the pitch. We just didn't do enough to win the tie and I felt they had the edge during both legs. It was my first real setback and was a bit of a reality check. It taught me a lesson in preparation and I said to myself, "If we get into Europe again, I need to be ready for it.

It wasn't a very happy memory, but looking back it was a lesson I think I learned from. I still blame myself and not the team, but it was an experience, although it was one that hurt for a long time. However, months afterwards, every time I went to see the chairman in the boardroom, he'd say something like, "Brian, Brian, come over here. This tie I'm wearing today cost me a million pounds, you know. Yes, this is a Helsingborgs tie. They knocked us out of the UEFA Cup and it cost us a million pounds, Brian, didn't it?" Very often, Mr Ellis would wear that very same tie and he'd say to people, "Do you like this tie?" and the other person would comment, "Yes, it's a very nice tie. Where's it from?" Mr Ellis would then make a point to tell them where it came from, and he'd tell them right in front of me, "It's a Hesingborgs tie. It's very expensive, this tie because it cost me a million pounds, because they knocked us out of the UEFA Cup, and that's how much money I lost with going out of the European competition." To be fair, it was his way of having a bit of a joke, but at the same time it was a dig at me, and in his own way, it was a way of saying to me, "Brian, if we are ever in Europe again, you must do better." It didn't bother me too much and the amount of times he reminded me of that result during the season was untrue. Still to this day, Mr Ellis reminds me of Helsingborgs, but those are the sorts of things you have to live with when your chairman is Doug Ellis.

We were also poor in the domestic cups. We lost to Wimbledon in the League Cup fourth round, In the FA Cup, we went out to Derby in the fourth round. It was a big disappointment after the tremendous run we had had in both competitions in the previous season. So, we fell flat on our faces in all the three of the cup competitions.

That second season in the Premier League went reasonably well and we finished a respectable fifth which was an achievement, but overall the season was a bit of a let down, after the marvellous season we'd had previously. One or two things during the season changed the dynamics of the group; however, we'd proven we were competitive and had proven ourselves in the Premier League as a solid, well-drilled team; we finished above Chelsea and Tottenham and we were really amongst the top teams. One of the games that stuck out most during that season was the game against Kevin Keegan's Newcastle side early in the season, when Mark Draper got sent off, Yorkie got a hat-trick and we still ended up losing 4-3. It must have been one of the most open games of football of that season. Despite the fact we lost the game, I thought we played magnificently well. Stevie Staunton played left-sided centre-back and had more possession than anyone else and also he must have passed the ball more than anyone else. We've had a conversation about that game many times since, with Steve saying I wasn't happy with his performance. As a centre-back, his job was to stop the opposition scoring, yet we leaked four goals and we have had friendly arguments about it several times. Steve was obviously thinking of his overall personal performance, and I was thinking of the four goals we let in, but that was always going to be a slight difference of opinion between us. Steve was a terrific footballer. His left foot was like a magic wand, but in that game, although he played well, I wanted my three centre-backs to defend. We will forever agree to disagree on that particular performance.

The 1997–1998 season promised so much and I remember saying to shareholders that we could kick on to bigger and better things. I'd learned a fair bit from the previous season and I felt we were ready for Europe. I made a point of spending time watching European games on DVD, so not to repeat the disaster of the previous season at Helsingborgs.

I was really looking forward to the domestic and European campaigns. However, there were two areas I needed strengthening. Firstly, we needed a bit more energy in the middle of the park, so I brought in Simon Grayson from Leicester to strengthen our squad. I had brought him to Leicester from Leeds so I knew all about 'Larry'; he was what you'd call a utility player, because he could play right back, centre-back and sometimes in midfield so I knew he'd be a good addition. I'd also been watching out for a lad called Lee Hendrie, who'd been in and around the first-team squad. At the time, Lee was still maturing and I'd been talking to him about being a local lad and a Villa fan and how he needed to look after himself. Maybe I didn't think he was quite ready, and I was sometimes criticised for not playing him more. The second weakness I felt we had was up top, in the striker department, but more about that later.

The players and staff flew out to America for our pre-season tour, but I stayed behind for a couple of days to conclude a deal which would see the clubs' transfer record broken. I'd had several conversations a couple of years' previously with the football agent, Paul Stretford about one of his players, Andy Cole, because I was really interested in signing him. Paul kept telling me for what we wanted to pay, I wouldn't get Andy Cole, besides, he was going to Manchester United. However, he also kept telling me that Stan Collymore was the man I needed, so he advised me to keep an eye on him at Liverpool during the 1996–1997 season. He had been in and out of the Liverpool side during the previous season and wanted to play, week in, week out. In all fairness, when I lost out on Andy Cole I started to watch Stan play for Liverpool alongside Robbie Fowler. They were incredible and I kept looking at their performances and how they were playing, and genuinely came to the conclusion that Stan was the right person to come to Villa, even regardless of the fact he was a Villa fan, and I still don't think I was wrong with that assessment.

I'd made my mind up that Stan was our man and encouraged the chairman to get his chequebook out. It was a lot of money, and the fee would break the then Villa transfer record. In the end, we signed Stan for around £7m. The deal was concluded between Paul Stretford, Mr Ellis and myself and then Stan and I flew out to LA to join the rest of the team. The long transatlantic journey was a chance to get to know Stan the person a little bit. When you talk to Stan, you find that he's quite deep and very clever. You simply can't doubt his intelligence and we got on really well and still do. I must admit, I was mega-impressed with him as a person, in terms of how he would sit down and talk about all sorts of things and as a footballer he was dynamite so I was well happy with the signing.

The only question niggling me was how would I come to terms with accommodating Stan, Dwight and Savo, because I couldn't play all three. Or could I?

Stan didn't need much introducing to the team, as he knew most of the lads reasonably well, especially the home-based players. The tour itself went well and we played some games out there and from an introductory point of view, Stan's first few weeks went extremely well.

The season started, but it didn't go quite to plan. In previous seasons, we got off to flying starts and surprised a few teams. Teams were looking up to us and respecting us. First up, was a short trip to Leicester City on a scorching hot day and a full house at Filbert Street and they were all still baying for my blood and we lost a close local derby, 1-0, with a first-half goal by Ian Marshall. We then got battered 4-0 at home by Blackburn and they beat us at Ewood Park 5-0 later in the season. We ended up losing the next two games in the Premier League, making it four on the bounce, although three of the four were away from home and the fourth was a narrow 3-2 defeat at White Hart Lane, where Stan scored his first goal for the club, after we went 2-1 up after 58 minutes. We were well and truly on the back foot; it was probably the worst start the club had had in many years, certainly in Premier League history and for the first time in my managerial career at Villa Park, I felt a bit of pressure.

Shortly after the four defeats, we lost Andy Townsend, my captain, to Bryan Robson's Middlesbrough for £500,000. Having made 134 league appearances and scoring eight league goals, he was a massive loss to the team as he was a leader on and off the pitch. I would go as far to say, Andy was the most influential player I've come across. He wasn't loud or dominant, but he just had an incredible way in the dressing room.

When I look back at the situation at the start of that season with no John Gregory, no Andy Townsend I realise those guys were big misses for me, and the team. They were both important people for me and pretty much irreplaceable and most certainly, their departures had some negative affects on the season. It felt like we'd have to rebuild again to some extent.

Although my mind was set at playing 5-3-2, I began to rejig the squad a wee bit; for those first four games, for some reason I reverted to a flat back four, which was totally against my philosophy. I was a bit confused and said to myself, it wasn't the way I wanted to continue playing. In hindsight it's easy to see I was wrong but at the time, I couldn't work it out. The change in my staff had something to do with it. I didn't get the nudge of approval or disapproval from the likes of Greggo, I'm not blaming anyone other than myself as I've always done things my way. However, in one particular game, I partnered Stan with Yorkie, but it was a partnership that never quite clicked and never really worked. Some days, I'd have Savo and Dwight up front with Stan playing the number 10 role, but on that day, I had Dwight and Stan up top. The number 10 role had been vacated by Tommy Johnson, who was a totally different player, one who was a grafter who closed the full-backs down and ran all over the place. Both Stan and Dwight were intelligent players who were at their best, right amongst the defenders; Savo was never a number 10, he just wasn't that type of player. Dwight had exceeded all expectation following the previous two seasons as an out and out striker, and he was good enough to play the number 10 role. In fact he was good enough to play anywhere.

If I look at the three of them, I believe they were all good being close to centre-backs and marked by centre-backs. In the previous nine seasons in football management I had been successful playing with three centre-backs, but I started that season with a

4-3-3, which was so unlike me. I often wonder why I started the season with all three strikers playing up top, players who were all better off being out and out strikers, but it's easy to look back and say, "Do you know what? I had three top strikers but I tried to get all three into the team at the same time." In all honesty, it just didn't work, although there were signs at times that it might.

When I'm talking to people about Stan Collymore, I'd always stand by him and back him. For me, he was brilliant, on and off the pitch and lived up to expectations. The only thing I'd say is that he probably wasn't in the right set up but as a player, he was technically brilliant. Looking at the partnerships we had: Stan and Yorkie, and Stan and Savo, he could have played with either of them, but maybe not both of them. One of the things about building your squad is that you need to have back-ups and in Julian Joachim, we had a good replacement for Yorkie. We were trying to build a team to win the league and we hadn't been that far away from competing in the previous two seasons. I'd never really built big squads or done squad rotation before, and in all fairness, I really didn't handle it too well, even though it was becoming more important if you were to be successful in the Premier League.

I soon reverted to my favoured formation, so I re-introduced Steve Staunton at the back, to play alongside Gareth and Ugo to make us more solid. Our first win came at home to Leeds, a 1-0 victory in front of 39,000 expectant fans. I was very pleased with the result and the performance, but it masked the problems we had floating around the place, but it settled the ship a little bit, at least. We followed that up with another two back-to-back wins in the league.

However, the season itself turned out to be fairly disappointing. There was the odd game in the league where we played especially well, like against Spurs when we won 4-1 and also in the European campaign ironically enough. We had a good UEFA Cup campaign and we had learned from our mistakes in the previous season. We were ready for the fact that still being in the game in the second leg was the most important thing. Conceding that goal against Helsingborgs hit me and the team hard so I was determined to make amends and learn from that experience.

I think because of what had happened during the previous season, I prepared better for the new European campaign and it sparked me into life. I was more aware of the European game and I really wanted to get it right and do well. I think teams in the Premier League were starting to suss us out a bit more, but in Europe we were still an unknown quantity so that probably gave us an advantage. In the first leg of the first round in the UEFA Cup, we played in Bordeaux and we were solid and drew 0-0, but by then I'd gone back to playing three centre-backs, although I was still accommodating the three strikers. We played well in France against a well-disciplined side and Stan could, and should, have won the game for us late in the match. However, it was a really fine result. It seemed we were back to being a solid, organised and disciplined side again.

In the return leg, we won 1-0 after extra-time. I played all three of our strikers and they were outstanding on the day. There was always one of them playing that number 10 role in a 'diamond' formation, behind the two strikers. All three of them could have scored that night. In fact it was Savo who did get the winning goal for us, deep into extra-time and that, in itself, showed we had bottle. It was a brilliant night of football.

After that, we played Athletic Bilbao, who incidentally were probably my favourite European side. I loved the way they played, and I'd had actually played in a tournament there in the 1970s, and for some reason I had a real affection for them. As a manager, for my team to knock them out over two legs was special and a great achievement. For me it's a fascinating club and, still to this day I follow them. I think they have a fantastic ethos as a club, the way they produce their own players from the area and move them on. Their old ground, they now have a brand new stadium, was tight and had a fabulous atmosphere and it was a great place to go and play football. We drew the first leg 0-0, a brilliant result again, but we saved our best performance of the season for the return leg at Villa Park. We went two goals up in the 50th minute, with goals from Tayls and Yorkie; Savo was again, outstanding. I remember Steve Staunton was immense, and he even took a shot from about 40 yards forcing the 'keeper to make a great save. It got a bit edgy towards the end as they pulled a goal back, but we held on to win 2-1.

Our European campaign was really on the way, and it kept our season alive and brought the smiles back to the faces of the fans and the players, too.

In the next round, we faced Steaua Bucharest away. We didn't know a lot about them so I asked our chief scout, ex-Villa legend

Peter Withe to go and watch them before our trip to Rumania. We knew it would be a big test of our character. We trained on the pitch in front of thousands of their fans on the day before the game and our lads got some horrible abuse, including some racist chants. Back then, you just ignored it and got on with what you were doing, but now it would be different, the authorities wouldn't tolerate that sort of behaviour. The noise wasn't confined to the training pitch, though; the hotel was horrible and there was noise all day and night long.

Steaua Bucharest were by no means a poor side and the atmosphere on the night was very intimidating, probably one of the most intimidating I've encountered in a football match. Our lads again got verbally and racially abused, and we got criticised for bringing clothes and food for local orphans, as a gesture of goodwill. Their fans jeered us as we walked onto the pitch. The game itself was open and competitive and they came at us, but we went at them also and that made for a great game. However, they scored twice in three minutes and we suddenly found ourselves 2-0 down within 33 minutes. It wasn't that we were poor, no chance! They were outstanding. They were an unbelievably talented group of players. Their second goal, however, was probably one of the best goals scored in any European competition that season, an overhead kick from 15 yards out. It was simply an incredible goal. Then on 54 minutes we got the lifeline we deserved, when Dwight scored with a free header from a Savo cross, and that gave us a real chance in the return leg. For us, that was a great scoreline, getting an all-important away goal but I thought we were very unlucky to lose the game, against a very good side.

We won 2-0 in the home leg and suddenly we were through to the quarter-final. We could (and probably should) have won the game 5-0 because we were that good on the night. I've watched that game a few times over the years and I remember the camera panned in at me towards the end, putting my hands on my face; I was tired and the stress was wearing me out. I couldn't put my finger on why the performances were so inconsistent and it was bugging me. I was interviewed on TV with Stan Collymore after that game. Stan was getting a bit of flak in the media, but he was magnificent on that night, and I can now see there was a tiredness in me. I was normally a low-key type of person at the time. I didn't get too carried away with good or bad results, but after that game I was thinking too deeply into why we put in performances like that for the European games, but in the league we were up and down.

In the league, we had some decent results, but were in mid-table by Christmas. We had one hell of a side, showing our best face for the big European nights, but we were under-performing in the domestic competitions, which was disappointing. When we played with the 'diamond' formation, we were tremendous, but when I tweaked the formation it didn't always work. However, I must stress here, it was only the odd game that let us down in the league. Was it down to me? Yes, I in hindsight I think it probably was. One game sticks out more than any that season. We lost at Blackburn 5-0 and I went into the dressing room speechless. I had nothing to say and I felt empty inside. One of my first games as Villa manager, we were beaten 4-1 by Wimbledon and I went into the dressing room and addressed the players and told them they would now do things my way but I couldn't this time. I've always been able to talk and always been able to hit the nail on the head, but on that occasion I had no answer. Being the sort of person I am, I was genuinely blaming myself for what I'd just witnessed. We were absolutely butchered that day and I can't remember that ever happening to me as a manager before. I knew something was wrong that day, but I couldn't put my finger on it. I've always had people come to me and say, "If you're alright Brian, then the team will be alright." On that day, I was really low and kind of lost. It can be said that a manager who makes a certain decision and it doesn't go for them, is immediately under pressure and can result in a defining moment in their career. For example, when Ruud Gullit left out Alan Shearer that was a defining moment in his managerial career. For me that result against Blackburn was a real defining moment in my time at Villa. I really wished it had happened at the end of the season, that way I could have walked away, there and then. It's hard for me how I felt at that time. I genuinely can't describe my mood, although in hindsight, when I look at videos of me, I can now see in my mannerisms I was a troubled person. When I look back now, I can have a chuckle to myself, but at the time I felt really down. However, I didn't really have anything to worry about. I was manager of an incredible football club who were mid-table in the Premier League and in the quarter-finals of the UEFA Cup, but I still wasn't happy.

We were well beaten twice during the season by Blackburn and Liverpool in the first five months of the season, but no other team had battered us. In the month of December, we played six games and only lost once, 1-0 against Manchester United, so that wasn't a bad period. At the end of that month, my unbeaten record was around 61%. I've often analysed myself in this way, by using my unbeaten record as a guide of where my team is at.

Attilio Lombardo was Crystal Palace manager for a short time in 1998 and he tried to sign Saša Ćurčić cheaply before the close of the March transfer deadline. He rang me one day and offered me something like £1m and I said simply, "No, absolutely no chance." There was no way I could have sold him for a £1m – Mr Ellis would have gone barmy, I think. However, it would have been his shout to sanction that deal, if it had been Palace's only offer. I then quickly got my thinking cap on and said, "And don't you dare ring my chairman and go behind my back," knowing the chances were, they would ring Mr Ellis. Of course, he did ring Mr Ellis. However, I pre-empted the call and told the chairman he might be hearing from them and said, "Tell them they can have him if they give us £3.5m, but my manager is going to go up the wall. He won't be happy about it." When I got another call from Palace, I played the "I'm not letting him go" card, while the chairman went along the lines of, "If you give us the money we want, you can have him tomorrow." There was a bit of kidology about it, but in those days you had to use every trick in the book. That situation showed how manager and chairman could work together, even if they both don't always see eye to eye all the time which it was hard to do at times.

Saša apparently attacked me in the press, saying he was fed up with the way he'd been treated by me, not allowing him an opportunity to show what he could do on the football pitch and said I didn't play him in the right role, so my relationship with Saša had deteriorated to a point of no return, but I still wasn't prepared to sell him cheaply.

During a two-month period after Christmas, we'd slipped up in the league. I especially remember losing 1-0 to local rivals Coventry City at home in the FA Cup. I'd never lost to Coventry before and that really knocked the stuffing out of me. That was the first of three back-to-back defeats; Manchester United scored two late goals to beat us, but by the time we'd played Wimbledon at Selhurst Park on 21st February 1998, that unbeaten record had dropped to 57%.

That defeat at Wimbledon finally finished me off. I didn't talk to anybody at the time and I felt fairly isolated, even though there were people who were important to me. Maybe if I had confined in those people, they could have talked me round. I'd made up my mind that I'd had enough. I needed a breather, and the sooner the better, so I resigned from my position at Villa Park, one week before an important UEFA Cup quarter-final against Atlético Madrid.

I rest my case here and now, that there was nothing wrong with the team. It was more to do with team selection and that was down to me. I felt genuinely tired, almost running on empty after ten years of non-stop, hard slog in football man-agement. The day after the Wimbledon game, I went into the office to see Mr Ellis. He was brilliant and advised me not to make any hasty decisions. He told me to have a little breather, but he also said he'd be willing to fetch Greggo back to help me out and lead the team for a few weeks, to take the pres-sure off. I understood his concern and where he was coming from, but I just couldn't accept that scenario. I acknowledged that John had left to become his own boss at Wycombe. I also said that if John wanted to come back, he should come back as the manager of Aston Villa, as a replacement for me. I'd always encouraged John to become his own boss and I couldn't see a situation where he would 'baby-sit' my team; I could have accepted it if I'd wanted to, but I didn't see any mileage in it. Without a doubt, that would have been a simple fix, but at the time, I felt if I was going to stay on I needed a nice long holiday, but we were nearing the end of the season so that wouldn't have been possible. Looking back at that situation, I could have changed it and stayed on as Villa manager, but I didn't feel that was the right thing for me to do. I remember saying to Mr Ellis and Steve Stride that I needed to go away, but I also said I didn't know what I wanted to do in the future.

Wycombe were performing well in February 1998 when John quit to take the role I vacated back at Aston Villa. He was a close friend of Steve Stride, the Villa Operations Director and Steve was a close friend of mine, too. I couldn't think of a better person to take over from me. He had the energy, commitment and desire to push the team forward. Sometimes, a team needs a manager who's in outstanding form and looking back, when I see John's enthusiasm when he came into the job in February 1998, and how clear he saw things in the early days, it demonstrated that he was the right man for the job. We've spoken about this so many times since, and for John, it was unexpected and came as a shock to be asked by Mr Ellis to replace me at the helm.

I left a great team in a poor position in the league (15th), but in the quarter-final of the UEFA Cup. It needed something fresh injected into it, but it was the end of three incredible years of my life. That great team needed a manager in form to take them forward, and that wasn't me at that particular time. John came in and immediately helped improve Villa's league form during the final three months of the 1997–1998 season. His first game in charge saw the team beat Liverpool 2-1 at Villa Park. Something I had always found difficult to do was to beat the Reds. That was followed by the UEFA Cup quarter-final away to Atlético Madrid, which ended in a 1-0 defeat, but in the home game the expectant Villa faithful witnessed an amazing game, where Stan Collymore struck a wonder shot in front of the Holte End to earn us a 2-1 win. However, that dreaded away goal sealed our fate and we cruelly went out of the competition. When you look at the results until the end of that season, I felt justified in my decision to resign and let John take over because Villa finished seventh in the Premier League and they qualified for the UEFA Cup again, with John at the helm.

Incidentally, Saša didn't last long at Villa after I left; later that year he was sold to Crystal Palace after all for £1.35m in March 1998. Sadly, his time at Villa was more remembered for his wild lifestyle and eccentric behaviour than anything football related.

I was more than happy with my spell as manager of Aston Villa FC and it was a brilliant period in my life, but like everything, it came to an end. People often ask me if I regretted leaving when I did; I will never regret anything about what I'd achieved at Aston Villa. I don't stop and regret anything that I've done in my life. Whatever I've done is done because I've felt that I needed to do it at the time, and that really sums up my per-sonality I guess. At the end of the day, if you're big enough to make a decision for yourself the one thing you shouldn't do is let others make decisions. So, I don't have regrets, simple as that, but should I have done it? Well, again, that's something I did and I'm happy with that. The only disappointment I had when I quit was the situation I left Allan Evans in. As a three, we worked well, but John and Allan needed me in the middle so there was no way they would ever work together as a two. However, I was delighted that John got his opportunity to manage Villa. I would say, when he left for Wycombe, he couldn't have imagined he'd be back so soon.

****

Like I've said before, Mr Ellis was fantastic with me and regardless to what some people may think, he did not sack me and I hope my explanation of the situation will put that argument to bed. In fairness to Mr Ellis and people close to me, they could probably see I was tired and in need of a break. When you work with Mr Ellis, you know you've worked for three years, even though it feels more like five. I've known worse and harder times. At Leicester City, we had a Board meeting once a month and I had to be in that meeting all day, listening to commercial activities, promotional activities, listening to this conversation, that conversation and anything to do with Leicester City; to get something passed, there was a sub-committee appointed to look into it before something was done about it. At Aston Villa, there was only one door I needed to knock on, and that was the chairman's door. All I had to do there was to walk down a corridor, knock on a door and say to Mr Ellis, "I want to do this or that..." and I'd either get a "Yes", or a "No", and we'd sit down and sort it out. No matter what anybody thinks of Mr Ellis, and yes, he was involved with everything at the club, even down to signing off petrol receipts in the early days, all I had to do was to knock on his door to get an answer. I've sat in his office from 3pm until midnight talking to agents, players, or chairmen, trying to sell or sign players.

Working for someone like Doug Ellis will always be difficult. I'll try and explain the pressure I was under with him as an example. At the end of my first season when we just about survived, I wanted to sign players, left, right and centre. I received a call from Mr Ellis who said he had a player coming over to Birmingham and he was going to talk to him. I knew nothing about it or the identity of the player, so I quizzed the chairman. He'd been speaking to an agent and he agreed to bring his player over but was cagy about who it was. At the time, I was in his office and he was on the phone, so I asked him who the player was, and as he started rustling papers around, and said, "He's Dutch. His name is, er Danny Blind". I stood back in amazement, "Danny Blind? He's the captain of Ajax! Danny Blind is the captain of Holland. He's a great player. But, we've got Paul McGrath, we've got Ugo, we've got Gareth Southgate and we've got kids coming through. Why am I going to leave one of those centre-backs out? I fully except that Danny Blind is an international footballer, but why's he coming over?" Strangely, Mr Ellis didn't know the answer to that simple question, but just said, "Well, the agent gave me a call and I've invited them over." I just couldn't understand it and said, "With the greatest respect, we're not going to sign Danny Blind so why are you doing it?" Mr Ellis got a bit excited and said, "He's coming Brian. He's coming into Birmingham, tomorrow." At that stage, I put my foot down and refused to meet him, and to that, Mr Ellis put a spanner in the works, "Well, if you don't come down I'll sack you." so that well and truly put me in my place.

So, the next day, Danny Blind flew into Birmingham just as he'd said, was greeted by Mr Ellis who entertained him through-out the day; he took him to the Belfry for lunch and then drove him around some of the sights of Birmingham. In the evening, I reluctantly joined them at Villa Park and we talked around the table for about two hours when Danny's agent asked a ques-tion, "Emm, Mr Ellis, err, what about the contract? We need to talk about the contract." Typical of Mr Ellis, and without batting an eyelid he said, "Yes, I'll tell you what, I'll speak to Brian, my manager, who's sitting there, and if we want to sign Danny, we'll give you a call one day." In fairness to Danny Blind, he said, "Mr Ellis, I've had a wonderful day. Thank you very much." and walked out of the room, and that was that.

Now, that story may seem far-fetched to some, but it was abso-lutely true. Mr Ellis told me he had agents on the phone every single day and that's something, as a manager you have to deal with when you work for him. It wasn't a problem for me, and I took it all with a pinch of salt. There is something quite unique about Mr Ellis; however, there is a history of Villa managers lasting around three years, and I can see why they only lasted that long, but to be honest I got on with him really well, still do to this day, even though he's into his 90s. Yes, we got into some scrapes, had a few arguments and some difficult times, but we also had some great times together, too. I can't knock him and I never will, but there were some really hard times. I've never sat with such a great negotiator as Mr Ellis. He could talk forever, go away from a subject and then come back to it, and by then he'd knocked £50,000 or even £250,000 off the value when he was trying to buy a player. To listen to him negotiate a contract with an agent or a player, the only words I can used to describe his tactics are that, he bore them down to submission and that's a compliment.

****

Hours after resigning, my good mate and journalist, Peter White, (his name often got mistaken for the Villa legend, Peter Withe) and I went to a casino in Birmingham city centre. The ironic thing was, I'd never, ever been to a proper casino before, so why we went to one that day, God only knows. Obviously, I was spotted by several fans, who asked me if I'd resigned, but the very fact I was in such a place, summed up my mood and mentality at that time. It was just not me. It was probably to release the pressure of working my socks off for 10 years and I needed to get it all out of my system.

Within a few days of leaving Villa, I jumped on a plane to Majorca. I had an apartment in Puerto de Pollensa in the north of the island and I'd always wanted to do something different, so after a few days relaxing I decided to cruise around the island on my Yamaha Virago cruising motorbike, which I had shipped out there. I am a massive fan of motorbikes and motorbike racing so, when the bike arrived, I ended up having the time of my life, cruising the island, spending days at different resorts, spending the day on the beach and enjoying the beautiful scenery, food and culture of the different areas. I was just chilling out and it was a brilliant spell in my life and it lasted for three months. I needed to get away from football; I needed to get away from life; I needed to recharge my batteries big time!

That trip did me the world of good, and it was long overdue. During the previous 10 years as a football manager, I genuinely didn't have a habit of going away during the summer break as I was always dealing in the transfer market. The job was full on, 24/7. It was worse at Leicester, because we were in the playoff finals until the end of May three seasons running, which didn't leave much time for a break before the players reported back during the first week of July.

Going away for that period of time actually helped my career and opened the next door for me. I did have the odd contact with people back home and one phone call in particular unexpectedly changed my life. While I was in Majorca I got a call from Phil Smith, a football agent I'd known for some time and he'd heard I was in Majorca and he was on holiday in Spain too. We arranged to meet and have a drink, some tapas and a chat together in one of my favourite places in Palma.

When we met, we talked about why I was in Majorca and what I was going to do in the future, then Phil got to the crux, "Well, Brian I've been asked by Stoke City to find somebody". I knew Stoke were a good club who had been relegated to the third tier that season, but they had just moved into the Britannia Stadium as it was called then, from the old Victoria Ground. Phil explained the condition of the club, in terms of finances, which wasn't very good if I'm honest. Phil asked me to consider talking to them. In all honesty, right at that time I wasn't ready and told Phil I still needed time. However, he was persistent, "Brian, do me a favour, just come over with me and meet them and we'll go from there." So I reluctantly agreed. I was reluctant because I was enjoying my relaxation; it wasn't that I didn't want to do the job, I did, because it was a club I nearly joined when I was 14 or 15 years old. In that respect, it was a club that I knew and had a lot of time for so I felt quite relaxed with the thought of going to talk to them.

Of course, I went over there, met the owner and chairman, Keith Humphreys, along with some of his board members, including Peter Coates and Jez Moxey. I hadn't seen the new ground before and I was very impressed by it, and the set-up they had there. The talks went well and the prospect appealed to me very much. As it turned out I agreed to become their manager there and then on a two-year deal and I was delighted.

I went back to Majorca to finish off my break and joined the preparation for pre-season at the start of June. I'd had my three or four months off and now I'd thrown myself into a new, unexpected challenge to get Stoke City out of the Third Division.

Chapter 9

RULE BRITANNIA
Stoke City manager: May 1998–July 1999

"I'm not sure if I can do this for another year"

Stoke City entered a new era at their 28,000 all-seater
stadium in the third tier of English football with heavy
debts of around £5 million, which was a lot of money back
then. It came as a bit of a surprise to both the fans and
myself when the chairman, Keith Humphreys, appointed me
as their manager.

I felt refreshed, raring to go and immediately that Stoke was
the right sort of place to re-ignite my management career. It was
a good club and I'd always had hard games against them in the
past as a player and a manager, so I felt as though I knew something about them from day one.

At the time I took the job, ITV Digital's attempt to renegotiate
the rights to Football League matches sent football in England
into meltdown as the TV money started to dry up, and that filtered right down the leagues, including Stoke City. My job
was to move out the lads who had reasonably paid contracts,
because the money just wasn't there to pay them anymore, and
I was asked to bring in players on lower-paid contracts. It was
something I was familiar with, as I'd done something similar at
Darlington, and at Leicester to a lesser extent. I thought that the
situation would be good experience and a challenge for me, one
I'd relish. I knew it would be a total restructure and rebuilding
job, and that I was the best person for the job.

However, the club had no divine right to bounce straight back
into the Second Division so we were in for a long, hard season.
Lots of things were going on in my head, on and off the field. I
was living in Leicestershire at the time, but knew Staffordshire
and quite liked the Stone area, so I'd already planned to move

there on a permanent basis. One of the first jobs I did when I started work there was to change all the training arrangements from a facility near the M6 to Keele University. The old facility didn't belong to the club and it didn't take me long to decide I didn't like it. Straight away, I started to think about all the positives to try and get the club back up.

I had a lot of transfer dealing to do before the pre-season started. In a very short space of time, there was a turnover of around 25 players, coming and going. To mention just a few of the names that went out of the club: Justin Whittle (£50,000), Ally Pickering (free), Steven Tweed (£150,000), Paul Stewart (free), Ray Wallace, Danny Tiatto and Neil McKenzie. It wasn't anything to do with their playing quality, but it was simply a financial exercise to balance the books; if it was about their playing quality, it would have dictated that they should have stayed. The level of players that we were in the market for were from that division or lower, or possibly hadn't played in the third tier before. I brought in the likes of: David Oldfield, Gavin Ward, Nicky Mohan, Paul Connor, Phil Robinson and Ben Petty, Bryan Small and Lee Collins from Villa. A lot of the lads that were brought in, I'd dealt with before from different clubs, so that was interesting. I also pushed up the ladder some young lads, the likes of James O'Connor, Clive Clark, Steven Taff, Steven Woods and Ashley Williscroft. My job was to get the club pretty much back to basics. There wasn't any pot of money and there was no chance of bringing in any foreign players. I think I eventually brought in around 11 new players all on free transfers. We had to form a brand new team, whether I liked it or not. I also brought in a new backroom staff in Allan Evans and Tony McAndrew, who also came with me from Villa; however, I wanted Kevin McDonald from Villa as well. That meant I had to have a chat to Alan Durban, who was the caretaker manager and had done a fine job before my arrival. I explained that I wanted Allan, Kevin and Tony to work with me, and those chats are always the difficult ones. I felt for Alan because he was an older person who'd been around the game a long time. However, I couldn't pretend to want him on my staff, so he eventually left.

Another difficult chat was with the physio. During the 1980s and 1990s, the job of the physio was a nightmare, because they had to deal with every type of injury and the rehab to go with it. I'd been told the physio room was a busy place during the previous season and there was some history which had to be dealt with. I think if you're going to meet someone, your new manager for example, you'd think about how you dressed for the meeting. The young physio who was already at the club walked through my door, he was wearing a sleeveless tee shirt, a pair of shorts and flip-flops. Anyway, he slouched down in front of me, I said my piece, and truth be told, the meeting didn't even last five minutes. I think he wanted to leave anyway and indeed, within a week he'd found another job. I'd decided there and then that I needed a new physio, so he was out of the door. I can't believe anybody would go to an important meeting wearing what he wore, but he did; it reminded me of the story about Graham Fenton and his interview with Blackburn.

It didn't take long to find his replacement; the new physio was a local lad called Rob Ryles, who was the complete opposite and a brilliant lad.

I quickly got well organised and introduced a set of fines, similar to those that I had set up at Darlington, if and when players got sent off, turned up late for training or forgot to wear flip-flops in the shower. Also, all the things I believed in were implemented, like dress code, no phone usage in the dressing room and no gambling on the team bus. By and large, the new rules went down well with the players.

So, we had soon established a good setup and a good group of players and staff to start the season with, but nobody knew what we were going to do with all these new faces.

We had a great pre-season; I enjoyed the fact we had use of Keele University and there was a good buzz around the place, with other people around so it wasn't all our own. It was a little bit different in that we were in amongst the students, so it took us away from being locked in the training ground, where the public weren't allowed to watch. It was interesting, to say the least.

My new look side started the 1998–1999 season on fire. It was a strange start to the season because after the opening 3-1 win at Northampton, we played Macclesfield three times in the first four games. We lost 3-1 away from home in the League Cup, but the very next game we beat them 3-0 at home in the league. In the next game, the second leg of the cup, we beat them 1-0, and we went out of the cup in the first round. That defeat in the cup didn't go down too well with the board, because they had budgeted for us to reach the third round at least, and I was reminded it cost the club around £150,000. The fact was, out of the first four games we'd won three so that one defeat proved costly.

A terrific 4-3 win at Preston followed the cup exit. It was the start of David Moyes' managerial career and I recall how good a side they were under David's control – he'd obviously made an impression. Victories against Oldham and Colchester followed. Before the Colchester game, I was doing my team talk about 10 minutes from kick-off, telling them what I needed and all the lads were dressed and ready to go. It was the old Colchester ground and it was on a slope; it was always a difficult place to play and it was never the best ground in the world; it was like stepping back in time. All of a sudden, a mobile phone rang and I felt a sense of embarrassment from the players and most of them drop their head, until Lárus Sigurðsson turned round without a care in the world, picked his phone up and off he goes, talking in Icelandic to the caller. I think there were a few sighs of relief from the other players when he picked up his phone, to be honest. Lárus stood there for five minutes rabbiting away as if nothing was going on, then when he'd finished he put the phone back in his pocket. I stood there looking at him, ready to give him a roasting and said, "I hope that was important?" and he replied, "Yes, and my wife is now having a baby." God bless him, he'd travelled with us knowing his wife was due to go into labour, but he just needed to know and said he had to get home straight after the game. That was probably the one and only time I didn't get annoyed with somebody not sticking to the rules, and I credit him for it, and for being at the game, when his wife probably needed him more.

We actually won that game, making it five straight league wins. In fact, we only lost two out of 10 league games from early August to the end of September; a defeat at Blackpool and a 1-0 defeat at Fulham, and by then, we'd come from nowhere to becoming favourites to win promotion. I won the Manager of the Month award for August 1998 for winning six games in a row. It was an incredible period and our new players like Dean Crowe were scoring goals for fun. It was a period nobody expected.

During the opening period, there were a couple of special games for me. We played York City at home and the interest in that game surrounded the fact that my brother Alan was their manager. I don't recall too many brothers in the English game who have managed opposing sides. So, on 21st November 1998, four days before my 46th birthday, I beat his team 1-0. Unfortunately, just weeks later, Alan got the sack from York. I was pretty gutted for him, in all fairness.

By the end of November, we had won all five games in the month, and I became Manager of the Month again and we were up towards the top of the table. It looked like that we would be too good for our Second Division opponents. I was loving my time at Stoke; I'd changed things around in such a short space of time and everything was going smoothly. I look at the likes of Fulham, who'd spent £2m on one player in Barry Hales and they were managed by no other than Kevin Keegan; that was what we were up against. We had a midfield, although it was strong, that cost next to nothing. I kept the same system with three centre-backs, three midfielders, two strikers and two wing backs; it was a system that made us very competitive. Up until Christmas, things were going really well again, it seemed a matter of when and not if we would gain promotion. However, the club were put up for sale in the middle of the season and uncertainty ruled the roost.

The second half of the season was also a massive setback. January in particular was an absolute nightmare, so the less said about that the better. We began to lose ground on the likes of Fulham and Manchester City and our form completely dropped off, registering just one win from the end of November to March. There were some real disappointments during that second half of the season, like losing 2-0 to Millwall in February, when they had two players sent off. After that game, I said to the media it was the worst game I've ever been involved in from a personal point of view. Another game that I hated was when we lost 4-0 to Bournemouth and likewise losing 4-1 to Burnley at home, after we'd beaten them 2-0 earlier in the season at Turf Moor.

At the end of the season, we finished the season in eighth place on 69 points, missing out on the playoffs by seven points, which I suppose wasn't bad. At the start of the season most fans would have settled for that, in view of what we had had to deal with. On reflection, looking at the financial restrictions I had to deal with, having to slash the wage bill and play a lot of young players, I didn't do too badly I suppose. We just didn't have the finances to push on and compete with the bigger teams in that league.

One of the interesting games was against Walsall on the last day of the season. Not only was it a local derby, but my old Villa teammate, Ray Graydon was their manager so it got a lot of media attention in the local area. Ray did a great job by taking Walsall up that year by finishing second, in front of Manchester City. Incidentally, Fulham won the league that year. Following that 2-0 win against Walsall, I remember sitting down feeling low and thinking to myself, "I'm not sure if I can do this for another year." I didn't want to be in Division Two again. I wasn't sure if I was going to have restrictions for the following season, even though we had done better than expected on the pitch, we could have been right at the bottom of the table if we had started the season as we finished it. The club needed new money; it needed new investment and it needed new blood. However, none of that was forthcoming and it just wasn't right for me.

During the summer of 1999, I decided to resign from Stoke due to personal reasons, and was replaced by Gary Megson several weeks later. It was a particularly interesting period for me when I look back at it, and I still think it was a good club and the right sort of club for me to manage at that time. In hindsight, the bottom line was probably I came back from my break a little too early. Having said all that, I still have a great affection for Stoke City FC. It's still a really good club that I have a lot of time for.

Chapter 10

STITCHED UP
West Bromwich Albion Manager:
August 1999–March 2000

*"You named me in the team today, but
I'm signing for Sunderland"*
Kevin Kilbane

There were a lot of things going on at Stoke City that made
me feel very uncomfortable and unhappy; there were a lot
of changes about to happen behind the scenes that I wasn't
happy about; there were also a lot of things going on in my
own personal life, too. Having said all of that, I felt I did well
enough in my first season to take the club forward. The club
were also changing ownership and I just felt I needed to get
out while the time was right.

At the end of that season, I went back to Majorca for probably
two months on my own to sort my head out and decided what
to do next. On my return, I'd decided to leave the club; I needed
another breather from football – or so I thought at the time. I
remember speaking to Jez Moxey, the CEO of Stoke City, and
explained I needed to take some time out of the game. To be fair
to Jez, he didn't want me to leave; if I had something planned
then I'd be walking out of a contract so he advised me to think
about my next move as I'd be in breach of contract if I was going
to move into another job. Quite honestly, I had nothing planned
so I was happy to sign an agreement with the club that stated
if I got another job in three months time, Stoke deserved some
sort of compensation as I'd left my contract, so I signed it. I just
needed a breather.

With my personal life upside down, I bought an apartment in
Sutton Coldfield on my own; a lot of things needed to change in
my life and I just needed to be on my own for a while. However,

while I was in Spain, I had some contact from West Bromwich Albion, who had just sacked Dennis Smith in July 1999, during the pre-season, which I found quite odd. If a manager is sacked during the summer, prior to a new season, it may tell you what's going on inside a football club; obviously things weren't overly good at West Brom.

I was well known in the Midlands and moving back to the Birmingham area I was very keen to meet the West Brom board. I didn't really contemplate the rivalry aspect of moving to West Brom, after being Villa manager a few years previously, and less so, being the Wolves caretaker boss. It didn't worry me at the time; after all, it was just another job to me. All I cared about was the fact that another club wanted me to be their manager. The only thing that worried me was what was happening behind the scenes at West Brom.

I met the officials from West Bromwich Albion over lunch in a small village in Staffordshire. We discussed my footballing philosophy and all the usual stuff and I think they were suitably impressed. I was relaxed and felt good about the interview. I hadn't looked into the history of what was going on at the club. I knew the chairman was under pressure from the other directors, but that was about it. The directors I met were Tony Hale and Joe Brandrick, and they must have been impressed with me because they offered me the job. I soon accepted the position and became West Bromwich Albion manager at the start of August 1999.

John Gorman was still at the club as caretaker manager and coach before I arrived. He was a fantastic coach and I liked what I saw when he was working with the players so I was happy for him to stay at the club. We had similar ideas about how the team should play, and he had developed a very good relationship with all of the players, which was fantastic for me. It was a very comfortable situation and John was absolutely first class. I looked at every session he did and they were outstanding. However, John himself was disappointed he wasn't offered the job on a permanent basis. At the start it wasn't a problem, although in the back of my head I knew John might want to look at that type of position somewhere else in the future. I also knew he was very close to Glen Hoddle, who would have almost certainly asked John to work with him if and when he returned to football management.

When you come to analyse situations at clubs, you ask yourself why has the manager been sacked during the pre-season. The team were steady enough and there were a good bunch of players, although they had found it hard to score goals in the previous season. I knew early on, making them hard to beat would not be difficult, but turning them into a winning team might well be problematic though.

I decided to call all the players into a meeting during that first week at the club, one week or so before the start of the 1999–2000 season, to try and lay out a game plan and to outline my thoughts on how I wanted my football to be played. We ran through my trusted system and what I expected from that formation, what everybody's role was, and how the system changed if I decided to tweak it, and I thought I'd put it all across to the players really well. It was a long, long meeting because I didn't have a lot of time on the training ground to stamp my authority on the team before the season started. Almost everywhere else I'd been, I had a full pre-season and an opportunity to set up what I wanted from the team, but I had to do all of that in one meeting. As it happens, it went really well and I could tell most people were attentive and enjoyed what they listened to. I felt the players warmed to it.

During a meeting like that, talking in front of people, I could usually tell who listened and who didn't; who was interested and who wasn't. I always built up an impression of my own of what people thought of me, what I've said and what I've done and vice-versa. As a football manager, as much as you want to get across your points, you also make sure you have the courage to look people in the eye and pick up vibes from them, as well as them picking up vibes from you. Looking around at the faces in the room, I picked up little hints that some people weren't interested about what I was talking about, but some were listening to every word. I specifically remember looking at Kevin Kilbane, who I picked out as being a very important player for us, and I was pleased, because I saw there and then that he listened and took in what I'd said. I think I got my point across to him, especially well. Another player who I thought would be important was Richard Sneekes, a player who I admired from afar, but when I met him and as I got to know him, I realised what a great person he was; he was massively talented and very intelligent; he a was multi-lingual speaker and he was a great help to the young players like Enzo

Maresca. Besides his native Dutch language, he spoke English, Italian and Spanish. I couldn't quite grasp the idea how easily he learned all of those languages. I'd spent two years in college doing Spanish, but as soon as I got to a hard bit, I couldn't grasp it and found it too difficult. It's easy to ask for a beer or a loaf of bread, but once you get into the grammar it's unbelievably hard.

Out of all the meetings I've held as a manager, I would say that was the most important meeting I've had in terms of it being such a unique situation. It was a week before the start of a new football season and the club expected me to hit the ground running with a team that struggled to win games and had finished mid-table in Division One (second tier) the previous season. Not only that, I was a manager who had managed two of the club's local rivals.

The success of that meeting brought back memories of a similar meeting I had at Darlington – only in reverse. I was determined to do well there, but when I looked around the room I saw so many people who were not interested in what was going on. When I compare the Darlington dressing room to the West Brom one, I have to say they were massively attentive.

If you look at the players that were there at the time, the likes of: Richard Sneekes, James Quinn, Micky Evans and Lee Hughes, there was a lot of quality. A lot of faith was put on Lee, who had an unbelievable time at West Brom, scoring at a rate of nearly one in every two games. However, during the period I was there, Lee was having a tricky time off the pitch. He was a local lad and had lots of mates, but was probably going out with them a bit too much. He was a top-drawer kid, but questions were being asked about his lifestyle. During my period there, he did have a barren patch and that made things really tough. Other players in the squad included Fabian de Freitas, who wasn't a prolific goalscorer; Justin Richards really didn't hit it off and anybody thinking he'd make it as a footballer during my time there were wrong; he probably got one game, if that; Kevin Kilbane, from a wide area was another good lad, but again a goal ratio of one in ten wasn't good enough. Looking at the strikers I had at my disposal, it was no wonder why the team struggled for goals.

In all of my teams, I built a solid foundation with a couple of strikers who would contribute with goals by allowing them to be out-and-out strikers. At West Brom, we didn't really have that. However, I felt that meeting I held before the start of the season had a big impact on the players and that showed during the first 14 games, we'd only lost two games, but we'd won only three, drawing the rest. It must have been one of the most solid starts to a season any of my teams had. We were solid, without being adventurous, but struggled like crazy to score goals and that put pressure on the rest of the team. In some of the games we drew, we were by far the better team and had chance after chance but didn't finish teams off.

However, the wheels came off a little bit after the first 14 games when we lost two home games on the spin, both 1-0. The first one was against local rivals, Walsall, a team who weren't supposed to be on the same level as West Brom. If I'm correct, my old Villa teammate, Ray Graydon was still their manager. The other defeat was against Queens Park Rangers.

My preconception about the team proved correct. We were a solid group, but we just couldn't score goals.

I always felt there was an undercurrent surrounding the chairman, people on the board wanting to change things and people wanting to invest more into the club. However, I was allowed to bring in two players, although, I couldn't bring in a striker as we couldn't afford it. Firstly, I signed Lárus Sigurðsson who I had at Stoke, because I needed a player who could play with three at the back. I also took Andy Townsend from Middlesbrough, who was my captain at Villa and was an outstanding individual. I thought those guys could help the system I wanted to play. We needed another centre-back and we didn't have a natural left-footed central midfielder, so those two guys fitted the bill.

Around the Christmas time, Tony Hales stepped aside as chairman and was replaced by Paul Thompson. There was some irony in that, because on 14th December 1999 we played at Grimsby Town, and that date stuck very much in my head. Leading up to that game, John Gorman left the club, and that was a massive loss for me. He'd been an incredible coach and his relationship with the players was massively important for me, but he wanted to go off and do something different. On the field, we'd lost two games in a row before Grimsby, so we lacked a bit of form, and the pressure was beginning to mount. We travelled up on the day of the game, having a pre-match meal in a hotel. At that point, we were mid-table, had played around 22 games, losing only six, but as I've said before, we weren't winning enough. We always held a 40-minute pre-match team meeting at the hotel, after lunch and that day was no different. The team and subs were announced and I briefed the lads on what the game held and what we needed to do. Bear in mind those were the days before analysts and all the facts and stats football clubs have now. All we had was a written report on the opposition. My way of thinking was to relay all the information we held on the opposition just before the game. If you tell players facts and figures days before a game they will forget what they've been told and so sometimes it loses its validity.

There was nothing unusual about going to Grimsby; however, during the team meeting I was well and truly shafted by the club on that particular day and I don't use that word lightly. I got the team to sit down for the meeting. I was just about to talk about the game and go through the team, one-by-one and telling them about their individual roles. However, immediately after naming the side, I knew I'd said something that had made a stir amongst some of the lads. Having managed a good few hundred games by that time, I just sensed something wasn't quite right, so I began to think if I'd said something wrong. It was at the back of my mind for the entire 40 minutes of that meeting. I felt uncomfortable about something. At the time, I couldn't have told you what it was, but now I can disclose what it was that ruffled a few feathers in the dressing room.

I came out of the room, after the meeting, and started to walk down the corridor, thinking to myself, "What is going on? There's something going on here." After walking twenty yards, I sensed someone following me. It was Kevin Kilbane, "Gaffer. Can I have a word with you, please?" I told Kevin that I thought something wasn't quite right and he replied, "Yeah, you named me in the team today, but I'm signing for Sunderland."

I was the only person in that room that didn't know the club had agreed to sell Kevin Kilbane to Sunderland for over £2m and I was the manager of the team. That was probably the worst thing that could happen to a manager and it happened to me. Fortunately, it was the only time it ever did.

As it turned out, that was the beginning of the end of my time at The Hawthorns.

From that very day, irrespective of what anybody has said on the subject since, I lasted another three months. I don't know how I lasted that long, if I'm honest. It just killed me; it utterly destroyed me, the fact that I was the only person at that club who didn't know one of my players had been sold, and I'd named him in the team. I didn't know what was going on behind my back.

In fairness to Kevin, it wasn't his fault in any shape or form. You won't come across a better professional, in fact and he was absolutely gutted and embarrassed for me. To this day, he's been fantastic to me, but I think even he realised that there had been a shift in the directors' power in terms of the chairman moving to one side and Paul Thompson coming in. From that day on, I was hanging out to dry and I never recovered from it.

Fortunately, the players were OK with me. They knew I'd been stitched up. The game itself, we drew, but the result wasn't important to me, because I wasn't really in charge of anything at West Bromwich Albion after 14th December 1999.

A few weeks after Christmas, Enzo Maresca was sold to Juventus for £4.3m, which was another blow. Not surprisingly, I didn't have any say in that transfer either. However, whilst I knew it was happening, the club couldn't say "No," to that sort of money. He was a young, talented lad, who was in and out of the team, so it made sense for the club to cash in. However, there was no way I was going to get any of that money to spend on players. With the sale of two players worth £6.3m, I never got a penny of it. If I'd had a say in how that money was spent, maybe, just maybe I could have made a difference, bringing in some fresh faces, but it wasn't to be.

Probably the last thing I did at West Brom, and was of some value to them, was to sign a Danish goalkeeper called Brian Jensen. I was allowed to sign him because everybody was saying to me how good he was. At the time, I had a good friend called Dougie George, who had done some scouting for me at several clubs and we'd played together in Aston Villa's youth team, back in the 1970s. Dougie had spoken to me about a Brian, who he described as an, "immense character, at the early stages of his career, but could be somebody who could do well for West Brom." When I met Brian, I can say Dougie was spot on with his assessment. At six foot five inches tall, he was a big, strong and an immense character, but slightly unorthodox and inexperienced. He was a shot-stopper and there was something about him. We had him on trial at first, and signing him up was probably one of the last things I did. The club actually paid £80,000 for him; they could also sense there was something about him.

My last game in charge of the club was a home game against Birmingham City, a local derby and we lost 3-0. The ironic thing was it was also Brian's first game for the club. In the next game against Tranmere, West Brom won 2-0 and he became an overnight sensation. The fans called him 'The Beast' because of his size. He was the type of player I would have brought into the club, given the opportunity to have spent some of the £6.3m. He subsequently had a great career in football, including 10 years at Burnley.

At least I left something behind in my heritage at the club.

After that game against Birmingham City, I basically challenged the board to make a decision about my future. I was being hung out to dry aftrer every single game that passed; I didn't feel anybody on the board had any confidence in me, certainly from the time the new chairman came in. Having worked at a club just down the road and been successful there, when things don't go right, it tends to get more difficult and that's where I was. I guess if you get it right, then the fans tend to forget where you have managed previously to a certain extent.

To be fair to the board, they did do something about my challenge. They sacked me the very next day on 4th March 2000 and ironically replaced me with Gary Megson, who had taken over from me at Stoke City. It probably was the correct decision, given the fact I wasn't wanted there, especially by the new chairman, but that's life, I guess. You move on and take it as another experience. You look back and say to yourself, "Gosh, I didn't enjoy that" and boy that was one such experience.

The significance of December 14th to my career at West Bromwich Albion was immense. Upto that date, I had steadied the ship and my unbeaten record was 72%; however, after that day they undermined me, it fell to 46% and a win ratio of nearly 20% and that's poor. Those figures aren't relevant to how I managed other clubs all over the country, where my unbeaten record was around 72%.

The fact of the matter was the Board hadn't addressed the issues on the pitch before they sacked Dennis Smith, and they wouldn't allow me to address them either. We had a lack of goals in the team and that was there for all to see. I also stand by the fact they undermined me. Without a doubt, given the right tools, I would have made a significant change to the situation on the pitch. Losing John Gorman was a major blow to me, but selling £6.3m worth of players and buying a goalkeeper for £80,000 isn't the backing you need as a manager trying to improve his team and bring success.

Chapter 11

WALK ON THE WILD SIDE
Hull City Manager: April 2000–February 2002

"Wow, what have I let myself in for here?"

I fancied a new challenge in the Spring of the new Millennium, and I wanted to get away from the Midlands and start afresh somewhere; the experiences at West Brom and Stoke City had pulled me down a bit, so I was grateful for the opportunity to meet the owners of Hull City.

I agreed to meet the Sheffield-based business consortium consisting of Nick Buchanan, the chairman, Stephen Hinchcliffe, the owner and Andy Daykin, the Commercial Manager, shortly after I'd left my job at the Hawthorns. They were very powerful people in many ways, and larger-than-life in some respects. It was a little bit frightening at first, being introduced to such powerful people, but at the same time it was an interesting meeting, and in late April 2000, just one month after leaving the Hawthorns, I was appointed manager of Division Three (fourth tier) strugglers Hull City on a two-year deal.

There was only one game left of the 1999–2000 season and I had three or four days to prepare for it. I thought it was important that everything was sorted out with the players. There had apparently been some uncertainty about what the previous manager Warren Joyce had done and why he was no longer the manager, so I just wanted to introduce myself to the players and try and prepare them for the game. The first day with the players was quite unique because, what the owners hadn't told me was that Warren had a playermanager contract, so the last person I was expected to see in the dressing room was Warren who I knew anyway, so I stood there in front of the players thinking, "What's Warren doing here? I thought he'd lost his job?" I was quite taken aback really, and felt a bit uncomfortable to start with, but he had been advised by the PFA (Players Football Association) to carry on playing until his compensation had been sorted out. I've never come across that scenario before or since, so that was my first challenge.

After I'd had a chat with Warren in person, he said he was prepared to roll his sleeves up and get on with it, until the time came for him to leave the club. I didn't think that was ideal so I went to speak to the owners as I thought it needed sorting out, one way or the other. As it turned out, Warren had two or three other players who travelled with him in his car from the Manchester area to Hull and that caused some issues, so I had to sort that situation out too.

The first few days flew by and it was matchday at the old Boothferry Park ground, which was a rundown shack of a ground. The Tigers had been hit by huge debts and had previously been locked out of the ground for one game by the landlord, former tennis star David Lloyd, at some stage of that season, so the club were struggling financially. The new consortium was apparently renting the ground from Lloyd, so that was a strange setup in itself.

My first game and the team's last of the season was against Hartlepool United at home and it was a bit of a struggle, but I thought the players did OK, under the circumstances even though we lost 3-0. The result was incidental because it wouldn't have made much difference to our league placing of 14th. However, sitting in the dugout for the first time, I heard some unbelievable comments from fans behind me. One chap shouted, "Oi Brian, every time our goalkeeper has to dive it's a goal. I'm just warning you, mind. I'm just letting you know." That comment didn't fill me with much confidence I must admit. The people of Hull were very open and honest, and I liked that and it was a real eye-opener, that 3-0 result on the last day of the season and it taught me some of the things I wanted to do; I knew already I would be planning for my favoured formation for the start of the next season; I knew I needed to settle in and plan for the pre-season; what sort of players should be coming in; what sort of player should be going out, all the usual things a manager has to think of.

Then on the 3rd May I think it was, the landlord, David Lloyd, locked all the staff out of the ground again because the club hadn't been paying the rent. That was another unique experience.

We were effectively homeless until somebody came up with the money. It was the end of the season and there would normally have been an opportunity to have had a little break, but I wanted to get started straight away, but I couldn't get into work, and it was just the start of a really interesting period for me.

Fortunately, it didn't take too long for them to sort it out and the owners came to some temporary arrangement with David Lloyd. We had a facility at the university to do the training and that's where we did our pre-season work. The first job I had to do was to form a management team, so I asked Kevin Smith, who was my captain at Darlington, and Dave Moore, who also played for me at Darlington for a short time, to join me and we worked closely with the group during pre-season.

I received a phone call from the board a week of two before the season started. They wanted to have a board meeting in the afternoon and they wanted to meet the local press, then they wanted us to meet some of the fans for a local radio show in the evening. It seemed like an eventful day indeed. The agenda arrived the day before and the board meeting was planned to be in a local pub on the seafront, where they'd booked a room. It was all well organised. When everybody arrived for the board meeting, we started off by talking about the plan for the new season; what type of players we were looking for; who the new players were that had already come in; we talked about potential targets; we talked about the style of play, and I got told about my travel arrangements, as the owner had bought the club's own bus to travel in. I hadn't had a chance to bring in too many new faces, with the exception of Lee Philpott, who played for me at Leicester City, joining us early doors. The board also reassured me that the ground situation had been sorted out.

So, all of those things and more were talked about and the meeting lasted a good two hours – that was all well and good, but it was shortly after all the talking had been done that I began to see the fun side of them, because at the end of a serious board meeting, Stephen, the owner said, "We've had enough of this right now, let's just relax a little bit. I'll tell you what, I'm going to have a pint…"

I think we left the pub at 4:30pm, which wasn't the suggested time the meeting was going to end and we had to meet the press at an Italian restaurant at 5:30pm, so I suggested I needed to go home to get freshened up first, while there was a little time to kill. We met the press on time, and of course the board members had already had a few drinks by then and were relaxed while entertaining the journalists. We sat down to eat some nice Italian food, while talking to the press boys and we were well looked after by the chairman and the owner. For me, I hadn't had a drink, but by the time we had finished with the press, which was about 7:30pm, you could tell they'd had a few and I could sense it was going to be carnage by the end of the night.

From the restaurant we went to the fans' meeting with the local radio station, which was due to go out live on local radio. I have to say the press lads were great, and I've learned over the years wherever I've managed, that they like to have a laugh and a joke and get to know any new owners and managers. I must say the board members were also great fun too, and were in their element; however, it ended up bordering on the rowdy.

At the fans' meeting, the room was full and the evening really went down well, mainly because everybody knew the board members had been drinking. Even though it was live on local radio, one of the board members ended up unwittingly swearing in response to a question from the fans. I think the question centred around finances, "Where would we have been if we hadn't had the cup tie with Liverpool?" He was talking about the two-legged League Cup tie with Liverpool in the September before I had arrived and the club had made some good money out of it and kept the club afloat. When asked that question, the chairman used quite a few expletives to confirm how brilliant it was, forgetting of course it was going out live and he continued, "and we would have been completely and utterly in the f***ing shit" Well, his answer brought the house down and I think everybody in the room knew he'd had a few too many. It started to get a bit messy from then on.

When the meeting had finished, I went back home thinking to myself, "Wow, what have I let myself in for here?" I say that, not in a bad way. They were just fun-loving guys who were very wealthy and loved their sport, but they also had a non-serious streak in them that was so evident on that particular day in the summer of 2000, and that wasn't a bad thing.

I've mentioned briefly about the owner, Stephen Hinchcliffe purchasing a team bus to travel to and from away games, but it kept breaking down. I think there was a hole in the radiator and the bus could only travel for short distances because we had to stop at service stations to refill the tank with water. When travelling to away games we couldn't have pre-match meals, unless I'd personally been given cash off the club to pay for the food. Apparently, the club had a poor reputation with regards to cheques bouncing when paying for pre-match meals. In fact it was so bad that it got to the point that I had to pay in cash before we had the food because hotels and restaurants wouldn't accept anything other than cash from us. There were also times when the lads had to take their own food as a pre-match meal. Things were pretty desperate.

With the new season upon us, we didn't start well. After a good pre-season, our first game in the 2000–2001 season was against Blackpool. It was a tough game for us in many respects and we lost 3-1. The first few games weren't too bad, although we drew too many games, but we looked solid; people could see what I was trying to do and the players themselves were buying into the system. However, it was another eight games before we won again, winning two and drawing five. Even by then, we knew there was a good feeling and spirit around the place. We had a great group of players whose mentality was fantastic. We rallied together and given all the problems with the finances of the club, which were farcical if I'm honest, we even made a joke about it; I think that was what we really needed to do in that situation. We maintained a great work ethic throughout; a great team unity, and we all gelled and bonded superbly. In those situations, a set of people can either become stronger or weaker as a group. We became stronger; we laughed a lot; we joked a lot; were worked hard, and we all knew what we were trying to achieve.

Apart from being knocked out of the League Cup by Notts County, by November we'd only lost three games, beating solid teams like Darlington and Hartlepool; by Christmas we'd only lost five games in the league, so we were beginning to make a little bit of a mark for ourselves. We played Leyton Orient early in the season away from home and we drew 2-2, which was a great result for us, because they were flying at that time. Teams like Cardiff City and Brighton were in the league. Now they are in the Premier League and it just tells you how far they have come. I remember Brighton giving us a beating by 2-0, and that proved to be an eye-opener for us; it was a game that was just a little bit too much for us.

During the course of the season, we managed to bring in some new players. We brought in Justin Whittle from Stoke. It was great to bring him in again. He must have thought, "Here's Brian again, he's already sold me once before," but he was a great lad, and 20 years on, he still lives in Hull. The team were a good bunch it has to be said, and as time went by, I managed to add to the group, but during that first season, it was by and large the same group I'd inherited.

The situation at the club didn't unsettle us as a group, but we were unsure what was happening at times, and if we had any information, we made sure everybody knew exactly what was happening, leading up to every game. Up until November time, we didn't really know how grave the situation was, on and off the pitch, but something hit us and it got a little bit too serious. From that time until about mid-January 2001, we won only two of our nine games; we lost five, won two and drew two. Even though the camaraderie was still there, the seriousness kicked in. It was just a case of keeping everybody informed as to what was going on off the field.

Before the Leyton Orient game in mid-February, it was announced in the press that the club was going into admin- istration; Nick Buchanan, the chairman, had announced he would step to one side, and he was prepared for other people to come in. That was the time the seriousness really clicked with us; however, it was also a time we found something else, which was truly amazing. In a situation like that, you either sink or swim – and we definitely started to swim. The proof of that was quite simple, because from the start of February until the end of the season, we drew six, lost two and won 14 of our 22 games. We lost to Brighton, who went on to win the league, and we lost to Cardiff, who finished second – we had some incredible results.

However, training took a turn for the worse; getting the group together on a regular basis became pretty difficult for various reasons. We had players living all over the place; we had Kevin Francis living in Birmingham; Rodney Rowe lived in Huddersfield; Gary Brabim lived in the Blackpool area; we had players living in Manchester and all over the place, so we had to give these fellas some time off. We also had a lot of local lads, too, but the main thing was, all of the lads stayed with us and were terrific throughout the season.

CHAPTER 11: WALK ON THE WILD SIDE

On the day the club went into administration, David Lloyd, who had purchased the club in 1997, claimed it was for the safety of the club and was probably unhappy with how it was being run at the top. When the administrators were appointed, I had to have a daily call from their office in Leeds and had to make several journeys there to talk to the administrators to discuss where we were at and how the team was doing. I told the administrators that we needed players and we were eventually allowed to bring a couple in. They couldn't guarantee whether or not they would get paid, but we did some business, never the less.

It was an incredibly inspiring period. We managed to find something from within because we were all very honest with each other. One day, I was watching TV at my house and I had a knock on my door. It was a fella from a supporters' group, offering me a massive amount of money, thousands of pounds in fact and he wanted me to take it off them, there and then. He was literally stood at my door with a large bag of cash. I couldn't take it and I didn't, even though it was an incredible gesture from the supporters who had collected the money. I'm not sure what happened to that money in the end.

The good feeling around the club and around the area remained throughout that uncertain period. We were getting good gates of 6,000 and up to 11,500; for a team in administration and in the fourth tier of English football it was amazing.

If I remember rightly, there was an American consortium interested in buying the club, but in early March 2001, a boardroom takeover by former Leeds United commercial director Adam Pearson eased the club's precarious financial situation and all fears of closure were banished. He effectively became the saviour of Hull City. You could strsaightaway tell how serious he was to make things work at the club. He was young and enthusiastic and wanted to make an impression. He came in and immediately started to tidy things up, paying up around £1.5m of debts off and making sure the players were paid. There was a period before Adam came in where the players hadn't been paid, for two months I think, so he made a promise to sort that situation out. It was a huge boost to everybody and he was a breath of fresh air. From my point of view, in no time at all I got a company car, a fuel card and things like that became the norm.

One of the shrewdest moves I made was to sign a lad called Andy Holt from Oldham, who was probably a bit of an unknown quantity, but he probably had one of the longest throw-ins in the football league at that time. Thinking about that, we did a shadow game during training one day. It was eleven v eleven where the second string team were passive and didn't have any contact. I stopped the game at one point and asked Kevin Francis to go and stand in the box and then asked Andy to, "Get the ball and show them what you can do." I don't think anybody in the team knew who he was and what he could bring to the team. So, Andy took the ball and threw it from the halfway line into the box, and everybody looked up and went, "Oh, wow!" It turned into a great weapon that we used during the latter part of the season. It meant we could go from the halfway line into the opponents' box in one move. The other thing was, we had six-foot, seven-inch Kevin Francis in and around the box and it made us very strong. We played the game to win; we had a winning formula we still played good football, but we had an alternative to be direct if we wanted to.

On the pitch, we'd ended the season on a high, in sixth place and we were in the playoffs and Adam was very bullish about our chances. We were drawn against Leyton Orient in the semi-final, who had finished one point above us in the table, and in the home leg we were absolutely outstanding. How we only won 1-0 through a John Eyre goal, I will never know. It wasn't a big enough lead. We should have won by at least three or four. We had a crowd of 13,310 for our home leg, which was unheard of, and the old ground was bouncing. Unfortunately, in the away leg, we lost 2-0 and went out. I remember how disappointed Adam was after that game. He was ambitious and our defeat was hard for him to take. It was a real eye-opener for what was to come.

Looking back at that season, with everything that went on, I still think it was a great time for me personally. I have to say, Hull City was one of my favourite places to be. It was one of my favourite seasons ever, and it was an adventure and a great experience, to say the least. I often go back to the area and talk to the fans who got right behind us and they all say it was an enjoyable period in the club's history and they could see that we, as a club, were trying our very best to be competitive in what was a difficult period. It was fear-free football; we had nothing to lose. I couldn't wait until the next season.

The prospects for following season were good. Adam was very excited and was keen to help. He was fantastic initially, he really was. We brought in players like Gary Alexander and Lawrie Dudfield for good money, two strikers who were well thought of; we also brought in Dave Beresford and Ryan Williams, two wingers; the decision to sign them was influenced by watching Chesterfield during the previous season, and they caused problems using two wide players. We also brought in Scott Kerr from Bradford and Richard Sneekes from Stockport. We really pushed the boat out and spent a good amount of money to improve the side, and it really built up the expectations amongst the fans.

Looking back on that second full season, I can honestly say, "It really wasn't me." What I mean by that is, my most successful periods in football management have been when I adopted the 5-3-2 formation, and when I look at Lawrie Dudfield and Gary Alexander, they were the perfect partnership for me, but where I went wrong was to employ two little out-and-out wingers. It didn't really work for us. Having said that, we started the season fantastically well. We went down to Exeter and won and drew a couple of games and beat the likes of Kidderminster, York, Swansea and Rochdale. Even going into November time, we beat Cheltenham Town 5-1, and we were more than capable of scoring goals, but we were also conceding them at the other end. There was something in what I was trying to do, but I never really felt I was 100% comfortable with working with a team that was playing 4-4-2. On reflection, it could have been a go-to situation or a plan B for me. We became a bit hit and miss and a little bit inconsistent, and Adam became a bit chewy with me. He was always concerned on how hard we were working in the training ground. My argument was, I worked with what I was given; it was all about preparation; we were fit enough, and as long as they gave everything on a Saturday, we'd be OK. In fairness to Adam, whatever I asked for, he tried his best to provide. We struggled for proper training facilities, but we built a little facility around the ground at Boothferry Park, after previously using the university facility. However, there was an impatience about him. He wanted everything yesterday and he wanted promotion and you could sense the frustration in him.

I wished I had addressed the inconsistency in our results earlier, in say the November time when that little bit of doubt was creeping in. I should have reverted to my favoured formation. Looking back on it now, I regret not changing it. What held me back was the fact we were a good side and we had some terrific performances. It all came to an end leading up to a defeat at home to Macclesfield on the 22nd February 2002. We'd lost only once in the previous five games; we played them on a Friday night; we played reasonably well; we'd done nothing wrong; everybody worked extremely hard; the team was in good knick, but we lost a game of football. After the game, I told the team we'd come back in on the Monday and prepare for a trip to Swansea on the following Saturday.

Adam was very disappointed with the Macclesfield result, and I received a call on the Monday morning, just as I was leaving home for the training ground. Adam wanted to see me in the office, and that wasn't a problem. He voiced his disappointment in not having the players in over the weekend, not having worked them hard after losing on the Friday night. He made it clear I should have brought them in over the weekend, as a punishment as much as anything else. He felt the players were disappointing, but I couldn't agree with him, in fact I couldn't disagree with him more; I genuinely thought, as the manager, that my team gave 100% and I know when people have let me down, but that night wasn't one of those days. Maybe that's a little bit old-fashioned, I don't know. I made my view clear to Adam, but in the back of that conversation, he asked me to leave the club. He also said he wanted my two assistants, Kevin Smith and Dave Moore to leave as well. I responded by saying, "Well, if that's the way you feel, that's fine. From my point of view, I could sit here and argue or I could go to the LMA and claim this, that and the other." But to be honest, we were too far apart on the situation it wasn't worth the hassle. If I'd argued and got my point across there would have been too much of a rift between us, and I didn't have anything to agree with him about. I stick by my decisions to this day and so we parted company. Before I left the room, we agreed a very small amount of compensation. I had a two-year contract and I didn't argue about that. I could have stretched it out, but I didn't want to do that. The club had been great to me and had looked after me, and I looked after them in very difficult circumstances. I left the room without shaking hands with Adam, but left feeling I'd been very harshly treated.

Certainly, my contract wasn't paid up and I'd left with a very minimal amount of money as we'd agreed, but I was happy with that. I was gutted, heartbroken even and still am in some respects as I'd formed an affection for Hull, so I didn't want to start taking money off the club, money they didn't really have.

Ironically, around six months on from me leaving the club, I received a letter through the post from Adam, apologising for his behaviour and his misjudgement. I still have still that letter to this day. He stated in that letter he was very harsh and he took a decision he later regretted. You know, sometimes in life you just need to sit down, take stock and perhaps listen to other people's reasons and arguments, but it wasn't to be. It was a damn shame, because I had a great affection for everybody at the club. Maybe when Adam came in, he thought he'd get it right straight away, but it's not always the case. Given a bit more time, I would have adjusted that formation and tweaked the team a bit; it was a learning curve, and sometimes in football you become very close to something, but you don't get a chance to see it through. However, I respected the fact that he had the decency to write and apologise to me.

Still to this day, I think I'd have got it right. Ironically, just before I left, I cut the first piece of soil for the new KC Stadium to be built with the Lord Mayor of Hull, and if I'd have held out until the end of that season, I could have moved my team into the new stadium, and perhaps got them moving forward.

The bottom line was, after I'd left, Jan Mølby came in to replace me and they only won one game until the end of the season and finished in 11th place in the Division Three.

Chapter 12

THE ROVERS RETURN
Tranmere Rovers Manager: October 2003–May 2006

"How can any team score five goals against us at home, especially, when we were good enough to score four goals ourselves."

After Hull City chairman, Adam Pearson wrote to me and apologised for sacking me, saying it was the worst mistake he'd ever made, that gave me a bit of confidence to find another job in football; however, I was enjoying my punditry work so much I decided to do it for longer than expected. I'd been out of work for two full seasons since I left Hull City, and during that time, I did a lot of Sky TV work, radio commentary for Radio 5 Live and Irish radio and TV commentary for Setanta Sports in Ireland, amongst other things. I'd actually watched more games in that two-year period than at any stage during my career.

During the early autumn of 2003, I received a phone call, out of the blue, from the Secretary of Tranmere Rovers, and it came on the back of the team struggling in Division Two as it was then; I think they were fourth from bottom of the third tier of English football. I wanted to work and knew I had still something to prove. I believe the club had contacted Dave 'Ned' Kelly, who had previously played for me at Leicester City. Ned was the assistant to Neil Warnock at Sheffield United at the time and the Tranmere board made a formal approach to United with a view to his becoming their manager, but it wasn't right for him and he recommended me instead. I believe he said, "Why don't you look at Brian Little; look at what he's done at Hull City; he's perfect for Tranmere." Subsequently, I received a phone call from the club's Secretary, who asked if I'd like to meet the lady chairperson and other members of the board.

CHAPTER 12: THE ROVERS RETURN

I was enjoying my time out of the game, but at the same time, the call hit me on a day when I thought I was ready to go back into football management. I certainly felt my education had been kept alive by talking about football on TV and radio. Sometimes when you're out of the game and working in the media you tend to think more deeply about football and you try to look for different things to say and you're looking at different things during the game. I was doing the Football League Show with George Gavin as well as doing commentaries for several different media outlets. Some may say you don't learn anything, but commentating on games helps you analyse what's going on in the game and helps you think differently about a game while you're watching it. I think it's a good education.

More often than not, you get offered jobs while you're still in football. However, when you're in the media it isn't a bad thing because you're still being educated about the game and on this occasion, I was lucky to be asked about a job inside the game. I accepted the invite and I remember having a conversation, up on the Wirral, prior to them playing Plymouth in a mid-week match. I think they had previously just lost a couple of games and were obviously in a bit of a mess in the league. I knew I wasn't going to get offered the job there and then, but looking at the fixture at the weekend, I thought to myself it would be a baptism of fire, if I were to be offered it.

I had an interview with some of the board members, and went through my CV and all my achievements at all the clubs I'd managed and I genuinely felt that my stock was still high, even though I'd been sacked by Hull City two years previously. I then spoke about the system I like my teams to play and the fact I knew the league, as I'd covered it with Sky. The whole interview went really well and they were listening to every word I was saying. I made a point of saying the most important thing when you go into a struggling club is to try and stop the club struggling. I said you couldn't suddenly change a team that had lost games, left, right and centre into a team that would win games for fun. There had to be a process, which ultimately saves the club at the end of the season. It's more about being unbeaten and hard to beat, rather than winning every game, but the process was to steady the ship and climb your way out of trouble. It's very rare that a team at the bottom of the table suddenly wins five or six games in the row. You have to have a strong mentality; you have to have a game plan; you have to believe in your game plan and if you lose a game early on, you can't suddenly change the system. You have to have belief in what you do and what you want to achieve. I said all those things in my interview and I went home feeling happy with what I presented. They didn't offer me the job there and then, and I assumed they were speaking to other people, which was fine. I accepted the fact that I might have to go through several more interviews before I got another job, but I was relishing that challenge.

The days passed and I'd heard nothing from Tranmere, and I carried on working that weekend for Sky. As it happened, Tranmere lost 6-0 at Plymouth that weekend and as I saw the scoreline I remember thinking I would get a phone call in the next 24–48 hours; if I didn't, somebody else surely would. The 6-0 hammering was a scoreline that dropped them right into trouble. The club was desperate for a new manager. I'm not sure who managed the team that day – it may have been John McMahon, the youth team coach. John was an exceptional young coach, but he wasn't ready for the step up to the first team at that time.

Lo and behold, I got that call from Tranmere on the Sunday and they asked me if I'd accept the job. Obviously, I needed to speak to them again before I accepted, given we hadn't discussed contracts so I suggested I go up to Merseyside to meet up with the board members. When we met, we quickly mapped out an 18-month contract that was acceptable to me, and I became the new manager of Tranmere Rovers.

When news broke that I had become their new manager, it was described on Sky Sports News as the most difficult job I'd had to date, even more difficult than managing at West Bromwich Albion, which I found surprising, but that's how some people looked upon it at the time.

The club initially asked me to keep Ray Matthias as my chief scout after they had sacked him. To be fair to Ray, he'd been around the club for a long time, but with the greatest respect, I didn't feel it was the right thing to do. He knows that, but sometimes when you've had the sack as a manager, to get another job within the same club isn't easy and in my mind, isn't the right step for the club to take. Whether I'd done the correct thing or not, I will stand by my decision.

One of my first signings was to bring in Richard Hill as my assistant manager. He was great friends with John Gregory and it was great to take him to Tranmere. I didn't know him particularly well but he came well recommended.

I'm pretty sure my first game in charge was a LDV Vans Trophy game, away at Blackpool, who were managed by Steve McMahon. I didn't have too much input prior to that game and we found ourselves 3-0 down by half time. I wasn't going to blast the players in the dressing room at half time, but I told them I didn't want to play the same way, so I changed a few things round and gave them a different outlook on how to play the game, with three centre-backs. Although, we still lost the lost the tie 3-2, we effectively had won the second-half by scoring two goals. After the game, I told the players we could work on the new system moving forward. The game was an eye-opener, but at the same time I did get a response from the players in the second half, which was a positive start and gave me some encouragement.

I'd inherited a team that had just lost 6-0 and in my first game, we had let in another three goals, so there was a defensive issue and I knew I had to make my mark on the team, change a few things and make us stronger pretty quickly. It is impossible to go from a losing team to one that wins every game in the space of a few weeks. I knew it would take time, but I also knew that by playing my way, we would eventually get stronger. I knew exactly how I wanted the team to play and I knew I had to make them hard to beat. It wasn't about how many games you win, but about how many games you don't lose when you're a team at the bottom. It is a grind when you're rock bottom. I knew there was something wrong inside that club, given their position in the league. Anybody who says they can go straight into a club, play dynamic football and win every week is talking rubbish. It's just not possible. At every struggling club I've been to, it's all about working at a system, giving very little away and trying to gradually work your way out of trouble. Not many teams at the bottom of the league win seven or eight games on the bounce. If you're in the bottom four or five by October or November after 11 or 12 games you've got something wrong at your club and you need to work hard to grind out results. If you have only won five games all season, there's no way you're going to win three out of the last five games of the season.

My first league game at home against Oldham sticks out in my memory, mainly because I started with the three centre-backs and brought in a young lad called Paul Linwood to link up with

Sean Connelly at right-back and Gareth Roberts at left-back. Micky Mellon was in midfield and we also had the likes of Ian Hume, who was an outstanding player. It's funny how people come back to haunt you in life, because within 30 minutes of the kick-off, we went 1-0 down through a goal by John Eyre, whom I sold when I was Hull City manager and I think by his reaction, he enjoyed scoring against me. We battled on and worked hard, and eventually clawed ourselves back into the game and scored two late goals. I really think that second half at Blackpool helped us become stronger at the back.

Something else stuck out in that game because Oldham had a young centre forward on loan from Newcastle called Calvin Zola, who played really well against us. After the game, I walked onto the pitch and congratulated him because of the way he played, even though he played for the opposition. I didn't say anything else other than, "Well played young man. You played really well against us today." He stuck in my mind for the rest of that season, because at the start of the next season I actually signed Calvin. That little chat I had with him must have stuck in his mind, too.

During that season, we had a magnificent FA Cup run, which saw us beat the likes of Chesterfield 3-2 at home and Hornchurch 1-0, in a game that we had got battered in for long spells. Then we came across Bolton Wanderers, who were a Premier League club at the time and we drew 1-1 at Prenton Park, but in the replay at the Reebok Stadium, we beat them 2-1, with Ian Hume getting the winner. We went on to beat Luton 1-0 in the Fourth Round and then Swansea 2-1 in the fifth round. Suddenly we found ourselves in the last 16. In the quarter-final, we played out a goalless draw against Millwall at The Den, but in the reply we came unstuck at home and lost 2-1. As it turned out, Millwall actually went on to play Manchester United in the final that year.

The great thing about Tranmere at that time was that there were some really good young players in the likes of Ryan Taylor, Danny Harrison, Steve Jennings, Chris Dagnall, Ian Hume, Paul Linwood, Neil Ashton and Alan Navarro. I had a good opportunity there to give these young players a go in the first team and they certainly didn't let me down. One of the best signings I made was a lad called Ian Goodison, whom I've already mentioned as he had played for me at Hull City. He was a legendary Jamaican International and he was a terrific player.

Commentating on the
2011–2012 Europa League Final
in Bucharest between Atlético
Madrid and my favourite
Spanish team, Athletic Bilbao

With the League Cup, celebrating
140 years of Aston Villa FC in 2014

Press conference at Hull City with Dave Capper
(left) and Steven Hinchcliffe (right)

Mr. B. Little
Manager
Tranmere Rovers Football Club
Prenton Park
Prenton Road West
Birkenhead
Wirral CH42 9PY

Our Ref: AP/2717/lvh

16th October 2003

Dear Brian,

I am absolutely sure that I am the last person you would want to receive any platitudes from. However I would still like to offer my most sincere congratulations on your appointment as manager of Tranmere Rovers.

Hindsight is obviously an easy attribute to possess, but it was obviously an extremely rash decision that I made eighteen months ago and one that I regretted almost immediately.

I wish you and your family well and I am sure you will have great success at Tranmere Rovers in the near future.

Kind regards,

Adam Pearson
Chairman, Hull City AFC.

Official Club Sponsor

THE HULL CITY ASSOCIATION FOOTBALL CLUB (TIGERS) LIMITED

The Kingston Communications Stadium • The Circle • Walton Street • Anlaby Road • Hull HU3 6HU
Tel: 0870 8370003 • Fax: 01482 304882 • www.hullcityafc.net • email info@hulltigers.com

Registration No. 04032392

A message sent by former Hull City chairman, Adam Pearson, six months after he sacked me in 2003

The quickest way to Wrexham and back –
me and my Honda Super Blackbird

Me with one of the Leicester City
favourites, Alan Birchenhall

Me with the 1990–1991
Division Four Championship
trophy while at Darlington

Stanley Victor Collymore
was my biggest ever signing
at nearly £8m for Villa

Me with Ian Ormondroyd
before the 1994 playoff final

John Gregory, Allan Evans and myself during the last
few minutes of the 1994 playoff final at Wembley

With the Midlands press at Leicester City, talking about my departure from the club

Looking worried as Tranmere manager

A thoughtful moment as Gainsborough Trinity manager - probably thinking, "I'm not sure if non-league is for me"

Being appointed Stoke City manager in 1998

First day as Leicester City manager with my new backroom team,
John Gregory (left), Steve Hunt (middle) and Allan Evans (right)

Penny for my thoughts - during a
press conference at Leicester City

I raised a few eyebrows when
I signed David Speedie - I'd
rather have him on my side than
playing against me, though

The famous Hell Station in Norway – it brought us good luck

A lonesome figure in the dugout. Sometimes
you just need five minutes alone

In fact, I remember Ian had called me, prior to me going to Tranmere, and he told me he'd had a nasty injury, which meant he'd left Hull City and he had gone back home for a while; he was desperate to come back to the UK and play football. After speaking to Ian, I contacted Danny Wilson at Bristol City and told him about Ian with a view of giving him a trial and of course, Danny agreed. Ian then flew over and we met to go to Bristol so he could hook up with Danny's side for a week. After not playing for a while, Ian wasn't as fit as he needed to be and he required games under his belt; Danny didn't have any opportunities for him at Bristol City so that was that. Anyway, a few weeks went by and by that time I had taken up the Tranmere job and I told our first-team coach, John McMahon, about Ian and if he'd help him do some extra training to get him up to match fitness. I was convinced Ian could do a good job for us, but he needed a lot of time to get fit. John agreed and the first training session Ian took part in, John came up to me and said he was like "Bambi on ice" and "he was all over the place". John said there was no way I could sign him and he was convinced the injury had a massive affect on him. John even told me not to be sentimental about it. I took on board John's advice, but asked him to give Ian two or three weeks and I promised if he didn't improve, I would let him go.

As the weeks past, Ian slowly improved, but he hadn't completely convinced any of us that he could be useful for us. However, I gave Ian an opportunity and signed him. The irony of that is he became a legend at Tranmere and stayed over 10 years.

After signing Ian, I also signed two more talented Jamaican internationals in Theodore Whitmore and Paul Hall. I signed Paul on loan when I was West Bromwich Albion manager so he was another player I knew all about.

As it turned out, we won our next game against Swindon and it was another few games before we lost again, against Barnsley. Some games that stick out in my mind included a 5-1 away win at Bournemouth. If you think where they are in the Premier League and where Tranmere are now, out of the Football League, it shows you just what can happen in football. It's just an incredible situation, looking at some football clubs and where they have gone in such a relatively short space of time.

As the season went on, we became hard to beat and in fact we were unbeaten in 33 of my 41 games during that season. I wasn't overly interested in the win percentage, but to come into a team that was fourth from bottom of the league and to be unbeaten in so many of those games was a remarkable recovery and we actually finished the season in 8th place. It was a pleasure to work with those players and they helped me settle in really well. I really believe that my work outside of football played a massive part in the success we had during that season, helping us restructure the club. It was a great start to my career at Tranmere.

The irony was that Plymouth, who had beaten us so convincingly the game before I arrived at Prenton Park, actually won the league that season.

In my second season, I secured the signing of Mark Rankine, a midfielder who had great energy but was coming towards the end of his career. I also went out of my way to sign Calvin Zola, as I've mentioned before. It has to be said, he had a lot of problems. He was classed as a refugee from Zaire and as it turned out we discovered issues with his visa, due to his background. We worked hard to get him his papers and he was unable to play for us until a solution was reached. It effectively kept him out of the whole season. Unfortunately, it was quite a lengthy process that lasted until May 2005, when at last he was granted a full permit and returned in time for training for the 2005–2006 season.

I also signed Jason McAteer, who was also coming towards the end of his career. I was often asked to be a studio guest on The Championship, a TV programme featuring the goals from the Football League, even when I was the Tranmere manager and on one occasion the other studio guest was Jason. We had a chat off camera and he was saying he was thinking about retiring, even though he was only 33 and playing for Sunderland at the time. I got the feeling he really wanted to go back home to Merseyside more than anything else. I remember saying to him, "If ever you want to come over to Tranmere, let me know" and left it at that. It was a bit tongue in cheek to be honest, but lo and behold, I got a call a few months later from Jason's agent, and he referred back to the chat I had with him. I later arranged to sit down with the agent, and if truth were to be told it wasn't an easy thing to sort out. Jason had a long history of playing in the Premier League and in international football and possibly had a contract to be sorted out at Sunderland, but we eventually managed to get a two-year deal done. I even made him club captain and he intended to do his coaching badges while with us.

We signed a lad called Michael Jackson, a centre-back from Preston and came highly recommended. I'd watched him loads of times and seemed like a solid professional and he was available on a free transfer. I also signed David Beresford from Plymouth, who had played for me at Hull City. The squad was slowly increasing, with the new transfers and the emergence of young talented players from the youth system, but more importantly, it was getting stronger. Of course, we lost a few players. Micky Mellon for one went to Blackpool, more by choice as he was offered a better contract. He was a great lad, was good around the dressing room, had a great sense of humour and always had something to say. He was a loss, but that's football. You have to change things around some times.

I was full of expectation for the 2004–2005 season and the beauty of it was I'd have a full pre-season with them, which is something I didn't have the previous campaign. Pre-season always makes a difference and I loved it. Going back to my first ever pre-season as an apprentice at Villa, it taught me what not to do. While I understood the work ethic, sometimes you test people because it helps team-bonding by pulling each other through hard training sessions, but I said to myself I'd never, ever put anybody through training sessions that I couldn't do myself, wouldn't do myself or wouldn't enjoy myself.

We had Les Parry as our physio and he was an unbelievable character. At that time, Les was pretty much 'Mr Tranmere'. He was a very talented, intelligent guy and highly qualified. Les had been at Tranmere all his life and knew the area, so he knew the places where were could do things differently or in a different environment. The beauty of being on the Wirral was that we had the beach, which was always a great place to train. We had the estuary, so when the tide was out, we could run across it for miles, before the tide came back in, of course. He was a great physiotherapist, that good in fact that none of the players wanted to get injured, they wanted to be on the training ground. His rehab work was tough and one that meant nobody would pretend to be injured, that's a certainty. I've been in football clubs over the years and prior to the modern day when sports science really kicked in, it was easy to say you had an injury and players could miss a day's training. Throughout my career in the 1970s, 1980s and 1990s as a player, coach and football manager, you could often look at somebody and say, "He's pulling a fast one today."

But Les was one of those physios who could see right through whoever was trying to pull a fast one, and believe me, they didn't do it very often. Les was one of those people who could develop a work session that was not only hard, but also beneficial to you. Nobody ever skived off training sessions because of it.

Incidentally, Les later became the manager of Tranmere after I left. I think he now works for Manchester United, which is testament to his ability and how highly thought of he is. I was blessed to have him there with me.

We had a brilliant pre-season that consisted of short and sharp work sessions, with the occasional longer session, just for that team-bonding exercise, where I'd set them off together and they try to finish off as a group. I really enjoyed the pre-season on the Wirral; it was a wonderful place to be, and Richard and I were delighted with the group we had put together; we had a group that were there to help each other and had a great team spirit amongst the lads.

The season started at Peterborough and we lost 1-0, which put a dampener on it, but they became a bit of a bogey side of ours throughout the season. The next game we played Hartlepool and beat them 2-1, to get us under way. A ten-game unbeaten run followed before we were beaten again, against Bradford City in one of the weirdest and most outrageous games I've ever been involved in. We played at home and lost 5-4 and I went home thinking, "How can any team score five goals against us at home, especially, when we were good enough to score four goals ourselves." I think we were 4-2 down at one stage and scrambled our way back to 4-4, but in the 91st minute, they scored the winner.

We'd made a real solid start to the season, which was great. However, there were some disappointing results along the way, though. Two of the worst games we played in that season were against Hull City, where I'd been sacked a few seasons previously. Peter Taylor was their manager, a quality coach and we lost both games, home and away, and it wasn't easy to take, either. They scored nine goals against us in both games, including a 6-1 thrashing in December at the new KC Stadium. That was another weird game, because we actually had two goalkeepers carried off. John Achterberg, our main 'keeper got injured when we were 2-1 down and he was replaced by Russell Howarth. Lo and behold, having being on for less than 10 minutes, Russell got injured and he got carried off. Of all the places where I wanted to do well, we were without a proper goalkeeper and losing the game. To be honest, absolutely nobody wanted to go in goal, but out of nowhere, Theodore Whitmore stepped up to the plate and took the gloves. It was as though the rest of the team threw the gloves and goalkeeper shirt at him. In all fairness, Theodore would have been everybody's last choice to keep goal. That game was almost comical, and if you could laugh at a football match, that would have been it. Theodore, bless him, let in four goals during the time he kept goal. I don't recall him picking the ball up once, except out of the net; if the ball came anywhere near him, he'd dive to knock it out with his feet; if there was a backpass, he'd boot it out or would dribble it out of the box. He was a marvellous talent, but he was no goalkeeper. In the return game at Prenton Park in the March, we lost 3-1.

Hull got promoted that season, which wasn't surprising, but we finished third in the newly formed League One; 55 games played and unbeaten in 41 of those, which was immense. To be unbeaten in 41 games is fantastic in any league and to get the team into the playoffs was a great achievement. I knew we had a decent team; we weren't that far behind the likes of Hull City and Luton Town, to be fair. We did well against the top six sides and we deserved to be in the playoffs. I think we finished with 79 points, seven points behind Hull, which wasn't bad.

We'd beaten Hartlepool twice in the league, but in the playoff first leg, we lost the away tie 2-0, but at Prenton Park, in front of 13,356 fans, we won the game 2-0 to take it to extra-time. Their goalkeeper was six foot four inches tall, a huge fella and he stopped almost everything we threw at him that night. Unfortunately, the score remained tied after 120 minutes and it went to penalties. What did us was the fact that Ryan Taylor, who was an unbelievable striker of the ball, missed our first penalty and that put us on the back-foot. With the scores 5-5, Ian Sharp stepped up looking nervous and it made me nervous too, looking on from the sidelines. Lo and behold, their 'keeper pulled off a great save and that left Ritchie Humphries to slot home the winning penalty to make it 6-5. Regardless of the score, it was an unbelievably exciting evening. Besides the results in the league, the playoffs prove it's a bit of a lottery and anybody can win on their day. In the final, Sheffield Wednesday beat Hartlepool to get promoted to the Championship.

With another pre-season under our belts, I was hopeful for the 2005–2006 season in League One. Our first game was at Swansea and the very first at the new Liberty Stadium. Although we played really well and were the better team, we lost the game through a single Adebayo Akinfenwa goal. There was a great atmosphere amongst the 17,000 fans, and they had the likes of Garry Monk, Roberto Martínez, Lee Trundle and Leon Britton. When you look at my team, it was fairly solid, but we'd lost Ian Hume, Calvin Zola, Paul Hall and Theodore Whitmore and Ryan Taylor, although we brought in Chris Greenacre from Stoke and Sam Aiston from Shrewsbury, among others. In fact, Chris Greenacre cost £40,000 and that was the only money I'd spent in the two years I had been at the club I think. Because we had sold Ryan Taylor for over £1m, we felt we had to spend some of it.

By the end of August, we'd lost two, won three and drawn one, but for the next six weeks we couldn't win a game for love nor money; nine defeats in 12 games just wasn't good enough. It seemed like the wheels had come off. The stats looked poor when you consider we didn't score a goal in eight games out of the first 14. If you're not a free-scoring team, those things tend to catch up on you. I couldn't put my finger on what went wrong, but sometimes, just one or two changes altered the whole balance of the side. I made some loan signings, taking in Nicky Summerbee and Alex Bruce and they were outstanding for me. Alex was one of those players I signed after I saw playing against us (at Oldham) and I shook his hand to congratulate him on his performance, merely my way of recognising a decent player has had a good game against my team. For me, it's more like break-ing the ice with a player, who may or may not recognise the fact I had taken notice of him. When you're a lower league player, to be recognised by a manager could benefit you in the future, and on several occasions that tact helped me seal the deal with players. There were also players that I recognised on the pitch, but I didn't sign. I also signed Simon Francis on loan, and when you see what Simon has done since, playing for Bournemouth in the Premier League, it was a privilege to have him around the place. When I looked at the teams I put out, I'd often say it wasn't a bad team on paper and I didn't do too much wrong in the transfer market, but I knew the dynamics of the team wasn't quite right. Sometimes, it can be right under your nose and you think the team has improved; you can argue the players we signed that season were actually better players than those we had before and there was the makings of a good team there, but they just didn't gel. That can happen in football. It's a crazy situation. It was unusual for me because I normally pick players, not just for their ability, but also for their camaraderie and the type of person they are, on and off the pitch.

I really liked Jason McAteer and was a big fan of him as a player and a person, and I knew he was desperate to get into the coaching side. As a right wing-back, he had incredible energy and I would have liked to sign him for one of my previous clubs when he was younger. I think Jason found it difficult to adjust to life in League One. Everywhere he went he got so much stick it was untrue and unfair. Sometimes, taking a player of that calibre to a lower division actually winds up the opposition crowd and players. I think there was a bit of friction between my assistant Richard Hill and Jason. He'd stepped down a couple of levels after leaving Sunderland in the previous season and he had been thinking of a coaching career and I don't think they really hit it off. Sometimes when those bits of friction go on in a football club, you know they're there but, as a manager, you find it hard to deal with.

There were some games during the season that I think to myself, "How did we lose to them?" Some of the results were quite embarrassing. When I look back, there were some big teams in that league. Nottingham Forest were in League One, for instance and so were Bournemouth, who weren't a big team back then, but are now. We couldn't score against them in either game, even though the season before we'd got four points off them and beat them 5-0 in one game.

The poor start then turned into a hard season. I knew I had to reinvent myself and build us up again, just like I did when I first came into the club. I decided to do just that and work at my system on the training ground and make the players work harder than they would normally do in the middle of a season.

From the 19th November I was wise enough to have reinvented myself; I recognised that something needed to be done and we went back to basics and got the players to play my system again, and the results showed. Up to 25th March, we had only lost five games in 20, and that was from a point at being at the bottom end of the table. However, we had a horrible period at the end of the season when we only won two out of the last seven games and found we were under pressure again. The group had potential, but there was something fundamentally not right about it, which was a surprise to me. Unlike in the previous season, when we finished third, we never really had that balance.

I never really changed that squad during the season. I had done my transfers during pre-season, but a couple of the characters weren't as close to each other as they should have been and there was an obvious tension between Jason and Richard. In fairness, Jason got booked and sent off a couple of times when he shouldn't have and Richard took offence and sometimes took it out on him. Losing Paul Hall before the season started took its toll and made people think why Chesterfield could pay him more than we could. In the end, there were a few things that went wrong and weren't quite right which ultimately made it more difficult for a manager to get the results we were looking for. There's a fine dividing line between success and failure and sometimes, as a manager you just can't put your finger what went wrong. Sometimes, because it's all around you, a manager can sense something is wrong, but you can't really get stuck into it until the end of the season.

There was a significant game towards the end of that season, at Milton Keynes Dons, and it turned out to be quite a defining moment in my Tranmere career. Just after losing four games in a row, we went there and won and that victory made us safe. I remember getting on the bus after the game and Lorraine Rogers, the chairperson, and the club secretary travelled back with us and I recall thinking there was something not quite right about it. They knew I didn't allow the players to drink alcohol on the team bus, but they had brought some beers for the lads, and for once I took a blind eye to it. They asked me if I wanted a glass of beer and I agreed to one. I think that was the first time ever I had an alcoholic drink on a team bus as a player or a manager. To be honest, I couldn't be bothered to make a scene and actually thought it would be nice for the lads. It was the end of the season and we'd avoided relegation, but I didn't think it was anything to celebrate. It was more of a relief for me.

It was only a few days later that I was asked to see the board members. We went through everything that had happened during the whole season; we talked about the changes that had been made; we talked about how we would move forward; we discussed the rift between Richard, and Jason. It was the sort of meeting a manager should have more often than at the end of a season. We never had board meetings and we never got together very often to discuss things during the season; as a manager I just got on with it, but I think discussing issues with the board is the right thing to do. It was quite obvious to me as the meeting came to a close and we all shook hands and left the room, they acknowledged my overall achievements in taking the club forward in the two years I'd been manager. I recognised where the problems were, but I believed in my system that was tried and tested. However, I sensed they wanted a change; I had sensed it from the time they travelled on the team bus back from Milton Keynes.

To finish that season as low as we did, they saw as a backward step. A couple of days later, I got a call from the club secretary who asked me to pop in and see him. As ever, I'm one who thinks if you're not wanted there's no point in falling out about it or staying in a situation you don't feel comfortable in, so during that meeting we came to a mutual agreement for me to move on. It was an odd situation to be honest.

I'd had a great time at Tranmere and I look at some of the results and it was brilliant, but sometimes things end up in such a mess it's untrue.

Ronnie Moore soon came in and replaced me and within two weeks had signed two players for £100,000 each, which seemed like a fortune as I'd only been able to buy one player for money (Chris Greenacre) during those two years and I was sometimes turned down when I wanted to sign somebody because it was £10 a week too much. I'm not criticising the way the club handled my transfers, I'm simply saying how it was.

I understand Ronnie was very keen to go back to the Tranmere way as he'd had a connection with the club for many years, and credit to him, I think they recovered in the following season and finished maybe, eighth.

Chapter 13

BACK TO WORK –
BUT NOT FOR LONG

Wrexham Manager: November 2007–September 2008

"Enough is enough"

I'd been out of work since I'd left my role at Tranmere Rovers during May 2006, so I was looking for some stability in my life and for another opportunity to show a club what I could do as a manager. I'd been previously linked with roles at Port Vale and Gillingham, but nothing materialised with them. However, I recall being at home one day in November 2007 and receiving a call from Jonathan Hassall, who was just starting up as a football agent; I'd known Jonathan's dad Brian for many years, so I was happy to have received his call. Jonathan called me to see if I'd be interested in trying to help Wrexham out.

As at every club, expectations were high for Wrexham for the 2007–2008 season, as there had been some good signings and a push for promotion was expected by the fans, following the disappointment of the previous campaign, which saw the club stave off relegation from the Football League on the last game of the season. However, the season kicked off in a similar vein; the first few games started badly, with the club rooted to the bottom of the table.

Following on from my brief discussion with Jonathan, I agreed to meet the chairman with a view of helping the club out, and as soon as I told Jonathan I was interested, I started doing some homework on the club.

The then Wrexham manager, Brian Carey, who ironically played for me at Leicester City, was a super lad; I thought a lot of him and he was a super player for me. Speaking to Jonathan, he told me the chairman strangely wanted Brian and his staff to stay at the club; he just wanted me in there to take over and guide them to safety in the league. It didn't sound like any job I had done before. However, I noted the squad was very much the same as it was in the previous season, barring a few new signings. I think, due to the fact they stayed up by the skin of their teeth, there had been a few massive celebrations and no doubt masses of relief too.

I found out that a lot of the lads actually had had their contracts renewed for the next season. I found it strange that most of the team remained unchanged. My take on the situation was, if you've had a struggling season, then change as many things as you possibly can, and as quickly as you can. At previous clubs who were struggling where I took over at, I tried to immediately turn the playing staff around as soon as I took on the job; I tried to move out the players who'd suffered the hard times; I tried to bring in fresh faces. At any club who is struggling, you need to bring in fresh faces, so in theory I saw the job in a similar vein, if I were to be successful in getting the nod.

On 6 November 2007 Wrexham Football Club released a statement saying that the club were looking for an "Experienced Senior Manager" to work alongside the current staff. So, I got the call from Jonathan to say the chairman wanted to meet me. Stafford wasn't a million miles from Wrexham so I went cross-country to meet him and some of the directors in early November. They were all very impressed with what I was saying to them, and I stressed to them that changing the playing staff was the most important thing that could happen for the club. When a team avoids relegation, you don't reward the players with new contracts just because they had kept the club up. I sensed the board were very loyal to their staff. Brian was a good person and a good manager, so I understood that. However, I also stressed that if there were players on two or three-year contracts, it would be very difficult to move them out. Players on long contracts tended to be fairly comfortable where they are, and I highlighted to the board that they might have similar problems on that front. I asked what the possibility was of bringing players into the club, and to my surprise they said it wouldn't be a problem. It was evident they wanted to stay in the Football League and would do anything to help me.

On reflection, I thought about it and decided it was a challenge I was willing to take. I had a smashing interview at a hotel on the Welsh border and they really appreciated what I had said, and more importantly, understood what I was saying. However, I could sense they weren't entirely happy with me wanting to change things immediately, but as I pointed out to them, they were in that position in the league because of how they played last season, not just this season. They had struggled because the team weren't good enough. It was as simple as that. I also suggested changing the backroom staff around, but they were adamant they were happy with the current staff.

I accepted the role, so on 15 November 2007 and I was named as Wrexham's new manager and the replacement to Brian Carey, who took the role of my assistant manager.

As soon as the news was announced, the first job I had to do was to speak to Brian. It was a hard thing for me to do, and hard for him to listen to me, because I knew Brian wanted to be the manager. He'd worked very hard at Wrexham for many years, as had his backroom staff, and was very happy there. Brian knew me, and he knew I was the not the sort of person to mess with and he knew I would be willing to change things if they needed to be changed.

I soon made time to meet every member of the backroom staff and all the players and made everybody understand that I was in charge, like it or not. I made it clear to everybody that I was quite serious in doing well in the role. I was serious about my football and that there was a right time and a wrong time to start messing about with both the playing and the backroom staff. I'm not the type of manager who has lots of fun in a situation where you're not enjoying it. For me, it's simple – results bring a smile to people's faces and can make the training sessions more enjoyable, so there was a time and a place for fun. I made a point to the staff that I wanted everything to be as serious as it could be, for the initial period at least, whilst I drilled into the players exactly what I wanted and expected of them. I sensed from my first meeting, that what I was saying wasn't going down very well. They all sensed I was ready to move people on, and they felt uncomfortable. Although I didn't want to make people on edge, or feel uncomfortable about the situation, I wasn't especially frightened about it. Having said all that, I'd had the backing from the chairman and given time, I knew I could turn the club around, but I could only do that with the help of the players and the backroom staff.

I had a little bit of breathing space as there was a break between matches so I had a good few days on the training ground with the players. Although they weren't totally set up to play the system I wanted to play, we adjusted things around and I worked hard for a week where I put my thoughts across in a positive way. Sometimes you go into a new club and there's a game the very next day or next couple of days, so you're under pressure immediately. This time, I had plenty of time to work on playing 3-5-2; we worked on that formation, day in and day out for that period of time.

From day one, I sensed things weren't right; I sensed there was an edge because of the uncertainty of the situation; there was a fear of change at Wrexham, and that it was just around the corner. The staff and the players were a very close group, but they weren't winning games and even if they were a close group, they needed to seriously consider what should be changing but that was just my opinion and they needed convincing.

My tenure started slowly. We started off with a couple of draws. My first game was actually on my birthday and a local derby against Chester. We drew 2-2. It wasn't an ideal result for me because I wanted to create a difficult team to beat, and on that occasion we conceded twice. My second game was at Rochdale and we came away with a clean sheet, and I was pretty pleased with that result because Rochdale were a decent side in those days. We then went to Bury, who were pushing for promotion and were near the top of the league and we won 1-0. We'd gone away from home and played with three centre-backs, not had a lot of possession, defended really well and we won the game. Things were going OK and the atmosphere in the dressing room after the game was unbelievable, I have to say. I almost sensed there and then, that I'd finally got to grips with the players and they were buying into my methods, but, unfortunately, that wasn't the case. In fact, it reminded me of my spell at Darlington, where I'd had people who were really attentive and bought into the change process, but in the end, they didn't have the courage to stick together and push on from a few great results.

After the first three games we were unbeaten, but we came crashing down to earth because we lost the next seven games on the bounce. There were a couple of games where we couldn't play my favoured formation because we didn't have the person-nel, due to injuries, and we ended up losing the points. It was at the end of that losing run, that I decided to sit down with the chairman and told him I needed to change things. He wasn't happy about that, but he had said to me he'd help me out, even if it meant players did have to move on. I was a little bit uncomfortable within the coaching area of not having an ally. Even though I knew Brian Carey, and we got on well, he'd been in my position only a matter of weeks ago and had moved down to become a coach. It's not an easy position for somebody to be in and I understood that. However, I just felt I needed someone to join me, somebody who I'd known for a long time and could be an ally for me in the dressing room. The chairman's response to that was simple. He told me it was my decision to bring whoever I wanted in, but at the same time, it was also my decision who to move on. That statement made me feel a bit uneasy, but I agreed nonetheless.

In the end, I chose to move on one of the younger members of the coaching team, in order for me to bring in former Port Vale boss, Martin Foyle, who I'd known for many years. On reflection, and in hindsight, what I did sent the wrong message out and from inside the club. People became even warier of me. Having said that, Martin was a great ally to me, just when I needed one and he and I could at least talk about the situation in a completely fresh light.

We went through a period of time where we tried to move some of the surplus players on. I also spoke to the chairman about bringing people in to freshen up the squad, and to his credit, he backed me on that front. We actually managed to bring in eight new players: Sam Aiston, Phil Bolland, Gavin Ward, Danny Sonner, Paul Hall, Carl Tremarco, Drewe Broughton and Stuart Nicholson. Some of the lads had played for me before, the likes of Sam Aiston, Gavin Ward and Paul Hall, for instance. There were good young players at the club during my time there. I had a young lad called Neil Taylor, who's now playing for Aston Villa. As a very young lad there, he got quite a bit of game time. I also felt that a lad called Wes Baynes was going to be a good player; he played right wing back and he played quite a bit of football at that level, but he never kicked on. However, the only player I was able to move out of the club was a lad called Ryan Valentine. He was our best player, for that league anyway and he went to Darlington, and that proved to be a great move for him.

What I was doing wasn't anything new. I'd brought in new players at all the clubs I'd managed. However, what I wasn't doing was to move players on, and that brought about an issue. We had too many players in the squad and too few positions to fill. That meant there were too many players that wouldn't get a game, and that caused me a lot of issues, with players banging on my door to get a game. I always felt that every time I named a Wrexham team for a game, even before I'd met the press, that everybody in the town knew the side I'd be picking. A lot of the players were very close to the fans; many of the younger players were fans themselves, so I had this feeling that everything I did, word got around the place before information was disclosed into the public domain. That made me feel a bit alienated and I was uncomfortable with it. Whatever I did was met with not a great deal of pleasure, as if the town didn't want me there.

The job wasn't made easy for me from day one.

So, we had those seven defeats on the trot and that made my job even harder. However, we then went on a six-game unbeaten run, with good results against the likes of Milton Keynes Dons and Darlington, and only lost two out the next 11, which was OK, but it was a real mixed bag of results.

I did my best to appease the fans, by going out into the community, visiting supporters clubs, and Martin and I went all over the place trying to promote the club, trying to take ourselves into the hearts of the fans, but it just never, ever looked as though it was going to go for us.

It was an interesting period it has to be said. We played away to Peterborough that season, and they were top of the league and we played with the three centre-backs and we looked so solid to draw 0-0. The most frustrating thing was, when the players concentrated their minds on the football it was good, but they just couldn't produce it week in, week out, which again, was reminiscent of my spell at Darlington. When the players were with us, they were OK, but they very quickly turned against us. It was a very difficult period for me and I found it really odd. In stark contrast to the away game against Peterborough, we played them at home and Sir Alex Ferguson came to watch his son's team play, up in the stand, and his presence caused one hell of a furore, as you'd expect. Unlike in the away game, we were poor and lost the game 2-0 – we just couldn't reproduce the same level of performance twice in a few weeks and I found that inconsistency very disappointing.

Towards the end of that season, we played poorly and started shipping in goals again. It was just a crazy time and a crazy place to manage. In the last bunch of games, we lost eight out of 12 games and it was pretty dour to say the least. In the final months of the season many of my new players got injured and we suffered several defeats against fellow strugglers in the league and were also defeated 3-0 in a derby match against Shrewsbury Town. We were finally relegated following a 2-0 defeat away at Hereford United, ending the club's 87-year stay in the Football League.

At the end of the season, there was a lot of speculation as to whether I should stay or go. There were very mixed feelings as I can recall at the time, but I was adamant to try and have another go at it, to try and sort the place out and to make some inroads into the next division. I'd been relegated out of the Football League with Darlington with a bad group of players, and I didn't see any reason why I couldn't get the club back, just like I did with Darlington. I honestly thought it wasn't me that was the main reason for going down, so I made a pact with myself to give it another go, and spoke to the chairman about it. He was happy for me to continue into the following season.

I soon started thinking about the new season, with Martin as my ally. During the pre-season we tried to move some of the players on. We tried to move on one particular player, our highest earner who was on a three-year contract, which we did, but we had to make a massive pay-off to him, and I've never known that in my entire management career. In fairness to the chairman, he allowed me to bring in eight or nine new players, but that deal just congested the whole thing up, which on reflection now, I can see. If I was ever in that position again, there will be no way on God's earth would I sign players to keep another 10 players out of the team and have them remain at the club. For a club in the fifth tier of English football, it was an absolutely absurd. I remember another player who had a similar sort of contract and he wanted his contract paid up as well, claiming he wanted to go and work in a shop somewhere. He'd had enough of football, he said, and hadn't enjoyed the previous two seasons, and had lost his interest in the game. This was a senior pro, who had come in because he'd heard one of the lads had been paid off, knocked on my door and asked for exactly the same as his mate.

My response to him was, "If you want to pack it in. Just pack it in." He then backtracked and suggested if I wanted to move him on, he was offering his willingness to except a pay-off, if the club wanted to do that. We didn't pay him off, by the way. From the chairman's point of view, that created unbelievably bad feeling and a list of players queuing up to be paid off was embarrassing to say the least.

We managed to bring in a small number of new players, including Kyle Critchlow, a young lad who was playing down south, Darren Kempson from Shrewsbury, Matt Brown from Lincoln, Jefferson Louis from Mansfield who had done especially well for them against us and Tom Kearney from Halifax. Some of the young lads made the move up from the youth team and were brought in, including Shaun Whalley, who's still doing well in football at Shrewsbury Town.

We made a conscious effort to change things around and lo and behold, we made an incredible start to the season. Stevenage Borough, who were favourites for promotion because of the money they'd spent in the summer, were first up in the opening game of the season and it was live on TV and we beat them 5-0. It was an unbelievable result to start the season with. However, in the following 10 games we'd won only three, drew two and lost five. It was a topsy-turvy start to the season to say the least. We were left in a mid-table battle, only four points above the relegation zone and only keeping two clean sheets up to that point. Following a 3-0 home defeat against Rushden and Diamonds, the fans were calling for my head.

I'd had a few run-ins with several people leading up to the Rushden game. As I've said previously, there were still a healthy group of players who weren't part of the first-team still at the club. We'd never got the numbers down enough, and I remember receiving some abusive phone calls, late at night and I reported them to the club straight away. I recognised the voices, and they were the voices of players, my players, who were leaving pretty abusive and threatening messages on my voicemail. They were players who weren't connected to the first team, the players who had been discarded as such and obviously they'd had a few drinks before they made the calls. It wasn't nice at all and I've never had that sort of thing happen to me in my life before. After I reported the phone calls to the club, a message came back to me along the lines, "Leave it for now, but if it happens again then we will do something about it..." I was very disappointed with the club's attitude towards it but left it at that.

Knowing there were people inside the club, inside my playing staff, who knew where I was and knew my private mobile number, obviously made me a bit unsettled. I couldn't say 100% who they were, but I had my suspicions; perhaps the Safety Officer at the club knew who they were; perhaps the Club Secretary knew who they were, but I was asked to leave it, and I reluctantly agreed to.

We then played Grays away from home and we lost 2-1, which was a poor result and we were pretty average at best. I remember Iwan Roberts, who played for me at Leicester City, was at the game, doing the Welsh speaking commentary for local radio, and I thought he was a little off with me when he came to interview me. He apparently found it difficult to interview me and was disappointed for me. He could tell the players weren't playing for me and probably felt a little embarrassed. He knew how things were at Leicester, and how good things were with that group of players and I could sense he'd rather not speak to me. He was commentating on local radio and as you do, he was criticising the team and criticising myself for how the team played. That really upset me. I knew he had a job to do, working for the media, but I was struggling and it was a real nightmare of a spell at Wrexham. As it happened, I had a similar experience at the end of the previous season when one of the Sky Sports reporters who I'd known for many years was very disappointed with me, and how my team had played at Shrewsbury. We had been beaten 3-0, and he said something along the lines, "I can't believe how bad this team is" or "I can't believe how bad the manager's doing." Things like that tend to get to you, especially when the comments come from people you know well or friends you respect.

The result at Grays had a massive effect on me, mainly because there were people I liked and respected who were finding it difficult to be polite towards me, so together with the abusive messages I'd received from my players, I was finding it extremely difficult to do my job. Then came the after match interview on the pitch at Rushden, where there was a big party of fans who were really abusive and aggressive towards me during the interview and it made me feel very uncomfortable, even more uncomfortable than before.

I remember the date was 23rd September 2008, the day I was confronted by my own fans and when I got home, I said to myself, "Enough is enough." However, I slept on it and gave myself a day or so to dwell on it, but I kept coming to the same conclusion.

It was a massive spiral of events that undermined my position at the club, and I told the club after that Rushden game that I was unhappy with what was going on. So, just eleven games into the season, and with the way I felt and the way people were feeling towards me, I told the club it would be the right thing to do for me to just move on. I don't think they were that surprised if I'm honest and I know it was in their minds to sack me. I didn't want to be sacked, so I spared them that job at least.

And that's what I did do; I moved on. In hindsight, it was the correct decision to make and just at the right time.

Within no time at all, Dean Saunders was ironically appointed as my replacement. I thought it was a great appointment, as he was a local lad who was unbelievably well thought of up there and he was inheriting a decent team. In fairness to Deano, the results that followed were incredible. Even though his first game against Forest Green Rovers ended in a victory, and in the subsequent 14 games they only lost once, Wrexham's first full season in the Conference Premier League ended in a disappointing 10th place. The following year, 2009–2010, ended in a similar fashion with Wrexham finishing in 11th position, well off the pace of the promotion battle.

I've been to a lot of football clubs that had their difficulties, but Wrexham was by far the hardest job I've ever encountered. No matter what I tried to do and no matter how hard I tried, I just didn't get the support of everybody I needed it from. I was never accepted there from day one. Whilst Martin Foyle was there for me, I genuinely felt that everything and everybody else was against me. However, I must say this: they really were a poor bunch of players to work with. In hindsight, I also think it was my fault and I sensed that was the case when some of the players were spreading bad things about me, saying they were unhappy with me; I felt they weren't happy with me from the start. I was never comfortable at that football club from day one.

Chapter 14

PART-TIME BOSS
Gainsborough Trinity Manager: August 2009–August 2011

"Do I really need people to speak to me like that?"

It was like venturing into the unknown for me; I'd not managed a side on 'part-time' basis or at 'semi-professional', 'non-league' standard, call it what you want. At the time, Gainsborough were in the Blue Square North division (now called the Vanarama National League North) so it would have been the lowest level I'd ever managed in.

It was Lee Philpott, an ex-professional footballer who had played for me at Leicester City and at Hull City who phoned me one day, while I was relaxing in Spain, and asked me if I'd ever considered working part-time in football. I was doing a lot of TV punditry at the time so I said it would be interesting to me if it fitted in with what I was doing for Setanta Sports. I told Lee I'd consider it, look at the fixture schedule and see what days the team train on. I wasn't against the idea, but I'd have to put a lot of thought into it if I was to consider it.

I enjoyed doing my TV work, as a co-commentator for Setanta Sports in Dublin, as it took me around the UK and Europe watching Premier League, Europa League and Champions League football. I also enjoyed doing my homework for each match, checking out who the players were and where they were from, but there's always times when somebody will mention something about a job that may interest you. It still happens to this day and I think it will never stop. Whilst I wasn't actively looking for another management job, I was always open to suggestions and still am. Every time somebody asks you about a job, it's very difficult to dismiss it straight away, and for me, I'd always have to have a conversation at least. It's something that's in my blood. On that particular day I received the call from Lee, and the natural answer was to say, "Yes,' to having a conversation about it at least.

Lee explained it was a 'part-time' job at a club that was a bit further away from where I lived in Stafford. However, he knew the owner and he was an admirer of me as a football manager. As it turned out, the owner and his family were all Leicester City fans, so that was a positive thing for me, I think. At first, Lee didn't mention the name of the club, but in subsequent conversations, the name of Gainsborough Trinity was mentioned.

Gainsborough had been struggling in the opening few games of the 2009–2010 season, so during one of the conversations while I was in Dublin, prior to me commentating on a Premier League game, Lee asked me if I was interested in meeting the owner. I agreed and Lee suggested he pass my number onto the owner, Peter Swan. Not long afterwards, Peter rang me while I was in a hotel in Dublin and said he'd like to meet me and talk to me about becoming manager of his club. He explained his ambition briefly, about expanding the club and making it into a full sports complex and trying to improve the stadium. There was an ambitious project in the pipeline, albeit still in Peter's head, and he wanted me to be part of it.

I welcomed the conversation and the chance to meet Peter and we did. He flew privately over to Dublin to meet me at my hotel. We hit it off straight away and the meeting went really well. There was serious conversation mixed in with general chit-chat, between two people who got on with each other. The outcome of the meeting was that, on return to the UK, I would pop up to Gainsborough and meet him there and see if there was any mileage in what we had been talking about.

A few days later, our second meeting took place and we spoke about my TV work and how I could fit it in with the day-to-day job of managing a football club, be it only on a part-time basis. I felt the schedule of training on Tuesday and Thursday, and mid-week and Saturday games, would be an issue and it would be impossible for me to change the training days to suit my schedule. I had to take into account the fact that most of the players had other jobs to supplement their income as footballers. The training schedule seemed to be pretty much set in stone. I had also to take into account that most of the players had arrangements with their employers to leave work early if there was an away game. It was a pretty complicated situation, to be honest.

My first thoughts were that I could continue my work in Dublin, but looking into it in a bit more detail, I'd have had to alter everyone else's schedule to fit in with mine and that was something I didn't want to do.

After another conversation with Peter, he expanded on his plans for the club; he potentially wanted to move the ground and build a sports complex, where the youngsters could come in from all over the local area and train on the pitches. It was a project that would be beneficial to the whole of the local community and I bought into his vision, and it was genuinely part of the reason why I wanted to work for him. The fact that there was a new project in the pipeline that at some stage I'd be involved in some shape or form was exciting. If it had been just a straight offer of working at that level, I may have thought differently.

Travelling to Gainsborough from where I lived was a two-to-three hour journey. It was an awkward journey too, given the M1 was under road widening construction, so that was an important consideration before I accepted the job. However, it was a project that interested me greatly and I wanted to be part of it.

Before I accepted the post, I did some homework on the club, and I was surprised how many ex-pros had managed there in the past. The list included Neil Warnock, who had managed the club back in 1980, Leighton James, Phil Stant, Dave Reeves, Ernie Moss and Adie Moses, whom I took over from. It was interesting to me that all those guys had a connection with the club, so that was another deciding factor for me.

A few days later, I accepted a two-year deal from Peter and started work as manager of Gainsborough Trinity in late August 2009. I took over after about three games of the new season; my first game was at Redditch and we won 3-0. I couldn't take any of the plaudits as I had hardly done anything with the team. I'd only just met the players and given them a few pointers for the game, but it all went swimmingly well. If I'm right, Matt Smith was playing for Redditch at the time, and he's now playing as a centre-forward for QPR. You could see he was a raw talent back then and had the potential to play to that high level. Early indications were good, and maybe the Redditch victory was a false awakening for me because the success didn't last.

Although it was the lowest level club I'd managed, I wanted to do it. I don't do things I don't want to do and I would have said to Peter straight away, if I had had any doubt. It was genuinely my choice to accept the job and I had no regrets in making that decision. I've never shied away from a challenge. Was this my biggest challenge? I don't think so. However, what it did do was put me in a position, that everywhere I went, wherever the team went, because of my background of managing at the top level I got loads of abuse off the opposite teams' fans and dugouts.

I had to learn the differences between managing at a top league club and managing at a non-league team, and I had to learn pretty quickly. In non-league grounds, you can buy a ticket to get in and basically move around the ground as you wish. If you wanted to stand behind the dugout and give the manager verbal abuse all game, then that was possible. That part of it was interesting because I was a magnet for the supporter who wanted to call me all things under the sun. The strange thing was, it wasn't just the opposite team's fans abusing me; a small proportion of the Gainsborough fans, maybe a handful of people who didn't like me for whatever reason I have no idea, had their own agenda and decided to give me dog's abuse. No matter what was going on, or what I was trying to do, these people didn't let up. There was one gentleman in particular, who was always in my eyesight and vision and on many occasions, he'd call me all the names under the sun. If I'd have said those sorts of things, I would have been arrested by the police. Nevertheless, it was an eye-opener, but I quite enjoyed it – I think.

Those non-league days bring back lots of memories for me. The league was very competitive, with teams like Solihull Moors (who are now in the Conference), Fleetwood Town (who are now in the Football League and were managed by Micky Mellon at the time), and Southport. We played Hinckley and Andre Gray played for them. He's now with Watford and he was outstanding on that day. His pace was unbelievable and at Hinckley, he really started to show people what he could do. Coming from the North East, one of my favourite teams was Blyth Spartans. They had a fantastic history in the FA Cup, so going to Blyth, with Mick Tait, who had played for me at Darlington, as their manager, was a thoroughly enjoyable day. Stafford Rangers were in the league, and living in the town, it was a big thing for their fans. I remember they battered us 3-1 at Stafford and I never heard the last of it. Travelling to Workington, I took the back roads and made a day of being in the Lake District. There was just something different being in non-league football at that time and it was quite enjoyable. It was like going back in time.

When you go and manage a football team, no matter what division they're in, you try and find out who their biggest rivals are, and straight away, I was told that Boston was their biggest game of the season. It was at my first game against Boston where I came across a young manager called Paul Hurst, who for a short while was manager of Ipswich Town, and whom I've watched very closely in the years since. When he was at Boston, he was part of a joint management team and Paul, although he never said that much, was always a perfect gentlemen. I remember when the game started, Paul's joint manager, I can't remember his name, was verbally abusing me for the whole game. It was horrible and verging on being obnoxious. I could see some of their subs almost squirming with embarrassment behind his back. All through the game, Paul was acting in the proper way, and I thought to myself he could do OK in the game. He was organised; he was disciplined; he knew exactly what he wanted from his team. However, Paul was working with someone who, in my opinion was holding him back and it subsequently turned out to be true. I've been in dugouts where managers or coaches have had a pop at you, or you have a misunderstanding and there's a bit of a chew between us, and that's commonplace, even in the football league, but this guy was relentless with his abuse and it began to grate on me. After that game with Boston, our goalkeeper, Gavin Ward, saw what was going on took hold of me and said, "Come and walk with me, Brian. Just walk with me and keep out of the way." There was no real need. I wouldn't have got involved in any tittle-tattle, but I'm glad Gavin led me away from that fella.

Incidentally, we beat Boston 3-1 on that occasion, and maybe that added to the abuse I got off this fella and for whatever reason, he just couldn't handle the occasion. I've been in dugouts in the past, where I sensed the opposing manager or coach had been on the booze before the game. I'm not suggesting that the fella from Boston had, but there was something definitely wrong with his behaviour. I don't know what I'd done to deserve that treatment, and I never questioned it, but the fact that my team had beaten his team convincingly, probably affected his behaviour. That day was the first time I began to think, "What am I doing here? Do I really need people to speak to me like that?"

I'd never met anybody like him before. He gave me dog's abuse like I've never received before from an opposing dugout, from which I'd have thought I would have received a little bit more respect and I certainly didn't show any lack of respect towards him, that's for sure. I was just shaking my head, along with everybody else who witnessed it. One thing's for certain, I would never have spoken like that to anybody. Apart from his behaviour, it was an enjoyable day for all of our players, staff and fans, but for me it was probably the oddest day I've ever had as a football manager. My saving grace was the fact we won the game. God knows what abuse he would have thrown at me if his team had beaten us. I think in the two years I was there, that was the most satisfying result, in terms of the way the game went and the way I had been treated.

In contrast to his co-manager, Paul's attitude and behaviour towards me was faultless, and since then, he has done well in football management. I'm also pleased to see Lee Philpott, the agent who recommended me for the Gainsborough job, now has a foot in his camp.

As it turned out, Boston beat us in the return game that season, 3-0 I think it was and it wasn't an enjoyable game for me, but that's football for you. I don't recall any abuse from the opposition's bench on that occasion I'm pleased to say.

My first season flew by and we did OK. We had periods when we did well and we had times when we struggled a bit, and we finished the 40-game season with 47 points, pretty much mid-table in 14th place. Our results and performances were very much up-and-down, and I put that down to the fact I wasn't as organised as I was in previous roles. I needed to be organised, but I found it difficult to get to grips with the training regime and schedule. I'd spent many years coaching and Thursdays had always been my players' meeting day, after training, but at Gainsborough, our training finished at 9pm or 9:30pm on Thursdays and I had a two to three hour journey to get back home. A meeting was the last thing on my mind, or on the players' minds for that matter.

So, because we didn't have a mid-week meeting, going into the game on a Saturday, I never felt we'd had enough time to work with the players and on our game. I never felt comfortable sitting at home on a Friday mapping out my team for the Saturday. I never got to grips with it and I never got into any sort of pattern or routine and I take my hat off to all the part-time football managers and coaches. The usual training regime started at 6pm or 7pm, so I'd usually leave home around midday to drive the two or three hours up to Gainsborough in order to plan the training session. The strange thing about the job was it was very rare did I have the full complement of players I wanted; usually one or two people would call in to say they were stuck on the motorway or stuck at work. It wasn't that they didn't want to come to the session, because they really loved their training, so I knew their calls were based on genuine reasons, but it was frustrating nonetheless. Quite a few of the lads in the group had been pro players before joining Gainsborough, and some had played for me or had played against my teams in the past, so they were decent lads and when they missed the training I knew they were genuinely gutted.

While the game at that level was very much about moti-vation as a manager and for the players, we did a lot of work around passing, keeping the ball, technique and the system we would play, but we never really got to grips with being ready for each game. I tried different things, like bringing in players from the local area and from some distance away. I tried to sign players I'd seen during my league management days, the likes of Leon Mettam. He reminded me of David Speedie, and I thought he was a player I'd rather have in my side than playing against me. He was a little bundle of energy, and was a thorn in the backside of my team, just as Speedie was, and lo and behold, I signed Leon when I was at Gainsborough. The problem with Leon's spell at Gainsborough was that I couldn't find a strike partner for him, although his goal record wasn't bad for us. I tried to sign big Jefferson Louis at a previous club. He was a six-foot, three-inch striker who'd had more clubs than Jack Nicklaus, 42 to be precise. He was a mountain of a man, quick, strong and I was obsessed with trying to sign him, even though he was from the London area. Peter Swan, our owner, backed me to the hilt and I eventually did get him. Peter had a flat in the town and insisted Jefferson use that while he was playing for us. However, even though he played nine times for us, it didn't really work out for him and he didn't use the flat, deciding on travelling to and from London for training and games. Even though I tried to sign local players where I could, signing Jefferson was a gamble because of the distance from his home. It was a shame, because he and Leon could have been a good pairing; Leon was a tiny fox-in-the-box type player, while Jefferson was a giant of a man and could have been a powerhouse for us, but that partnership never really materialised with Leon. Jefferson was an awkward character anyway, and wanted his own way a lot, like his own music in the dressing room, so it was a marriage not made in heaven.

Then on the other hand, I signed great people like Jamie Yates from Boston, who played brilliantly against us. I remember signing Mark Robinson and Darren Williams from the North East, and they were immaculate in every way as players and people. You go from one extreme in Jefferson, who let me down a lot, to the other extreme in Jamie, Mark and Darren who were brilliant lads and I loved them to bits. They travelled from the Whitby area and loved being at the club. There were other good signings that worked for us, people like: Mark Greaves, Nathan Peat, Ryan Williams, Shane Clarke were good lads from the local Humberside area, and we mixed that with people from a distance.

There were four of us who travelled up to Gainsborough from the Midlands together in my Citroen C4 Grand Picasso: Gavin Ward, Gavin Cowan and Sam Hasten came with me on a daily basis. The car had little tables in the back so the lads could sit in comfort and eat their packed lunch or dinner while we were travelling, and sometimes we'd stop for fish and chips on the way and having the lads in the car with me made the journey just about tolerable.

It's funny when I look back at that season, because I noticed a couple of players who stood out in that league, one being a centre-half called Aden Flint who played for Alfreton Town. I thought that he could become a great player, because his goal ratio for Alfreton was sensational, something like one goal in every two games – and he was a defender. Fast-forward to 2017, and Aden was playing for Bristol City and I recommended him to Aston Villa, who were in the Championship, and a couple of other people in the game. When I saw him play against us, I thought "Wow!" It wasn't just his size, six foot seven inches, but you just felt there was a powerful player in there who could cause teams damage. My point was proven correct, because he was signed by Middlesbrough in 2018 for a massive fee. It just shows that there are players out there in the lower leagues and in non-league football coming through the system, and given the chance, they could become stars. Jamie Vardy is the prime example. Another player was Cyrus Christie, who was playing against us for Hinckley. He came through the Coventry City youth system, and I remember thinking how good he was at wing-back. He was very quick, very lively and caused us all sorts of problems. He went on to play lots of league games and even played international football for the Republic of Ireland.

In my first season, we went quite a few games unbeaten and I was beginning to think my system was working, and I even won a Manager of the Month award. I think at every club I've managed, I had won some sort of personal award, and I'm very proud of that fact. The following season wasn't any better. In fact we finished in a worse position in 18th in the league. It was meant to be the big season for us. It should have been the start of something that was a little bit special, but it wasn't to be.

Before the start of the 2011–2012 season, I brought in Steve Housham to help me, because he knew the non-league scene inside out. I wanted him to have more of a role within the club so I appointed him as youth team coach. He was a local lad who knew the club, but was working as the manager of Brigg Town, so I saw him as a good fit to take some of the pressure off me. The season started at home on Saturday 13th August and we won 3-1 to Solihull Moors and on the following Monday night, we had another game, and that was the worst thing in the world for a part-time non-league team, to have two games in a matter of a few days. Now, as a manager of a football club, you don't know what your players do from the minute they leave you on a Saturday night until the following Monday or Tuesday night. Well, anyway, we lost 3-0 at Hinckley and then we lost 4-0 away to Stalybridge, who were a decent side. Things weren't going to plan. That season was meant to be the season we kicked on. After the second game, I had a bit of a chew with the lads after our defeat to Hinckley, questioning whether they were interested in playing for me. Although I wasn't totally in love with it, I still needed the players to perform for me, week in, week out, but I felt they weren't giving 100%.

So, in one week, we'd won one and lost two, and so I was relieved of my position at the club, with Steve Housham taking over my reign. I always knew Steve would take over from me at some stage, but not after three games. I knew the owner could see I was getting extremely frustrated with the job, but to sack me after three games of the season was a bit harsh, but probably understandable. The team I left was pretty decent, and they actually finished in the top four that season which was the highest they had ever finished. Whilst I can't claim any of the plaudits for the team finishing so high in the league, I had put that team together and I had brought in Steve Housham, so in fairness to him, he did a fantastic job. Thankfully, just after I'd left, Gainsborough didn't go backwards, although recently they have struggled.

So, after two years, almost to the day, my time as a part-time non-league manager had come to an end. I think Peter Swan knew I was a good person, but it just wasn't the place for me to be. It was an experience to say the least, and I'm happy to have done it, but in all fairness, I wouldn't want to do it again. The transition from being in work every day, in control of everything, to a situation where you just don't know how many players are going to turn up for training or indeed the game was totally alien to me. People don't understand that I actually enjoyed the job at times, even though I felt really uncomfortable in it as well. I didn't really get to where I needed to be, and in the end, I lost interest because I couldn't come to terms with the whole situation.

I had no regrets, though, none whatsoever.

MY FOOTBALL MANAGEMENT PHILOSOPHY

"I often see one or two of the top coaches these days now adopting the same 3-5-2 system and I think to myself, I was doing that in 1989. Did that make me ahead of my time? Maybe"

My principles and football management philosophy were nurtured at Middlesbrough, working for Bruce Rioch as the Youth Team Coach back in the late 1980s; however, my own principles developed and grew in my first management role when the door opened for me at Darlington.

If I was to give an overview of my management career, it would go like this: In the **sixth tier** of English football I won Manager of the Month awards; in the **fifth tier** I won the championship, Manager of the Year and Manager of the Month awards; in the **fourth tier** I've been in the playoffs, won the championship, won Manager of the Year and Manager of the Month awards; in the **third tier** I kept Tranmere up from relegation and took them to the last eight of the FA Cup and got them to the playoffs and won Manager of the Month awards; In the **second tier** I've been in three playoff finals, took Leicester City to the Premier League, won Manager of the Month awards; In the **Premier League**, I kept Aston Villa up in my first season, finished 4th and 5th in the league with Villa, been in the semi-final of the FA Cup, last eight of the UEFA Cup, won the League Cup with Villa and won Manager of the Month awards.

If I continue with the overview in terms of stats, I would say my philosophy has worked well and the stats prove that. I'm not a statistical man, but in the 910 games I've managed teams it would read like this: a win average of 40% and an unbeaten average of nearly 72%.

CHAPTER 15: MY FOOTBALL MANAGEMENT PHILOSOPHY

It must be highlighted here, that not one of the clubs I took over were in a healthy position; when I've gone into them. I've had to steady the ship, and how did I do that? Firstly, you need a game plan. Then, you need to change the mentality of the players there, and you have to start to make yourself a little bit resilient and the main reason why I was successful, was pretty much to change the style of play, and that system stemmed from the early 1990s and is now making a comeback.

Since I started out as a manager, all those years ago, 30 years to be precise, the role of the football manager has changed dramatically. Would I be a football manager in the Premier League now? Well, it would be a challenge, that's for sure, but I'm delighted with what I achieved in the tough era I achieved it in.

Throughout my managerial career, I have had a certain job to do and that was mainly to sell lots of players and bring in lots of fresh faces. I did that at Darlington in my first managerial role; at Leicester; at Villa; at Stoke City; Hull City and at Tranmere. It was all about recruitment, game plan and system. I had a football philosophy and a certain way I liked my teams set up, which was a 3-5-2 system, with three centre-backs, two wing-backs, three midfielders and two strikers, although I've been known to play a variation where there were two midfielders and three strikers, one big centre striker and two wider players, like I did a few times at Leicester and at Villa, most notably trying to accommodate Dwight Yorke, Savo Milošević and Stan Collymore. The latter formation seems to be the theme for more and more of today's teams, in the Premier League at least. My teams were all about protecting the goal, making sure the midfielders were working hard and protecting the centre-backs, but they were also about making sure the players were comfortable in possession of the ball.

However, there were some things that didn't work for me: either I didn't have the type of players who could play in that formation or, as in the case at Wrexham for example, I couldn't move the players on when I came in, and I was faced with a group of players who had been rewarded with two-year contracts for staying up on the last game of the season before I arrived. If I had been there and had just about avoided relegation, I'd have said to the chairman, "It's time to change". That tiny bit of success, and staying up was success to them at the time, and they then go and reward people. If you start doing that, chances are you'd have to do the same the year after, which proved to be the case.

During the years I was managing, I needed to have a ruthless streak in me and work miracles in a short space of time, trying to get the balance of the side right. It wasn't only the playing staff I'd change; I'd often have to change the system and the mentality of the players, too. While you go into some clubs and integrate the players at your disposal, sometimes that doesn't work, because the players aren't able to do that. One of the most important things to do as a manager is having the ability to change things around and work the market. It was important to know the transfer market and get players into the club that could do a job for me, and at the same time, ship out players who I didn't feel would suit my style of play or who didn't want to play for me.

Player recruitment was as important as moving players on. I looked for players who fitted the system. It wasn't about having the best 11 players in the league. It was more about having a group of players to complement each other. For example, at one club I had a wing-back who preferred to be more attack-minded, but could defend and I had a left-sided centre-back who could cover for the wing-back, and so we could still operate with the centre-back shuffling over a bit if the wing-back was exposed. Those were some of the intricacies of the system, and there were a lot more as well.

Nowadays, I believe managers need to be a bit more patient, because the transfer window shuts at the end of August and the end of January, but in my day, the transfer window remained open until the third Thursday in March, and that was a major advantage to me during my entire management career. If there were players who needed to be moved on, I'd sit them down and have a chat about it, and in most cases, I could move them out. The market made it more flexible to do business. There were also lots of cases where people didn't want to move, but that's another story. Again, doing your recruitment early makes it a different ball game altogether. My player turnover at the nine clubs I managed was incredible. I think I worked it out that I must have made over 350 player changes at first-team level with around 40 players at each of the clubs I managed. That sort of thing doesn't happen these days, because of the length of the window doesn't allow it. It would take several years to shift that many players these days, whereas I was doing it in a season or less. I played my role as manager of every football club I've been at, to the rules as they were.

CHAPTER 15: MY FOOTBALL MANAGEMENT PHILOSOPHY

Talking about recruitment and how it can influence the success of a club, I often wonder why a club like Aston Villa went from the third tier of English football in 1970–1971 to winning the European Cup within the space of 10 seasons and I maintain it was all down to positive recruitment. As a football manager back in the day, I've always said that recruitment is the most important key issue; getting the balance right; getting the right personalities in. It's all about doing what's right at that club and for the team. I know it's different now, where some, if not most managers have their recruitment done for them, but I can only talk about when I was a manager. At Villa in the 1970s, there was some great recruitment done by managers like Vic Crowe and Ron Saunders, who always wanted to make the team stronger. I can think of some key signings made, like Ian Ross coming in from Liverpool, Chris Nicholl from Luton Town, Leighton Phillips from Cardiff City and Ken McNaught from Everton, all had a massive impact on the defensive side at Villa. Then you've got players like Allan Evans, who when he came into the club was a centre-forward, but he was converted into a centre-half. We've had laughs about that since, but Ron Saunders was very shrewd and knew what he was doing when he recruited Allan.

Then you've got the youth policy, which was obviously different back then. I can think of players like Bobby McDonald coming through the ranks as a midfielder, but who was developed into a good left back; John Gidman who was signed as an 18-year-old, and was then developed by the club as a right back; Gary Williams came through the ranks. Then there are signings who made an impact as full backs, the likes of Kenny Swain, John Robson, Gordon Smith, who were scouted from other clubs. When you talk about the midfield, I can name people like Alex Cropley, Gordon Cowans, Frank Carrodus and Des Bremner, people who covered the pitch from top to bottom; those boys were fantastic, coming into the club and doing a great job. In the striker department, people like Keith Leonard came in from the local environment but made a great impact on, not only the team, but me personally; Andy Gray, what a great signing he was; Peter Withe was the missing piece of the jigsaw for Ron Saunders, and we all know what impact he made for Villa. Striker development during that period found players like John Deehan and Gary Shaw who came through the ranks. In the wide areas, there was Tony Morley; what a signing he was. When you talk about goalkeeper recruitment, two players that stood out for me were Jimmy Rimmer and John Burridge, both great goalkeepers, but also great for the dressing room. They influenced other people in the team, which was important too.

All of those guys I've mentioned, and there are more, did a fantastic job for the club, and that sort of recruitment and development continued throughout the 1970s and into the early 1980s when the proces was at its absolute best. Could that be matched again? Of course it could, but it would take some doing. I must make a mention of the manager – Ron Saunders was instrumental in a lot of this, but Vic Crowe before him played his part, without a doubt. Tony Barton, who took over from Ron in 1982, was the eyes and ears of the club and was also an important part of the recruitment and development of some of those players.

Moving back to my own experience as a manager, obviously, I had to be careful of what I was doing, and there were occasions where the policy didn't work. Take Darlington as an example. They were bottom of the table in the February, when I joined the club and hadn't won a home game all season. I had to play 4-4-2, because they didn't have the players to adapt to my system so I spent time working on them. However, we beat Rotherham away 2-1 who were top of the league and I thought that was great. However, that's when I found out what was wrong with that club. It's important that you find out what's wrong with each club. The Monday after the game, most of the players didn't train, probably thinking, "We did well on Saturday so we don't need to train." Straight away, that alerted me to what was wrong, but I could never get to grips with what was really wrong there. In that case, I couldn't do anything because there was no money to do much business in the transfer market, and I just couldn't move people on. Ultimately, later that season, we were relegated at Scunthorpe, into non-league football.

The beauty of that was at the end of the season, out of the 24 players I had on the books, I released 20, which straight away gave me the scope to develop what I wanted to do. The next season started with a new system and new players who weren't sick of the club and who weren't disappointed at being relegated, so they all had something to try and achieve and all my targets were reached because we gained promotion.

That first full season at Darlington was probably the ultimate in terms of getting the right people in at the club, because my scouting skills were put to the test as we tried to get local players in who were hungry, or players who I'd seen at Middlesbrough and had liked what I'd seen; Bruce helped me on that front, with the likes of Gary Gill and Mark Prudoe. I tried to get a bit of quality in there, because every club needs that. In a four-week period, from the end of the season to pre-season, I'd turned over 36 players. The team were brand, spanking new and we went on to win back-to-back championships, and it was all down to my philosophy.

That success at Darlington gave me the opportunity to move to Leicester City, so when I went there one of the things I asked for was the previous season's video. They had conceded 83 goals in the 1990–1991 season, which is almost two goals a game and that meant the team had to score three goals a game to win a football match, and that was quite bizarre. It was dead simple for me and that was they couldn't defend. Leicester had always been identified as an open, attacking side, but when you concede that amount of goals, the team has problems.

Again, the most important thing there was recruitment, but starting at the back. It was important for me to recruit the right type of centre-backs. I had to change the system of play, but I had most of the pre-season to do that so it was easier to make the change. That time, I had people who I knew and trusted in John Gregory and Allan Evans, who I took to the club with me, so I knew straightaway they could work with me and help integrate the players into the system. Buying the right players to play in the system and to move players on was again high priority. There were obvious defining moments at Leicester, like selling Paul Kitson to Derby at a time when he was probably the most talented player at the club, if not in the league. However, with his sale, I managed to bring in several players with the likes of Simon Grayson, Ian Ormondroyd and Michael Whitlow, so I was again using my scouting experience to the full.

I had a continuation of trying to improve Leicester City over the course of three seasons, which culminated with two playoff final defeats, followed by an eventual playoff final victory against Derby at Wembley. So, what did we do following on from the two Wembley defeats? Did we let the disappointment hit the players? No, we never let them wallow in defeat so we gave them a strategic plan to work to and improved the squad every season in order to achieve what we wanted, and that was promotion to the Premier League, and we didn't let anything hold us back.

I had to drill into minds of Allan Evans and John Gregory the fact that we had to do everything together, from the scouting and coaching to instilling all of those old-fashioned values that were really important to me.

Moving to Aston Villa was by far my biggest job, but also one of my most difficult ones, because we had a lot of experienced players there when I arrived and they knew I would be changing it. It was something I had to do. I had to go in there a little bit softly-softly at first, which was hard for me, but it wasn't long before I stood up before the players, following a big defeat, and said something like, "It's my way or no way." That was when I started to integrate the system of three centre-backs and making my moves into the transfer market, with signings like Gareth Southgate, Gary Charles, Ian Taylor, Mark Draper and Savo Milošević, to name but a few, being drafted in. I knew then that I had to integrate the new players, but on that occasion, I had to be careful because of the experience I had at the club.

I had a game plan at Villa to sign players who were mainly under-21 internationals, players who had played a lot of games in Division One or if possible, existing Premier League players. I managed to bring in a complete new wave of people who would fit into my system and way of playing. Again, there was a massive turnover of players. I brought in 14 new players, plus giving 5 youngsters their debuts. I moved on 29 players during my time at Villa. The biggest decision I had to make in my first year was about the strikers: Dean Saunders and Dalian Atkinson were top quality players, but I spotted Dwight Yorke had a role to play, and even though he probably saw himself as a second striker playing alongside Dalian or Deano, I had to make him my number one striker. I needed to choose the right players in their right positions who would stick to, work with and accept the system and the game plan.

I've had the same game plan at all of the clubs I've managed, and in the main, it's worked successfully. In fact, the clubs where it hasn't worked for me would be the ones where I wasn't able to change things around, and I could identify Wrexham as being one of those clubs. If I'd had the opportunity to have changed the players at Wrexham, where I'd always had too many players there for such a small club, things may have turned out differently.

I had the same game plan at Wrexham, of playing a 3-5-2 (or 3-4-3) system, and I felt that was my strength as a manager. I think because I was a forward in my playing days, and because I knew I hated games that I wasn't involved in, my biggest sentence was to keep the forwards involved in the game and make sure they enjoyed playing in the game. I always remember the games we lost when I played; it was always because we, the strikers, be it Andy Lochhead, Keith Leonard, John Deehan or Andy Gray, hadn't been in the game enough, and I used that principle with all of my teams, wanting to make sure that we kept the players in the game.

I can look back at Wrexham and genuinely say, "I wish I could have done better." I know I should have done, but I couldn't get them to play the way I wanted them to play. Even in that second season, I made the mistake of playing 4-4-2 in the first game of the season in the Conference and we won 5-0 against the favourites and so I never changed it; nine games later we were still playing 4-4-2 and we started losing too many games. For me, if my mentality had been right; if I had had the right players around me; if the system had been right, we would probably only have lost two of those nine games at best, playing 3-5-2. I can look back at that and say I was wrong.

In contrast to Wrexham, in my first season at Hull City we were in administration for most of the season; we had no money; we had nothing, but we played with three centre-backs, three midfielders, two wing-backs and two strikers, and we managed to bring in players from time to time. We had a 17-match run in the second half of the season that took us into the playoffs and we should have got to the final. I was fortunate there that we had a really good, strong group of people who understood exactly what the system was.

In our second season at Hull, new owners had come in and we'd been given some money to spend on players in order to change things and I had reverted to 4-4-2. I keep looking back at that and I say to myself, "Why did I do that?" I signed a couple of little wingers that season, influenced by how Chesterfield played in the previous season and stuck with the flat back four system. However, in the first 12 games we only lost once, but then we had a bad run of results and we couldn't stop the opposition scoring against us.

When I sit here today and reflect on my time at Wrexham and Hull City, two clubs where it didn't work out well for me, I still can't believe I changed my system from 3-5-2 to 4-4-2. I cannot believe that. I wish I could go back and look at what was going on in my head at that time, and whoever or whatever was influencing me, because it had a massive effect on my game plan and how well I did at those clubs. Then I look back at my short spell at West Brom, where I didn't do so well but I played the way I wanted my team to play, I just didn't have the strikers who could score the goals for me, barring Lee Hughes, who was probably having the worst spell of his career at that time. When we played OK, we tended to lose games.

So, as you can see, I have a very strong view on how I should manage and approach the game of football. Will I ever do it again one day? Well, I don't crave it, but I often see one or two of the top coaches these days now adopting the same 3-5-2 system and I think to myself, "I was doing that in 1989". Did that make me ahead of my time? Maybe.

Football management has changed so much since I was last in a job. It doesn't allow people to go into a football club and make a major difference to a team. You see a lot of managers being changed now, and the new manager having the same set of players as the previous regime; managers having the same problems as the previous manager. The fact is that they have pretty much the same players to work with, whereas in my day, you go into a football club as a new manager and the players knew there would be change. The clubs that benefit from it are the so-called 'big clubs', who buy the better players and generally speaking they are going to perform reasonably well, whereas the clubs who are less prepared in terms of finance have to gamble at the start of the season, and once the season starts and you start losing three or four games, everybody loses their confidence; everybody loses confidence in the manager and the manager tends to get the sack. When the new manager comes in, he has the same problems as the previous manager. For example, if I was going into a team who are bottom of the league, I would be inheriting what is there now; therefore, I wouldn't be able to do the things I was able to do when I was managing. I respect the fact that it's a completely different game now, but my answer to a lot of people who may read this is that it has been done in the past, and occasionally it's done now, that managers can make a massive difference, but it's fewer and farther between that somebody goes in and make a difference when teams are struggling. In the main, teams struggle because the playing staff isn't as good as it needs to be. Moreover, managers, or coaches as they are now, aren't the ones changing the personnel around. Somebody else does that now, maybe a Director of Football, but when I was a manager, I'd go and watch three or four games a week looking for players and I'd be searching for new players, day-in, day-out and I'd buy those players myself.

I generally believe it's more difficult for a manager or coach to change the fortunes of a team at the wrong end of the table than it ever was. Just look at the Premier League in 2017–2018; Stoke City changed their manager, but nothing changed and they got relegated; West Bromwich Albion changed their manager and they got relegated. The teams who didn't change their managers, the likes of Huddersfield, will probably stick with the same manager for the following season. There are exceptions, like Crystal Palace, who sacked Frank de Boer after four defeats and brought in Roy Hodgson and he did well and kept them in the division and even finished half way up the Premier League. They had enough quality to stay up, whereas the other teams obviously hadn't. The fact is, most teams who are in trouble usually stay in trouble during the season. In my view, I don't think any team in any division has a great advantage in changing their manager mid-season, although every now and again, one team will climb out of trouble and that will probably inspire others to change their manager mid-season.

I've mentioned before that I had to bring in players who had the right mentality and I believe that is the hardest thing for a manager these days to change; I thrived on those sorts of challenges and my stats stand up to support that.

Chapter 16

PEOPLE WHO HAVE INFLUENCED MY CAREER

"I am what I am, and I am who I am – I want to be who I am"

There have been a number of people who have either influenced me or have played an important part during my playing and managerial career; people who were great for me when I was a coach, and coaches who were good for me when I was a player. I'd like to take this opportunity to mention those people and let you into the reasons why they have been an important part of my life so far.

Frank Upton
Aston Villa youth team coach, 1970–1977

Six months into my apprenticeship at Aston Villa, we had a massive change in personnel; Graham Leggat went off to Canada and Frank Upton replaced him as our coach. When you first saw Frank, it was hard not to be intimidated, not in a bad way, but because he stood six foot four inches tall, and stood above most of us youngsters. It wasn't surprising he was known as 'Frank the Tank' when he played for clubs like Chelsea and Derby as a tough tackling, no-nonsense centre-half.

Frank wasn't the sort of person who I thought would be an ideal person to learn from, being a hard-natured former centre-half. I wouldn't say Frank was abrupt, but when he spoke, you stood up and listened to him, and when he asked you to do something, you just did it. He was very organised and very disciplined so one of his jobs was to check that the apprentices were doing our jobs correctly. He was in charge of us, basically.

CHAPTER 16: PEOPLE WHO HAVE INFLUENCED MY CAREER

At first, I wasn't sure about Frank and I told myself I didn't need him telling me what to do. In hindsight, I have to say that Frank taught me so many good habits it wasn't true. Every day he came to work he was clean-shaven and always wore a shirt and a tie, until he started coaching and then he'd put his training gear on. He always kept himself prim and proper. I think that rubbed off on me at the start of my coaching and managerial career, because I found myself coming to work in a shirt and tie at first, but then found my training gear more comfortable after a while.

In fairness to Frank, he always had time for the apprentices and found time to talk to us. After one particular game, he said to me, "Look, I know you're a midfield player and you love playing out wide, but I watch you train and I look at your first touch and the way you can go past players. You're quick and you're an intelligent player, but I just feel that sometimes you're missing out on games in the middle of the park. I want to try and play you up-front." That in itself, was the making of me in many ways because it made me realise I had the potential to be a striker. Although I had the qualities of a midfield player; I could pass the ball; I could pick a pass to the striker, but he felt I'd be far more effective in the final third of the field, rather than the middle third. That was a massive thing he did for me, by recognising that, perhaps I wasn't playing in my natural or best position. He also said I was calm in front of goal and if I had a chance to score I could take those chances. It was evident I wasn't getting enough chances from midfield, but I recognised I was creative enough in the final third of the park to cause people problems with creativity and pace.

That more or less started my career as a striker, or someone who played off the main striker. I worked tirelessly with Frank, doing a lot of shadow play work where the ball would be passed across the back and similarly, it would also be passed to the right or left full-back and their first touch was out of their feet for me and my alternative striker, either Greg Fellows or Tony Betts, would have to do the right type of run to get into the channels. We believed in channel runs back then, which could have been called 'direct' football, but at the same time it was football with a purpose. That's where I learned about keeping the forward players in the game and Frank very much taught me that. His philosophy was to never give the ball away, and when you've got the ball, make sure your strikers were interested in playing it.

He also did that because he was a centre-half in his day and he didn't like running around and was quite happy in playing it into people's feet. I also learned how to spin into channels, and he encouraged me to use the ability I had and never once criticised me when I tried to flick the ball over my head or try something different. He was happy for me as a striker to do those things and encouraged me all the time to try new things. Frank could sense when I was feeling a bit down and he'd pull me to one side and we'd have a chat, making sure everything was OK. Even he recognised that I was one of those people who was away from home and I needed someone, an adult, to talk to from time to time and that was very important for me in that first year or so.

Frank was not only a massive influence on me as an apprentice, but when I was appointed manager at Leicester City, he worked for me as a scout for the three years I was there and I also took him to back to Villa Park, also as a scout. I guess it was a way of paying him back for the time he spent teaching me how to become a striker. I respected him that much and it was a huge compliment to him, coming in as one of my trusted scouts. I liked a lot of the things Frank did, especially the way he was so regimented as a player and organised as a coach, and how he allowed his strikers to be free to express themselves on the pitch – he gave me an awful lot of freedom on the pitch.

I will always remember when I'd just turned 17 and Frank said to me, "Your hair's too long", and I replied, "No it isn't. My hair isn't so long that it stops me playing football." I hated having my hair cut in the 70s and for anybody who has seen pictures of me when I was young, I used to try and keep my hair out of my eyes at the front. That stemmed from going to the barbers with my brothers when we were kids and we'd have to have short, back and sides and a lot off the top, and I hated it. That stuck with me forever. Anyway, Frank told me to get my hair cut and I replied, "I'm not having it cut. Frank, can you give me a good reason why you want me to get my hair cut?" Frank didn't really give me a reason, but just said, "I just want you to be tidy and smarten up a little bit." Again, I wasn't having any of it, "To be honest, I'm comfortable having my hair like this and I'm not having it done." Frank thought about my reply and said, "I'll tell you what. You ARE having your hair cut and I'm going to take you down to the barber's now." The barber's he was referring to was where all the lads went to get their hair cut except me; however, Frank took me down to the barbers because he didn't trust me to go on my own, but I wasn't happy about that either.

The barber's shop was right next to the number 7 bus stop, where I caught my bus home. In those days, the buses had open backs and no doors so people could just hop on and off. Frank and I were walking towards the barber's shop and must have been about 30 yards away from the shop and I noticed a bus just starting to pull away from the bus stop, so I decided to sprint towards it, hop on, and left Frank to stand and watch in amazement. I don't know why I did it, maybe it was an impulsive reaction, but as you can imagine, Frank wasn't happy. When I arrived back at my digs, I said to my landlady, Mrs Mallard, "I think I might be in trouble tomorrow..." and told her the story. As always, Mrs Mallard was really sympathetic and said, "No, you'll be all right. Don't worry." I told her that Frank didn't let people off with anything and said I was going to get called into the manager's room. I began to worry that the club would fine me, or even worse, sack me. I knew Frank wasn't messing about and was adamant I had to have my hair cut.

In the morning, I packed my clothes in my holdall, caught the bus to the ground and walked into the changing rooms. Frank was waiting there and immediately said to me: "The manager wants to see you, Brian." I was thinking to myself, "Oh my God. Here we go. My mam will cry and my dad will slaughter me if I get sacked. I've really messed up here." Even when I walked into the manager's office, I was adamant I wasn't going to say sorry, not in an arrogant way, but I just felt comfortable with the way my hair was, and I didn't want it cut. I was trying to think of excuses why I jumped on that bus, but I couldn't. In the end, I said to myself, "I am what I am, and I am who I am – I want to be who I am." If I felt getting my haircut would have made me a better footballer, then I'd have got it cut. If my hair was getting in my way of my eyes, I would have done it, but it wasn't. I was prepared to stand my ground with the manager, again.

I got the call to see Vic Crowe, knocked on the door and Vic shouted, "Come on in." The manager asked if I was OK and I said I was fine. There was no mention of Frank, no mention of my haircut and he just said, "Oh, OK Brian. Well, here it is, sign here." Vic handed me a contract to sign me up as a professional. So, I began to realise as I signed my contract, that Frank only wanted me to get my hair cut so I looked smart for when I was handed my professional contract and had my picture taken with Vic. I felt a bit of a fool to say the least, but at the same time, it gave me a reminder just how good Frank was to me, how he was a decent bloke and only wanted the best for me.

After all the formalities, I walked out of the manager's office and Frank was waiting there and gave me a big handshake; my God, when he got hold of your hand he almost crushed it. He then said to me, "I only tried to get you tidied up." I apologised to him and said I shouldn't have argued my corner and shouldn't have run away. My respect for him grew even further that day.

Frank was really good to me and he's one of the very few people to whom I owe an awful lot in my career. It could be said, without Frank, I might have stayed as a midfield player, or I could have easily have been released by Villa at the age of 18.

My brother, Alan Little

Alan joined me at Villa as an apprentice a year after I did. He was always an unselfish person and I'm very lucky to have a younger brother who totally looked after me. He looked after me in all sorts of ways, just by being by my side. Alan was a totally different player from me, and to be honest, he got used to me getting all the praise and him doing all the work.

When we lived at home and we were both given jobs, he'd always do mine as well. He was a brilliant lad and I had huge respect for him, and still do. Having him around me when we were at Villa was magic and helped me settle in during my second year, when he moved into digs with me after Roy Stark had moved out.

Not only was he always around me, we even played up front in the youth team together. Although he was a midfielder, he could also play centre-back and as a striker. Alan was a really settled character, hard as nails and a no-nonsense, no-thrills sort of person who made me focus on my training and made me work and concentrate harder.

Alan has never got too many mentions when it came to my career; however, when I go to Barnsley, the first thing their fans will say to me, "Your brother was better than you, Brian." That goes to show that, wherever he's been he's had a massive influence. His professional playing career was centred around playing central midfield or as a holding midfielder, and he has a tremendous reputation at Barnsley, Halifax, Southend, Doncaster, and Hartlepool, where he finished playing.

Thanking Alan isn't a long "Thank you" and it's one I can't really expand on, but it's one that only he and I will understand. Anybody who has brothers, or sisters, and I have two brothers, will know that when you get together you realise just how close you are. When I left home that first year, there were periods in my life when I was all over the place, so him being around me was genuinely a massive influence on my life and on my playing career.

John Gidman
Former Aston Villa full-back 1971–1979

Giddy and I had so many great years together at Villa from the age of 18 through to our mid-20s, before he went off to play for Everton, then Manchester United. Giddy came from the Liverpool youth system at the age of 17, but we then played together for Villa in the youth team, the reserves, first-team and also played together for the England youth team, and later in our careers, he came to Darlington with me for a short while. We trained together, warmed up together and we also roomed together everywhere we went, and that is testament to the great friendship we had. It could be said we'd be pretty inseparable in those days.

In our youth days, we'd both run out onto the pitch singing 'Maggie May' by Rod Stewart. We were a right pair of crackpots. It's always good to have someone who you can release yourself on because being a footballer is hard work; you go into train- ing working your socks off, day in, day out so to have somebody there to release all that energy on and to help switch off from football is something special, and Giddy was that person.

Giddy was also a terrific footballer and we were just made for each other in those early days, both on and off the pitch; I was quiet compared to him, but while we got into a few scrapes together, I think he'd turn to me to use my sensible head in sit- uations that could have got out of hand. We had some great nights out together, whether it was down the pub or playing snooker, and we'd often get back in a little bit too late and get into trouble for that.

The one thing I remember about Giddy that always stuck in my mind was that he'd always have a better car than me. When I bought my first brand new car, a Vauxhall Viva in deep metallic blue, I thought it was great, but then I saw Giddy turn up for training in a brand new, yellow Ford Cortina; I was gutted, because his car was twice the size of mine, and better too. I know it sounds daft, but we'd kill ourselves laughing at things like that.

Later on in our careers, when I retired from playing football in 1981 and Giddy was at Everton, I was at a stage in my life where I wasn't sure what I would do for the rest of my life. Giddy would call and ask me to come and see him. At the time he owned a sports shop in Liverpool and every time I went up there to see him, we'd always visit his shop and just before I left, he would make sure my boot was full of sports kit. He'd always look after me. That's a sign of a really good pal, someone who was still in the game, but recognised the fact I had retired and that resulted in a really nice gesture from a friend who looked after me and was worried I didn't have enough sports gear to wear.

Giddy was a top lad and having a good friend during those years was very important and he will always remain very special to me. As we got older, we sadly drifted apart, which is part of life I suppose, although his friendship stays very special with me to this day.

Andy Lochhead
Former Aston Villa centre forward 1970–1973

Andy was a lot older than me when I joined Villa as an apprentice, but little did he know, he would soon became a 'mentor' to me, both on and off the field of play.

The best way to describe Andy Lochhead was that he was a 'man' – a big man, and a hard man at that. You just didn't mess with Andy and most people were quite weary of him, but I was unbelievably lucky that he took me under his wing. He'd talk to me about playing as a striker; he'd talk to me about playing off the striker; he taught me to look at his strengths and accept that he was different from me; however, I also learned that in a partnership, we could both be very effective, and it could be said we formed a 'Little and Large' partnership.

We didn't play a great deal together, but Andy was the person who taught me that I needed to read what was going on in a game of football. If the ball was hitting the striker, I learned to look at the game and, yes, you gamble where the ball drops after the centre-half or centre-forward challenges for it and flicks it on. You still have to read the game to see what sort of ball it is – a high ball or a drilled ball, if there's going to be a clash and where the ball's likely to land. Andy kept persevering on all those bits and pieces and drilled those things into me. Obviously, sometimes it didn't come off, but if you were active, on the move and thinking about it, then it's better than standing still and watching. It's all about trying to be aware of what's happened and what's about to happen, which seems simple, but it's not that easy when you put it into practise. I sometimes made runs off Andy that came to nothing, but there were lots of other times when you could sense there would be a big scramble and the ball would drop next to Andy and the centre-half and I'd be close by, where the tough stuff would be going on, and I came out with the ball. I also learned to always be on the move so to make Andy's pass a simple one, rather than him trying to find me, which made the game easier for both of us.

When I look back at those early games playing alongside someone who'd been in the game a long time; someone who'd played in that position for many years; someone who had given me a few rollickings at the right time, in the right way but with the right amount of threat in there, I still think it was a fantastic experience for me. Andy was a brilliant man to learn from and to play alongside.

I thank Andy for being honest with me, for liking me and for allowing me not to be frightened of him – and a hell of a lot of people were frightened of him, even his own teammates. When Andy spoke, everyone listened to him and if he had a bit of a chew at somebody, they were frightened. He was a menacing character, both commanding and demanding, honest and hard working, but I worshiped the ground he stood on. He was hard as nails and what you'd call an old-fashioned centre-forward who had an incredible appetite for football. Without him, I wouldn't have been the sort of player I became.

Davie Gibson
Former Aston Villa inside-left 1970–1972

I've mentioned it before, but Davie always picked Giddy and me to play alongside him in our small-sided games in training. In those days, not many players spent much time talking about the game when they were off the field of play, but once you were on the field with experienced players they were forever talking to you, getting on to you and always on your back, whether we were winning or losing. Along with Giddy, Davie was the first senior pro that we came across, who took the pair of us under his wing and talked about football, the theory of football and the relativity of why we were doing certain things.

More so on the training ground than during a game, Davie would speak to me about football all the time. If I was running in the wrong direction he'd stop me or after our small-sided games, he'd be talking to me about all the little things I should have done during the game. Davie was a true professional, who advised me to look after myself, and do the right things off the field of play. On the pitch, he'd talked about slowing the game down, speeding the game up at the right times, looking at a situation and either getting involved in it or moving away from it. I had a great education from him from the age of 17. He was a very special person during my development and we still see each other to this day and chat about those times we spent together at Villa.

Keith Leonard
Former Aston Villa striker 1972–1976

Keith came into the professional game very late in his career, having played non-league football until the age of 22, and that in itself earns my respect. He was a big unit, six foot two inches tall and not the most mobile player in the world, and a very different character to Andy Lochhead, whom he replaced in the Villa team. Keith deserves a great amount of praise for the successful partnership we had, especially during the 1974–1975 season. It was unfortunate that he got injured and it could be said that Ron Saunders may not have had to buy

Andy Gray if his career hadn't have been cut short and there lies a twist of fate, because Andy later became another hero and friend of mine.

Keith was a quiet lad off the field, but put him on a football pitch and he was as tough as you could get. Ron Saunders drove into Keith all the time about contact with the centre-half and making it difficult for them. Ron encouraged that old-fashioned battle between the centre-half and the centre-forward and made Keith and the other centre-forwards get in amongst the defenders; in fairness, he did it really well, too.

Although Keith spent the best part of four seasons at Villa, he only had one great season, but he was an absolute diamond of a player to play alongside, nonetheless. It could be said that although he was a younger version of Andy Lochhead, he was also different in many ways. Like Andy, he messed centre-halves around, and not only did he score goals, he created goals for me. He was definitely the focal point of that team and that was a feature of Ron's teams. Ron encouraged his team to get the centre-forward involved in the game early doors and to make contact with the opposition, and that was Keith's job on the pitch. One of Keith's best features was to pin the centre-half by blocking him out and shielding the ball so they couldn't get it off him and he did that incredibly well. In fact, there was only one centre-half who got the better of Keith and that was Tom Walley of Orient.

I don't think I would have survived in the game if it hadn't been for players like Andy Lochhead and Keith Leonard, especially in the early 1970s. The size I was and the way the game was back then, I'd have been picked out of the game easily – I needed a centre-forward to play alongside and a big man to play off. I needed players like that to take all the knocks, even though I got rattled quite a bit myself from time to time, in terms of movement and players being late into tackles. Without the Keith Leonards of the time, it would have been impossible for me have made my name in the game, that's for sure.

It's a great shame that Keith hasn't been written and talked about a lot more because he deserves credit in the history of Aston Villa and in my career. He made a massive contribution in the promotion season, getting the club back into the First Division during that 1974–1975 season.

Dennis Mortimer
Former Aston Villa captain 1975–1985

Villa always had a good midfield in the 1970s, with the likes of Alex Cropley, Frank Carrodus and Gordon Cowans, but for me, I loved the way Dennis Mortimer carried the ball from box to box. It's true that Frank could run all day, Gordon could pass a ball and Crops was a good passer of the ball as well, but Dennis could run with the ball at his feet and I always admired him for that. He not only ran with the ball but he was strong with it. There were times he had the ball at his feet and he'd pass it to me, then I'd put it in a position for Andy Gray to score and that was a great sight to see.

I also respected Dennis for being very single-minded. – He'd only do what he wanted to do, and that's not an easy thing to do in football, especially being managed by Ron Saunders. If he didn't think something was right for himself, he just wouldn't do it, that's similar to myself in some respects. While most of us did things together, Dennis kept himself very much to himself and that showed he had a very strong mentality. He was very professional in his attitude towards the game and I admired that side of him. Dennis and I never socialised together, which wasn't a problem but we got on well, and from my end there was a massive respect for him. That respect stemmed from how he played and how he conducted himself on a football pitch. I can look at the goals in the 1977 League Cup semi-final against QPR when Dennis carried the ball from the edge of our box, right up to their box, and the goal that I scored in the final, where he passed to Gordon Smith who squared it for me to finish off are both good examples of the way he played. Later on in his career, after I had retired, I watched the team win the league and the European Cup. He was just immense.

Still to this day, like many other people, I can't believe he didn't play for England. He was capped by England at youth and under-23 level and England B, but was never capped for the full England team, and was often described as the best player never to play for England. When you look back and you think, here's a fella in the team that I played with and who was absolutely outstanding, and led the club to the European Cup Final in 1982, that makes him a hero of mine.

Andy Gray
Former Aston Villa striker 1975–1979

I remember big Keith Leonard was struggling with injury before Ron told us he'd signed another big centre-forward. When I first saw Andy, I thought to myself, "Where's the big centre-forward?" and in fairness to Andy, he was just a touch under six-foot, but by God he made us sit up when we watched him play.

My first game with Andy was away at Middlesbrough, not an easy place to play at that time. They had a centre-back called Stuart Boam, who was huge to say the least. During the game, I remember a couple of balls flying into the box and seeing this fella flinging his arms on top of the centre-back, climbing all over Stuart Boam and heading the ball towards goal. Although the game ended up 0-0, I thought to myself, "Crikey, I've got a lad here and all I have to do is put the ball in front of him and I'm convinced he'll score a goal or two." That was an understatement, because without a doubt, he was the bravest centre-forward I've ever played with. I've played with some tough ones, and that's not to say Andy wasn't tough, but he was brave. If Andy sensed there was a ball coming into the penalty box and there was a sniff of a chance for him to score, he would be right in the thick of it.

A lot of people have asked me, what did I enjoy about playing with Andy and the answer is simple. I looked where Andy Gray was on the pitch, I looked where the goal was and I knew, that if I put the ball somewhere in that region, in between Andy, in between the goalkeeper and in between the goal itself I knew he would be fairly close to getting his head or foot on to it. He was a joy to play with because he had energy, enthusiasm, commitment and his total enjoyment of the game, and I think he was the first centre-forward I've played alongside who actually celebrated his goals with what you'd call nowadays a goal celebration. I think he introduced goal celebrations, to be honest, with his trademark raised arms celebration. He loved all that; he loved the attention and Andy absolutely loved scoring goals. Just look at some of his headed goals and you'd agree there was nobody better than Andy Gray. During the two seasons between 1976 and 1978, John Deehan, Andy and I scored 120 goals between us, with Andy scoring 49 of those during that incredible period at Villa.

Andy was totally infectious and the great thing about him was that when he was there, you knew he was there. He was unbelievably bright and loud, which doesn't do him a disservice, but when he walked in he lit the room up, especially after he'd been at the club for sometime. Just like on the pitch, he'd be straight amongst the action, whether it was a bit of banter or whatever, he'd be amongst it.

He was brilliant for me and I totally enjoyed my time playing with Andy, but sadly we both had injuries that were not great for us.

Bruce Rioch

Former Aston Villa midfielder 1969–1974 and
Middlesbrough manager 1986–1990

Bruce was manager at Middlesbrough, who had just come out of administration and were in the Third Division when I got the call to join him on his coaching staff. The call came as a shock, and at the time, I was living in Sutton Coldfield so I thought it would have been a bit of a jaunt to get there. However, I wanted to learn more about football management and it seemed like a good opportunity to work with a player I admired greatly and a person who I looked up to, so I agreed to join him in the North East.

Bruce and Colin Todd coached the first-team and I coached the youth and reserve team. During the week, though, on a Tuesday we would all go off, along with Barry Geldart, to watch football matches up and down the country, well two of the closest games to Middlesbrough. Two of us would get dropped off at one game and the other two would watch another game. After the games had finished, we'd all meet up and drive back to Middlesbrough. On a Wednesday, we'd do the same and on a Thursday we'd all do schoolboy coaching. More often than not, regardless of the weather, Bruce and I would go to places like Scunthorpe or Stockport on a Friday, if there was a game going on. It was more than a full-time job watching football matches and coaching players, but we enjoyed every minute of it.

Bruce was the only manager I've ever known who didn't want to be called 'boss' – everybody called him 'Bruce', which seemed strange, but everybody knew exactly who he was, and everybody knew he was the boss. His commitment to do things properly and his demands from the players were second to none, and his discipline with the players was incredible. Bruce didn't believe in hammering people and it wasn't a necessity to fine players heavily; moreover, he'd give his players little guidelines and rules to stick to, almost to the point of creating a bit of fun surrounding them. The little things like wearing flip-flops in the showers or wearing tracksuits wherever they went were examples. There were also rules like being into training on time and being dressed appropriately, so everyone looked neat and tidy. I loved the way he went about his job and I loved the way he got the respect from his players.

Bruce was not only a great manager, he was a great coach and during the three years I was at Middlesbrough with him, we got promoted from the Third Division to the Second Division and then to the top tier. It was an immensely incredible and successful period and I was watching a fella that was, not only coaching the first team, but also honest enough to coach the schoolboys on a Thursday night. Bruce led us all the way through that period and I learned so much from him. It was unbelievably tiring, I have to say, but we didn't have massive squads in those days and there were lots of games going on so we went away and watched lots of football matches. We never stopped working, but we all prospered from it.

For me personally, he was a great mentor and he had a massive influence on me, in terms of how I would manage my teams in my subsequent management career. Having worked with a lot of different types of managers as a player, I realise just how much of an influence Bruce had on my managerial career in the years that followed. He taught me how hard I'd have to work to become a football manager, because football management wasn't second nature to me in those days. His format for being successful was simple: discipline, organisation, hard work and going out and watching players he wanted for his team, so he had a good knowledge of who was out there and those are the things I took on board throughout my managerial career.

Ron Saunders

Former Aston Villa manager 1974–1982

Ron and I struggled to get along with each other if I'm perfectly honest, but that doesn't really matter. In hindsight, while I was working under Ron Saunders, I didn't realise how much I was taking in, but there were a lot of things he did that I would never do. My total belief is to treat people how I would like to be treated myself and Ron was quite hard on players and that's not the way I treated my players when I was a manager.

What actually surprised me, and where Ron and I had similar views was on the training ground. He had a system of play that he liked and he worked at it until it was embedded into the players – and that's just what I did when I became a manager. As a manager we'd practised that formation during pre-season and up to a point, during the season. We did lots of drills where we'd work on that defensive unit and we'd have the strikers on the field. However, when I was working under Ron at Villa, he'd start with the defensive unit then bring the strikers on later, but, as a slight variation on his method, I'd like to start with the strikers, defending from the front. When I was not involved in the training as a player I'd very often get bored with watching, so I guess I looked at that and changed the method slightly when I became a coach or a manager. I didn't want my strikers to feel left out as I did when I was as a player.

I worked at how to stop the opposition playing and that was the real premise behind my method of playing, which was exactly the same as Ron's way – make sure you know how to defend, and have strikers in your team who could win you games. I did so many training sessions that were similar to Ron's sessions and I used to find myself saying things that Ron said, which was quite bizarre; I couldn't get it out of my system for a while, thinking I was beginning to sound like Ron Saunders and that was worrying.

The fact is we just didn't get on, but he had a massive effect on me after I retired, more than I ever realised when I was a football player. I remember some years ago, I met him at a get-together for the European Cup winning team, a function I wasn't officially invited to but was asked to attend by Allan Evans as his guest. I saw Ron there that evening, plucked up enough courage and made my way over to him to say, "Mr Saunders, it's nice to see you again. I know we had our problems when I played, but I just wanted to say that I realise now that I'm older some of the difficulties you have as a manager, and I understand the way you have to get on with players. I just want to say that I used a lot of your methods in my training and management time, so thank you for that." Ron just looked at me and went, "OK", turned around and walked off. I don't think it went down overly well with him, but at least I said it to him and I had the satisfaction in saying and knowing that I had the courage to say, "Thank you" in a weird sort of way.

It was probably ten years too late that I realised that Ron was actually good at his job when he managed us at Villa. Ron genuinely had an effect on me and I think I used as many of his good traits as his bad ones. I dismissed what I thought were his bad methods, but I thank him very much for all the things he did teach me, which I was able to turn my own little slant on.

Kevin Smith
Former Darlington captain 1989–1993

After a very brief spell as Caretaker Manager at Wolverhampton Wanderers, my first real job in football management came when I was appointed manager of Darlington on a temporary basis at first in February of 1989, with the club bottom of the Fourth Division.

I had a thankless task on my hands but I almost pulled off a miracle in saving the club from dropping out of the League. We were relegated, but it didn't prevent the owner from handing me a two-year contract.

The first job I had after being relegated was to release a lot of players, but I needed a leader most of all – somebody who might attract players to the club. Even though that player I had in mind wasn't a well-known name, I knew he was the one I wanted. It was Kevin Smith and he was playing at York City at the time, my brother Alan's club. Kevin had played 245 games for Darlington between 1979 and 1985 as a defender and he was from my part of the world: County Durham. People at the club were saying to me that Kevin had been a great player for them and wished he could return. So I went out of my way to make it happen. I first spoke to Alan to see if I could have permission to speak to Kevin, and it was granted. Kevin had been in the top division and part of the Coventry City FA Cup winning squad in 1987 before signing for York City. When you dropped out of the League in those days it was like falling off the end of the earth, so I was asking a lot of him to drop down a division to the Conference because only one team would be promoted and so it was a tough ask.

I had several long conversations with Kevin's team and a lot of negotiating was done, and he was close to not signing on a few occasions, basically over £20 or £30 a week, which sounds ridiculous, but when you're at that level it is a lot of money for the club. We, as a club, had to balance a fairly even matching salary cap for all of the players. However, I eventually managed to speak to Kevin and he signed for me. It was a big coup for a club like Darlington, because lots of lads who had played at that level knew he had gone to Coventry a few years earlier, and on the back of the deal, we signed lots of local players who wanted to come back and join us.

So, I had my man and he turned out to be a brilliant choice as captain. I likened his character to Jimmy Cumbes, who had a tremendous ability to organise the players off the pitch, as well as on the pitch. Kevin had unbelievable enthusiasm for team spirit and team bonding and made sure we stayed together as a team.

During those two years at Darlington, Kevin was massively important for me, because he was a leader and loved the club, as well as being a good footballer. He felt he'd missed out at Coventry because he'd been injured a lot and only played a handful of games. It was like he was coming home and had something to prove.

Kevin was a cheeky chappy and didn't escape my wrath when sometimes he overstepped the mark, like when he'd take the players for a night out at the wrong times. In fairness, everything he did was with good intentions, but sometimes he got carried away and I'd have to jump on him every now and again.

To have someone like Kevin in your side was brilliant. He was six-foot four, led from the front and was an unbelievable defender who organised his team on the pitch. He was a super player for me. He was captain of the side who won two championships in a row. To win the Conference the first time round and then to win the Fourth Division in the next season was brilliant.

Kevin had a huge influence in my first proper management job in football, and nearly 30 years on, we still keep in touch and that in itself shows that you appreciate what somebody has done for you.

Mick Tait
Former Darlington striker 1990–1992

When I turn the clock back to that period managing Darlington, it was a brilliant time for me personally and when you go through those good times, you need great people around you.

I realised we needed a bit extra in defence when we got promoted from the Conference to the Fourth Division. I remember getting a call from someone who asked me if I knew a fella by the name of Mick Tait. I had heard of him, but didn't know him personally at the time. He was another Geordie lad who had played at clubs like Hull City, Portsmouth and Reading and had been around the league scene for sometime. Mick had a reputation of being a proper 'man' and I couldn't resist the temptation to meet him with the view of signing him for Darlington. As soon as I met him, I knew I'd got a player who was as hard as nails and would do a job for me.

Mick was capable of playing in midfield or as a central defender in a three, a player who would read the game and didn't have to be the quickest in the world. He was one of those players who would give his all and probably score an 8.5 out of 10, and he was probably capable of playing anywhere at any time. He was brilliant and respectful to me. He never shirked anything and everyone in the team looked up to him and listened to what he said. I'm not saying anyone's commitment was any different from Kevin's or Mick's, but for those two years at Darlington, I had two great characters and two players who would get the respect from everybody in the team, would fight for the shirt and made us hard to beat, which were a few reasons why we won the Fourth Division championship.

Barry Geldart
Chief Scout, Middlesbrough and Darlington

Barry was a scout at Middlesbrough under Bruce Rioch, so when I took charge of Darlington, I asked him to come and join me as Chief Scout because he had such a good knowledge of local talent. He was a wonderful character, had a great way about him and everybody knew and liked him at the club. He was also fantastic off the field and often helped me in certain situations. He was a massive influence in the signings of people like David Cork, David Corner, John Borthwick, Drew Coverdale and Michael Trotter. Barry knew the type of player I liked and all of those guys were players I liked. Bear in mind, there was no lower league football on TV, let alone Conference football; we had no idea how teams played, so you had to scout the players and those people were massively important. Of course, I went out to watch games when I could, but usually I left it to the likes of Barry.

We had great success at Darlington, but I can't claim all the success myself because it was partly down to people like Barry, who recommended the right type of players for the football club at that time. He became a fantastic asset, a huge influence on myself and the team. He also helped me personally at times, because he'd sometimes look at me when I looked down and say something like, "You all right, Brian? What's happened? Are you worried about something?" So, I owe a big thank you to Barry for the part he played during those two years.

Richard Cordon
Former Darlington Chairman

Richard wasn't the chairman when I took charge of Darlington. He became chairman the day before the penultimate game of the season, away at Scunthorpe, with us bottom of the Fourth Division. We lost the game 5-1 and got relegated out of the Football League. He probably wondered what he'd taken on. Everyone at the club was gutted and in those days, dropping out of the Football League was the worst thing that could happen.

After that game at Scunthorpe, with our fate already known, Richard came into the dressing room and said he wanted to have a word with me. I thought the worst, that it was the end of my time as a football manager. We went outside and found a couple of seats in the main stand, sat down and he said to me, "Well, Brian, if you go I'm going as well." Now bear in mind it was his first game in charge as chairman of the football club, it was a bold statement indeed and probably the greatest sentence anybody has ever said to me in my entire football career. In reply, I said, "Well, what are we going to do then?" He had obviously been thinking about things during the game and we talked for a good half an hour about a two-year plan to get us back into the Football

League as a full-time football club. He did say, though, if after the two years we weren't in the Football League, the club could possibly be left in a big mess, so there was no pressure on me there.

Of course, everything that happened after that day is history. The club went on for the next two years with back-to-back promotions. Throughout those two years he was brilliant to me. He'd always ask how I was, he'd stick up for me if anybody was having a pop at me and became a great chairman and a friend of myself and my family; he'd often turn up with a couple of presents for my two boys, which showed how much he cared about my family too.

When I eventually moved to Leicester, he simply said to me, "I don't want you to go, but I'm not going to stop you. You deserve an opportunity to go. You've worked hard and you've been brilliant. If you go, I'm going to be gutted, but obviously I would allow any move that you need." I really appreciated him saying that to me.

Richard Cordon was probably the ideal football chairman and I thank him for that, and for delivering the greatest line ever.

Steve Walsh
Former Leicester City defender, 1986–2000

I had three incredible years at Leicester City, getting to three playoff finals in a row was just unbelievable, but there were several people who were inspirational in that success.

Walshy was an incredible character, a complex person who needed a bit of care and attention from time-to-time, and he needed a bit of encouraging, shall we say. His leadership qualities were simply how he played the game, the fact that everybody knew he wasn't an easy person to play against, and because of that, people used to wind him up. He'd sometimes jump in there with both feet and that landed him in hot water, so much so I had to take the captaincy off him at one stage. To do that you'd probably think I didn't think much of him as a player, but I had to think of a way of stopping him getting sent off or into trouble with the referee. He was always falling out with the centre-forwards he played against; that was his mentality. He had that winning desire on a matchday and had some unbelievable scraps with players like Steve Bull. I remember him being sent off once, and it began to get to the point where it promoted the club publicly in the wrong way so it was hugely important that I did something about it.

Walshy didn't like training, and that was probably the start of me having to handle people who played at the higher level a little differently. He reminded me of some experiences I had when I was a player and the way I was as a player, someone who probably needed to be handled in a different way. However, most managers weren't prepared to do that with me. He'd had a few injuries and had trouble with his back so I had to look at Walshy throughout the week, and there were particular training sessions he didn't like so I had to tread very carefully with him in that respect. I also knew on a Friday that I probably couldn't name a team until I'd spoken to him and sometimes he'd say he was struggling; however, if I spoke to him first thing on a Saturday morning, he'd be raring to go and couldn't wait for the game.

Even though he was a centre-half and his major strength was defending, Walshy would never work on the defensive side of his game in small-sided games. The only way you'd get him out to train would be to play him as a centre-forward in those small-sided games. Nobody liked playing against him. He was majorly competitive and would probably run through a brick wall if I'd ask him to. From the centre-half position, he was an influence on the team because of his never-say-die attitude and he could also score goals. Fast-forward to one of the playoff finals, I actually played him at centre-forward, mainly because he had a problem with a new injury and hadn't played many full games for a while. That decision raised a few eyebrows, but Walshy was a goalscorer after all, and he loved scoring them. He was a real threat, so there was always a temptation when we were behind in games to play him up front.

Walshy was fantastic for me, even though as a manager he gave me a testing time; as a captain, he led from the front and probably got too involved in the end, but that was his major strength, rather than a fault. Although he was unbelievably aggressive on the field, he was a terrifically nice guy off it.

Gary Mills

Former Leicester City captain 1989–1994

Gary had been part of the great Brian Clough side at Nottingham Forest who had won two European Cups before he signed for

Leicester, just before my arrival at the club. He was a model professional who had been around the team a bit before he took over as captain from Walshy; Gary was probably the polar opposite of the big man.

I think the best thing I did for Gary was to play with three centre-backs and give him a wing-back role. He absolutely loved that and I think he saw football in a different light, certainly different from the way Cloughie played. He was dynamic pushing forward in that role, dependable in terms of his work rate, getting back to deep positions to defend and he was a perfect clubman. He was a good man in the dressing room and a great example to the younger players. Gary was that personable, approachable captain I wanted at the club; the type of person the club liked; what the fans liked and what the press liked. Gary was brilliant for me, week in, week out. Unfortunately he couldn't play in the 1993–1994 play off final because of a problem with his big toe which was the worst injury you can have as a footballer, let me tell you. We had to give him an injection to freeze his toe every week, but for that game it got that bad he couldn't play so I asked him to lead the team out for the final as a gesture for all his help in getting us that far.

John Gregory and Allan Evans
First-team coaches at Leicester City and Aston Villa

It could be said that John and Alan were absolute opposite, as people; I don't think they'd ever go out socially with each other, but I often reminded them that their differences were something I wanted around the place and that I needed their diverse approaches and opinions. I soon realised they were completely different people, and often talked to them on a one-on-one basis, but whenever I wanted us to be a three, they both always responded in the right way. It was a situation that I managed and handled in my own way. I needed a combination of people who worked well with me, and although John and Alan were poles apart, both of them together seemed to combine well.

While I did the team building in terms of the pattern of play, John did a lot of the general coaching and Alan, as a top-class centre-half himself, was a an immaculate person, a perfectionist and really good at organising and talking to the defensive players. He loved being organised and made sure everything was in place for training on a day-to-day basis, or when we travelled away, he'd make sure everything was ready for us. He just enjoyed having things in place.

Alan was the one who I'd talk to about any problems I might be seeing or issues I was thinking of, or situations where I thought about changing the team a bit. He was my 'go-to' person for those sorts of things and became a wonderful friend of mine.

John, on the other hand, had an incredibly infectious character and had a nickname for everyone in the dressing room. I don't know where he got them from, but that was just his way. He was my right-hand man around the training facility and in the dressing room, where he had great way with the players, but they also knew when to keep out of his way. He could get quite angry at times, especially when we lost games. After a defeat, he'd have a chew and when he sat down, everybody knew not to go near him otherwise they might have got both barrels. Having said that, I loved his moodiness; loved his enthusiasm for the game; loved his ability to get on with people and his ability to give a little rollicking, every now and again. In the dugout, he was fiery and at times he'd kick a bucket full of cold water and I thought that was great, because it showed passion. There were times when he kicked that bucket and it either went onto the pitch or drenched some poor supporter who sat behind the dugout.

Ultimately, for the six years we worked together at Leicester and Villa, we did some tremendous things: we took Leicester to three playoff finals, including one promotion to the Premier League; kept Villa in the Premier League; took them to fourth and fifth in the Premier League; won the League Cup with Villa; got to the semi-final of the FA Cup and took Villa to the quarter-final of the UEFA Cup. Both Alan and John played their part in all of that and I will always be grateful to both of them.

Dwight Yorke
Aston Villa striker 1989–1998

There was always trouble on the horizon for me at Villa Park, based on the team knowing I wanted to change things around, and it was all about trying to recognise what I wanted and didn't want for that second season in charge. Obviously, I needed the club to stay in the Premier League and there were players who needed to move on, not because they were bad players, but because it was time to change things. There was one player that impressed me so much, that I knew I wanted to build a team around him. In fact, there was one specific performance that during that period that I knew I needed to do something that was both brave, and may raise a few eyebrows.

I remember we played Leeds United at Elland Road, and Dalian Atkinson was unavailable so I paired Dean Saunders with Dwight Yorke up front. That day is cemented in my memory because it was the day I decided I had to build the team around Dwight Yorke. His performance that day was absolutely outstanding, because I really needed a hold-up player. OK, I had Dean Saunders and Dalian Atkinson when fit up-front, but I wanted Dwight to be the main part of the striking partnership and to free him from being the secondary partner. I don't think Dwight had been given the opportunity to be the main striker before, in front of Deano or Dalian, but he was happy to play in any position.

Everything about Dwight's game against Leeds was immense and he did everything I looked for from a striker. There were lots of things I felt I could encourage and make him believe he could do; he'd already played a lot of games in a few different positions, including wide positions, midfield positions and as a striker, but he was still young enough to develop into a top-class player. Seeing Dwight play that day cemented in my mind that if we were to stay up and I was still in charge, Dwight would be massively important to us. However, right near the end of the game, Carlton Palmer scored for Leeds and I dropped to my knees, thinking we were being dragged back into a relegation fight and my plans would remain on hold. Fortunately, we didn't get relegated.

Without a doubt, my plan proved to be the right thing to do. I found a role for him in the team and I gave him my full backing. He knew his own strengths, and I encouraged him to play on other players' weaknesses. I'm not claiming I found Dwight Yorke or made him better, but I just felt it was the right time for him to be given his time and it was the start of a period when he became hugely important for Aston Villa; he just needed someone to guide him a little. As a player, I had things said to me or done to me that I didn't like; I said to myself I would make sure that Dwight wouldn't get any of that and he had the full commitment of the manager from there on in.

Dwight remains one of my all-time favourite players and he did things for me that justified the faith I had in him. Looking back, I am very proud I had the courage to make that move and give him the opportunity to pay back the faith I had in him. I think I was right in many respects to make that move, and that's no detriment to Deano or Dalian, who were both fantastic players in their own rights, but it was the right time for a young player to be given his opportunity.

Gareth Southgate
Aston Villa centre-back and captain 1995–2001

The player who gave me the most pleasure in signing was Gareth Southgate from Crystal Palace during the summer of 1995. I recall being in Doug Ellis's office, telling him about the player I wanted to sign most of all. At the time, Gareth was a holding midfield player, and in all honesty, that was the main position I wanted to sign him for, even though I'd seen him play at full-back and he'd also played at centre-back at times. He had the right sort of background for me; he was able to play in a number of positions; he'd played international football for England Under-21s and he was an experienced Premier League player by the age of 25. He was definitely the right type of player I was looking for.

I was in the office listening to Crystal Palace chairman Ron Noades and Doug Ellis arguing about the cost of Gareth's proposed transfer; it was toing and froing from £2m to £2.2, then to £2.5m and it seemed strange to me hearing two chairmen quibbling about £50,000, but eventually they agreed on £2.25m.

That pre-season, we tried to keep it as low-key as possible. We played quite a few 'behind closed doors' games at Bodymoor Heath, so I could stop the game if we wanted to and give new players the opportunity to play. There were no fans watching so we weren't under any obligation to adhere to any rules or regulations and we could do pretty much what we liked. There was one particular game where I experimented playing three centre-backs and three midfielders, and I saw Gareth very much as one of those midfield players. However, during the game, I asked Gareth to drop in as a centre-back, in between Paul McGrath and Steve Staunton and within five minutes of taking that position, Alan, John and I were standing watching in total amazement. We stood there, looking at each other and knew we'd stumbled upon something. It was uncanny the way Gareth read the game from the back; it was just outstanding to see how he anticipated what was and wasn't there. I never told him what to do, I simply said, "Go in there and play." We had a structure and our centre-backs knew how to play the formation, and that we weren't playing with a sweeper. We had talked about those situations all the time; we didn't want two people to be marking all the time; we had a zonal starting point, but if you had to follow a person and didn't have time to pass it to the other centre-back, then you stayed with him, and the other centre-back would go into your position. It was a quite simple, open and well-balanced method, and Gareth got to grips with it straight away.

Gareth was just an unbelievable signing for us, and a great character too and it didn't take us long to see that. If you add to that Gareth's personality, his professionalism, his integrity and his ability to get along with people and talk sensibly to the media he really was the ultimate footballer. Not only that, he joined in the fun and games we had in the dressing room which he needed to at that time.

It wasn't long before Gareth had been selected for the full England squad and we were all delighted for him.

Gareth was a massive plus for us, and his signing goes right to the top of the list in terms of the players I signed. He was arguably the best player I'd ever signed for any club I managed and I think lots of people agree that was the case.

Ian Taylor
Aston Villa midfielder 1994–2003

There were three players who I signed for Villa who I called 'the Three Amigos' and to be honest, I can't separate Ian Taylor, Mark Draper and Tommy Johnson. Together, they were a delight and probably the best three players to be around in terms of enjoyment, pleasure, arguments, and disagreements, but ultimately, they ended up laughing at each other. They all lit up the dressing room with their energy, humour and enthusiasm. It was beyond anything I have ever sampled before.

I should have signed Tayls when I was manager at Leicester City. A friend of mine who was a scout, told me to watch this young lad called Ian Taylor, who was playing for a non-League team called Moor Green in Birmingham, but I never got round to watching him and he then went off to Port Vale. I did watch him a few years later, playing for Sheffield Wednesday and he played in a wide position and I thought that was totally the wrong place for him to play, even though he was a great athlete. I thought if I was his manager I'd play him in the middle of the park, because he'd get from one box to the other pretty quickly and with power and that's just what I did.

Tayls had bags of energy and a massive amount of ability. In fact, he didn't know how good he was, and lo and behold, he was the first player I signed for Aston Villa.

Mark Draper
Aston Villa midfielder 1995–2000

Drapes was as daft as a brush. He was the clown prince of the three, if not the club. Tommy and Ian rubbed it into him like nobody's business, but together they made the dressing room bounce. One story that sums up Mark Draper happened at White Hart Lane, where he shouted to Ian Taylor for the ball, but Tayls didn't see him at all and Drapes wasn't happy with him. There were two huge screens at both corners of the ground at the time and the footage was almost running at the same speed of the game. At half time, I saw Tayls laughing his socks off so I asked him why he was laughing, "It's Draper, he wants me to watch the television so I can see where he is on the pitch, because I should have passed to him." Drapes was convinced that if Tayls watched the big screen while he was playing, he would be able to see who to pass to and who not to pass to. He was an absolute lunatic but in a good way; how on earth anybody could believe that would happen? He once famously said that he wanted to play for Barcelona in the Italian league. He was a fruitcake, but I loved him to bits and all the lads loved him.

Tommy Johnson
Aston Villa forward 1995–1997

Tommy was probably the best one-on-one finisher I've ever managed. He had an incredible ability to rifle the ball past the goalkeeper, time and time again and usually with his left foot. He was a bundle of energy and always wanted to be part of what was happening. He was probably used as a substitute too many times for me, but he was always on to me to get him on the field. I reluctantly sold him to Celtic because I couldn't guarantee him game time, and I owed him that much.

Sir Stanley Matthews
Former Stoke City, Blackpool and England outside right

When I was about 13 years old, the first club I ever went to for a trial was Port Vale, and Stanley Matthews was the manager there. I remember they had a theory to bring on young players through their scouting network, and one of the places they scouted was around the area I lived in County Durham.

One day, I went all the way to Port Vale on a bus with my dad and two brothers, and about another dozen or so young footballers and their parents from my local area. The idea was give us a trial for a week in the hope Port Vale would take us on. He was there to try and sell the whole idea and the club to us. We usually trained at Leek Town and every day during that week Stanley Matthews was there, giving encouragement to us young hopefuls, and I will always remember he went out of his way to speak to me. He'd find time to come and speak to me and he'd also speak to my dad and I found it quite brilliant that he found time to take an interest in us. He spent a lot of time watching us play little games and training sessions. To think Stanley Matthews was the first famous footballer I ever met is quite amazing; he was one of the most iconic footballers in the world at the time and he was watching me. I was so impressed with him as a person and that stuck with me.

I think Stanley Matthews left Port Vale after a year in 1968, shortly after I went there for a trial, but I would have seriously considered the move. However, when I was Stoke City manager, in 1998, he was around the club at the time and we met up and talked about my trial week at Port Vale. On the back of that, we pretty much talked weekly, mainly about football and it was great to think, here I was, the manager of Stoke City and Sir Stanley Matthews would come in and make his way to see me and talk football. He always made the time to stop and chat to me about football and it was just a great experience for me being in his presence. He was a tremendous ambassador for Stoke City and for football in general, a tremendous football person and a person who had a dream of bringing in young footballers and progressing them through the club. Unfortunately, his managerial days only lasted a year and his dream didn't come to fruition.

I was very much influenced by Stanley Matthews, as most young boys were during the 1950s and 1960s and he had a lasting affect on me, as someone who pursued a football career myself. I am very proud to be able to say I knew him and that is something I will cherish for the rest of my life.

Theodore Whitmore
Hull City, Tranmere Rovers and Jamaica international midfielder, current Jamaica national coach

Theodore had the ability to change a game on his own and I still can't understand why he didn't play in the top flight. He was very much a major talent. He was six foot two inches tall and stick thin, but was a wonderful athlete with the ball at his feet. I've talked about how Dennis Mortimer carried the ball from one box to the other, but Theodore could not only do that, he could dribble and do tricks as well while carrying the ball at his feet. I'm quite sure if you saw Theodore play for Hull City, you would have said he should have played at a higher level.

He was a wonderful person, a quiet man, very respectful and always had a smile on his face. On the pitch he had an eye for a pass and he was unselfish with the ball, and every time he would put the final pass into the path of the striker to score. Theodore was probably the start of the influx in Jamaican talent coming through into the English game, and perhaps it was just their naivety, but they played the game in a way that it was fresh and enjoyable to watch and that made people start to take notice.

I not only brought him to Hull City, I also took him to Tranmere two years later, and he was marvellous for me there, too.

Ian Goodison
Hull City, Tranmere Rovers and Jamaica international defender

Ian was probably the total opposite to Theodore; a very casual player and probably the most laid-back footballer I have ever dealt with. Nothing fazed him and nothing hurried him up, unless he was playing football. However, when he played football, he could play in any position in the defence, midfield or in a holding position. He'd always call me 'dad' and used to say to me, "I'll play anywhere for you, dad."

Physically, he probably looked clumsy being six foot three, but had the temperament to try things, and he was an incredible athlete, who worked really hard, and you'd always find him in the gym, working out, keeping his fitness levels and physique in shape.

Although I didn't get the best out of him at Hull City, mainly because of his injuries, he was always willing to play when he was fit and played some great games for me. I think he was a far more talented player than anyone would give him credit for. He must have been pretty good, because he played 128 times for his country.

When I took him to Tranmere, he was 32 and he'd been injured for a while, but to be fair to him he was still playing for Tranmere into his 40s. In fact, I had the honour and pleasure of being his team manager for his testimonial at Tranmere when I managed the Jamaican international team and that must have been the funniest dressing room I have ever been in. Their humour and their carrying on were just superb.

As a pair, I just loved Ian and Theodore to bits, both quality players and I think if they could start their careers over again, the way the game is progressing and with the Jamaican lads knowing more about football these days, I really think they could have played in the Premier League. They are both iconic figures in Jamaica and they are two players who were totally underestimated by top-flight clubs in this country, but I owe them a tremendous amount for what they did for me.

CAREER STATISTICS

Playing Career

Aston Villa 1971–1980

Season	League			FA Cup		League Cup		Europe (UEFA Cup)		Total	
	Division	Apps	Goals	Apps	Goals	Apps	Goals	Apps	Goals	Apps	Goals
1971 - 1972	3rd Division	2	1	0	0	0	0	0	0	2	1
1972 - 1973	2nd Division	19	3	1	0	0	0	0	0	20	3
1973 - 1974	2nd Division	37	8	2	0	1	0	0	0	40	8
1974 - 1975	2nd Division	34	20	2	1	8	3	0	0	44	24
1975 - 1976	1st Division	20	1	0	0	2	0	1	0	23	1
1976 - 1977	1st Division	42	14	4	2	10	10	0	0	56	26
1977 - 1978	1st Division	40	7	1	0	3	1	8	3	52	11
1978 - 1979	1st Division	24	1	0	0	4	1	0	0	28	2
1979 - 1980	1st Division	29	5	6	1	2	0	0	0	37	6
Career Total		247	60	16	4	30	15	9	3	302	82

Management Career

August 1986–August 2011

Team	Date From	Date To	Games	Record			
				Won	Drawn	Lost	Win %
Wolverhampton Wanderers	Aug-86	Oct-86	8	4	3	1	50.00
Darlington	Feb-89	May-91	106	54	30	22	50.90
Leicester City	May-91	Nov-94	178	76	58	44	42.70
Aston Villa	Nov-94	Feb-98	164	68	51	45	41.46
Stoke City	May-98	Jun-99	52	23	22	7	44.23
West Bromwich Alb on	Aug-99	Mar-00	41	8	15	18	19.51
Hull City	Apr-00	Feb-02	97	41	28	28	42.27
Tranmere Rovers	Oct-03	Jun-06	147	61	43	43	41.50
Wrexham	Nov-07	Sep-08	32	7	16	9	21.88
Gainsborough Trinity	Aug-09	Aug-11	85	25	19	41	29.41
Career Total			910	367	285	258	40.33

MAJOR HONOURS

As a Player

1970–1971 FA Youth Cup Winner – Aston Villa

1971–1972 Third Division Championship Winner – Aston Villa

1974–1975 Football League Cup Winner – Aston Villa

1976–1977 Football League Cup Winner – Aston Villa

As a Manager

1989–1990 National Conference League Winner – Darlington

1990–1991 Fourth Division Winner – Darlington

1993–1994 Division One Playoff Winner – Leicester City

1995–1996 Football League Cup Winner – Aston Villa